THE FINAL TESTAMENTS

VOL. 11 – STARK REALITIES OF SPIRITUAL REBIRTH

by

Uche Ephraim Chuku

Gotham Books

30 N Gould St.
Ste. 20820, Sheridan, WY 82801
https://gothambooksinc.com/

Phone: 1 (307) 464-7800

© 2024 *Uche Ephraim Uchuku*. All rights reserved.

No part of this book may be reproduced, stored in a retrieval system, or transmitted by any means without the written permission of the author.

Published by Gotham Books (May 11, 2024)

ISBN: 979-8-88775-918-0 (H)
ISBN: 979-8-88775-916-6 (P)
ISBN: 979-8-88775-917-3 (E)

Because of the dynamic nature of the Internet, any web addresses or links contained in this book may have changed since publication and may no longer be valid.

The views expressed in this work are solely those of the author and do not necessarily reflect the views of the publisher, and the publisher hereby disclaims any responsibility for them.

CONTENTS

DEDICATION v
ACKNOWLEDGMENTS vi
INTRODUCTION viii
    Discover Your True Self viii
    Standard Bible Reference Format xii
    Use of *Jehovah* Instead of *Yahweh* in This Volume xii
ABBREVIATIONS xiv
CHAPTER ONE: Life, Sin, And Death; Repentance, Salvation, And The Resurrection 1
    Echoes from the Proverbial Prodigal Son's Experience 1
    True Status of Human Spirits 3
    Unique Role of Jesus Christ in Our Salvation Race 20
    Incontrovertible Facts Relating to True Spiritual Salvation ... 23
CHAPTER TWO: God of Genesis: Man or Myth? 29
    When the Gods Walked Freely on the Earth as Men 38
    Who the father Really Is 48
    Who the Father Is Not 49
    God of Genesis: Creature, Not the Creator 50
CHAPTER THREE: Birth of modern human beings 60
    Jehovah's Corrupted Breath Did Not Create Human Spirits ... 75
    Woman Is Also an Individual Spirit 80
CHAPTER FOUR: Garden of Eden: Impossible Paradise within the Shattering Universe 85
CHAPTER FIVE: Human Nature: Perfection Versus Sheer Ignorance 98

CHAPTER SIX: Human Nature: Captivity of Human Spirits ... 115

CHAPTER SEVEN: First Battle of Eden: God of Eden Was the Real Venomous Serpent ... 124

CHAPTER EIGHT: Body-Spirit Interface ... 135
    The Sin Within ... 135
    Pollution Within and Without ... 147

CHAPTER NINE: Gift of Abundant Foods for the Human Body: Generosity or Sheer Sadism? ... 159
    Differentiating the FATHER and His Perfect Provisions ... 163
    Generosity or Sadism? ... 170
    Foods for the Stomach ... 172
    Foods for Sensual Gratification and Mental Self-Imaging ... 178
    Actual Value of Jehovah's Material Blessings ... 186
    True Fasting and What It Means for Our Captive Spirits ... 190
    A well-nourished body is a badly starved spirit and vice versa ... 191

CHAPTER TEN: Fallacy of Human Comfort and Happiness ... 198

CHAPTER ELEVEN: Fallacy of Human Rights ... 213

CHAPTER TWELVE: Finding the Right Way Back to Our Heavenly Home ... 239

CHAPTER THIRTEEN: Battle Against the Odds ... 260
    Ignorance, Fear, Religion, and the Gods ... 260

CHAPTER FOURTEEN: Walking by the Holy Spirit ... 325
    Walking by the Holy Ghost ... 358
    Christ's Promise of the Holy Spirit of Truth ... 363
    Jehovah's Promised Outpouring of His Ghostly Spirit ... 368

CONCLUSION ... 372

SELECTED BIBLIOGRAPHY ... 375

DEDICATION

I dedicate the book solely to Jesus Christ of Nazareth, my able heavenly Restore Guide; he is *the name above all other names ... in heaven and on earth and under the earth.*

ACKNOWLEDGMENTS

My profound gratitude goes to my ever-loving Father in heaven for his miraculous love and grace upon my undeserving spirit; and to my heavenly Redeemer, Jesus Christ of Nazareth, for granting me the special privilege to be named among his privileged disciples in the world.

I am eternally grateful to the following angelic persons—both dead and alive—whom the Father positioned at crucial stages of my life to love and groom me for this great task of testifying the special love of Jesus Christ in the world: Mama Comfort Chuku (my late mother), Mama Eunice Nwanebe Okoro (my late grandmother), Chief D. T. Okoro (my late grandfather), Late Mazi Okeke (Azibuaku) Chuku, Late Mama Ogbenyeanu Okamigbo, Mazi Sylvester Okamigbo, Late Mazi Nnaa Okafor, Mazi Nwankwo Okafor, Mr. E. Obijiaku, Late Prince John Ik. Okonkwo & Mama Theresa Okonkwo, Late Mazi Sabastine Nwankwo, Ms Dorothy Ibe, Ms Rose Ogbuewu, Mr. Sunday Igwegbe, Mr. Sunday Ojiaku, Mr. & Mrs. Onyemelukwe, Mazi Christian Igbo, Mazi & Mrs. Emmanuel Okwukogu, Cdr. & Mrs. John E. Okeh, Lt. Cdr. Eborho, Mazi C.O. Enuke & Late Mama Elizabeth N. Enuke, Mr. David Manuwa, Mr. T.T. Lasisi, Ms Chinwe Rapu, Mr. P.C.C. Uche, Capt. Clifford Okoro & Auntie Debbie Okoro, Mazi & Mrs. Willie Okoronkwo, Engr. & Mrs. C. Ibia, Capt. S.O. Runsewe, Mr. Herbert Ukwuajoku, Engr. Ojuroye, Sis. Ernie of Sumatra, Mazi Greg Iheme Mbadiwe, and Mr. Allen Johnson. The miraculous love these liberated minds bestowed on me formed the basis of my unwavering conviction in the redemptive power of the divine love of Jesus Christ for the entire humankind.

I am particularly grateful to my wife, Enderline Njideka Chuku. It would have been nearly impossible to overcome all the difficulties and come this far in this momentous vocation without her relentless spiritual and moral support.

My special appreciation also goes to my daughters, Gem Uzoma Chuku and Ruby Chiamaka Chuku, and to Flora Famakinde, Simeon Inyang, and Ben Mbonu for their invaluable contributions to the progressive editing of the manuscript, from the preliminary draft to the final script.

Strange as it may seem, I am equally grateful to the small group of temporarily *misled* individuals who were secretly incited by Jehovah to try to distract my spiritual focus on the true gospel of Jesus Christ—even those closest to me, including my parents, brothers, sisters, relatives, and friends whom I loved so dearly—just as my Savior had forewarned. I thank them, because they unwittingly provided the physical tribulations and religious challenge that rather sustained my confidence and resolve to hold on to the love and guidance of my heavenly Redeemer, Jesus Christ. No doubt, they felt religiously justified to hate me for my extraordinary conviction, but I was sure that they knew not what they were doing. Therefore, I pray that *my* Jesus Christ would, at the right time, reveal himself and his perfect loving Father to each one of them, and help them to see that Jehovah whom they serve is none other than the dreadful Antichrist.

INTRODUCTION

DISCOVER YOUR TRUE SELF

Any kind-hearted person would safely guide a child who has lost his way back to his home, providing the child possesses the right information. If the child knows his own name, his father's name, and the correct address of his father's residence, he would eventually be home and dry. Captive human spirits are in a worse kind of situation. Rebellious spirits that fell out of the realm of perfect spirits presently animate human bodies in the material universe. Incapacitated by the fall from eternal glory of perfection, they are spiritually dead, and are presently held captive by world processes. They are lost and totally blank in mind. They do not know who they are. Neither do they remember who their true Father is nor where he dwells. Worst of all, they do not even know that they are lost.

The inevitable first step for any genuine seeker of true spiritual salvation, therefore, is to rediscover his true self. A lost amnesiac must first find himself before he can find his way home. He must first come to his senses and realize that he is not at home. If he does not know where he came from, he cannot know where he is, and he would not desire to return to where he does not know.

The second step is to seek and identify a genuine guide and friend who can help direct him on the right pathway. Jesus Christ is the tried and tested true Redeemer of all lost souls in the world. He has the divine mandate of our heavenly Father, and he is willing. False Christs and false redeemers abound in the world. Therefore, genuine seekers of true spiritual redemption must first seek out the true Christ, and then hold firmly to his divine precepts.

INDIVIDUALITY OF EVERY HUMAN SOUL

The most humiliating aspect of human nature is ignorance or lack of knowledge of one's spiritual pre-existence. The saddest knowledge of all is that though the god of Genesis decreed ignorance for humans for his own ulterior ends, ignorant religious operatives blame Adam, Eve, and the heavenly Spirit of Knowledge for it.

We are individuals in the world—whether as fallen spirits or as human beings—and our spirits are ageless. Every individual human being should be able to define himself. Unfortunately, so many people cannot because of the programmed debilitating effects of human nature. Attempting to correctly define oneself should be the starting point of genuine aspiration for true spiritual salvation.

As for me, before this world was born, I am. This is not a statement of personal *religious belief*—certainly not one that people may either *believe* or *disbelieve*. It is a statement of fact, informed by the clearer understanding that I have of my true spiritual status as a fallen spirit being. This has been made possible by the ongoing, universal spiritual re-awakening of blinded *immortal* spirits in humans, started far back in Eden by the redeeming Spirit of our heavenly Messiah.

I was not only there on the foundation-laying day of the universe; I was also a co-creator of it. This may sound so strange, even sarcastic to some uninformed minds, but I am certainly older than the universe. Somehow, most people already know that the Father is eternal Spirit and that their own spirits are a part of him, yet they find it hard to understand that their own spirits are, in essence, ageless as well. This is abnormal indeed.

Surely, something went terribly wrong with me. Something is still terribly wrong within and around me. Here I am, feeling so *newborn*, so little, so *knowledgeless*, so lost and *Fatherless*. Bubbling thoughts and plain walls are the only realities known to me now. I cannot even imagine all that I ought to know as an ageless spirit being. Under the spell of human nature, I *believed* whatever I heard with my ears to be true and *accepted* whatever I saw with my eyes to be real. Nevertheless, my inner self never stopped longing for the things that I ought to *know* as a pre-existent spirit being. Although I speak of me, it is true for all human beings on earth. Those who reach this realization will see the greater picture clearer.

When Jesus Christ said to his Jewish audience, "Truly, truly, I say to you, before Abraham was, I am," he was trying to enlighten them about the ageless nature of the human spirit, relative to the transient nature of the human body, and of the material world in general. Unfortunately, his hearers, being in total ignorance of the basic status quo, tried to stone him to death. They did not understand his gospel truth and were not prepared to. Hence, they remained oblivious of the need to rediscover their true selves and to find their way home.

It is so unfortunate that the human mind, as predestined by the primordial blueprint, identifies solely with one's physical personality and sense perceptions, but man's invisible self, spirit, or soul is the real person. Hence, when I speak of "me," I speak not of my physical being, but of my spiritual self. As Jesus Christ says in John 6:63, "it is the spirit that gives life; the flesh is of no avail." When the Messiah spoke of being in existence before the biological formation of the human android, Abraham, he meant that his Spirit, the heavenly Christ, existed before his physical body, named Jesus, whom the Jews supposed was the great-grandson of Abraham.

The reason Jesus Christ came into this world was not to perfect the physical man, but to **salvage** and eventually **resurrect** the "real person" in every willing human being to true spiritual life. The fact that this real person in man needs both spiritual *redemption* and *resurrection* means that he is both *lost* and *dead* to his true spiritual self. It is obvious, therefore, that every human being does have a redeemable past that transcends his physical personality and worldly experiences.

For this spiritual redemption and restoration to past glory to be possible, however, one must first incline himself to seek heavenly wisdom, which human nature strongly abhors. He must be willing to encounter and adopt radically opposed realities from the ones predicated on worldly norms. Then, he must discover his *only* true heavenly Guide, Jesus Christ, and firmly resolve to learn from him. Only Jesus Christ has the heavenly mandate and the willingness to impart true guidance to lost spirits in our present worlds of darkness.

Anyone who finds the true Jesus Christ will surely know it, for he dispels all doubts and fears. He gradually overrides the false programming of the human mind, replacing it with spiritual information from the soul's memories. He activates and strengthens the human conscience, making it the point of contact between the human mind and the indwelling Holy Spirit of truth. Only by his guidance, therefore, can the captive human spirit truly rise above the smothering influences of carnality and materialism.

The journey of a lost spirit toward total self-rediscovery can only be made possible by Jesus Christ. Only he can assist the captive human spirit to recollect obliterated memories of his past glory, and only such assisted recollection of his true nature will make it possible for him to understand and define himself. It will help him to appreciate the alien nature of his present captivity and make it easy for him to choose wisely between spiritual resurrection and eternal death in the outer darkness. What we already know about the horrifying nature of our present world of darkness as human beings, should spur us to seek and hold on to the true Jesus Christ for divine guidance toward true spiritual redemption.

The world will assuredly hold anyone who finds the true Jesus Christ in contempt. So-called friends and family members will desert such a person. They will literally disown him, but he will prosper greatly in his spirit. He will feel special peace and genuine accomplishment deep in his conscience. For the true friends of Jesus Christ, what human nature counts as rejection, humiliation, and defeat before men, he reckons to them as heavenly beatitude. Thus, Jesus Christ enjoins his true friends to be very glad in such situations, knowing that their reward transcends material prosperity.

He re-assures them with these positive words: "God blesses you when people mock you and persecute you and lie about you and say all sorts of evil things against you because you are my followers. *Be happy about it! Be very glad!* For a great reward awaits you in heaven. And remember, the ancient prophets were persecuted in the same way." [Matt. 5:11–12 **(NLT)**]

STANDARD BIBLE REFERENCE FORMAT

As in the previous volumes, my main reference Bible for this volume is still the *Revised Standard Version*. Other versions of the Bible used in this work are mentioned in brackets at the end of the quotations. For example, Matthew 5:11–12, when taken from the *New Life Translation* version of the Bible, would appear in the bracket at the end of the quotation in this way: [Matt. 5:11–12 (NLT)].

USE OF *JEHOVAH* INSTEAD OF *YAHWEH* IN THIS VOLUME

Most people who read the previous volumes seemed unfamiliar with the fact that "**Yahweh**" and "**Jehovah**" are but two artificial variations of **YHWH**, the personal name of the tribal god of the Jews. Some readers in Nigeria asked me if the Yahweh I wrote about was the same as "Jehovah Almighty," god of Israel.

Well, YHWH is the transliteration of a four-letter Hebrew name of the god of the Jews that he personal revealed to Moses. It is also known as the Tetragrammaton, because of its four letters. The Masoretes who reproduced the original texts of the Hebrew Bible from about the sixth to the tenth century, mechanically replaced the vowels of the name YHWH with the vowel signs of the Hebrew word *Adonai*, thus forming the artificial name **Jehovah** (YeHoWaH). However, early Christian writers, such as Clement of Alexandria in the second century, had used a form like **Yahweh**. Although Christian scholars after the Renaissance and Reformation periods used the term Jehovah, in the nineteenth and twentieth centuries, biblical scholars again began to use the form Yahweh, thus making that the modern form in use. Other Greek transcriptions also indicated that **YHWH** should be pronounced Yahweh (YaHWeH).

However, since the majority of customary Christian laity in Africa and other parts of the Christian world seem to be more familiar with the form Jehovah, I decided to revert to that in this volume to make sure that no reader is left in any doubt as to which deity I refer to in my books.

ABBREVIATIONS

The Holy Bible:
Good News Bible—With Deuterocanonical Books/Apocrypha (GNB)
King James Version (KJV)
New International Version (NIV)
New Life Translation (NLT)
New Revised Standard Version (NRSV)
Revised Standard Version (RSV)

*As noted in the Introduction, my main reference Bible for this volume is the *Revised Standard Version*. Thus, when no abbreviation is given with a Bible citation, my source is the *Revised Standard Version*.

CHAPTER ONE

LIFE, SIN, AND DEATH; REPENTANCE, SALVATION, AND THE RESURRECTION

ECHOES FROM THE PROVERBIAL PRODIGAL SON'S EXPERIENCE

Most often, people ask me to explain how the Father could be so loving and still abandon us in the world to be tormented by Jehovah, the devil. Their answer lies in the life experiences of the proverbial prodigal son, but most Bible readers never bother to make sense of it. The Father did not abandon us in the world; rather, we abandoned him and chose the world. Even then, he has not abandoned us to the devil; rather, we are self-tormented in the world. Jesus Christ used the parable of the prodigal son to teach human beings the true meaning of life, sin, death, repentance, salvation, and the resurrection.

The prodigal son abandoned home for the *distant country* because he believed that a better life existed out there. He willfully left behind everything that made him a prince and the son of a great king, severed the sacred bond of love that bound him and his father's royal household, and thus forfeited his father's natural shield of love.

His life in the alien country was a complete deviation from the natural life of a royal personage. Deprived of his natural royal restraint, he lived recklessly while he struggled in vain to find the kind of inner peace and happiness that he had taken for granted at home. As every unnatural thought or action is bound to bring dissatisfaction, pain, and unhappiness, he soon became extremely frustrated, hungry, and broken. The scripture says in Luke 15:14 and 16 that "he began to be in want … and no one gave him anything"— a situation that had been unthinkable for him when he was in his father's house. Eventually, he discovered the hard way that the only condition beyond **life** *at home* is **death**.

While he lived *a true* **life** at home as a beloved son, the scripture says emphatically that he was *dead* and *lost* in the distant land of his meaningless dream. The prodigal son became firmly convinced that he was being self-afflicted the moment he *rediscovered* his true self. Hence, he made a resolute choice to live again. He positively stopped wandering and soliciting for *alternative salvation* within the world of his self-affliction; *no one gave him anything* worthwhile anyway. Therefore, he abandoned the spheres of the world, where he had died, and headed back home—the only place he knew he would find true resurrection.

Indeed, the moment he set foot on his natural homeland and came face to face with his loving father, all his pains and anguish vanished like a bad dream. True life returned to his whole being. Immediately, his loving father instructed his royal attendants to restore him to perfect peace and happiness. Literally, the prodigal son became *born anew*. "Quick!" his father said. "Bring the finest robe in the house and put it on him. Get a ring for his finger, and sandals for his feet. And kill the calf we have been fattening in the pen. We must celebrate with a feast, for *this son of mine was dead and has now returned to life. He was lost*, but now he is found." [Luke 15:22–24 (NLT)]

In other words, the prodigal son lived, sinned, and died; then he repented, returned home, and lived again. Although his father's love for him remained steadfast, he lived again *only* because he returned *home* to the natural sphere of influence of his father's love. It is clear from the above that life and death, like light and darkness, belong to two eternally opposite situations. There is no mid-way between them. The prodigal son could enjoy true life only at home; life outside his proper home meant death.

TRUE STATUS OF HUMAN SPIRITS

Every spirit being in existence is *immortal* or eternal, whether in life or in death. A spirit being is either living in perfection in his Father's sphere of positive influence or dead in his Father's sphere of negative influence. The choice to live or die, for every spirit being, hinges directly on the heavenly norm of perfection, which states, "the soul that sins shall die." This can be seen in Ezekiel 18:20. If a living spirit abides by the heavenly norm of perfection, he lives in absolute bliss in the realm of perfection. But he dies the moment he willfully deviates from the norm, as a matter of natural recompense. He automatically forfeits both the natural heavenly ambience and all the glory of spiritual perfection and descends into the realm of total darkness. Even though he continues to *live* in the lifeless realm of darkness, it is in anguish, and as a shadow of his true self.

In other words, **there is no finality in death for any fallen spirit**, contrary to what deluded religious dogmatists insinuate. Therefore, "the soul that sins shall die" is a permanent reminder to every living spirit of the only two possible modes of existence, it is either *life in absolute bliss in the Father's heavenly kingdom* or *death in utter anguish in the outer darkness*. As one would expect, the heavenly norm confers divine endowment of absolute free will on every living spirit.

No one kills or subjects a spirit that sins, that violates the norm, to eternal suffering. He is self-condemned to a life of misery and pain when he yields to his improper, loveless desires. It is erroneous to insinuate that the Father punishes or that he would torment unrepentant spirits in a certain hell fire. The Father does not kill or punish sinners. It is not in his perfect nature to do so. Rather, he patiently encourages fallen spirits to return to the natural sphere of his divine love to regain their perfect spiritual heritage. The Father's perfection is absolute. He is Love, and Love is Life. As the Blessed Tree of Life, he gives perfect eternal life, not the life that is marred by suffering and death. As we have learned from his perfect envoy, Jesus Christ, "The Father is never tempted to do wrong, and he never tempts anyone else." [James 1:13 (NLT)] That is the straightforward way to define the Father's perfect nature.

The prodigal son experienced life in his father's house and death in the outer world, and he decisively made his final choice. He chose to return to the natural domain of his father's love, and that choice automatically rekindled him. Walking out on his father's love and eventually returning to it were both *his* choices. No one forced him to abandon home, and he knew the possible implications of his fateful decision. Hence, no one caused him all the pains and anguish that he experienced outside his father's home. Certainly, his loving father never wished him any harm, but patiently waited for him to rediscover, in his own way, that life was impossible outside his proper home. He was, therefore, self-afflicted.

Such is the case of the fallen human spirits in the world. We are strictly self-tormented. As living spirits in the perfect spiritual kingdom of the Father, we knew the norm well enough, and we enjoyed absolute free will. Lucifer represented the erotic allure of the uncharted distant country, such as the one that lured the prodigal son away from true life in his father's kingdom. We knowingly chose to abandon our Father's heavenly household for the selfish life of total abandon in the realm of "anything goes."

We are the real prodigal sons. Yet the Father's love for us remains steadfast. He has never stopped loving us and desiring that we come back to our senses. Hence, he sent us his living Son, Jesus Christ, as a *heavenly Guide* to lead us back home. Indeed, if we were wise like the proverbial prodigal son, we would have seen clearly that life outside our Father's heavenly home is death. We would have willingly embraced the special love of the Father in Jesus Christ that steadfastly draws us back to himself. This is why friends and true disciples of Jesus Christ are the only truly wise people in the world.

In our case, as fallen spirit beings, spiritual death means dwelling outside the perfect spiritual kingdom of our Father. It means totally abandoning our proper place in the Father's spiritual household and plunging into the distant realm of total darkness, beyond the natural domain of his steadfast love for us.

A spirit dies in the sense that he practically falls away from the realm of perfection. He loses the true essence of his natural potential as a *living* spirit. He literally becomes a *fallen* spirit, and therefore, the direct opposite of everything the perfect Father represents. For instance, his life ceases to personify true love, light, life, and holiness. Therefore, a dead spirit continues to "live" in the faraway alien world of darkness, just as the proverbial prodigal son did in the distant country, but as a Fatherless son and prince.

Captive human spirits are prodigal sons of heaven. The scriptural books of Jude and Genesis clearly tell the story of our collective spiritual rebellion, death, and *new life* of anxiety and anguish in a chaotic universe. Human beings need to understand that they are, indeed, *the angels that did not keep their original position [in the Father's spiritual abode] but forsook their own proper dwelling place* in perfection and died. That spiritual death is the only death that matters for our individual fallen spirits. The programmed cyclic, physical death of mortal human bodies on earth means absolutely nothing in spiritual terms. With that wrong choice of abode, our rebellious spirits were automatically spewed out of the Father's heavenly kingdom and plunged into the lifeless outer darkness. We lost our true eternal life at that same moment.

The cataclysmic explosion that brought about our restless universe took place within the *primordial* outer darkness and represented the actual beginning of our universe. Scientists have called that fatal explosion the *Big Bang*, and they are correct. It was, indeed, the initial collective outburst of the entire heavenly dropouts, aimed at sufficiently disturbing the natural state of tranquillity that characterized the lifeless realm of darkness, to create a state of constant motion within which they hoped to invent artificial light, recreate themselves, and explore alternative life forms. What we call the universe is, merely the expanding debris of matter and gas caused by that initial mystical outburst—much like the giant mushroom-shaped cloud of dust and debris caused by a nuclear explosion. Human earthen bodies are composed of the floating debris of matter and gas contained within the universal mushroom and animated by the false lights of our fallen spirits that radiate from specific solar grids.

That should tell human beings the spiritual status of all the spirits involved with the eventual making of the humans' world. The so-called Genesis creation account in the Jewish Torah is a calculated religious propaganda, invented by Jehovah for his own ulterior motives. No real creation took place in Genesis; planet Earth and its solar system evolved naturally from astronomical activities triggered by the *Big Bang*, which was the collective exploit of all the fallen spirits about 13.7 billion years ago.

What followed the *Big Bang* was the formation of universal superstructures and natural evolution of lifeforms on various biospheres. Gradual evolution of ideas, principles, and inventions thrived on planet Earth; obviously, because it presented the right conditions that favored organic innovations. The very first two verses of the Jewish-doctored Genesis account reflect these facts clearly. They read, "In the beginning **when [Jehovah] began to create** the heavens and the earth. The earth was formless and empty, and darkness covered the deep waters. And the Spirit of [Jehovah] was hovering over the surface of the waters." [Gen. 1:1–2 (NLT)]

The planet Earth, with the deep waters and darkness that covered its surface, was already in existence before the so-called Genesis creation. The surface of the earth remains covered with the deep waters and darkness today, exactly the way it was before Jehovah's so-called creation.

The Genesis cock-and-bull tale rather presents positive indication of sudden homelessness on the part of the groping spirits. The groping spirit of the so-called god of Genesis was as homeless as the rest of the fallen spirits within the barren expanse of darkness and matter. If he and his Jewish publicists were truly wise, they would not have tried to make him out to be the sole inventor of the universal superstructure within which his spirit continues to grope helplessly. By admitting that his spirit was *floating* over the surface of the deep dark waters that covered the surface of the planet Earth, they also acknowledged that he was indeed, stranded, powerless, and helpless in the beginning. In fact, he is still *floating* in his general outlook. Scriptural accounts of his deeds and utterances in human history show that clearly. He is still as stranded, powerless, and lost as the rest of the fallen, dead spirits in the world.

For as long as the universe remains outside the Father's realm of perfection, every spirit being associated with it remains spiritually dead. Both the so-called gods and rulers of the universe and their subservient human captives are dead spirit beings within the imperfect world. There is only one perfect option for every fallen, dead spirit outside the Father's heavenly kingdom, and that is genuine repentance. Only those who willingly choose to return to their proper dwelling place in the Father's perfect heavenly home will live again. The Father has already mandated his living Son, Jesus Christ, for their resurrection.

Thus, the scripture makes it explicit that death is not a state of outright mortality, but rather that of spiritual degeneracy. For, though it says, "the soul or spirit that sins shall die," it also says that the resurrection of those who repent is in the Father's divine emissary, Jesus Christ, the heavenly Messiah. "For the wages of sin is death, but the *free gift* of the Father is eternal life through Christ Jesus our Lord," says Rom. 6:23 (NLT).

Surely, if death of the sinful spirits were final the way human minds understand it to be, then the idea of *repentance* and *resurrection* would have been unimaginable. If the dead spirit beings in the world were not redeemable through the present dispensation of the Father's grace upon them, Jesus Christ would not have come into the world. Unfortunately, the human mind is not readily attuned to this fundamental fact, and misleading activities of worldly religions have sustained a permanent state of human ignorance on the matter;

the hidden agenda being to discourage people from persevering for spiritual resurrection.

Customary Christianity, for instance, teaches its gullible adherents that, "each person is destined to die once and after that comes judgment." [Heb. 9:27(NLT)] That teaching is necessarily dubious because it is meant to apply to the physical death of human beings. It is entirely false in the context of reincarnation or the cyclic process of human life and death on the earth, which is indisputable. It is also technically false regarding our spiritual death, because the Father presently *preserves* us and expects us to persevere to regain true life within the protracted period of grace that he granted for our repentance, redemption, and resurrection.

Indeed, "the wages of sin is death, but the *free gift* of the Father is eternal life through Christ Jesus our Lord." What this means is that the Father has not written off any one of us, irrespective of whether we are presently dead or alive as human beings. So, Jehovah and his religious abettors have no rights, pretending to be in the position to have sealed our fate already.

Contrary to insinuations by human religion, even death of the physical man cannot be described as final. The *missing* matter of the decaying human corpse does not necessarily die; it simply transforms into other forms of matter—solid, liquid, or gas, depending on the kind and intensity of energy that acts upon it. In cremation, for instance, heat reduces the human corpse to gas and ashes.

In fact, every substance in existence, whether material or spiritual, is infinitely indestructible. Science recognizes this fact, stating that matter is infinitely indestructible, but merely changes in state or form. In his theory of relativity, Albert Einstein came up with a simple equation to demonstrate that energy can be infinitely transformed into matter, and matter into energy: $E=mc^2$; where E=Energy, m=mass and c=the speed of light (a constant=3×10^8m/s).

This is why we can recycle things like cans, glass, and paper. It is easy to understand how matter simply changes form by looking at what temperature variations do to ordinary water. Water is normally liquid, but varying its temperature will transform it into solid or gas. Nature recycles too. Water cycle, for instance, is a complex system of continuous circulation of water within the Earth and atmosphere in different states. Liquid water evaporates into water vapor, condenses to form clouds, and falls back to Earth in the forms of rain, snow, or hail. In this way, water on earth is constantly recycled.

Likewise, a rebellious spirit does not necessarily *die* or vanish out of existence when he violates the heavenly norm of love and drops out of his proper place of eternal bliss. Rather, the incongruous conditions of his alien abode automatically transform him into a frustrated, self-afflicted, miserable being. Outside the Father's perfect spiritual kingdom is a world of acute limitations. Every being in the universe is miserable, frustrated, and self-afflicted because we are all self-seeking. We are all preoccupied with dreams of vanity, because we are spiritually dead and presently dwelling outside the natural sphere of the Father's divine love and guidance. Nevertheless, his divine grace upon us at present makes the world seem merely like a kind of spiritual remand home. We do not yet know or feel the full impact of spiritual death.

Jehovah, the celebrated god of Genesis, is the most frustrated and miserable of all the fallen spirits in the world, because he is the most obsessed about meaningless worldly glory. In his falsely exalted ego, he adamantly struggles to become what he could never be, especially in his present state of spiritual folly. As he permanently struggles in vain to crown himself "God" over the rest of the fallen, dead spirits in the world, he adamantly "opposes and exalts himself above every so-called god or object of worship ... proclaiming himself to be God." [2 Thess. 2:4]

Unfulfilled desires bring about frustration, grief, and inability to think clearly. Unsurprisingly, Jehovah spoke freely and even acted out his utter frustration and grief throughout the Jewish Torah. He just could not help that. Because he could not think clearly in his present circumstance, he also spoke about taking vengeance and pouring out his wrath on other individuals for his own failures. His ungodly outbursts paint the clearest picture of self-affliction. He desired what he could never get, and so he grieved.

In the book of Ezekiel, he pronounced the heavenly norm of perfection—*the soul that sins shall die*—to try to explain away his frustration and unfaithfulness to the battered Jewish exiles. By that, he intended not only to distort the true meaning of the sacred statement in the minds of the disenchanted Israelites, but also to mislead the entire human race on the true meaning of **life, sin,** and **death** through his protracted Jewish conspiracy. He merely alluded to physical life, sin, suffering, and death, which are entirely unrelated to the heavenly norm. Meanwhile, he deliberately avoided stating the fact that the Father freely grants spiritual resurrection to every truly repentant spirit in the world. Of course, he was not addressing fallen human spirits that matter, but mortal humans that live once and die forever.

For generations without end, he battered the helpless descendants of Abraham, invoking a jungle standard of justice that permitted him to *"visit the iniquity of fathers upon the children to the third and the fourth generation"* of people who resisted his impure, selfish desires. In so many vicious ways, he made it obvious to the Jews that he was simply a god who enjoyed destroying both the sinful and the just. His lopsided standard of justice was so notorious that it became a commonplace saying in Israel that *"the fathers eat sour grapes, and the children's teeth are set on edge."* [Ezek. 18:2]

To save face, he merely pronounced the divine standard of justice, *"the soul that sins shall die,"* which he never really believed in. His so-called *new* policy on universal equity and justice stated that, "the son will *no longer* suffer and die for the iniquity of the father, nor the father suffer and die for the iniquity of the son; the righteousness of the righteous shall be upon himself, and the wickedness of the wicked shall be upon himself." [Ezek. 18:20] But that still turned out to be an empty talk, coming from an unrepentant lawless lawgiver. Injustice and inequity remained Jehovah's standard norm in the earthly world that he rules, as he remained "a jealous *God* that visits the iniquity of the fathers upon the children to the third and the fourth generation" of those who disagree with his lawless nature. It could not be otherwise in a godless world such as this.

The context of *individual responsibility* that he conveyed in the book of Ezekiel to the Jews and their teeming religious followers worldwide does not reflect the true meaning of the heavenly norm that pertains to true *life, sin,* and *death* of heavenly spirits. "The soul that sins shall die" is the fundamental norm of a heavenly life of perfection. It should be obvious to all that the norm strictly addresses spirits that are living, not ones that had already violated its tenets and died spiritually. The heavenly norm of perfection is simply inappropriate for beings within any sphere of the sinful material world that is populated by already dead spirits. It is particularly not applicable in the human situation, whose natural portion is already suffering, injustice, and death. Every *living* man is twice dead spiritually. He is merely the mortal physical cloak of a spirit that had already sinned and died.

It is very important that human beings understand the true meaning of spiritual life, sin, and death. If they do, they can appreciate the full implications of spiritual regeneration—*repentance, redemption,* and *resurrection*—that the Father offers all of us through Jesus Christ, his heavenly Envoy. The true meanings of life, sin, and death are not what the human mind has been programmed to think that they are. For instance, they have absolutely nothing to do with a permanent obliteration of the physical and spiritual elements that make up the physical man. Certainly, they have nothing to do with the universal cyclic process of reincarnation or physical re-embodiment of transmigrating *dead* spirits within the chaotic universe. Death is not the cyclic cessation of physical activities randomly experienced by mortals in the world; it is the basic state of the universe and everything in it.

The process of life and death of man, as worldly religions have impressed upon the human mind, represents artificial reality. They are, but two processes of the unreal world. The gods craftily intend that to distort humans' understanding of the spiritual death that matters, and to confuse them about the true meaning of eternal rest. They have no place whatsoever within spiritual reality. That is why human beings think of themselves as *living* when they are merely moving carcasses of dead spirits. That is also why some religious people believe and teach that *righteous* men die and proceed to a place of eternal rest in heaven. Such a statement represents a vivid symptom of spiritual oblivion.

Death is the mode of existence of every being who dwells outside the Father's spiritual realm of perfection. Physical death on the earth does not lead to eternal rest; it leads to another page of spiritual bondage. True life or eternal rest is practically impossible within any sphere of the precarious universe because the universe is outside the realm of life and eternal rest. The entire universe is dead and lost within the massive spiritual emptiness of the outer darkness. Everything in it is lifeless through direct involvement.

The composite man is dead even when he thinks he lives, because he is strictly of the same unstable nature as the universe. Even when he shades his physical body under the worldly makeshift process of physical re-embodiment, his spirit continues to hover in anguish within the chaotic universal. Eventually, he would return to the physical plane, as a newborn *animal* in its due season, as the only life possible for the animating dead spirits within the present material world is animalistic. Meanwhile, the captive human spirit subconsciously continues to seek spiritual salvation, whether in the physical body or out of it.

True spiritual life means eternal rest. Therefore, it cannot exist in a chaotic situation. Neither can death exist within the realm of perfection. True life is absolute peace and happiness, or the total absence of danger, anxiety, and pain. Spiritual death is the exact opposite of that. If I put it another way, true life is love. To love is to live; and to live without love is spiritual death. This marks the basic difference between the mode of existence in the perfect spiritual kingdom of the Father, and the life of permanent strife and anguish in the chaotic universe. Our displaced, prodigal spirits presently wander about in calamitous, mystical orbits of artificial life and death within the dead universe.

This should help human beings to understand clearly that the Father who is Life himself does not dwell anywhere within the lifeless universe. Because he is Love also, danger, anxiety, and pain cannot possibly exist within his sphere of positive influence. Jesus Christ makes us understand that "perfect love casts out all fears." The entire universe is therefore godless because it is loveless. If our perfect heavenly Father dwells anywhere within the universe, there will be absolute peace, order, and happiness in every sphere of it. The entire universe will be eternal Paradise indeed.

People ask, "Why doesn't the Father do just that?" Well, it is like asking why the father of the proverbial prodigal son did not go and transform the distant country to make his lost son feel at home there. The realm of perfection is the eternal domain of our perfect heavenly Father; our present universe is a travesty within the eternal realm of darkness. Lost sons of the Father here must return to their heavenly household to experience perfect eternal life, just as the proverbial prodigal son did.

Jesus Christ told the story of the prodigal son, as a parable, to help human beings appreciate that there can be no alternative to true spiritual salvation and resurrection within the spheres of the chaotic universe. For true spiritual restoration, every dead spirit in the world must make an outright reversal in his choice of eternal abode. Our spirits have all experienced the two extreme modes of existence—*life in absolute bliss in the Father's heavenly abode* and *death in utter anguish in the precarious universe*, just as the proverbial prodigal son did. The Father now presents each one of us with the same gracious opportunity that the prodigal son had—to finally decide where our spirits will spend eternity.

Just as the prodigal son had to return to his father's household to experience the full effect of his fatherly love and to regain true eternal life, truly repentant spirits must renounce the world and return to their proper dwelling place in the Father's heavenly kingdom to regain full spiritual restoration and true eternal life. Any fallen spirit that does not make that positive choice now will not make it back to the spiritual realm of perfection, and he will never regain true eternal life at the end of the present dispensation of the Father's grace. That is the gospel truth.

Since true life is impossible in any sphere of the imperfect universe, the wise ones already know that they must look beyond the world, its gods, and religious institutions for true spiritual salvation. This is where the mission of Jesus Christ, as the Father's divine Envoy, beckons thorough understanding. While the proverbial prodigal son remembered his way home and had no extraordinary hindrance on the way, very wicked spirits who constitute themselves into principalities, false authorities, gods, and lords of the universe vehemently hinder captive human spirits in their genuine efforts at returning to the Blessed Tree of Life.

The Father spoke his Word of Life for the benefit of all the dead spirits in the world, but this wicked clique determinedly hinders the disadvantaged ones from receiving that divine privilege of a second chance. They do not only reject the divine offer themselves, but they are also terminally committed to stopping other fallen spirits from availing themselves of the gracious opportunity.

This ruthless clique of mystical banditti poses nearly insurmountable opposition to true spiritual salvation of human spirits on earth. Hence, captive human spirits inevitably need the gentle but supreme authority of a *heavenly Guide* to walk them home through the clustered mine fields of the repressive world order. No captive human spirit can make it back to the Father's heavenly kingdom without special heavenly intervention, in the person of Jesus Christ. He is the sole heavenly Messiah or Liberator of all oppressed spirits in the world.

The Father sent him into the world first, to give us the *Good News* about the Father's gracious offer of eternal resurrection to every repentant dead spirit in the world. Second, he came to *liberate* our captive spirits from involuntary bondage in the hands of the false gods, overpowering influences, and chieftains of the universe. Finally, he would guide the *redeemed* ones back to the Father's heavenly home in safety. Jesus Christ came to help us regain our lost eternal life. That would eventually be consummated on the day of resurrection, when he would have finally guided us back to the only place where true spiritual life is possible—in the Father's domain of perfect existence.

The scripture makes it clear that Jesus Christ is the true redeemer of all dead spirits in the universe. His is the true *way* back to the heavenly Blessed Tree of Life. Only he has the Father's mandate and authority to overcome for us the antics of the ferocious principalities. He is the heavenly *Good Shepherd*. Only lost spirits guided by him will make it home in the end; and only those that make it back to the presence of our heavenly Father will be *restored* to true spiritual life. The Messiah confirms this in the scripture by reiterating the solemn will of the Father: "For this is the will of my Father," he says, "that everyone who sees the Son and believes in him should have [regain] eternal life; and I will [resurrect] raise him up on the last day." [John 6:40]

All religious salvation initiatives by the world that are not rooted in Jesus Christ, the Good Shepherd, will ultimately lead to *second* eternal death at the close of the period of the heavenly grace. Every worldbound salvation program, such as Jehovah's "New Jerusalem" and "dry bones will rise again" gambits, are calculated spiritual fraud, purely aimed at oblivious religious soul-sleepers, like the Jews, customary Christians, and Muslims. By expecting that Jehovah would invent the world anew for them for instance, **the Jews** and their teeming religious surrogates worldwide, are literally expecting a refurbished *pig farm* where they would eventually continue their present miserable occupation of feeding the swine and eating of the seed pods meant for animals.

The **Jehovah's Witnesses** sect is not only expecting to live together with lions, goats, snakes, and scorpions in the wild, but also to chew grass as every other animal in the so-called *New World* that Jehovah promises his ignorant religious slaves. It might help them to understand that animal life will not exist ever again when the present universe and its suns have ceased to exist. The present universe will eventually stop expanding and *die* a natural death. When that happens, organic existence, as we now know, will cease to exist forever. Everything in the universe will ultimately revert to the primordial state of total darkness and eternal serenity. Since organic life depends solely on solar energies, how then do Jehovah's Witnesses hope to continue living as human beings in a non-existent animal world?

The **Seventh-day Adventists**, on their part, are not only unable to appreciate that Jehovah's seventh-day redundancy injunction does not lead to true spiritual salvation, but they are also expecting to continue to be slaves to the moon phases in his utopian *New Jerusalem*. They are surely living in some cloud-cuckoo-land at the present.

Roman Catholics and their popes make a mockery of true spiritual salvation with their institutionalized fallacy of sainthood—a purely human process of *nominative righteousness*. Catholics believe not only that the pope is *infallible* and that he can *declare* a dead human being saved and living with *God* in heaven, but they also believe that idolizing and praying to, or through, such a *dead* religious *holy man*, can improve their own physical and spiritual conditions on the earth. That is certainly, a worse kind of spiritual delusion.

Occultists and **blind mystics,** too, think of transient mystical experience of astral travel to some imaginary heavens as true spiritual liberation. They readily succumb to all kinds of dehumanizing *exercises*, all in the name of trying to fraternize with the god that dwells in one imaginary dark orb and rules our present world of darkness. They believe that the *burnished* image and likeness of human form "with eyes like the flames of fire" that every throne mystic sees at the end of his swift nocturnal flight seated "on a likeness of an electrocuting metallic throne" is the Father. They also imagine that the spiritual kingdom of the Father is the world-like orb that deluded, eccentric mortals like them can zoom in and out of at will while remaining earthlings.

What sworn cultists would never openly admit is that the so-called heavens and the images of their orchestrated mystical experiences are purely of human and worldly nature. Luckily, they are not the only ones who have travelled to these so-called heavens and seen the mundane images that they deliberately misconstrue. At least, visions of Jehovah's *heavenly* throne seen by the prophets of the Bible should help ordinary people, who may have never experienced the mystics' world of caricature spirituality, to reason things out for themselves.

Ezekiel saw, "seated above the likeness of a throne ... a likeness as it were of a human form." [Ezek. 1:26] He did not see the Father who is the Infinite Spirit. Isaiah saw the same long-robed elderly man sitting on the throne of the world within a concrete temple building and among human and animal creatures. He stated emphatically, "I saw Jehovah. He was sitting on a lofty throne, and the train of his robe filled the temple. Attending him were mighty seraphim, each having six wings. ... They were calling out to each other, 'Holy, holy, holy is Jehovah of Heaven's Armies! The whole earth is filled with his glory [or rather his pugnacious reputation]!' Their voices shook the temple to its foundations, and the entire building was filled with smoke." [Isa. 6:1-4 (NLT)] Isaiah did not see the Father who is Absolute Spirit—"who alone has immortality and dwells in unapproachable light, whom no man [or prophet] has ever seen or can see." [1 Tim 6:16]

The so-called *God* who sits on the throne of the world is merely a man of war. No wonder his worries and preoccupation are strictly of mundane human matters that directly affect him and his subordinates on the earth. Isaiah's report corroborates this fact. His testimony reads, "Then I heard Jehovah asking, 'Whom should I send as a messenger to this people? Who will go for us?' I said, 'Here I am. Send me.'" [Isa. 6:8] Then, Jehovah sent Isaiah to his beguiled Jewish slaves, as he had sent many other religious spokespersons before him, with interpolative words, against the true prophetic inspiration from the coming Messiah. Isaiah eased Jehovah's immediate worries on that occasion, thus proving that he is neither self-sufficient nor fully in control in his so-called worldly kingdom, as religious people insinuate.

Even after Jehovah had abducted and indoctrinated Apostle John, he also saw and described the same *mystical man* that sits upon the fiery throne of the material world. John reported that Jehovah "was someone like the Son of Man," and that "He was wearing a long robe with a gold sash across his chest. His head and his hair were white like wool, as white as snow. And *his eyes were like flames of fire*. His feet were like polished bronze refined in a furnace, and his voice thundered like mighty ocean waves." That was quite typical indeed! [Rev. 1:13–15 (NLT)]

It is so pathetic what organized religion has done and still does to its unsuspecting *believers*. Indeed, ignorance is the greatest exponent of spiritual death. Human beings earnestly need to imbibe heavenly wisdom, which is entirely predicated on selflessness. They need to learn to live the life based on true love, which is alien to our present loveless world. Only learning to love again can form the right foundation for true spiritual restoration to the realm of perfect love. Love is the divine fuel for life. One can, therefore, express the divine norm of perfection in a different way: **"the soul that runs out of love runs out of life."**

It is pertinent now to streamline the definitions of **life, sin, death, repentance, salvation,** and **the resurrection** so that people might cultivate the right mental attitude toward their deep-rooted inner yearning for true spiritual rebirth:

- **Life** is the mode of existence of perfect spirits dwelling within the Father's perfect spiritual kingdom. Profound love of the Father fuels and sustains heavenly life.
- **Sin** is the willful rejection of the heavenly norm of perfect love. Selfishness is the root of all sins. Selfishness was the

only sin committed by the proverbial prodigal son. It is the original sin committed by all the fallen, dead spirits in the world.
- **Death** is the mode of existence of every being dwelling outside the Father's realm of perfection. It is the outcome of selfishness or the willful rejection of the divine norm of true love.
- **Repentance** is the resolute re-acceptance and persistent observance of divine tenets of true love, even as human beings. Learning to live selflessly in human communities is practical repentance. Jesus Christ, the heavenly Messiah, showed us that we can live selflessly in the world, even as human beings. He proved to us that we can all repent and be resurrected, and that none of us is beyond salvation.
- **Salvation** is the unwavering acceptance of the Father's divine arrangement, through Jesus Christ, for the rebirth of one's fallen, dead spirit. Inwardly accepting Jesus Christ as one's heavenly guide is salvation itself.
- **The Resurrection** is the total reversal of the demise of a fallen, dead spirit, culminating in his ultimate return to his original dwelling place in the Father's perfect spiritual kingdom. Only the *resurrected* Christ has the Father's divine mandate to perform that final process of spiritual rebirth for every repentant dead spirit in the world. "For it is my Father's will," says the heavenly Messiah, "that all who see his Son and believe in him should have eternal life. **I** [not Jehovah or any other Fatherless spirit in the world] **will raise them up at the last day.**" [John 6:40 (NLT)]

UNIQUE ROLE OF JESUS CHRIST IN OUR SALVATION RACE

It is equally pertinent here to make as plain as possible the unique role of Jesus Christ in our salvation race. He is the Father's sole redeemer for all the dead spirits in the universe. Being able to distinguish and inwardly accept the love of Jesus Christ as one's *only* personal guide for this crucial return journey to spiritual restoration is the very crux of salvation. At the core of the concerted universal hindrance to our spiritual salvation lies our inability to make that distinction. The world and its religious agencies work tirelessly to keep unsuspecting human beings in perpetual ignorance of the true nature and purpose of Jesus Christ in the world.

Normally, it is not difficult for people who dwell in darkness to see and embrace light when it suddenly shines among them. The Father sent Jesus Christ into our world of darkness to be the light of our salvation, but the wicked principalities that oppose the Father's gracious gesture have cast a spell of three-fold blindness over the minds of their human captives. They have cleverly invented and sustained falsified understanding of the unique position of Jesus Christ as the only true Savior in the entire universe, relative to any other entity known as god among men. Ultimately, customary religions of the world have become official pillars of illusion for the gods over beguiled humans.

The *Good News* that the Father meant for all his fallen, dead sons in the world is that though "*the wages of your sin is death,*" he has granted "*the free gift of eternal life in Jesus Christ, his heavenly Envoy*" to all. Every spirit that accepts the special love of the Father through Jesus Christ will regain true eternal life. As far as the issue of spiritual rebirth of our dead spirits is concerned, the scripture makes it plain that Jesus Christ of Nazareth is our *only* true guide on the crucial journey from death to life. He is the only bridge between our present world of dead spirits and the Father's perfect spiritual kingdom of living spirits.

There is absolutely no alternative to Jesus Christ in the entire universe, whether in the name of man, god, or object of human worship on the earth. There is no alternative to his new commandment of love. The scripture states these facts plainly. It says, "There is salvation in *no one else*! the Father has given *no other name under heaven* by which we must be saved." [Acts 4:12 (NLT)]

The emphases here are on *"no one else"* and *"no other name under heaven."* Here, *under heaven* clearly means *in the universe* or simply *outside the Father's heavenly domain*. The same special emphasis on Jesus Christ being the Father's sole Envoy in the entire universe is repeated in some other verses of the scripture. Philippians 2:9–11 (NLT) for instance, reads, "Therefore, the Father elevated him [Jesus Christ] to the place of highest honor and gave him *the name above all other names*, that at the name of Jesus every knee should bow, *in heaven and on earth and under the earth*, and every tongue confess that Jesus Christ is Lord [of our spiritual salvation], to the glory of the Father."

Here again, the emphases are on *"the name above all other names"* and *"in heaven and on earth and under the earth."* It is obvious here also that *"in heaven and on earth and under the earth"* clearly means *in the entire universe*. Sadly, customary Christianity has effectively falsified the straightforward meaning of the verses in the minds of its followers.

Because customary Christianity propagates Jehovah, the tribal god of the Jews, as *God Almighty* on earth, when its ministers read the verses, they make their adherents assume that Jehovah is a name beyond the bounds of the universe. Yet they acknowledge him as the heartbeat and chief god of our earthly world. Of course, they had already brainwashed the people into believing that the universe has two distinct regions—*the heavens* and *the earth*. Hence, it is easy for them to compel the churchgoers to presume that Jehovah dwells in heaven, and that *under heaven*, therefore, means *on the earth* or simply *among human beings*.

That is a very deceitful nuance indeed. That is not what the verses are saying at all. Jehovah's name is in no way excluded from the names *"in heaven and on earth and under the earth."* As the *first* man on the planet Earth and the chief ruler of the present world order, he is indeed, the first name among all the names *"in heaven and on earth and under the earth."* Once people understand that Jehovah resides wholly here on the earth, both **as fallen, dead spirit and as a man**, they will no longer have a problem understanding why Jesus Christ is the only true Savior for all captive human spirits.

The truth is that the universe is *one* vast expanse of shattering matter within the outer darkness. It is the chaotic abode of all the fallen, dead spirits in the outer darkness. Jehovah is simply the most notorious one on planet Earth. The Father's perfect heaven is not here in the universe, and the universe has no separate heaven, as purported by religious propagandists. Scientific proofs abound to that effect. If religious people call outer space heaven just because they are standing on the surface of planet Earth, then they must agree that worldly heaven is indeed relative. Earth would appear equally as heaven to any being standing on the surface of Mars or on the moon, for instance. The idea of worldly heavens and earth is merely an imaginary *partitioning of convenience*, just like the imaginary geographical lines of divide between countries on the surface of the earth. These do not really exist.

Nevertheless, even if Jehovah, the mountain god of the Jews, resides in one of the so-called *heavens* within the universe, his name is still not excluded from the names *"in heaven and on earth and under the earth."* In all matters concerning our spiritual salvation, the name Jesus Christ is still above the names of Jehovah and all the other solar gods and co-rulers of the universe who dwell in the various other worldly *heavens*. That is the plain truth, which customary Christianity has deliberately twisted in the minds of its deluded adherents since Paul founded it to serve the will of Jehovah, who is the well-known Antichrist. The Father's heaven is not a part of the so-called *heavens* of the universal wasteland. It is very important that people should know this.

INCONTROVERTIBLE FACTS RELATING TO TRUE SPIRITUAL SALVATION

Keeping in mind the clear lessons drawn from the parable of the prodigal son, as well as from relevant verses of the scripture, we can now firmly state some incontrovertible facts relating to true spiritual salvation:

- There are *only* two eternally opposed realms in existence—the realm of perfect Light and Life, and the realm of perfect darkness and lifelessness; the former is spiritual, while the latter is material.
- The realm of perfect Light is the eternal domain of the Father and the heavenly abode of living spirits who emanated from him. The Father himself is the Absolute Divine Spirit. He is the supreme embodiment of Life, Light, and Love, which are the defining factors of perfection. True spiritual life is only possible in this realm.
- Our present material universe, which is just a tiny *malignant tumor* within the perfect realm of darkness and lifelessness, is presently the abode of fallen, dead spirits that were spewed out the realm of Light and Life. These include Jehovah and his ruling partners in crime who blindly claim to be *gods* and those of us who have perforce become their religious slaves. True spiritual life is impossible in this realm. Hence, spiritual redemption is necessary for *every* fallen spirit within this realm, as it was in the case of the proverbial prodigal son in the distant country.
- Naturally, any spirit that sins will remain eternally cut off from the heavenly household of the Father. However, infinite love of the Father miraculously draws us back to himself. Hence, spiritual salvation is a miraculous process by which the special love of the Father retrieves a corrupted spirit from eternal spiritual death in the outer darkness and

returns him to the heavenly household of the Father. It was the everlasting love of his father for instance, that drew the prodigal son back from death in self-captivity to a rekindled, blissful life at home. Love is the spiritual gravitational attraction that inwardly pulls his own to himself. Indeed, it is the love of the Father that gives true spiritual life. Nothing in the entire universe can replace that. No kind of religious ritual, performed in the name of Jehovah by men of uncanny dispositions, can replicate that.

- Unlike in the case of the prodigal son, the human situation required the physical incarnation of the Father's love, because human nature represented a complex level of spiritual degeneration. It literally amounted to a second degree of spiritual death. At the height of our spiritual anguish, Jesus Christ of Nazareth became the physical incarnation of the Father's life-giving love in the universe. The scripture expresses the divine miracle this way: "When we were utterly helpless, Christ came at just the right time and died for us sinners. Now, most people would not be willing to die for an upright person, though someone might perhaps be willing to die for a person who is especially good. But **the Father showed his great love for us** by sending Christ to die for us while we were still sinners." [Rom. 5:6–8 (NLT)] When we appreciate Jesus Christ as the physical embodiment of that *great love of the Father*, sent to draw us back to our rightful place in the heavenly household of the Father, it becomes easier for us to understand why no one else is like him in the entire universe. All the spirits in the universe are dead and lost; naturally, only the living Son of heaven can guide the lost ones back to the kingdom. All the prophets of old who were inspired by the Father's spirit of love prophesied, even before his physical appearance on earth, "that everyone who believes in him will have their sins forgiven through his name." [Acts 10:43 (NLT)]

A dead spirit whose sin is forgiven is divinely cleared for ultimate restoration to his original perfect status. The Father has already forgiven all the fallen spirits in the world. All that a forgiven spirit needs to do is to accept the Father's offer of spiritual rebirth and willingly allow his heavenly Envoy to retrieve him from the realm of spiritual death to the realm of light, love, and eternal life.

Jesus Christ came in human form so that the spirits who had further degenerated into physical humans would be able to see, touch, feel, and believe *that* special love of the Father for them. The scripture explains further: "Because the Father's [fallen] children are human beings [now]—made of flesh and blood—the Son [the love of the Father] also became flesh and blood. [For only as a human being could he effectively communicate with human beings.] For only as a human being could he die, and only by dying, could he break the power of the devil, who had the power of death. Only in this way could he set free all who have lived their lives as slaves to the fear of dying [physically]." [Heb. 2:14–15 (NLT)]

Indeed, Apostle John summarizes the efficacy of the physical appearance of the Father's love among the humans in his testimony in the first Epistle:

> "We proclaim to you the one who existed from the beginning, whom we have heard [of] and seen. **We saw him with our own eyes and touched him with our own hands**. He is the Word of life [from the Father]. This one who is life itself was revealed to us, and we have seen him. And now we testify and proclaim to you that he is the one who is eternal life. He was with the Father, and then he was revealed to us. We proclaim to you what we ourselves have actually seen and heard so that you may have fellowship with us. And our fellowship is with the Father and with his Son, Jesus Christ. We are writing these things so that you may fully share our joy." [1 John 1:1–4 (NLT)]

Apostle John further explains, "And this is what the Father has testified [by the physical appearance of his Word of Life]: He has given us eternal life and this life is in his Son. Whoever has the Son [therefore] has life; whoever does not have the Father's Son does not have life." [5:11–12 (NLT)] It is as plain as that! Jehovah was the chief god on the ground at the so-called beginning of the earthly creation. He dwelt on earth when the living spirit of the heavenly Christ first appeared into the world in the Garden of Eden. He still dwelt on his Temple Mount in Jerusalem when the heavenly Christ returned in human form and made his historic triumphal match into Jerusalem. Jehovah remained here with us in both body and spirit, even after the heavenly Messiah had accomplished his earthly mission and returned to the Father in heaven. Jehovah is, therefore, an *earthman.*

In fact, as the principal and everyday ruler of the imperfect world order, Jehovah is the biggest player and stakeholder here on the earthly scene. Therefore, when the scripture says that there is *"no one else"* like Jesus Christ *"in heaven and on earth and under the earth,"* it explicitly means that not even Jehovah is like the living Son of the Father. He is just a dead and lost spirit, like every one of us.

Jehovah poses as *God* before ignorant human beings, only because human nature almost completely stifles the memories of human spirits. We all know him very well; only we cannot quite remember fine details in our present state of forced spiritual oblivion. Evidently, people who still look up to Jehovah as *God* are still under his *three-fold spell of ignorance* that he alludes to in various *ayahs* of the Qur'an. People who look up to him for spiritual salvation have not yet discovered that he is just a powerless, dead spirit like every one of us. Jehovah is of no consequence to the spiritual salvation of our captive spirits, except in his notorious capacity as the tempter and dreadful Antichrist.

In Matthew 25:30, the Bible refers to the region outside the Father's perfect spiritual kingdom as "the outer darkness." Qur'an 77:30 speaks about "the shadow falling threefold," as the final abode of unrepentant sinful spirits. However, part of Qur'an 39:6 reads: "He [Jehovah] created you [human beings] in the wombs of your mothers, creation after creation, *in three-fold darkness.*" Judging from the context of the entire *ayah* 6, as well as other related *ayahs* of the Qur'an, the phrase refers to the total darkness surrounding human nature. Jehovah's three-fold spell of ignorance is thus a reflection of the programmed ignorance of the Edenic human being, the concerted blindfolding activities of worldly religions, and the resultant self-delusion of unenlightened minds.

Jehovah is openly opposed to *the great love* of the Father for our lost spirits. He is the pretentious god of Eden who obstructs our way to the Father of life. Documented evidence shows that he barricaded the only way to the Blessed Tree of Life with "*demonic creatures and a flaming sword,*" his express intention being "*to keep anyone from coming near [the Father who symbolizes] the tree that gives life.*" [Gen. 3:24 (GNB)] People should not overlook this fact. Jehovah is the devil who hinders human beings from understanding and responding positively to the special love of our heavenly Father that beckons us to return home. He is also the one who has subjected ignorant human beings to *lifelong bondage* to fear of artificial mortality, which is what the worldly cyclic process of human life and death is.

Jehovah is the fear of ignorant minds. All the so-called fathers of our religious faith who looked up to Jehovah as *God*, did so purely out of fear—not because they were truly convinced that he behaved like *God*. In fact, most of them were inwardly convinced that he had nothing of spiritual value to offer anyone, both in the present world order and in the impossible one that he promised his deluded religious victims. Of course, he never pretended to say that he has anything good to offer anyone. They also knew that he would never change.

Most of them feared and propagated the *fear of Jehovah* as a virtue, because they had not encountered that invincible, life-giving love of the Father in Jesus Christ that drives away all fears. The gospel truth is that Jehovah is just a spiritual weevil. Jesus Christ, our heavenly

Messiah, has the right pesticide against him. Even though he has successfully proclaimed himself the chief god of the universe, he is just an earthbound spiritual bug. He is completely powerless before the meek and gentle Messiah. Jesus Christ is the ultimate hope of captive human spirits who seek spiritual salvation.

I say all this emphatically and will stand to defend it wherever and whenever I am called upon to do so—*"in heaven and on earth and under the earth."* People should not be afraid to broadcast the *Good News* to the four corners of the universe. True spiritual salvation is a battle of righteousness against the spiritual weevils of the world who have riddled our spiritual resolve for so long. It involves outright *spiritual revolt* against the world, its gods, human nature, and all spiritually repressive human traditions that are inspired by Jehovah. Furthermore, it is a battle of conscience. Only honest and courageous spirits will win this battle.

Now is the time for people to be brave and to stand up for their spiritual rights, holding on to the only victorious name that the Father has approved of. The reason Jesus Christ came into the world in human form is to physically disarm the principalities—to crush in pieces the so-called *flaming sword* of the lawless man of war that hinders the captive human spirits from reaching the Father.

The scripture clearly says that Jehovah is the lawless man of war, and it affirms that, "The Good News about the kingdom will be preached throughout the whole world, so that all nations will hear it; and then the end [of Jehovah's oppressive worldly regime] will come." [Matt. 24:14 (NLT)] "Then [Jehovah] the man of lawlessness will be revealed, but the Lord Jesus will kill him [merely] with the breath of his mouth and destroy him by the splendor of his [third and final] coming [into the world]," says 2 Thess 2:8 (NLT).

CHAPTER TWO

GOD OF GENESIS: MAN OR MYTH?

Jesus Christ states plainly in John 17:3 that true spiritual salvation is only possible for people who can correctly identify our true heavenly Father. He says, "This is eternal life, that they know thee **the only true God**, and Jesus Christ whom thou hast sent [as sole emissary into the world]." With this statement, the Messiah stresses the fact that a major false *God* resides in the world and presently deceives the entire humankind. Indeed, it makes no sense for someone seeking true spiritual restoration to be wasting his time seeking the face of the god of mundane worldly matters, which is what Jehovah is.

A *God* that is in *image and likeness* of human beings is strictly of the world. He may be able to grant material *breakthroughs* and *prosperity* but will be deliberately misleading in true spiritual matters. He cannot possibly grant anyone true spiritual salvation.

Since the beginning of the world, various customary religions have solely preached the god of material blessings. Before now, people never really understood the true meaning of spiritual rebirth or the need to distinguish and identify with the Father who grants spiritual salvation, rather than with the false *God* that is strictly concerned with perishable worldly goods.

Even in our present generation, heavily deluded church ministers, for instance, still preach the rusty old god of Genesis so powerfully to multitudes of *religious believers* who merely believe in and seek material prosperity in the world, and not outright spiritual deliverance from spiritual death. Most of these believers do not even know that there can be outright spiritual redemption from the entire spheres of the imperfect world and its gods. Evidently, they also do not yet understand the real substance of the true gospel of Jesus Christ.

Some people look up to Jehovah, the rusty god of Genesis, as the Father, simply because *most* people do. But genuine seekers of true spiritual salvation should sincerely answer this simple question today to determine where their individual captive spirits stand in the ongoing battle for true spiritual emancipation: **Is Jehovah really a man or myth, considering that we, as human beings, are in his exact image and likeness?**

What the Jews, customary Christians, and Muslims have deliberately taken for granted about Jehovah, the god of Genesis, is the fact that the historical account of his tactical ascension to the false position of *God Almighty* on the earthly scene is clearly documented in the annals of human history. If it could be proven that Jehovah started life on earth as a man, like every other human being, and that he is strictly concerned with mundane worldly matters, then he is simply the false *God*, and, therefore, of absolutely no use to any genuine seeker of true spiritual salvation.

While Abraham, Moses, Elijah, and the Jewish patriarchs of old did not have the perfect external standard by which to judge the authenticity of Jehovah's systematic claim to the status of the true *God Almighty*, Jesus Christ has provided all the answers to people of our present generation. I strongly doubt that any human being on earth today questions whether Jesus Christ is the worthy emissary of the Father in the world. The scripture states emphatically that "No one has ever seen the Father; the only Son, who is in the bosom of the Father, he [alone] has made him known [in the world]." [John 1:18] "We [the whole world] have seen and testify that the Father has sent his Son as the Savior of the world." [1 John 4:14]

Men and women who are truly wise should endeavor to appraise Jehovah's bogus claims with the heavenly standards that have been duly exemplified by the worthy Messiah. In his unique position as the divine Envoy of the Father in the world, Jesus Christ duly demonstrated the Father's eternal attributes to the entire humankind. He made us understand clearly that **the Father is not a man**, and that he is not in any way involved with the mundane aspects of the imperfect world of humankind. Of course, the Father sent his living Son, Jesus Christ, into the world because he does not dwell in the world. The Messiah also showed us that the Father is the **Living Spirit.** He proved by personal examples that he is also **Love**, **Light**, and eternal **Life**.

Even a toddler would understand the true meaning of these simple words. It should not be difficult for any honest person on earth to see that the Father does not dwell within any sphere of our chaotic universe, which is eternally characterized by materialism, lack of love, darkness, and death. No doubt, if the Father dwells even in the remotest part of the universe, his eternal nature will prevail all over it. Hence, the Messiah concluded by saying, "If I had not come and spoken to [people of the world], they would not have sin; but now they have no excuse for their sin [for believing in the false *God Almighty*]. He who hates me hates my Father also. If I had not done among them [unique] works [of love] which no one else [ever] did [in the world], they would not have sin; but now they have seen and hated both me and my Father." [John 15:22–24]

Usually, religious interpretations of reality are calculated affront on common sense. The religious notion of Jehovah, the groping god of the Genesis, being the Perfect Living Spirit who is true Love, Light, and Life is surely fraudulent. Even with all the sound, documented evidence to the contrary, religious propagandists still expect rational thinkers to *believe* that the groping spirit in the Genesis account eventually emerged from the primordial darkness that totally encompassed him in the beginning to become the true *God Almighty*, "who alone has immortality and dwells in unapproachable light, whom no man has ever seen or can see." [1 Tim. 6:16] That is the calculated myth about Jehovah, the notorious entity whom the scripture clearly shows to be the very *first* human being on earth.

Jehovah's preeminence among human beings can be simply likened to that of the ostrich among birds. The ostrich is exceptionally big and outstanding in the world of winged animals. It is the largest and strongest of all known birds in existence. Its Latin name is *Struthio camelus*, reflecting its likeness to a camel in terms of shape and size. A gullible little child might even see it as a feathered dinosaur. Indeed, the ostrich is related to the prehistoric *Ornithomimus*, a gigantic, toothless, beaked carnivorous dinosaur that lived in North America and Tibet about 65 million to 97 million years ago. In fact, the ostrich is the king of the birds. Nevertheless, because it has wings and feathers, and lays eggs like every other bird in existence, it is nothing else but a bird. In the same way, Jehovah is just an oversized human being.

Jehovah, the god of Genesis, is both a man and a myth. The Qur'an has ninety-nine names and attributes for him that generally try to portray him as the biggest and strongest being on planet Earth. Five times every day, Muslims are summoned to mandatory prayer sessions (*salat*) with chants of "*Allahu Akbah!*" (Allah is greater!). This is a very crafty statement indeed! Is Allah greater than whom? They leave the answer open, for obvious reasons. It is a purely psychological tactic of permanently impressing on the worshipers' minds the erroneous idea that Jehovah is the greatest being in existence. In truth, Muslims are merely claiming unconsciously that he is *greater* than other human beings on earth.

Finally, the last *surah* of the Qur'an states that Jehovah is "the Lord of mankind, the King of mankind, and the God of mankind." [Qur'an 114:1–3] This simply means that he is an outstanding figure among humankind, just as the ostrich is among the winged species. Here, the strong emphasis on *humankind* clearly tells the whole story about the true nature of Jehovah. Jehovah's lordship or kingship is over fellow human mutants that presently populate planet Earth, not over perfect *living* spirits that dwell in the perfection realm of unsearchable light beyond the bounds of our imperfect, physical universe.

It is a natural fact that every king rules among his own kind. The king whale rules among lesser fishes and creatures in the oceans, the queen bee among the bees, and the village chieftain among his own kith and kin. Therefore, Jehovah, the self-invested king of human*kind*, rules over human beings that are under his mystical spell of authority, because he is human. It just cannot be otherwise.

A true spirit can only preside over his own kind—the living among the living, and the dead among the dead. The Father of Jesus Christ is the Sovereign Living Spirit; his Kingship is not among dead human mutants on planet Earth, but over living spirits that dwell in his perfect spiritual kingdom. His kingdom completely transcends the mystical kingdoms and principalities of the world, presently dominated, and ruled by a few opportunistic, dead entities.

Jesus Christ proved that he is a truly living spirit when he firmly rejected Jehovah's cryptic offer of earthly kingship in league with the earthbound principalities. Jehovah is human, and a very desperate one at that. The so-called archangels are equally humans. Hence, Jehovah presides over the council of the principalities that rule over unconscious humans. If he were indeed living spirit, he would not have been completely engrossed in mundane human matters. He would not be terminally obsessed with the despotic desire to become king over all human beings at all costs.

The Jewish Torah talks about a certain *wandering miracle worker* who sneaked into the life of Prophet Abram, pretending to be a friendly kinsman, and stealthily enslaved his mind and those of his unsuspecting religious descendants. He predicted that Abram would become a very rich man in the land of Canaan, that his wrinkled old wife, Sarah, would become pregnant and bear him a son, and that his descendants would become nations of people on the earth. Most of his predictions came true, and so Abram mistook his wandering shamanic friend to be the omniscient and omnipotent. That was where the whole mistake started.

He also showed Abram very cheap, magical signs and wonders, like making a smoking fire pot and a flaming torch to appear from nowhere and consume carcasses of sacrificial animals that Abram had laid out before him. He thus captured Abram's undivided allegiance. Subsequently, promising to make him exceedingly fruitful in material riches and offspring, he unceremoniously changed his name from *Abram* (the Father is exalted) to *Abraham* (the father of many nations). Thus, he altered the spiritual focus of his captive spirit away from the Living Spirit and from true spiritual pursuits toward materialism and pure idol worship.

Using Abraham as his prototype of religious stooges, he proceeded to set some spiritually enslaving precedents that enabled him to gradually re-dominate the liberated sons of Adam, vowing to be king over them at all costs. The scripture captures the desperateness and the mundane nature of his ultimate ambition. "As I live," vowed Jehovah, concerning the lost sons of Adam, "surely with a mighty hand and an outstretched arm, and with wrath poured out, **I will be king over you**." [Ezek. 20:33]

Abraham's wandering shaman later became *god* over his direct Jewish descendants. However, history clearly shows that he did not become god and king over them legitimately. He overpowered them purely through guile and terror. He knew that the true spiritual posterity of Adam within the biological descendants of *Abraham* would never trust or willingly accept him as *God*. They would inwardly continue to uphold the name of the Father who is the exalted one.

However, with the Jewish nation effectively subjugated, Jehovah began scheming to become king over the entire human race. Relying entirely on his concerted Jewish conspiracy, he now vows to usurp universal kingship from the rest of the principalities and rule humankind directly from his throne of violence in Jerusalem, in human form. To that end, he predicts, "And [Jehovah] will be king over all the earth. On that day there will be one Lord—his name alone will be worshiped." [Zech. 14:9 (NLT)] His claim ultimately went beyond being merely the *God of humankind* to being the *Living God Almighty* and Father of Jesus Christ. The scripture speaks plainly of the rusty god of Abraham and his sick ambition in the second book of the Thessalonians 2:4(NLT): "He [Jehovah] will exalt himself and defy everything that people call god and every object of worship. He will even *sit in the temple of God*, claiming that he himself is *God*."

Surprised by the thought of Jehovah sitting in the temple of the Father, my daughter, Ruby, asked me, "What temple and which *God*; for I know that the Father does not live in man-made temple structure, and it is impossible for the evil *god* to sit in a true temple of the Father?"

Indeed, that Jehovah would *sit in the temple of God* is a cryptic way of saying that he would openly *appear bodily in his human form*. This notion is standard with most Bible writers. When Jesus Christ spoke of the coming of the Father's Holy Spirit into his disciples, he meant that their bodies would become temples of the Father. Where the book of John quoted him as saying to the Jewish religious authorities, "Destroy this temple, and in three days I will raise it up," it quickly added, "But he [Jesus Christ] spoke of the temple of his body." [John 2:19, 21] In the same vein, Paul wrote in the first and second books of Corinthians, "Do you not know that you are *God's* temple and that *God's* Spirit dwells in you?... Do you not know that your body is a temple of the Holy Spirit within you, which you have from the Father?... For we are the temple of the living Father." [1 Cor. 3:16; 6:19; 2 Cor. 6:16]

The second book of the Thessalonians 2:4 directly refers to Jehovah's end-time prophesies of dominion, when he hopes to appear undisguised *in human form* among the Jews to rule as the sole king of humankind. Ezekiel 37:27–28 and Zechariah 14:9 are plain and explicit regarding what the Bible means when it says that Jehovah would appear in the temple of *God*. Jehovah says: "I will make my home among them [the Jews]. I will be their *God*, and they will be my people. And *when my Temple is among* them forever, the nations will know that I am Jehovah, who makes Israel holy. ... And [Jehovah] will be king over all the earth. On that day there will be one Lord—his name alone will be worshiped." Here, "*when my temple is among them*," clearly refers to his physical presence among the Jews, and not to a concrete type of temple that had always been among them.

One thing is obvious from the above at least; Jehovah is not yet the king of the entire human race. He is hoping to become in some uncertain future if his Zionist expansionist scheme works out as projected. As we should have already known, the Father is the only true King in existence, which is why his Son, Jesus Christ is known and called Prince of Peace. Regarding the world of human beings, however, Jehovah is still grappling with the thought of eventually becoming the *consolidated king* over it.

Jehovah is the entity that the scripture refers to as "the beast that was once a living spirit, but now is not," meaning that he is a dead spirit. His corrupted ambition has always been to forcibly assume universal kingship over the entire fallen, dead spirits in the world. The scripture makes it clear that he is just one of the eight desperate principalities that presently rule our lost world of hominines. The book of Revelation 17:11 (GNB) states clearly that "The beast that was once alive, but lives no longer, **is itself [only] an eighth king [of humankind]** who is one of the seven ..." Luckily, the scriptures speak clearly about the rest of these so-called kings, or rather principalities, of the world. They all started out on the earth as wandering shamans in the beginning, eventually becoming members of the supreme ruling council of gods of the world presided over by Jehovah. So, it is a question of who among them would eventually become the *consolidated king* over captive humans in the world.

The Bible documents incontrovertible evidence that Jehovah is one of the first human beings on planet Earth. It proves beyond doubt that he walked and still walks the surface of the earth, as a human being. Surprisingly, the Jews, customary Christians, and Muslims, who are the official custodians of these books of evidence, vehemently deny these facts, thereby making him seem like a special kind of *transcendent human king*.

However, no one on earth is more human than Jehovah, the god of Genesis. The Jewish Torah, which was chiefly inspired by him as canon of his worldly rule, documents clear evidence to that effect. Human history books also capture him vividly in human forms and as the most notorious player in human events. He is not just a man, but also as *the first and the last* of humans on the earth, he is the prototype of human organisms. According to the Torah, every other human being took his physical *"image and likeness."*

When he said to his seven closest companions with whom he later formed the council of eight principalities, "Let us make human beings in our image, **to be like ourselves**," he had not yet realized the need to play down the fact that he and his partners were already human beings. "So [god of Genesis] created human beings in his own image … male and female he created them." [Gen. 1:26–27 (NLT)] Surely, it is practically impossible for an entity who is not human to form men and women that are exactly like him. If the god of Genesis were a living spirit, he would have formed living spirit beings, not oblivious, mortal men and women who are but spiritual morons. The truth is that Jehovah is man, both in *form* and *character*.

The Bible also says that Jehovah planted a garden in the east of Eden, in the beginning, and called it a paradise. That action alone says so much about his real nature and limitations. In the first instance, a true spirit dwells in perfect spiritual paradise, where people do not need to own zoos, meadows, or pleasure parks. A true spirit does not plant a botanic garden; a true spirit has absolutely nothing to do with the meaningless aesthetics of a perishable, physical botanic paradise. Such vocations are strictly for *earthmen*.

Of course, Jehovah's so-called paradise on earth withered away long ago, as it should have, because it was only an earthly project. Nevertheless, the Bible makes it clear that he physically wandered about the garden, in human form, admiring the perishable beauty of it, and that he interacted with Adam and his family who tended it for him on a person-to-person basis, just as he later did with Abraham and his family members.

Where the Bible says that Adam and Eve "heard the sound of Jehovah walking in the garden in the cool of the day" for instance, it is not in any way suggesting that they heard the footsteps of a living spirit and not those of a human. A true spirit does not walk about, making sounds that human beings can hear with their ears.

It is implicit in the scripture that though Adam was the official keeper of Jehovah's garden, he was never his god, but his relative. The relationship between them severed irredeemably when he tried to dominate and turn Adam into an unthinking stooge, to advance his ambitious Zionist (expansionist) agenda through him.

When Jehovah decreed *knowledgelessness* and *disinterest in the divine Tree of Life* for him and his descendants, Adam realized that he was terminally opposed to true spiritual salvation for any fallen, dead spirit in the world. With the timely intervention of the Living Spirit of the heavenly Christ in the Garden, Adam promptly renounced Jehovah, his so-called Garden of Paradise, and his sick idea of worldly dominion. Adam opted for true spiritual redemption from the entire spheres of the world of sin through the divine mission of the heavenly Christ, and he became saved. Jehovah would later accomplish most of his evil intents through Abraham, his intimidated Jewish descendants, and their beguiled religious surrogates worldwide.

WHEN THE GODS WALKED FREELY ON THE EARTH AS MEN

What religious believers find difficult to reconcile in their minds is the fact that Jehovah is both a man and a spirit. Evidently, they do not know that they too, are both humans and spirits. With what we already know of the lifeless nature of the universal realm, and of the activities of the fallen, dead spirits that the Bible book of Jude alludes to, that puzzle should not be difficult for any enlightened mind to resolve.

As we already know, the universe is a sort of spiritual quarantine for the fallen, dead spirits that violated the norm of perfection in the

Father's spiritual kingdom. In their present corrupted nature, they invented and animated all kinds of physical organisms within the universal mushroom in a desperate attempt to mimic the lost life of true spirits. Every living organism in the world today, whether human or a microorganism, is animated by one of these fallen, dead spirits.

Jehovah's fallen, dead spirit animates human and other animal forms on earth, as does the fallen, dead spirit of the commonest human being in the street. The religious movement, Brotherhood of the Cross and Stars, has these to say about Jehovah, "He [Jehovah] appears lavishly in the dream to all men of goodwill all over the world. People pass him on the way and deal with him every day all over the world without knowing he is the one. He has manifested in various forms in different places at the same time. In the kingdom of fish, he is fish. In the kingdom of birds, he is a bird, he is an ant, he is a tree, a rock, and in the plane of humans, he manifests as a man, a beggar, a leper; in any form, as a small child, as a man, as well as a woman." Strangely enough, the Brotherhood also holds that "**the Father is not man, tree, mountain, water, air, etc. He is Spirit,**" meaning Jehovah who manifests in various animate and inanimate forms all over the world is not the Father after all. This should not be mysterious or difficult for people who genuinely seek the truth to understand.

Indeed, Jehovah is most likely multidimensional because of his advanced knowledge of occult science. Therefore, the obvious difference between him and the average person alive is his higher knowledge of the mystical formulas necessary for readily transmigration of spirits from one animal form to the other. If power is defined in terms of that, then Jehovah could be called the most powerful man among humans on earth. But that only makes him a higher mortal. It also makes him an advanced mystic, but not the Father.

He turned himself into a writhing snake for instance, when he appeared to Moses in the wilderness of Horeb, *snake* being one of his official mystical symbols of shrewd authority on earth. He was the *lion of Judah*, the *dragon* of the Chinese emperors, the Quetzalcoatl (*feathered serpent*) of the Aztecs, etc., but he is fundamentally human. He may have been "god of Abraham," and the "mighty one of Jacob," but he was also known as the "**Kinsman of Isaac**." Jacob revealed this during the final confrontation between him and his father-in-law, Laban, at Galeed as he fled Paddan-Aram with his wives, children, livestock and all his possessions in fear that he might oppose their departure. He said to Laban, "If the God of my father, the God of Abraham, the **Kinsman of Isaac**, had not been with me, you would have sent me away empty-handed. But God saw my plight and my labours, and last night he delivered judgement." [Gen 31:42(NJB)]

It was obvious that Jacob rightly saw Jehovah as his own mysterious but powerful *Uncle*, considering his knowledge of Jehovah's intimate familial relationship with his grandfather, Abraham, and with his father Isaac. The same innocent childhood mindset made Jacob wrestle with his mysterious *Uncle* at Peniel, refusing to let him go unless he blessed him, and he technically prevailed. To assure Jacob that he was indeed Jehovah, he changed his name from Jacob to Israel in accordance with his well-known practice, then he granted his request and blessed him. So, Jacob called the name of the place Peni'el, saying, "For I have seen Jehovah face to face, and yet my life is preserved." [Gen 32:30]

Even up to the time of Abraham, men needed not to become mystics to be able to see, talk with, and dine with Jehovah and the so-called gods of the world. The gods were men and were so proud to be. The only reason ordinary men looked up to them as gods was because they possessed magical powers that enabled them to appear and disappear at will, predict future events in peoples' lives accurately, and perform some magical "signs and wonders."

In the beginning, the earth was full of such men. They wandered about openly, like homeless shamans. Jehovah, the friend of Abraham, was one of them. Eventually, the divine presence of the heavenly Christ in the world drove the wandering *supermen* underground. Because of that, they founded human religions and inspired few blinded mystics and mediums, through whom they began marketing themselves as true gods to the multitude of uninformed humans. Nevertheless, they still walk the dusty streets of our ramshackle villages, towns, and cities, and they still talk and dine with their accredited mediums and friends, just as they did in the days of the Jewish patriarchs.

The cryptic story of certain *sons of God* who freely took wives from among the *daughters of men* and bore giants and extraordinary supermen of old still confuses so many uninformed Bible readers to this day. Genesis 6:1–4 (NLT) reads: "Then the people began to multiply on the earth, and daughters were born to them. The *sons of God* saw the beautiful women (daughters of men) and took any they wanted as their wives. ... In those days, and for some time after, giant Nephilites lived on the earth, for whenever the *sons of God* had intercourse with women, they gave birth to children who became the **heroes and famous warriors of ancient times**."

That was the story of some of the wandering gods who violated the code of their special powers that expected them to avoid unrestrained intimacy with ordinary humans as their aim was to play gods over them. One thing that should not be confusing to any reader here is the fact that the so-called *sons of God* were men with normal human genitalia. Although their offspring turned out to be giants, they were equally humans.

Evidently, the genes of the human gods proved to be more dominant in their offspring, which explained why they possessed and exhibited extraordinary strength in human battles. In fact, the inherited genes of the giants were those of **raw men**. Jehovah and all the so-called gods on earth were nothing but **unrefined men**. Only the divine light of the Father glowing in the conscience of a Christ-enlightened man defuses that brutal essence of the natural man. Jehovah and his colleagues resolutely rejected the Father's offer of spiritual salvation through Jesus Christ, and so have remained **natural men**, even to this day.

Genesis 18 reveals that Jehovah once came to Abraham by the oak of Mamre near Hebron, accompanied by two of his fellow wandering *supermen*. Abraham made them sit down and rest while Sarah prepared food for them, which they ate. The natural conversation that transpired between them, Abraham, and Sarah confirmed that one of the three men was Jehovah whom Abraham revered as his personal god just because he could predict the future and perform some magical feats. Strangely, no Bible reader seems particularly taken aback by the straightforward details of this revelation—not even present-day religious extremists who even stake their lives arguing that Jehovah is some invisible spirit muscle somewhere beyond the physical universe.

Evidently, there was no need for Jehovah and his partners to pretend not to be men in those days. Today, however, Jehovah has contracted the Jews and their religious surrogates all over the world to make it seem an anathema the fact that he had once wandered about the barren lands of Jerusalem and its environs as a mere homeless shaman.

Genesis 14:17–20 tells of a certain man named Melchizedek who appeared from nowhere and welcomed Abram with bread and wine after his return from the stage-managed war against king Chedorlaomer and the allied kings who were with him. The scripture calls him "**king of Salem**" and "**a priest of God Most High**." He did not only have the power to bless Abram, but he also had unspoken authority to tithe his war loots. Abram had no doubt about who he was, and so the scripture says, "Abram gave him a tenth of everything" he had recovered from the war. No doubt, Melchizedek was one of the wandering shamans that Abraham knew very well.

As we had seen, Jacob did not only see Jehovah, god of Abraham, *face to face* as a man sees another, he even wrestled with him *body to body*. The scripture confirms that the man that Jacob wrestled with was Jehovah himself, and no Bible reader seems to frown at that as sheer abomination. The following conversation that took place between them showed that **the man** had authority to change Jacob's name as well as the power to pronounce blessing on him:

> **The man:** "Let me go, for the dawn is breaking!"
> **Jacob:** "I will not let you go unless you bless me."
> **The man:** "What is your name?"
> **Jacob:** "Jacob."
> **The man:** "Your name will no longer be Jacob. ... From now on you will be called *Israel*, because you have fought with *God* and with men and have won."
> **Jacob:** "Please tell me your name."
> **The man:** "Why do you want to know my name [isn't it obvious to you]?" *Then he blessed Jacob there."*
> [Gen 32:26-29(NLT)]

The story may seem like a mere fairy tale to uninformed Bible readers, but the cryptic message is very clear. Jehovah was practically introducing himself to Jacob as the desert *man of war*, which he was. Just as he changed Abram's name to *Abraham* to demonstrate his power as the god who provides material prosperity for his friends, he also changed Jacob's name to *Israel* to prove to him and his descendants that he is also the god who fights human wars both against and for his people. "**Israel**" means "**El (Jehovah) fights.**" In other words, Israelites are a tribe whose god is a *mystical Warlord*. Moses, Joshua, Elijah, David, and most Jewish patriarchs would later dramatize the full reality of the mock seaside combat between their forefather, Jacob, and their militant god. The Father that Jesus Christ introduced to the world loves and makes peace; he does not fight human wars and he did not change Jacob's name to Israel.

The Bible says in Exodus 33:11 that "Jehovah used to speak to Moses **face to face**, as a man speaks to his friend." Jehovah personally confirmed that in Numbers 12:6–8 where he tried to make ordinary Jews understand the uniqueness of the man Moses to his ultimate Zionist scheme. "Hear my words," he said to them, "if there is a prophet among you, I Jehovah make myself known to him in a vision, I speak with him in a dream. Not so with my servant Moses; he is entrusted with all my house. With him I speak mouth to mouth, clearly, and not in dark speech; and *he beholds the form of Jehovah.*"

It is obvious, therefore, that the Jehovah that Moses knew was a man, for a spirit does not speak *face to face* or *mouth to mouth* with a mortal man. Moses called him a *man* of war because that was exactly what he was to him. Moses spoke the truth plainly. I only hope that religious believers will believe his testimony. "**Jehovah is a man** of war," he affirmed, "Jehovah is his name." [Exod. 15:3] He also clearly stated that Jehovah was merely the most prominent figure among the rest of the wandering gods on planet Earth. Moses sang and asked, "Who is like thee, O Jehovah, **among the gods**?" [Exod. 15:11]

Furthermore, Moses challenged the Jews to name another god who could match Jehovah's magical exploits. "Or has any [other] god, ever attempted to go and take a nation for himself from the midst of another nation [or from the territory of another god]," he asked them, "by trials, by signs, by wonders, and by war, and by great terrors, according to all that Jehovah your God did for you in Egypt before your eyes? [Deut. 4:34] Deluded Jews, customary Christians, and Muslims would later vehemently deny the existence of all the well-known territorial gods and partners of Jehovah in a desperate bid to try to transform him into not just the one and only god on earth, but also the only true *God Almighty* in heaven.

Furthermore, the *God* that all the prophets of Israel saw and spoke to in their dreams and visions, as recorded in the Bible, was also in the *image and likeness* of mortal man. He often disguises himself with flashes of lightning and peals of thunder, just to create the theatrical impression of being very dreadful and unapproachable. Isaiah reported that he "saw Jehovah sitting upon a throne ... and his train [the trailing part of his robe] filled the temple." [Isa. 6:1] Ezekiel also narrated that the Jehovah he saw "seated above the likeness of a throne was a likeness as it were of **a human form**." [Ezek. 1:26] He went on to add, "From what appeared to be his waist up, he looked like gleaming amber, flickering like a fire. And from his waist down, he looked like a burning flame, shining with splendor. All around him was a glowing halo, like a rainbow shining in the clouds on a rainy day. **This is what the glory of [Jehovah] looked like to me**." [Ezek. 1:27–28 (NLT)]

After his prophesied abduction, exile, and forced transformation in the rocky little island of Patmos, Apostle John also saw and described the same mystical man that sits upon the fiery throne of the material world. This time, Jehovah pretended to be the resurrected Jesus Christ while at the same time speaking of himself as "the Alpha and the Omega—the beginning and the end," and "the one who is, who always was, and who is still to come [in human form in the later days]—the Almighty One [of Israel]." According to John, however, "He was wearing a long robe with a gold sash across his chest. His head and his hair were white like wool, as white as snow. And *his eyes were like flames of fire*. His feet were like polished bronze refined in a furnace, and his voice thundered like mighty ocean waves." [Rev. 1:13–15 (NLT)] Now, a *sash* is the band of wide ribbon draped over one shoulder and across the chest by women in beauty pageants and by politicians as a symbol of rank or office. Remarkably, Jehovah still needed to wear the symbol of his self-arrogated rank among the secret council of gods, even within the haloed chambers of his supreme mystical office.

John's description of the throne and its official paraphernalia, including the personalities and official activities of the throne companions and attendants, in the so-called heavenly kingdom of Jehovah did not portray perfection or true spirituality. In fact, John did not see living spirits or anything spiritual. Rather, he saw masqueraded images of human and animal forms singing songs of infatuation and speaking mundane words and thoughts of average religious zombies on earth.

Revelation 4:5–11 reveals the things seen by John in the so-called heavenly kingdom of Jehovah:

- A throne surrounded by a rainbow that issued out flashes of lightning and rumble of thunder and someone sitting on it.
- Twenty-four other thrones surrounding the first, and **twenty-four old men** clothed in white and wearing gold crowns on their heads, sitting on them and singing false praises to the occupant of the main throne of illusion.
- Seven torches with burning flames, representing the homeless spirits of the seven collaborating principalities—the so-called archangelic companions of Jehovah—standing in front of the throne; and
- Four animalistic beings standing at the center and around the throne—the first looking like a lion, the second like an ox, the third with a human face, and the fourth like an eagle in flight—all continually praising the feted *superman* on the throne.

All the things that John saw were familiar worldly images, proving that Jehovah is just a disguised *earthman*. Of course, he would not know how to act out a true spiritual scene. In fact, one occultist I once knew assured me, saying, "As above, so below, you know!" He meant that the way things are here on earth is exactly the way they are in the imaginary heavens of the world. Yet, multitudes of religious believers solemnly look up to Jehovah and his illusory heaven as the goal of their spiritual pursuits. It is obvious, therefore, that spiritual oblivion forms the background of all world-bound religious movements. All worldly religious goals are nothing but fruitless alternatives to true spiritual salvation by Jesus Christ.

Exodus 24:9–11 is one of the portions of the Bible tactically deemphasized by religious believers who promote Jehovah as transcendental spirit. It speaks about the secret banquet held in the wilderness between Jehovah and the top elders of Israel. Moses had just successfully imposed Jehovah's covenant of eternal servitude on the bartered, floating population of Israel, and the banquet was to commemorate their official acceptance of him as the only god they would worship. The account reads, "Then Moses, Aaron, Nadab, Abihu, and the seventy elders of Israel climbed up the mountain again. There they saw [Jehovah] the God of Israel. ... And though these nobles of Israel gazed upon Jehovah, he did not destroy them. In fact, **they ate a covenant meal, eating and drinking in his presence!**" [Exodus 24:9–11 (NLT)] In fact, it was on that very occasion that they jointly drafted and adopted the Jewish Shema that Moses would later impose on the Jewish masses. The Shema reads:

> "Listen, O Israel! **Jehovah is our *God*, Jehovah alone**. And you must love Jehovah your *God* with all your heart, all your soul, and all your strength. And you must commit yourselves wholeheartedly to these commands that I am giving you today. Repeat them again and again to your children. Talk about them when you are at home and when you are on the road, when you are going to bed and when you are getting up. Tie them to your hands and wear them on your forehead as reminders. Write them on the doorposts of your house and on your gates." [Deut 6:4–9 (NLT)]

The aim of the Shema was purely psychological. It was intended to overwhelm the peoples' minds with the thought of Jehovah as the *only* god the Jews should look up to. The actual wordings of the Shema clearly reveal inferiority complex on the part of Jehovah, his fears, and the insincerity of his motive. The Jews knew that other gods existed as protectors of various other tribes, but chose, or rather were compelled, to look up to Jehovah *alone* as their own tutelary god. According to Jewish tradition, Jehovah also chose the Jews *alone* as his personal witnesses, just as they chose him. He became god over them on the strength of the blood treaty that obligated him to use his superior magical powers to fight, protect, and influence their material well-being on earth in return for their undivided allegiance, and for their unflinching endorsement of his false claim as *God Almighty* in the world.

The truth, therefore, is that Jehovah, the rusty, old friend of Abraham, is the *mystical handyman* of the Jews *alone*. He fights their wars and protects their nation, and they look up to him as *God*. Gentiles who cling to Jehovah as *God Almighty* are doubly deluded. Jehovah's testamentary words to the Jews in the scriptures are very clear. "You are my witnesses," says Jehovah to the Jews, "and my servant whom I have chosen, that you may know and believe me and understand that I am He." [Isa. 43:10] In Amos 3:2, he says, "You only have I known of all the families of the earth." I hope that customary Christians, Muslims, and the rest of the Gentile world will think seriously about this and endeavor to discover the Father who is for all peoples. What the human mind interprets as "gods" on the earth are simply intimidating physical objects, ideas, personalities, and influences that are somewhat beyond its limited scope of comprehension.

WHO THE FATHER REALLY IS

People often ask me to tell them the name of the true *God*, since I say that Jehovah is false. Well, I simply tell them what they already know, but never bother to think seriously about. The Father is **Love**. His name is very prominent in the New Testament of the Bible, yet most people who read the texts hardly take it to heart. He is the binding essence of perfection, which transcends the entire scope and bounds of our imperfect world of darkness.

The Father is All-encompassing Divine Spirit, who alone exists of Himself and is eternal and infinite in perfection. He is the Divine Tree of perfect Love, Light, and eternal Life that our fallen, dead spirits presently seek to return to through his worthy Envoy, Jesus Christ. Surely, he does not dwell in or approve of our world of sinful beings. Jehovah, the desperate, bungling *kinsman of Isaac* who rules the sinful world is not the Father.

The Father is the Source of all spirits in existence, both the living and the dead. Love is the true nature of every living spirit. The world is loveless because it is populated by fallen, dead spirits. Jesus Christ is the *only* living Son of the Father ever to have direct contact with our world of dead spirits. He defined the Father on earth by his exemplary actions and utterances. The scripture bears witness to that.

Usually, religious *believers* pride themselves as the only people who know *God*, but their uncaring utterances and actions toward their fellow human beings prove that they are utterly deluded. Everything about their individual lifestyles points to the fact that their knowledge is strictly restricted to Jehovah, the god whose image and likeness human beings share. Through their prayers and songs of praise, which are so openly pugnacious and self-centered, they clearly testify their actual allegiance.

The only people who know the Father are the ones who understand what true love is not. They are the ones whose day-to-day personal lifestyles reflect true love. "Anyone who loves is a child of the Father and knows the Father. But anyone who does not love does not know the Father, for the Father is love. … the Father is love, and he who abides in love abides in the Father, and the Father abides in him." [1 John 4:7–8, 16]

WHO THE FATHER IS NOT

Because the Father is Love, he is all-round purity of purpose; he is not good and evil as situations may demand. He is not any of what Jehovah, the god of humankind, is. The Father is the King of Peace; he is not the man of war. He dwells among blissful spirits in his eternal heavenly paradise; he does not rule our kingdoms of battered, homeless, hungry, sick, and dying paupers in a restless universe. The Father is not jealous, wrathful, and vengeful. He is not self-seeking; he does not enslave or extort worship and vainglory from blindfolded, lifeless human captives. The Father gives perfect gifts; he does not bestow enslaving material blessings or occasion human calamity. He gives perfect eternal life. He does not *kill to make alive*, and he does not *wound to heal* anyone.

Jehovah, the false *God* of the world, does all those things and more, and he proudly admits it. "I am the one who kills and gives life;" he says, "I am the one who wounds and heals; no one can be rescued from my powerful hand!" [Deut. 32:39 (NLT)] He also says, "I form the light and create darkness, I bring prosperity and create disaster; I Jehovah, do all these things." [Isa. 45:7 (NIV)] It should be obvious, therefore, that Jehovah, the bungling god of Genesis, who had long posed as *God* in the world, is nothing but counterfeit. He is perhaps the most unstable entity in the entire universe.

Jehovah's mind is clearly that of a *raw man*. With his domineering disposition and a mind so full of malice, wrath, vengeance, and terror, he is simply dead in sin. Looking up to such a *homeless desert shaman*, who presides over multitudes of miserable animals in a calamitous world pretending to be *God*, is perhaps, the most striking symptom of spiritual oblivion on the parts of religious-minded people. In fact, if Jehovah were not human in both form and character—if he were not spiritually dead and emotionally unstable—he would have not been proud declaring himself *God* over this kind of unworkable, violent, and sorrowful world.

GOD OF GENESIS: CREATURE, NOT THE CREATOR

Let me quickly repeat this here: **the entire universe is Godless**. This is not hard for anyone to see, except people who are under the blinding spell of religion. Even people who may choose to disbelieve this fact feel it deeply in themselves. The Father is perfect Spirit; he is infinite Light, Life, and Love. None of these unsullied divine qualities exists here in the world.

Certainly, if the Father dwells anywhere within this universe, there will be no need to publicize him. No being will be in any doubt whatsoever about his presence. If the Father dwells here in the universe, we will all be pure spirits, and true love will be natural to all of us. There will be no need for artificial light from the sun, and life will be truly blissful and eternal. Moreover, there will be no need for religion, no need for mediators or religious agents, and most especially, people will not have to pray for their daily needs or pay religious taxes to religious agencies, because the Father will be all things to all peoples.

Religion exists solely to disprove these obvious facts. It exists to compel people to deny what they see and feel. Religion is the propaganda agency of Jehovah, who spends all his time explaining why things are the way they are, rather than being *God* for everyone to see and appreciate. He seems to have all the best reasons to explain his ungodly actions and inaction, to explain why every human being is not able to feel him as *God* now, and why he has decided to invent a new world altogether in the future instead of rectifying whatever is wrong with this one now.

Jehovah is a remarkable *storyteller*, not *God* who lets his actions speak for him. No wonder he hires and trains multitudes of religious public speakers and he owns and hires radio and TV stations worldwide for his promotional jingles.

Religion is a spellbinder, and religious believers are woolgatherers. Hence, they impulsively disagree with any idea that calls into question their irrational congregational beliefs and dogmas. Even when they have genuine doubts as individuals, they still believe in whatever the sect believes. The fact that religion exists at all in the world for the purpose of trying to lead people to its *God* is the strongest proof that people do not readily notice or feel the divine presence of the so-called *God* in the world and around them.

The truth is that the god of human religion is none other than the groping spirit of the Genesis account. He is still lost in the thick darkness of the Genesis. People do not feel him as the Father because he is not the Father. He was not the Father in the beginning, he is not the Father now, and he will never become the Father in the future. This has nothing to do with human beings being disobedient or assertive. Human failures are not his vindication, but his own making. This is the gospel truth!

Religious propagandists have so aggressively marketed Jehovah as *God* and *Creator* of the universe on earth that even people who do not feel it believe it. Strangely enough, all the religious scriptures that he had largely inspired clearly portray him as corrupt, lawless, and ungodly. Ignorance is the only reason people mistake the gaseous glow of a burning nuclear furnace as light and are thrilled by the false goodwill of a fallen, evil spirit. But we are only sustained by the interim grace of the Father on the world.

As we have seen from the factual account of the fallen angels in the book of Jude, the Father tempered absolute darkness and evil with the limited measure of light and goodness necessary to help the heavenly dropouts with their expected spiritual reform. The Father intends to help them make informed choices, based on adequate knowledge of the difference between good and evil, between returning to perfect heavenly life and remaining eternally dead in the outer darkness. If there had not been some kind of reprieve to total primordial darkness, religion would not have had any platform upon which to begin to portray evil as good in peoples' minds. The presence of a little measure of goodness in the world is the only reason why some people can pretend not to see that Jehovah is just an evil spirit.

The *supreme principle* that governs the wicked world—what blind occultists call the *ultimate reality*—is based on harmonized *good and evil* within our present state of imperfection. While some speak of it as *even and odd*, Eastern religions call it the *yin and yang*. This does not mean perfection but simply says that Jehovah is *good and evil*.

Because every human being shares Jehovah's image and likeness, the best of us is equally good and evil by nature. This is what the Bible, the Qur'an, and all other religious books say. Sadly, exponents of these books still try to suppress the plain truth to protect the false position of their religious idols. It is evident that Jehovah lacked adequate intelligence, foresight, and power to censor or control the putting together of the wordings of these scriptures that today heavily indict him as an outlaw.

What Jehovah says about himself in these books would have said it all, but for men of "uncarved simplicity" who twist and deface obvious facts, with the hope of killing the truth forever. Jehovah told the Jews in plain words that he is both the god and the devil in their lives, and they understood him very well. When he told them that he "kills and makes alive" and "wounds and heals," and that he "forms light and creates darkness, and brings prosperity and creates disaster," they understood that he was not speaking in parables.

In other words, what people call the devil is but the inseparable half of Jehovah. Sadly, customary Christians believe that Jehovah is perfect, attempting to permanently obliterate or suppress the facts that are written in black and white in their own scripture. That is not possible, and they ought to know it. It is all a matter of time though. The truth will eventually triumph, for usually after nighttime comes dawn.

Jehovah is not All-encompassing Divine Spirit. He himself says that he rules the kingdoms of the world "for it has been given to me." [Luke 4:6 (NIV)] The Bible and Quran are not the only religious books that portrays Jehovah as a creature. The Taoist scripture, Tao Te Ching, erroneously calls the hovering spirit in the Genesis account of creation, *Tao*. It describes him as *the mother* of the earthly situation but makes it clear that he is a creature *mysteriously formed* by someone else. Chapter 25 of *Tao Te Ching* says, "(There was) something mysteriously formed, born before heaven[s] and earth. ... Perhaps it is *the mother* of ten thousand things [on planet Earth]. I do not know its name. **Call it Tao.**"

Thus, they named *it* Tao, which does not mean the Father in any way. It means the *hidden principle* or *process of nature* by which all things evolve, and which human beings need to discover and follow for a life of harmony on earth. The goal of Taoists is to search out this obscure *Tao* or *process of nature* and be in harmony with it and with the programmed nature around them. When defined as the *ultimate reality*, it still means the *universal principle* by which all things that happen in the humans' world are programmed and controlled. In time, blind mystics simply presume Tao to be the *universal energy* that made and sustains everything that exists in the universe. But I say that Tao is the '*Primordial Blueprint*' that was jointly written by the heavenly dropouts and launched into action with the *Big Bang*, and it formed the basis of all resultant cosmic activities within universal mushroom.

However, whether seen as the *universal energy*, or as the groping *god of Genesis*, the most important aspect of this revelation is the fact that *Tao* was created by a greater force, which is not even the Father who transcends the spheres of the imperfect world of ten thousand material inventions. It is obvious, therefore, that although human beings regard the god of Genesis as creator of the universe, he is most certainly, not the Father, who is the Divine Source of eternal spiritual reality. And though Jehovah claims to be the "Most High," and blind mystics regard him as "ultimate reality," he is only a little lost speck of the true Almighty Father. He is just an impostor on planet Earth.

The Taoists' emphasis on the *mother* nature of Jehovah's world is another important revelation. It proves that the so-called Genesis creation was not the Father's handiwork. The Bible confirms unequivocally that "all that is in the world ... is not of the Father but is of the world." [1 John 2:16]

The Muslim Qur'an describes the same groping spirit of the Genesis creation story in another way. It surprisingly depicts him as *a fallen light* originally kindled from the self-illuminating Blessed Tree of Light. Qur'an 24:35 reads, "Allah is the light of the heavens and earth. The similitude of his light is as a niche wherein is a lamp. The lamp is in a glass. The glass is as it were, a shining star. (This lamp is) kindled from a Blessed Tree, an Olive neither of the East nor of the West ... (This lamp is found) in houses which Allah hath allowed to be exalted and that his name shall be remembered therein. Therein [religious hypocrites] do offer praise to him at morn and evening ..."

This is the clearest and most honest revelation of all. Allah or Jehovah was a perfect speck of light from the Father, but following his spiritual downfall, he is now just *a dim lamp incased in a glass within a dark niche* **and** having the false appearance of *a shining star*. He was a true son of the Father, but now he is dead and lost in the outer darkness. He ultimately became the false light of spiritual hope, resident only in shrines, temples, churches, and mosques, where deluded religious believers mistakenly worship him as true Light.

As should be expected, the very first two verses of the Bible implicitly corroborate the true confessions of both the Tao Te Ching and the Qur'an, concerning the corrupted and inferior status of the principal groping spirit in the Genesis creation story. The Bible account makes it clear that he was just a fallen, dead spirit hopelessly floating in the primordial darkness. The material world credited to his ingenuity also speaks plainly of his spiritual limitations.

It is obvious that Tao, Jehovah, or Allah is neither the Father nor a creator in the right sense of the word. A creator that appears like a flickering lamp in a glass is a very impossible one indeed. Universal creation that was erroneously attributed to him is merely a cataclysmic outburst of darkened energies of corrupted spirits upon concrete dark matter of the primordial environment. Everything about the world and human nature amounts to utter futility in spiritual terms. The Bible calls entire worldly craftmanship "vanity upon vanity," and "an unhappy business given to the sons of men to be busy with." [Eccles. 1:2, 13]

Jehovah is just a high-handed opportunist. His love for humankind lacks conscience and goodwill, but human beings seem not to have noticed that. The cyclic process of human reproduction that reduces mature spirits into suckling babies is glorified as a blessing from Jehovah even though we all feel the worst for it. Incarnating into the physical stage as bland new babies is the worst possible cosmic intrigue against the fallen spirits in human beings.

Whenever a *new child* is born, people sing and chant praises to heartless incarceration of the human spirits, just because they lack knowledge of the cyclic agonies confronting the reincarnating spirit of the *little person*. Mark Twain (1835–1910), the American writer and humorist, once said, "Why is it that we rejoice at a birth and grieve at a funeral? It is because we are not the person involved." Human spirits are victims of human nature. They freely gulp the magic potions, scripted, and steeped in self-destructive passions by the primordial blueprint, and call it the love of *Mother Nature*. Meanwhile, human nature sustains spiritual death and captivity of human spirits.

The human mind is a slave to *Mother Nature* by deliberate design, which is why human beings deny their innate doubts and genuine distrust of the meaningless world order that permanently holds them in bondage. Human beings are in a terrible state of loss. They adore the enslaving allures of the magical world and worship their self-confessed captor as *God*, while finding it so hard to recognize their true friend and redeemer, Jesus Christ.

Human beings deserve genuine sympathy from honest minds. For their sake, the Father's period of grace has endured. Jesus Christ bore the bitter cross to try to awaken and inform captive human spirits. Many of his true disciples have equally paid the ultimate price for speaking out against concerted universal falsehood, and against its mastermind. Sadly, Jehovah remains "*God*" to multitudes of blinded religious zealots all over the world, and he will continue to be *God*, until human beings awaken themselves to the realities of their present spiritual bondage.

What people should appreciate at this point is that the realms of perfect light and perfect darkness exist as eternal opposites to one another. Darkness is an ineradicable feature of our present realm of imperfection, just as Divine Light is the eternal nature of the realm of perfect existence. Nothing can permanently eradicate physical and spiritual darkness from our present realm of darkness. Hence, even with the false rays of light from our dying star, darkness continues to overwhelm the planet Earth and the stranded beings on it. The scripture simply says, "This world is a dark place, and its people [all the displaced spirits in it] have no light." [2 Esdras 14:20 (GNB)]

The Father will never attempt to eradicate darkness from the realm of darkness. His Son, Jesus Christ, did not come into the world to turn it into a realm of eternal light, but strictly to redeem the fallen specks of heavenly light presently lost in the eternal satiety. Likewise, nothing can possibly sully the eternal light of the Father's realm of perfection. This is the basic status quo. Light and darkness will, forever, exist as the two extremes of reality. Living spirits within the Father's realm of light and perfection enjoys absolute free will. They can choose to either live in the light or die in the outer darkness. Any spirit that abandons the realm of light dies in the realm of darkness willy-nilly. The heavenly norm permanently reiterates absolute free will of all free spirits.

Right now, Jehovah, so-called archangels, and human beings are dead sons of the Father. Everything we can know and discuss about the universe, about Jehovah, and about ourselves concerns the realm of darkness and imperfection. The true heavenly kingdom of the Father is entirely beyond our scope of mental insight now. Our spirits continue to hover in thick darkness, despite the physical presence of the artificial light of the sun. The scripture captures Jehovah's perpetual handicap as it concerns his eternal loss of self-luminosity. It says, "Jehovah has set the sun in the heavens, but has said that he would [continue to] dwell in thick darkness." [1 Kings 8:12]

Jehovah continues to dwell in thick darkness as a matter of inevitability, because he had lost the true light of perfect spirits and rejected the Father's offer of spiritual rekindling. The darkness that overwhelmed him and all of us *in the beginning* is deep-rooted in spiritual dearth. It is not something that artificial light from some glowing balls of gases can assuage. The only way any of us can regain personal glory is to regain perfect spiritual selfhood. And that can only be possible for spirits that would willingly return to their proper dwelling place in the Blessed Tree of eternal light through the heavenly Christ. Unfortunately, Jehovah chose the path of opposition to divine mission of Jesus Christ who is the Father's sole heavenly Envoy, and who alone can help him find his way back to his divine origin.

No perfect spirit *hovers* in thick darkness. That is inconceivable. Jesus Christ exemplified the true nature of perfect spirit in our world of darkness. The scripture rightly calls him "the true light that enlightens every man" in the world. [John 1:9] His advent into the world literally dispelled the thick darkness that had blinded the mutated spirit beings on planet Earth. Adam and Eve willingly received the heavenly light and glowed within themselves. They ate of its fruit, "then the [spiritual] eyes of both were opened," and they began to see beyond the darkness that had encompassed them within and without. [Genesis 3:7] Hence, the scripture further says of Jesus Christ, that "the true light shines in the darkness, and the darkness has not overcome it." [John 1:5] No other light in the entire universe has ever shined as he has.

Right now, Jehovah is in harmony with darkness, so he cannot be anything other than imperfect. While he has never been able to shine forth since the so-called *beginning* of his earthly regime, our heavenly Messiah came and shined in ways that we all can see. Apart from his bodily transfiguration before his Apostles, his deeds and utterances revealed the natural glow of perfect Spirit.

The heavenly Christ came so that we may stop hovering endlessly in darkness. Accordingly, he speaks to us words of true spiritual rekindling that Jehovah or any of his cronies cannot. His words clearly define his divine mission in the world. "As long as I am in the world," he says, "I am the [true] light of the world [Jehovah is the dim lamp of groping religious daydreamers]. ... I have come as light into the world, that whoever believes in me may not remain in darkness. ... The light is with you for a little longer. Walk [away] while you have the light, lest the darkness overtake you [completely]; he who walks in the darkness does not know where he goes. While you have the light, believe in the light, that you may become sons of light [once again]." [John 9:5; 12:46, 35–36]

CHAPTER THREE

BIRTH OF MODERN HUMAN BEINGS

Life outside the realm of perfection is death. Organic life is an artificial process of astral projection that enabled the fallen, dead spirits in the outer darkness to animate organic matter in the material universe to experience a false sense of being *alive* outside the Father's perfect spiritual kingdom. The birth of modern human beings was the climax of evolutionary experimentation with animal existence on planet Earth. Humans are perhaps the most privileged animal organisms on planet Earth today, as animating human spirits stand a better chance of attaining spiritual enlightenment and eventual ascent from the unique earthen human cloak.

With enhanced grey matter, human organisms merely mimic heavenly wisdom, such that uninformed ones think of their own mortal form as essentially superior to those of other species of animals. However, human brainpower represents nothing but artificial intelligence. True wisdom is a faculty of functional human mind and conscience. Only the Father endows the humans with functional minds and transcendental good conscience through the divine office of the heavenly Christ. Only true friends and disciples of Jesus Christ are truly wise on planet Earth.

As the scripture shows, Jehovah, the god of Genesis, and the other so-called gods of the world donned the first human cloaks formed on planet Earth. Thereafter, they helped some other spirits to become like them. Thus, the *most high gods* cloned other human beings—male and female—in their own *image and likeness*. Multitudes of other spirits animated lesser forms of animal species. Thus, a natural hierarchy of worldly beings exists on planet Earth along the lines of levels of knowledge and mental consciousness. The humans were to dominate the *new* animal world order, with Jehovah and the so-called archangels acting as tutelary *supermen*. They would later pretend not to be humans like the rest of us; Jehovah would even gradually assume the false status not only of Most High God, but also of a perfect, transcendent spirit being.

Nevertheless, human nature is a second degree of spiritual degeneracy underwent by the self-seeking heavenly dropouts. It also turned out to be a complex process of bitter spiritual captivity for the less privileged human spirits. But the brave action of Adam and Eve in Eden liberated their captive spirits from false life of the world and from the repressive world order for ever. Their unexpected victory against divine enslavement in Eden set the precedent and gave impetus for humankind's gradual revolutionary match toward the blessed Tree of Life. Meanwhile, the gods schemed harder in attempt to reassert their false supremacy and to prevent the spiritual redemption of their human subordinates. To this end, they founded human religions of various creeds, and through them spread and sustained propagandas and erroneous beliefs about basic realities.

In keeping with the universal conspiracy, customary Christianity peddles very disruptive lies about the true nature of the Father, Jesus Christ, Jehovah, the so-called ruling gods of the world, and the human beings. Therefore, to make any meaningful progress toward true spiritual salvation, one must fully expunge all these religious lies from his overall mindset. Genuine disciples of Jesus Christ must seek and hold firmly to his true gospel of the Kingdom. For, as he says, those who meditate in his exact words "will know the truth and the truth will set them free."

The Church advertises Jehovah as *God Almighty* and *Creator* of the entire universe to ignorant human beings on planet Earth. It holds Jehovah to be transcendental, while at the same time saying that his permanent dwelling place is on one obscure Mount Moriah in Jerusalem, the so-called Temple Mount. According to David, "Jehovah, the *God* of Israel, has given peace to his people; and **he dwells in Jerusalem forever**." [1 Chron 23:25] In other words, Jehovah dwells forever in a kind of magical heaven that exists here on planet Earth. And as for David saying that Jehovah has given peace to the Jewish nation, extensive history of Jewish people says otherwise. On the contrary, descendants of Abraham have never known peace since their days in Egypt, and they will never know peace until they realize that Jehovah has been their archenemy, until they renounce him and all his works and turn around and say, "Blessed is he who comes in the name of the Father." [Matt 23:39] In fact, Jesus Christ says to the jews specifically, "Would that even today you knew the things that make for peace! But now they are hid from your eyes [by the one you call your *God*.]" [Luke 19:42]

Furthermore, the Church willfully elevated the so-called archangels or tutelary deities who belong to the world's ruling council that is presided over by Jehovah to the false status of *heavenly beings*, while angels are represented as some unquestioning winged sprites who minister to Jehovah in the invisible plane. Then, human beings are merely reduced to disobedient mortal beings that Jehovah formed by breathing atmospheric air into the nostrils of an earthen sculpture called Adam. In other words, the Church holds human beings to be mere transient chattel slaves of Jehovah that do not have preexistent individual spirits of their own. Yet, it says that Jehovah made the first human beings perfect. This is sequel to the notion that Jehovah also made ancient Jerusalem a paradise before *his perfectly created* Adam and Eve single-handedly pulled the plug and turned the place into an eternal land of horror, as the situation stands today in his present Jerusalem.

These are preposterous lies. Religious people who believe all this are very pitiable indeed. One thing is obvious at least; the so-called almighty Jehovah, the archangels, angels, the humans, and all other beings mentioned in religious exploits are all contained within this eternal realm of darkness. The whole story is strictly concerned with the material universe that we all see and can understand as humans, with the planet Earth being the specific theater of events. Nothing about Jehovah, archangels, and human beings transcends the sphere of planet Earth. None of the religious homilies is set in the perfect spiritual kingdom of the Father.

Therefore, no matter how hard religious propagandists twist and suppress the truth, people who cannot readily understand the truth can at least feel it. The entire universe is godless. The Genesis god-man epic is entirely hellish. These facts are commonplace. Remarkably enough, the Bible, upon which the Church claims to base its arguments, largely contradicts the claims of the heavily deluded clergies.

Facts from the Bible's account of the foundation of the world reveal the origin and nature of the spirit beings involved, the nature of the primordial situation, and the origin and nature of the first human beings on earth. These are very lucid and incontrovertible. As we can see from the book of Jude, verse 6, "angels that abandoned their proper dwelling in the Father's perfect spiritual kingdom were kept **in eternal chains in the outer darkness** until the judgment of the great day." This is a simple description of spiritual quarantine. That was the actual foundation or genesis of our present magical world.

That the fallen spirits were kept *in eternal chains* in the realm of darkness meant eternal limitations. It meant that the *fallen* spirits were strictly incapacitated in their *new, improper* abode. Fortunately, in his infinite love and compassion, the Father had magnanimously *reserved* them within a special period of grace for a second chance. It was meant to be a period of reflection within which they were expected to show genuine repentance and resolve to return to their proper heavenly dwelling, just as the proverbial prodigal son did. The Father would then send his heavenly Envoy to escort the repentant ones back to the kingdom for full spiritual restoration. The unrepentant ones would, however, remain eternally self-condemned in the outer darkness after the great day of the final roll call.

Thus, the Father's heavenly salvation program was explicitly stated right from the onset. Unfortunately, the heavenly dropouts refused to play by the life-giving heavenly precepts. Genesis 1:1–2 further reveals that the same group of *fallen* angels in the book of Jude were the inglorious spirits *hovering* in pitch darkness before the invention of the chaotic universe. They included the spirits of Jehovah, the so-called archangels and angels, the humans, and every other life form within the universal mushroom. It is clear, therefore, that the Father was not involved, and there is no true heavenly being in the entire universe.

True heavenly spirits are perfect sons of the Father. As sons of Light, they dwell in their proper place within the perfect spiritual kingdom of the Father. All the so-named heavenly beings, gods, archangels, and angels in the world are counterfeits; they all dwell in universal darkness, which makes them sons of darkness. The Bible depicts the so-called angels of this world as having wings with which they fly from place to place. That, itself, is a sign of spiritual corruption and limitation. True spirits are not restricted by time and space. They do not have wings or bodies that the human mind can imagine or represent. They do not look like human beings or fly about like birds, as the angels of the world do.

Limitation is the hallmark of imperfection and spiritual death, and it reflects in every aspect of worldly existence. It manifests in stunted capacity of minds and spirits, and in the general dispositions of worldly beings. Limitation means ignorance in the ultimate sense of the word, which expresses itself in acts that generally show lack of knowledge and deficiency in wisdom.

Limitation brings about anxiety and emotional tension, caused by fear or self-doubt about one's capacity to cope with his immediate natural disadvantages. The pressure of such a circumstance usually compels one to act in predictable ways. It compels one to hoard or monopolize resources, to seek social recognition, and to try to dominate and enslave others. The fallen, dead spirit of Jehovah epitomizes that frame of mind on earth. He got the upper hand and ultimately crowned himself god over the rest of his desperate kith and kin, and there is nothing godly in that.

Necessity, we all know, is the mother of invention. A finite world of limitations, such as ours, is one full of all sorts of imperfect ideas, inventors, and inventions. Every inventor in the world is self-seeking; he invents for some personal reasons. The aim is always tied to material aggrandizement, as well as the need to surpass other people. John Fowles identified that innate tendency of all humans as the *nemo complex* in his book, *The Aristos*: "It is necessary to make my name known; I must have power—physical, social, intellectual, artistic, political ... but power. I must have monuments; I must be remembered. I must be admired, envied, hated, feared. In short, I must endure, I must extend, and beyond the body and the body's life." [Fowles 1964] And so, the rat race goes on endlessly.

The spiritual kingdom of the Father is perfect and infinite. It is true paradise. Perfect spirits in the heavenly paradise have no limitations; they have no need to try to outwit one another. They, therefore, have no need to devise selfish ideas or inventions. Perfect love of the Father cares equally for all his perfect sons within the heavenly household.

In the realm of imperfection, an inventor may simply have an intense need of an implement or tool of work by which to confront or assuage his immediate disadvantage. The primitive man invented crude implements of raw nature to help him confront and survive the limited handicaps of his age and times. He did not know of today's types of scientific problems and so did not have solutions for them. Today, the modern man has invented all kinds of computerized and automated machines and gadgets to try to meet his ever-increasing needs in a scientific age, as well as to satisfy the *nemo complex* of the modern men. Yet the problems never disappear, but rather, they get worse because situations are ever-changing and precarious in the chaotic domain of corrupt spirits. Some people have even invented scientific gadgets that enable them manipulate others for their own selfish advantages. This is a natural aspect of living in darkness.

The perfect solution is always a mystery to every being in the realm of imperfection. There can never be one anyway. What applies to every imperfect human today, applies equally to Jehovah, for he is the prototype of all men. He too has continually had his trials, errors, failures, regrets, and griefs, which are clearly recorded in the annals of human history. He is still searching for the elusive perfect answer to his eternal problems; hence he proposes *New Jerusalem* in some uncertain future. That is already a bad dream though, because nothing perfect can ever take root in an imperfect realm.

According to John Scotus Erigena, as quoted in *The Aristos*, Jehovah does not even know himself well enough to be able to determine what could be the best solution to his personal problems. The quote states, "[Jehovah] is eternally partially self-ignorant. If he knew all of himself, he could define himself. If he could define himself, he would be finite. But all he knows of himself is what he has created. What is created is his knowledge, what is potential is his mystery: mysterious in him and to him. **All this applies equally to man.**" [Fowles 1964]

Just as ordinary human inventors fabricate complex electronic tools or robots to deal with their recurrent human handicaps by harnessing and transforming naturally available resources found on planet Earth, whatever ideas, or material inventions that Jehovah inspired or contributed to human civilization because of his higher level of scientific knowledge, were equally achieved by harnessing basic resources found in nature. And his motive, like that of every human inventor, was in no way selfless or Godly. All his inventions and inclinations were willfully aimed at enslaving humans by manipulating the innate weaknesses and hedonic desires of human nature to his ulterior advantages.

That Jehovah "formed man of dust from the ground and breathed into its nostrils the breath of life ... and man became a living being," as stated in Genesis 2:7, is a very dubious way of describing cosmetic transformation and domestication of primitive ape-man species on planet Earth. Nevertheless, the tale proves that

Jehovah was indeed human before he could make the ape-man human in his exact 'image and likeness.' He was not a true spirit; a true spirit neither sculpts mud, nor does he wear a mud cloak that is in exact image and likeness of humans. Jehovah is an original earthman, so there can be no real difference between his mode and motive of invention and those of any other human inventor. After all, the same eternal chains bind all of us in this eternal region of darkness—both the so-called gods and their *favored* religious slaves are equally in bondage of sin and death.

The heavenly Christ took on the imperfect human garb temporarily, just to be able to communicate effectively with us in our earthen human form. Jehovah, on the other hand, is permanently an earthman. The Father is perfect Spirit, he is not a man; he is the true Origin or Source of all perfect ideas, both physical and spiritual. The Father is Ultimate Nature within which his fallen sons harness natural resources to create or sculpt self-help implements to assuage their unrelenting predicaments in the outer darkness.

We may never know the criteria and exactly how the primordial blueprint allocates levels of consciousness, membership of organic species and apposite habitations to various fallen spirits. And how fallen human spirits found themselves donning the enslaving mortal garbs of iniquity can only be imagined by humans, giving our present level of consciousness.

Here again, we clearly see the sad effects of spiritual limitations at work. Anxiety is a major characteristic of the world of limitations. No one has the ultimate answer to common problems, so people *willingly* embrace other peoples' ideas and inventions at face values. Ideas and inventions are discarded only when they have been tried and found unworkable or disastrous. Thus, everyone suffers the harmful effect of an individual's invention before any improvement is made to it.

If we look around us today, we will see that most of the principles, ideas, and pieces of property we own and use in our everyday lives are other peoples' inventions. Some of these inventions make human existence easier, while some make our lives miserable. Most of them enslave and destroy our lives gradually. Yet we are perforce stuck with them. Motor cars, for instance, serve good purposes, yet they endanger human lives in so many ways.

Contemporary human civilization, inspiration of which has been largely credited to Jehovah, is gradually becoming the most palpable element of spiritual setback to fallen human spirits on earth. We cannot talk of modern human civilization without highlighting sophistications in weapons of mass destruction, proliferation of luxury inventions that encourage hedonism, corrupt leadership all over the world, get-rich-quick racketeering, cultism and ritualism, religious exploitations, collapse of family value systems, increase in sexual delinquencies, and general moral decadence in human societies. The fact that someone conceives and invents the most enslaving idea on earth should not make him *God* or *Almighty*. Author of human delinquencies should not be called *God*, but a felon.

Furthermore, every idea in the universe is governed by principles. Every inventor withholds or reveals his to whomever he chooses. That is called product patenting or copyrighting. This is also another aspect of limitations. If everyone knows what everyone else knows and has what everyone else has in this world, there will be no need for self-seeking inventions or patents or copyrights. Of course, that can never happen in our present realm of limitations and imperfections.

Perhaps, Jehovah holds monopolistic knowledge of the principle governing universal process of reincarnation and the principle that enables transmigration of fallen spirits from one animal form to the other. What makes the average human being seem like nonentity is that Jehovah has effectively concealed from him general knowledge of the cosmic principles that hold the world order together, including the principle that would have enabled him to move in and out of mortal bodies at will. Again, that does not make him *God* or the *Almighty*; it makes him an opportunist, a monopolist, and an enslaver.

Today, most occultists and blind mystics of the inner alcoves earnestly desire to yoke with him just to obtain limited knowledge of the same principle of *astral projection and transmigration*. With that, their corrupted spirits can temporarily squeeze into lesser animal bodies for some diabolic missions on the earth. I must quickly add here, however, that knowing how to astral project one's spirit in and out of one's physical body is just like owning and knowing how to fire a gun. It not only involves very serious personal dangers, but it also offers no spiritual advantage whatsoever to the occult practitioner. So many overambitious, dim-witted mystics have eternally willed away their priceless souls to Jehovah, the chief prince and custodian of the so-called *treasures of darkness*, just to have such meaningless mystical experience.

Animating spirits were originally tricked into believing that animating organisms in the physical plane would restore eternal happiness and serve as perfect alternative to lost eternal bliss of true spiritual existence. Meanwhile, the caucus that formed the *Cosmic Establishment* knew so well that animal existence was a trap, as well as a second degree of spiritual death for the transmigrating spirits. Thus, the primordial blueprint ensured that the majority were completely kept in the dark of the universal status quo, while the privileged few superintended and sustained universal masters/slaves dichotomy that exist in every domain of animal community.

The same colonial status quo exists here on planet Earth. The Edenic scenario that willfully kept Adam and Eve in the dark about the Father and the most important essences of possible spiritual rebirth was a vivid example. As Jehovah and the so-called gods of heavens and earth colonize ignorant humans on earth, privileged nation states likewise colonize and dominate the less developed ones, while ruling class and privileged individuals in various societies dominate and lord it over the common masses.

Thus, Jehovah has successfully generated multitudes of doubly handicapped religious followers who worship and look up to him as *God Almighty*, which he is not and will never be. His intents and actions have all been self-seeking, in tune with the spirit of imperfection. Literally speaking, Jehovah won his intrigues over the humans and took it all; and today, he practically enslaves the entire human race through repressive human nature and the enslaving achievements of human civilization.

While one can easily discard an invented mechanical appliance that endangers and enslaves his life, the human spirit can only cast-off human nature that incarcerates him by the help of the heavenly Messiah, Jesus Christ. For as long as one still wears the mortal human body, he remains enslaved to the imperfect universal setup. Even when one is truly *born anew*, he is still under some degree of bondage to human nature. The ultimate way out, therefore, is outright death to the entire processes and spheres of the universal order.

And only Jesus Christ can guarantee eternal death to the cyclic processes of life-death continuum to someone in the world. He does not only know all the hidden principles of illusory immortality invented by the groping gods of Genesis, but he also has the antidote for people who genuinely desire true eternal life. He is the authentic, heavenly *Ghostbuster*. So, we all need him in this tough battle against Jehovah, who is the dreadful Chief Ghost of our world. Jesus Christ is the only one who can banish Jehovah eternally from the cosmic aura of his true disciples; only he can grant eternal spiritual emancipation to captive spirits.

Jehovah is just an oversized human being, and he thinks and behaves like every other human being on earth who naturally shares his imperfect traits and temperament. After all, he first became human on earth before the rest of us who took his exact 'image and likeness.' It should be noted that "exact image and likeness" does not stop at actual bodily similarity, but also extends to natural attributes and general mannerisms, which include ethical, intellectual, and general behavioral tendencies. Jehovah is self-conceited, self-centered, jealous, irritable, wrathful, vengeful, and violent. He is ignorant, shortsighted, incompetent; and he regrets and grieves like every other human being. This should help *ordinary* human beings to understand that Jehovah is not the Father, but a charlatan and a mean opportunist.

But Jehovah is just one among other oversized *earthmen* that we erroneously revere as archangels or gods of heavens and earth. Genesis 1:26 (NLT) captures them as some faceless companions to whom Jehovah said, "Let us make human beings in our image, to be like ourselves." Customary Christianity elevated them to *gods of heavens and earth*, deliberately suppressing the fact that they are indeed men like every one of us. I call them the '*let us gang* of Antichrists.' Together, they are the wicked principalities alluded to in Ephesians 6:12 that stand in our way to the Blessed Tree of Life, that are terminally opposed to Christ's mission of spiritual salvation for our captive spirits.

The Church even claims that these inglorious *earthmen* represented the 'Holy Trinity' in the beginning, thereby implying that the Father, the heavenly Christ, and the Holy Spirit were equally humans before metamorphosing into Divine Spirits that we now know they are. Such a notion itself is blasphemy of the highest order. And for that reason, Jesus Christ states emphatically in John 4:24 that "The Father is Spirit, and those who worship him must worship in spirit and truth."

On the contrary, Jehovah and the inglorious *earthmen* in whose image and likeness other human beings were formed on planet Earth belong to the group of fallen dead spirits groping their way in primordial darkness in the beginning. They were none other than the eight wicked principalities that rule the eight mystical kingdoms of our present world of darkness. They are a gang that include Jehovah and the so-called archangels that is cryptically referred to in Revelation 12:3 as "a great red dragon, having seven heads ... with seven crowns upon his heads." These are the chief players in the sphere of human affairs, and they are well-known in person by initiates of certain occult orders.

The earliest reference to an order of seven archangels as a group appears in the *Book of Enoch*, where they are named **Michael, Gabriel,**

Raphael, Uriel, Raguel, Zerachiel, and **Remiel**. All their names end with *el*, which is the Semitic word for *god* or *deity*. Writers of the Old Testament equally used the word *El* both as a general term for *deity* and as a synonym for Jehovah. Although different sources disagree on the names and identities of the seven archangels, Michael, Gabriel, Raphael, and Uriel are universally renowned. "Various occult systems associate each archangel with one of the traditional seven 'luminaries'—the Sun, Moon, Mars, Mercury, Jupiter, Venus, and Saturn—but there is disagreement as to which archangel corresponds to which body." In addition, "the seven archangels figure in some systems of ritual magic, each archangel bearing a specific seal."
[From http://en.wikipedia.org/wiki/Seven_Archangels; retrieved 09/07/2008]

The NRSV (*New Revised Standard Version*) of the Bible describes these eight human-gods of the Genesis account in its footnote to Deuteronomy 32:8–9 not as the 'Holy Trinity,' but as "the divine beings who belonged to the heavenly court." (See Gen. 1:26n.) Then it added, "To these heavenly beings Jehovah delegated authority to govern other nations [of people], but Israel was claimed as *Jehovah's own portion*." Revelation 17:11 (GNB) refers to the same ignoble *let-us group* of eight in the Genesis story, not as the 'Holy Trinity,' but as the eight *beastly* kings of the mystical kingdoms of the world. It reads, "And the beast that was once alive, but lives no longer, is itself an eighth king who is one of the seven and is going off to be destroyed." Here, Jehovah is cryptically described as a *beast* that was once a living son of the Father but now is a dead entity.

As we have seen, Jehovah was and still is a corrupted spirit in thick darkness. All his ideas and actions were naturally flawed, and they still are. This is not a matter of religious belief. The facts around us are overwhelming. How the imperfect spirit of Jehovah could have sculpted perfect *mortal* beings using imperfect material substances in an imperfect earthly setting is the question customary Christianity should try to answer rationally. Jehovah is the prototype of all human beings. If he were perfect, Adam and Eve, who were formed in his exact image and likeness, would have been perfect as well. Unfortunately, he was not.

Jehovah was a blind explorer on planet Earth; he never knew what the ultimate effect of his day-to-day exploits would be. He still does not have precise knowledge of how tomorrow will unfold around him. Even going by his personal scrutiny at every step of his fictitious Genesis account of creation, we can see that he did not have prior knowledge of what the outcome would be. The scripture repeatedly says that *"he saw that it was very good,"*—at least, good enough for a desperate, powerless spirit seeking for any kind of respite from total darkness and eternal spiritual death. That *"he saw that it was very good,"*—meant that he never knew whether it would be *very good* or not. So, what else could have made a spirit being who ought to be eternally graceful, blissful, and self-illuminating to declare that artificial light of the sun was "very good," or that human nature was "very good," if he were not corrupted and debased?

What is the false light of the sun *very good* for, when the groping spirits could have repented and regained their true light of life in the perfect spiritual kingdom of their Father? And what is human nature *very good* for, when it only offers the comfort of a life of illusion on earth to the heavenly dropouts, while preventing them from seeking to regain true eternal life in the heavenly kingdom?

Human nature was a desperate alternative to the blunt realities of spiritual death that confronted the hovering spirits in the Genesis. It was a lose-lose situation. A dead spirit grappling freely with his handicaps in thick darkness was far better positioned to concentrate on genuine spiritual reform than one that willingly sank further into animated carcass of an earthen man. Human nature was an imperfect idea, and it turned out to be a deeper level of spiritual death.

In the original state of the fallen spirits, they were constantly reminded of their lost glory, the resultant handicaps they faced in the outer darkness, and the necessity for spiritual rebirth. It was easier for them to look back and desire to do something positive toward returning to their heavenly life of perfection. That stage in the life of the heavenly dropouts corresponded to the point in the life of the proverbial prodigal son where the scripture says that *"he began to be in want ... and no one gave him anything."* [Luke 15:14-16] It was better to have endured soul-reawakening predicaments in our primordial prison of darkness than to be enjoying something that is *very good* but entirely detrimental to our spiritual rebirth.

The fact that Jehovah had once judged any aspect of human situation to be *very good* showed how spiritually degenerated he had been. Human situation is a false alternative to perfect spiritual existence. It is spiritually inhibiting, thereby preventing humans from appreciating the necessity and urgency for genuine repentance and rebirth. Jehovah knowingly chose that wrong option for his own selfish desires, while the rest of us embraced the futile concept of *better life in hell* out of ignorance and desperation. Nevertheless, the Father granted us the second chance and Jesus Christ is our sole heavenly Redeemer. Jehovah opposes the Father's will for captive human spirits and never means well for us. He has never been a true friend but a dreadful foe.

Jehovah is the custodian of the *better-life-in-hell* idea on planet Earth; Adam and Eve were the first captive humans to see him for what he really stood for. Following their spiritual encounter with the heavenly Messiah in their Edenic captivity, Adam and Eve suddenly came to their senses, as did the proverbial prodigal son, and they did exactly what he did. They defied Jehovah and his vehement but empty threat of physical death and chose to return to their heavenly Father as lost sons. They *knowingly* revoked their original oath of allegiance to Jehovah and boldly rejected him, holding firmly to the special love and redemptive guidance of the heavenly Christ. Thus, they successfully reached the barricaded Tree of Life and regained their lost spiritual heritage in the Father. Their outstanding accomplishments represented perfect examples for all humans in our present circumstance.

Adam and Eve became the first fruits of Christ's interim paradise. They became the first *repentant prodigal spirits* retrieved from our present world of darkness, and the perfect examples of whom the Father expects all of us to be. Although Jehovah and his religious propagandists branded them sinners, those who know the truth now know better. Adam and Eve were rather the first fruits of the resurrected sons of perfection—of "those who are accounted worthy to attain to that age and to the resurrection from the dead on the last day" that Jesus Christ spoke about in Luke 20:35.

JEHOVAH'S CORRUPTED BREATH DID NOT CREATE HUMAN SPIRITS

The impression that Jehovah's breath animated every individual human being on earth is absolute nonsense. A mind-bending Bible homily has it that Jehovah sculpted man of miry clay, breathed air into *its* nostrils, and *it* became a living being. This kind of fairytale is not even sound enough to tell twenty-first century toddlers, let alone full-grown adults with common sense. What the story is saying, in simple language, is that man does not have an individual spirit or a preexistent spiritual personality. That is a very malicious lie willfully intended not only to deny the preexistence of individual human spirits, but also to suffocate the natural yearning in people for the spiritual liberation of *their individual spirits* from eternal bondage in the world and its enslaving processes.

As usual, Church ministers preach the sheer falsehood, and even supposed enlightened human beings accept it, just because it is written in the Bible. Somehow, religious *believers* always believe, even when religious teachings make no sense at all, because they have already been thoroughly brainwashed into accepting everything written in the Bible as true. Of course, religious enthusiasts are *believers*, not *thinkers*. That is the sad irony of *programmed intelligence*, which is what human nature offers.

On the contrary, not everything written in the Bible is true or right. The Bible is largely a book of the world. It was neither written nor canonized by perfect human beings, meaning it contains elements of both true and contrary inspirations. This is gospel truth, and I say it emphatically. People who genuinely seek to fish out the gospel truth from the pages of the Bible should first seek to have spiritual insight. Then, they will need to be courageous enough to read the lines rationally, and to stand up against erroneous traditional interpretations that do not agree with common sense.

The human earthen bodies, like those of innumerable other species of organisms in the universe, are naturally generated of organic matter in accordance with models conceived and scripted in the primordial blueprint that contains all principles and projected activities of the heavenly dropouts within the universal mushroom. Jehovah and his alien accomplices may have cloned and reprogrammed brains of aboriginal ape-men on planet Earth to suit their grand evil ploy, but he certainly did not create the human spirit. He just does not have the wherewithal. As a fallen, dead spirit, Jehovah is so lost and powerless that he cannot even exorcise himself of the inward and outward darkness that presently overshadows him. He can neither re-create nor rekindle his own corrupted spirit, let alone impart 'breath of life' into anyone else.

But even if, only for the sake of argument, we accept that Jehovah is the sole inventor of the human body, what is in that for him to be proud of? As a miry potter, he would have still been a very incompetent one at that. Even scriptural evidence portrays the human body as grossly imperfect. It is so flawed and disease-prone that it is extremely vulnerable and unguaranteeable. According to Mark Twain, "Man is a museum of diseases, a home of impurities; he comes today and is gone tomorrow; he begins as dirt and departs as stench." How can the inventor of such *a museum of diseases* be mistaken for the perfect Source of the immortal spirits in humans? Or what could have motivated an entity who claims to be a perfect creator to infuse his perfect breath into some earthen carcasses only to bring to life mortal beings who are but walking *homes of impurities*?

All spirits in existence—both the living ones within the heavenly realm of perfection and the fallen, dead ones in the universe—emanated from the Father alone, who is Divine Spirit. All spirits are immortal because the Father is eternal, and all have their individual identities. Human spirits are immortal members of the family of fallen spirits alluded to in the Bible's book of Jude. They all existed before the very foundation of this transient material universe, and before the evolution of the mortal android called man on planet Earth. They certainly did not originate from the lifeless breath of Jehovah, who is but a dead spirit.

Mortal human bodies are perishable earthen androids animated by *immortal* spirits of desperate heavenly dropouts to feel a sense of artificial existence in a realm of lifelessness. The disposable human cloak is nothing without the *immortal* spirit that animates it. Therefore, it is individual fallen, dead spirits that gave life to lifeless human organisms, and not the other way around. Evidently, human bodies represent terminal hindrance to spiritual wellbeing of the animating spirits, as it effectively locks them out of spiritual consciousness, which is necessary to engender genuine repentance and spiritual rebirth.

Jehovah is an individual spirit just like every one of us; we all belong to the great multitudes of the heavenly dropouts groping in the dark in the beginning. Jehovah's corrupted breath animates *only* his own earthen android, while other individual spirits animate theirs. Thus, we are strictly individuals in the outer darkness, whether as fallen, dead spirits or as human beings. In the beginning, we were desperate and naïve and just needed any kind of respite from total darkness. Some of the credulous spirits were eventually programmed into the *womb of the world* or the universal cyclic process of physical re-embodiment. Hence, the Father expects each one of us to seek out his own personal salvation. Jehovah ought to equally seek out personal salvation for his own fallen spirit.

Indeed, Jehovah concedes in very simple words that when it comes to spiritual salvation, every individual spirit in the world is entirely on his own, that he is independent of every other individual spirit in the world. "And whosoever striveth, striveth only for himself, *for Allah is altogether independent of his creatures*," he says. ... "He who groweth (in goodness), groweth only for himself, *(he cannot by his merit redeem others)*. ... Whosoever goeth right, it is only for (the good of) his own soul that he goeth right, and whosoever erreth, erreth only to its hurt. *No laden soul can bear another's load.*" Then he concludes by saying that the last day would be "a day on which no soul hath power *at all* for [or over] any (other) soul." [Qur'an 29:6; 35:18; 17:14; 82:19]

I only wish that chronic religious believers would stop believing otherwise. Even today, no spirit has real power over another spirit. Jehovah's spirit has no real power over any human spirit in the world. His power over human minds is purely manipulative and psychological. His religious propagandists have dramatized the fear of Jehovah over the years that it has become deep-rooted in peoples' subconscious minds. Jehovah is a toothless dragon in chains. People fear him just because they do not know the truth, and because they do not know their spiritual rights.

The truth is that Jehovah only dominates people by their own consent. He is strictly a *god of covenant*. He did not enslave Abraham and his Jewish descendants, for instance, until they approved his claim over their lives by the blood oath of allegiance administered over them by Moses. Even then, he first approached Abram, promising all sorts of material rewards—riches, land, and offspring—and he talked very friendly with him to win his undivided confidence. He only began to make demands when he had dominated and enslaved his mind completely.

Jehovah never forces anyone to worship or work for him until that person has made the pledge. So, he is a "wily good guy" in his own way. He did not force the Israelites to declare him the only *god* they would worship; rather, he conned them systematically. The snag is that the pledge is usually so subtle and seemingly harmless that his victims seldom realize it until they are already deeply entrapped. Very simple religious creeds—like the Shema, Apostles' Creed, the Shahadah, and other cultic articles of faith—represent such deadly pledges. They seem so harmless; yet, though Muslims, for instance, are said to be under obligation to recite the Shahadah only *once* in a lifetime, some of them recite it several times every day as a sign of religious piety, without realizing the spiritual implications and dangers.

Although the tall tale about how Jehovah's breath formed the human spirits may seem harmless to unenlightened minds, it was with that crafty maneuver that he decisively erased the spiritual identity of individual human spirits from human consciousness. The outcome of that is the humans' habitual apathy toward the gospel truth and toward spiritual matters concerning their personal spirits. If Jehovah had not successfully obliterated spiritual self-consciousness in the human minds, he would not have been able to turn human beings against their own true redeemer. He was able to manipulate Jewish religious believers into crucifying Jesus Christ because they did not understand the meaning of personal spiritual salvation that the Messiah preached.

Sadly, most people still do not understand Jesus Christ today. Religious believers have continued to violently harass and destroy people who disseminate the gospel truth in the world. They will continue to do so until they can understand and properly scrutinize even their own scriptures. The Qur'an, for instance, makes it explicit that true spiritual salvation is not a matter of group religious pursuit, yet Islamic tenets generally impress the direct opposite upon Muslims. As the Messiah said, religious believers do not know what they are doing. Spiritual enlightenment is a **personal** inward reflection for **personal** spiritual rebirth—it is strictly "for the good of one's own spirit." Even Jehovah's personal advice to believers on this matter reads, "O ye who believe! **Ye have charge of your own**

souls [alone]. He who erreth cannot injure you if ye are rightly guided." [Qur'an 5:105]

WOMAN IS ALSO AN INDIVIDUAL SPIRIT

Perhaps the most senseless story found in the Bible is about how Jehovah formed woman with a single rib from man's rib cage. It goes like this: "So Jehovah caused a deep sleep to fall upon the man, and while he slept took one of his ribs and closed up its place with flesh; and the rib which Jehovah had taken from the man he made into a woman and brought her to the man." [Gen. 2:21–22] Sometimes, even the most ardent religious believers do not know whether to take the story as factual or as a mere fairytale. Yet Church ministers seem to be under obligation to explain both the things that make sense to them and the ones that do not. I have watched some well-educated preachers ramble on for hours trying to give divine meaning to manifest nonsense.

Sequel to the notion that Jehovah's breath animated Adam, the man, is another malicious lie about the true personality of woman. It should not be difficult for enlightened minds to read the perverted mind of the god of Eden. Since he had successfully sold the impression that the man made of miry clay and animated by his lifeless breath has no preexistent spirit of his own, he expected blinded humans to conclude that the woman, formed from a single rib of the mortal man, must herself be subhuman. With that, it was easy for him to propagate the subjugation of women of the world under soulless men.

Of course, this formed the basis upon which customary religions of the world would eventually denigrate women, not only as spiritual nonentities, but also as ritual pollutants. The situation is the same in all customary religions of the world. The Buddha taught that there are no redeemable, immortal souls or spirits in mortal human beings. Yet, he personally ordained men of his inner circle into the *Sangha* as monks, who were concerned chiefly with attaining their own enlightenment and *nirvana* (a kind of spiritual liberation) by following the rule of his *dharma*. Women had no place in the Buddha's *Sangha*. It was with great persuasion that he reluctantly created a separate order of Buddhist nuns, which eventually died out in Theravada Buddhism around the fifth century, obviously because the Buddha never actually intended it to survive.

In the same way, religious traditions of the Jews, customary Christians, and Muslims explicitly encourage men to regard and treat women as nonentities, especially in spiritual matters. To the patriarchs, only men were made in the image and likeness of Jehovah. Yet, their Torah clearly records the truth about this matter. Men and women share exact 'image and likeness' with Jehovah. "In the image of Jehovah he created them; male and female he created them," says Gen. 1:27.

Jehovah used insensitive men like Abraham, David, Solomon, Muhammad, and others to institutionalize religious subjugation of women of the world. These men particularly took it upon themselves to try to prove that women were nothing but personal properties, sexual slaves, and physical possessions of men. Abraham used and discarded women without regard. David got his kicks by murdering other men and acquiring their wives. Solomon built brothels and officially turned many women into court prostitutes. Muhammad sexually abused a seven-year-old little girl and took unnecessary advantage of many helpless widows. He officially inaugurated sexual abuse of underage women in child marriages in Islam and institutionalized the worst kind of social segregation of women in Muslim communities, all because Jehovah gave him the misleading impression that he was something superior to women. The naked monks of the Digambara sect of Jainism, on their part, propagate the senseless idea that no soul or spirit can attain spiritual salvation from the body of a woman without first being reborn as a man. This is how extensive human ignorance runs among religious peoples of the world.

There is a bona fide spirit in a woman, as there is in a man. While there are minor physical differences between male and female bodies, there is no difference whatsoever between spirits in men and spirits in women. As a matter of fact, there are no female spirits in existence. The physical entities called *man* and *woman* on earth are, but interchangeable *mortal overcoats* worn by identical fallen spirits, purely for the transient purpose of operating on the physical plane of the physical world.

The only difference between man and woman is in superficial appearance due to body chemistry. The homology of male and female external genitalia during early stages of the fetuses is a biological fact. Before ten weeks, the genital tubercle is in the "undifferentiated stage" for both male and female fetuses. Sometimes, nature is not even definite on points of sex identities of newborn babies. It should be noted that there are many hermaphrodites or intersexes on the earth today. These are human beings having both male and female sexual organs, or characteristics of both organs, meaning they are both male and female at the same time. There are three categories of intersexes: *true hermaphrodite*—a person born with both ovaries and testicles and has both male and female sex organs; *female pseudo hermaphrodite*—a genetic female with external genitalia that are ambiguous or male, and *male pseudo hermaphrodite*—genetic male with external sex organs that fail to develop properly, resulting in female or male/female physical characteristics. *GotQuestions.Org* has this to say on hermaphrodites:

> "When babies are developing in the womb, they all begin with sex organs that look female [during the "undifferentiated stage"]. If the baby is male, he begins to produce testosterone, if the hormone reaches the tissues correctly, the external genitals become a scrotum and penis. Chromosomal or sex hormone abnormalities can produce an infant in an intersex state. It can also be caused by a condition called congenital adrenal

hyperplasia, which is a disease that blocks the baby's metabolism. **It is not as uncommon as we might think; about 1 in every 2,000 newborns is born in an intersex state."** [From http://www.gotquestions.org/hermaphrodite.html; retrieved 12/12/2008]

Corrective surgery is used to easily reconstruct the external genitalia of hermaphrodites in the early stages. With the help of science and advanced surgical precision, some hermaphrodites have successfully undergone sex change even as adults. Consequently, *men* now become pregnant and deliver babies in the United States. Thomas Beatie, 34, a former female beauty pageant contestant—better known around the world as the "pregnant man"—made cultural history as perhaps the first legally transgender male to give birth, bringing into the world a 4kg baby girl named Susan Juliette on Sunday, June 29, 2008. Beatie was born a woman, but he now lives as a man in Oregon after surgery and hormone treatment. He appeared on *The Oprah Winfrey Show* in April to talk about what he called his "human desire." He recently revealed to celebrity interviewer for ABC news program "20/20," Barbra Walters, in an exclusive interview that he is pregnant again with his second child. People who desire more information on the "pregnant man" can log on to www.google.com on the internet and search for the *pregnant man*.

The saying that "whatever a man can do a woman can do also" is correct. Most women even excel in stereotypical men's activities. Abundant scriptural evidence show that women are more spiritually alert than men. It should be noted that Eve is the actual pioneer of humankind's spiritual evolution. She was the first to decipher the redeeming value of the divine tree of knowledge of good and evil; she was also the first to receive and eat of its fruit before Adam. Therefore, she was the first disciple of the heavenly Christ in the whole world. She handed the batten over to Adam, the man, for obvious spiritual reasons; she indeed, made Adam the first prophet of the heavenly Christ. As shown in the scriptures, women were equally the most devoted disciples of Jesus Christ. The spiritual insight and resolute courage of Mary, the mother of Jesus Christ, Mary Magdalene and other women who ministered to the daily needs of our Messiah were outstanding.

Achievements of many women equally stand out in various other fields of human endeavor—in politics, science and inventions, medicine and nursing, social reform, writing, and so on. As heads of state, for instance, the names of Cleopatra of Egypt, Elizabeth I of England, Christina of Sweden, Queen Amina of Zaria, Indira Gandhi of India, Golda Meir of Israel, Margaret Thatcher of England, Corazon Aquino of Philippines, and others stand out among their men counterparts.

In general, male and female physical bodies are means by which the world continually belittles the Father in all of us. Our spirits are captives in the mortal earthen overcoats, and because we are divine specks from the Father, he miraculously knows our anguish. That is why he sent the heavenly Christ to help us triumph over human nature.

Men who subjugate and oppress women just because Jehovah and the Bible have portrayed them as inferior are utterly ignorant. Men and women who know the truth look beyond the physical being; they genuinely work as a team to vanquish a common enemy to free the Father trapped in their mortal bodies. Adam and Eve stand as shining examples. They loved and respected one another; they discovered the truth and pulled their energies together to overcome the dubious god of Eden for the good of their individual spirits. Twenty-first-century men and women ought to be spiritually enlightened in this matter.

CHAPTER FOUR

GARDEN OF EDEN: IMPOSSIBLE PARADISE WITHIN THE SHATTERING UNIVERSE

The human mind is, by nature, highly impressionable; external influences can easily mold it. A cat will not chew onion or eat any food that it hates, no matter how much its owner tries to influence it. Human beings do not possess such willpower. Experiences, opinions, and personalities of other people can easily make impressions on humans, even when they do not seem to make sense to them. Evident excesses of human religions, traditions, and customs thrive solely on this major aspect of human weaknesses.

It is really a shame that enlightened human beings have continued to believe in baseless assumptions about our meaningless world just because they conform to antiquated religious convictions, even when rational facts have become abundant and glaring. Human religion, in general, is purely an aggressive propaganda machine in the hands of the so-called gods of the world. It exists only to help the wicked gods turn the truth upside down in the human minds to the spiritual detriment of captive human spirits. In return, the gods reward their hired religious operatives with cheap fame and material prosperity.

Judaism, customary Christianity, and Islam have taught and sustained blatant lies about our present situation by sheer propaganda tactics. Not only have they successfully marketed Jehovah as the *God Almighty*, which he is not, they have also ratified all his blunders and outright infamy as *divine righteousness* in the minds of their teeming adherents. Their collective pretentious activities have made it almost impossible for their unsuspecting devotees to appreciate the clear difference between Jehovah's treacherous nature and the impeccable attributes of our heavenly Father.

We all know that Jehovah did not start his rise to earthly power as *God Almighty*. He was merely a 'wonder working' desert hermit that repeatedly waylaid Abraham in lonely pathways, promising him unsolicited material rewards for some unstated reasons. Overall records of Jehovah's utterances and activities within human history show clearly that he is a seasoned fraudster. He never fulfilled any of the bogus promises he made to Abraham, as documented in the scriptures. In fact, referring to Jehovah as *God Almighty* is sacrilegious. Yet human religion has successfully twisted the true meaning of righteousness in the human minds to suit Jehovah's false standards.

No one can dispute the power of advertising and the great influence it has over people's minds. Today, the media simply runs the lives of so-called civilized peoples of the world in accordance with public trends set by aggressive brand advertisements. It determines what people eat and drink, what they wear, what they think, believe, say, and do as individuals. Today, life is all about going with the views of the majority on topical issues. Although that has always been the case with Homo sapiens, one expects that there should be improvement with the twenty-first-century species, given the stage of human spiritual evolution in our time. Indoctrinating, market-oriented advertisements and the adverse influence of television and other advertising media have greatly affected the sanity and innocence of our young minds.

Sheepish adherence to irrational religious conventions has equally become the trendiest aspect of today's world, not only among the uneducated, but also among the so-called enlightened peoples. No doubt, religious marketers rank highest among the most aggressive brand advertisers in our societies today. Apart from shouting on top of their voices from loudspeakers mounted on housetops and disturbing the neighborhoods, both at night and in the day, they have literally taken over the billboards, radio, and TV stations. Of course, they have a lot of money to buy their way through.

Today, TV Pentecostalism is simply the name of a flamboyant religious propaganda outfit that has thrown caution to the wind in its end-time desperate attempt to promote the lowlife god of Eden into what he is not. It literally advertises Jehovah, its religious idol, as if he is a kind of delicious bottle of soft drink, and sadly, great multitudes of people buy and gulp it down without a second thought. When a very forceful teacher teaches what he does not understand himself and bullies his disciples into accepting whatever he says, both the teacher and the taught are doomed forever indeed.

For more than 1500 years, customary Christianity taught and enforced the belief that the earth was immovable at the center of the universe. Claudius Ptolemy advanced the Geocentric model—earth-centered universe—in the second century, which held that the earth was stationary and at the center of the universe and posited the following order for celestial objects in the solar system: Earth (center), Moon, Mercury, Venus, Sun, Mars, Jupiter, Saturn, and the so-called fixed stars. The Roman Catholic Church made that its official teaching, obviously because it agreed with the notion that the earth is the seat of Jehovah, whom the Church held to be the god of the whole universe.

Nicolaus Copernicus discovered and published the true position in the year 1543, stating that the sun is the center of our solar system, and that the earth and the other planets revolved around the sun. He declared that the earth turns on its axis once a day and goes around the sun once a year. He was sure that the way the earth turns makes it look like the sun, stars, and planets are going around it. The Church dismissed his findings as too radical and continued to teach and enforce sheer error.

Next, Galileo Galilei visually observed the Copernicus system with his telescope and published a book in 1632 that compared Ptolemy's and Copernicus's ideas, and he concluded that Copernicus was right. The correct order for celestial objects in our solar system is Sun (center), Mercury, Venus, Earth, Mars, Jupiter, Saturn, Uranus, Neptune, and Pluto, and not as Ptolemy had posited.

The Church adamantly stuck to its official error. The Inquisition summoned Galileo to Rome to stand trial for heresy, notwithstanding his pleas of illness and old age. He was forced to renounce the *truth*, and when he would not, the Church authorities sentenced him to life imprisonment, which they quickly commuted to permanent house arrest. The Church ordered his book, the *Dialogue*, to be burned, and the sentence against him to be read publicly in every university. Thus, customary Christianity openly dramatized the fact that it was vehemently opposed to human enlightenment; opposed to *truth* and people who work toward revealing it to humanity. The sentence of house arrest remained in effect throughout the last eight years of Galileo's life. He became blind and died of slow fever on his little estate on January 8, 1642, but the Church never subdued his spirit.

It was not until 1992, **350 years after his death**, that **Pope John Paul II quietly acknowledged that the Church was in error** to have convicted Galileo of heresy. In any case, that was a very remarkable confession of ignorance by the Church and its *infallible* pontiffs. It proved that the Church did not know much after all, and that Jehovah, its religious idol, was both perverse and ignorant too. Galileo's ultimate triumph over the Roman Catholic Church represented an outstanding defeat, not only against the entire Christendom, but also against Jehovah who inspires it against the truth.

Galileo had written a long, open letter on the irrelevance of biblical passages in scientific arguments, holding that interpretation of the Bible should be adapted to increasing knowledge and that **no scientific position should ever be made an article of Roman Catholic faith.** His famous quote on "religion" clearly portrayed the Church as utterly misguided. It reads, **"It is the Holy Spirit's intention to teach us how to go to heaven, not how the heavens go."** This means that the issue of true spiritual salvation for our fallen, dead spirits far transcends knowledge of how the universe works. It far transcends Jehovah, the Church, and its erroneous views on the order and actions of the so-called heavenly bodies. Human scientists can deal with that effectively; religion should restrict itself to issues of spiritual salvation of captive human spirits if it were true.

Victory of Adam and Eve over Jehovah in the so-called Garden of Eden was most decisive. It represented the mother of all Jehovah's continual failures in human history in the face of reason and the truth. Jehovah had cast a spell of ignorance over the human spirits, coercing them to accept the blatant lie that acquiring heavenly wisdom or *the knowledge of good and evil* would cause them to die. Adam and Eve debunked his irrational reasoning. But Roman Catholic Church freely offered itself as agent of falsehood in service of Jehovah who is the father of lies.

At the right time, the spirit of the heavenly Christ descended into Eden and inspired in Adam and Eve divine words of wisdom. He convinced them that Jehovah lied about the true importance of acquiring the fruit of knowledge. Knowledge does not lead to death. Rather, it leads to true spiritual life. He assured them and their posterity, saying, "You will not die!" That assurance still stands today for everyone who courageously defies Jehovah and his religious mind-benders to seek and publish true knowledge in the name of the heavenly Christ, as Adam and Eve did in Eden.

Keeping human beings in total ignorance of spiritual matters relating to their fallen spirits and to their true heavenly Father, safeguarded Jehovah's false position as god over them. And forbidding them from acquiring the knowledge of the difference between what is *good* and what is *evil* ensured that they could not readily distinguish between him and the Father who truly loves them. Of course, that was tantamount to forbidding them from seeking true spiritual salvation. It was a definite way of preventing captive human spirits from seeking the way to return to the Father who is the Blessed Tree of Life. He spoke his evil mind clearly in Genesis

3:23-24(GNT), which reads, "So Jehovah sent them [Adam and Eve] out of the Garden of Eden ... Then at the east side of the garden he put living creatures and a flaming sword which turned in all directions. **This was to keep anyone from coming near the tree that gives life**.

The scripture proves clearly that Jehovah lied, and that he could not be trusted. He assured Adam and Eve that knowledge would lead them to death, while the heavenly Christ promised them that knowledge would rather help them to regain true spiritual life. They received Christ's gift of the fruit of knowledge and instantly acquired the ability to differentiate between good and evil. That, in turn activated functional minds and the human conscience in them and awakened their incarcerated spirits, and that signaled the definite start of humankinds' spiritual evolution toward ultimate spiritual rebirth. Today, all of humanity delights in the knowledge of good and evil and earnestly aspires for ultimate spiritual resurrection as promised by the heavenly Spirit in Eden, being the noble dividend of Adam and Eve's victory over Jehovah who is the father of lies. Yet hired religious agents of the defeated god of Eden would not stop perpetuating his malicious lies on earth.

Knowledge of the difference between good and evil is the inevitable foundation for the spiritual journey of our fallen spirits back to perfect eternal life. Jesus Christ, our heavenly Messiah, makes it explicit that anyone who is not able to distinguish Jehovah from our true heavenly Father, will not be saved. He calls the ability to know and act on the difference eternal life itself: "This is eternal life, he says, "that they [beguiled human beings] know [and choose] thee *the only true Father*, and Jesus Christ whom thou hast sent." [John 17:3]

Sadly, instead of acknowledging defeat, as Pope John Paul II did in the case of the Church versus Galileo Galilei, Jehovah devised and propagated more and more lies through his self-seeking religious agents to try to cover his previous lies and save face before Adam's unsullied legacy. First, they branded the heavenly Spirit of

Knowledge serpent, devil and archenemy of humankind, even though scriptural evidence explicitly stated otherwise.

The scripture expressly convicts Jehovah as the liar in the Edenic impasse. Whichever way one looks at it, it is the real devil that is terminally opposed to humans acquiring knowledge. He is not in the business of disseminating life-giving knowledge, especially, not to captive human beings whom he sees as his eternal enemies. It was obvious, therefore, that Jehovah was the actual serpent, devil, and archenemy of humankind in the Edenic encounter. He was the one who forbade heavenly wisdom for humankind and barricaded the way to the divine Tree of Life, not the heavenly Spirit of Knowledge whom he maliciously termed the serpent.

Customary Christian propagandists had to device bigger lies to try to explain away Jehovah's persistent failures in human history since the collapse of his Edenic conspiracy. Instead of admitting that Jehovah is just a powerless, bungling *superman*, they tried to transpose all his failures on humanity. Whenever it suited him, they called him the "Almighty," but when he fumbled beyond excuse, it became the fault of his human slaves.

They taught and compelled their spellbound followers to accept that Jehovah made the Garden of Eden a paradise *in the beginning* before Adam and Eve's personal acquisition of heavenly wisdom abruptly destroyed everything beyond redemption. They were not even ashamed to concede that Jehovah could not foresee the disaster before it happened, could not stop it when it was happening, and when it had happened, could not rectify whatever it was that went wrong with his so-called paradise. What a powerless almighty and his volatile paradise! What a bungling dead spirit and his shameless lies!

In the face of abundant scriptural and scientific evidence available to enlightened humans today, one wonders how Jehovah, the father of lies, and his lying Church could have believed that they would keep up with the naked lies forever. A paradise on the surface of the unstable planet Earth was and still is practically impossible.

A true paradise means a **place or state of perfect eternal happiness**—a place, situation, or condition in which somebody finds perfect eternal happiness. Perfect happiness also means eternal rest, which is the hallmark of true spiritual eternal life. Such a place or state cannot exist anywhere within the restless universe. It is impracticable.

The universe is a gigantic expanse of exploding debris of matter, and Earth is just a very tiny, unstable ball of rock gyrating on its axis and floating in space around the sun within the universe. The universe has never known rest since the *big bang*, and neither has the tiny planet Earth. How then could Jehovah have made a localized paradise park on it, at any point in time, where anyone could have truly found eternal rest?

Looking at the planet Earth from outer space, one sees irregular patches of water and land, with a thin blanket of clouds enveloping the entire sphere. If one could cut open the earth, one would see three layers of highly unstable matter. The crust, the thin outer layer, includes all land and the ocean floors. Below that, is the mantle, a thick layer of hot rock, some of which is so hot that the rock is soft and sticky. The center of the earth, the core, is the hottest part of the planet. The outer part of the core is liquid metal, while the inner core is a ball of solid metal. The earth is naturally unstable. It simply does not possess the natural characteristics of a true paradise. It never did and it never will.

Furthermore, life on earth emerged from a protracted process of natural evolution, which is entirely dependent on the activities and effects of the sun on it. Without the sun, there would never have been life or any so-called paradise on planet Earth. Therefore, the sun had to be a paradise first, for a true paradise garden to exist on earth. Unfortunately, the sun has never known peace since it originated from swirling clouds of gas and dirt within the shattering universe.

The sun itself is a huge ball of hot burning gases—a giant nuclear furnace. Temperature at the center of the sun is about 16,000,000°C, and at the surface, about 5,500°C. We live this meaningless life on planet Earth because the sun dies. The sun started to die the very day it started to shine, and its death will become final the day it uses up its stock of hydrogen fuel and no longer shines. At which point, therefore, could anyone reasonably argue that the sun had been a paradise? The sun is simply hell. The only reason we are standing on the surface of the earth and talking about some long-forgotten, dreamy paradise of Eden is because, at 150,000,000km, we are far enough removed from the main heat of the sun to enjoy its quasi benefits.

Saying that a paradise of Eden existed on planet Earth is like arguing that one could fetch a cup of chilled water from a particular section of a big iron pot of boiling water. The only paradise possible on planet Earth is a dream one. Only dreamers can find perfect happiness in a raging inferno. Customary Christianity is the household of such dreamers, while Jehovah, their religious idol, is the most incorrigible dreamer in the entire universe.

What religious people call paradise on planet Earth are gardens of vanity. According to the scripture, the so-called Edenic paradise was merely a portion of well-watered grazing land amid the arid region of ancient Middle East. It says that Jehovah put Adam and Eve in it *"to till and keep it."* Obviously, that did not paint the picture of people living in perfect eternal happiness; Adam and Eve were some kind of *regal gardeners*. Jehovah was a dreamy rancher; Adam and Eve were his hired gardeners. Living sons of the Father do not walk about *naked and shameless*, they do not *rear and "dominate" animals* in zoos, and they certainly, do not *till and cultivate* gardens in the perfect spiritual kingdom of their Father.

What people have taken for granted is the fact that Eden is a well-known geographical location on the surface of planet Earth—a place that has been continuously inhabited by various peoples since the emigration of Adam and Eve. **Eden is the present-day Jerusalem.** People should be very clear on that.

From facts available to us today, we know that the present site, Jerusalem, was occupied during the Stone Age, but a people who had advanced into the Bronze Age drove out the Aboriginal inhabitants in the period from 5000 BC to 4000 BC. The invaders, called Canaanites in the Bible, were a mixed people among whom Jebusites were dominant. Archeological excavations have shown that a settlement existed on the site south of the Temple Mount. A **massive town wall was found** just above the Gihon Spring, which determined the location of an ancient settlement. Again, an ancient city marked by the presence of *a massive town wall* did not paint the picture of a true paradise, but rather that of a prison yard.

The Genesis account locates Eden around the Gihon Spring, and that correlates with the site of the ancient *massive town wall* excavated by archeologists. Genesis 2:10–15 reads, "A river flowed out of Eden to water the garden, and there it divided and became four rivers. The name of the first is *Pishon*; it is the one which flows around the whole land of Havilah. ... The name of the second river is *Gihon*; it is the one which flows around the whole land of Cush. And the name of the third river is *Tigris*, which flows east of Assyria. And the fourth river is the *Euphrates*." This account gives the precise location of the so-called paradise of Eden. The rivers are permanent landmarks; they still flow in the same locations today, so people cannot pretend not to know where the defunct paradise was situated.

Urusalim is the earliest form of Jerusalem, apparently meaning "Foundation of Shalem" ("Foundation of God *of Eden*"). As the mountain god of Eden, Jehovah dwelt on the Temple Mount in the days of Adam. He dwelt on the same spot in the days of Abraham and the Jewish patriarchs. He still dwells on the Temple Mount today. It was on that very spot that Abraham nearly sacrificed Isaac to him. Solomon built him the first temple on the same spot, later replaced by the second and last temple built by Herod; and finally, by the Dome of the Rock, completed in AD 691. It was on the same spot that Muhammad of Arabia was purported to have ascended to Jehovah's mystical heaven. Nothing in archeological records suggests that Jerusalem was ever a true paradise. It has never even had enough potable water for its inhabitants. Rather, it has always been *"a land that devoured its inhabitants."*

Jerusalem has meant nothing but misery and pain to its inhabitants, both in the past and in the present. The land meant eternal spiritual enslavement to Adam and Eve, until the Holy Spirit of our heavenly Messiah redeemed them from it. The lost sons of Adam have never known peace in it since Jehovah tricked Abram into coming back to the wasteland. The blood of many prophets, apostles, and true disciples of our heavenly Messiah was shed on that soil. Jesus Christ was brutally murdered there in the presence, and by the direct instigation of Jehovah who permanently dwells there in person.

Jerusalem is simply a city of unending human calamity. In the very words of the three courageous Jewish spies under the leadership of Moses, "**Jerusalem is a land that devours its inhabitants.**" [Num. 13:32] Jesus Christ grieved over it, calling it "**the city that kills the prophets and stones the Father's messengers!**" [Matt. 23:37] History speaks clearly on that fact too. *The Preacher*, one of Israel's most influential kings, sums it all up this way: "I the Preacher have been king over Israel in Jerusalem [the present-day Eden]. ... I have seen everything that is done *under the sun*; and behold, all is vanity and a striving after wind. ... What is crooked cannot be made straight, and what is lacking cannot be numbered." [Eccles. 1:14–15] This is the gospel truth! Both scientific evidence and practical human experience firmly correlate that.

Perfect happiness is only possible for perfect spirits within the realm of perfection. No other realm of perfection exists beyond the transcendent spiritual kingdom of the Father. Unlike the so-called Garden of Eden, true paradise is eternal. The heavenly kingdom automatically spews out spirits that sin, so their sin and spiritual death do not affect its eternal state of perfection. Thus, the kingdom of the Father remains a paradise forever. The entire outer darkness represents the realm of imperfection. Our planet Earth is a very tiny place within the universe, which is itself, a small region within the infinite outer darkness.

All the spirit beings within the universe are corrupted; they are rebellious spirits spewed out of the Father's heavenly kingdom. The only life possible in their present state is that of eternal suffering, being the natural wages of sinfulness. It is practically impossible for any fallen, dead spirit to experience true paradise within the outer darkness. Human life on earth vividly typifies the *best* form of life possible within the restless universe. It is practically full of trouble and emptiness. The Qur'an says plainly that *"the life of the world is but comfort of illusion."* This has nothing to do with Adam and Eve suddenly acquiring heavenly wisdom against the express wishes of the selfish god of Eden. The world is outside the Father's heavenly realm of perfection. It naturally cannot sustain true eternal life.

The Good News, however, is that the Father has granted spiritual redemption to all repentant fallen sons of heaven within the universe. Jehovah and his customary Christian abettors seek only to distract genuine seekers of true spiritual salvation with their fruitless argument about some transient paradise in hell that existed in Eden. Serious-minded human beings should not waste their precious time on human religion and its spiritually regressive insinuations. For perfect eternal life in the true heavenly paradise, people should focus all their genuine efforts toward discovering Jesus Christ, the way Adam and Eve did. Only Jesus Christ has the will and the Father's divine mandate to reverse our eternal fate for good. "So, if the Son makes you free, you will be free indeed," says John 8:36. If Jesus Christ holds your hands, you will surely make it back to the true heavenly paradise.

People who wait on Jehovah to recreate his dreamy paradise of Eden in his so-called New Jerusalem after our sun has died, are hopeless dreamers indeed. They will all end up in eternal pitch darkness on the last day. All the stars and suns in the universe will eventually die out, never to shine again. All the moons and satellites that reflect their light will darken, and all forms of organic life and activities sustained on the planets by solar energy will wither away forever. This has nothing to do with religion or peoples' religious convictions.

Nevertheless, for the benefit of adamant religious minions, even the scripture confirms in Matthew 24:29 that there will be a great tribulation toward the last day, at the climax of which, *"the sun will be darkened, and the moon will not give its light, and the star will fall from heaven, and the powers of the heavens will be shaken."* When that happens, every worldly dream will revert to pitch darkness. How religious believers read and understand this today will determine the eternal fate of their individual spirits on the last day.

CHAPTER FIVE

HUMAN NATURE: PERFECTION VERSUS SHEER IGNORANCE

Religious people have persistently argued that the original world and human beings formed by Jehovah were perfect until Adam and Eve acquired knowledge of the difference between good and evil. In other words, they are insinuating that ignorance is perfection. But even their own scriptures say the direct opposite.

The Bible is explicit about the true nature of the Edenic human beings. Their minds were not originally programmed with the ability to distinguish between what is good or evil. So, they could not have been perfect beings. Knowledge is the foundation of perfection. Therefore, without knowledge of good and evil, Edenic humans were simply spiritual imbeciles. They did not even have any idea about what perfection or imperfection meant. True perfection means that someone knows what is good and what is evil, but consistently chooses to do that which is good. Indeed, the scripture says, "Without eyes there is no light; without knowledge there is no wisdom, [and without wisdom there is no perfection]." [Sirach 3:25 (NRSV)]

Genesis 2:9, 15–17, 25 (NLT) states: "In the middle of the garden [god of Genesis] placed the tree of life and the tree of the knowledge of good and evil. ... [He] placed the man in the Garden of Eden to tend and watch over it. ... But [he] warned him, 'You may freely eat the fruit of every tree in the garden—*except the tree of the knowledge of good and evil. If you eat its fruit, you are sure to die.*' ... *Now the man and his wife were both naked, but they felt no shame.*"

In the first instance, the biblical notion that Jehovah personally planted the two heavenly trees of life and knowledge of good and evil in the middle of the Garden of Eden is absolute nonsense, deliberately intended to fool uninformed minds. Clear-thinking people should wonder why a reasonable deity would take such a risk, knowing that doing so would eventually destroy his entire paradisal project forever. No sane farmer knowingly plants weed among his treasured wheat. The truth, however, is that the tree of life and the tree of knowledge represented the Father and the heavenly Christ respectively, which explains why god of Eden forbade, and still forbids, their fruits for his blindfolded human slaves. The two divine trees are not of the world; they certainly did not stand in the middle of the defunct paradise of Eden. The Living Father and his Son transcend the entire spheres of the rickety worlds of the heavenly dropouts.

It is clear from the above that Edenic human beings lacked *basic wisdom*. They lacked the natural ability to understand or choose wisely between what was morally right or wrong for them. Hence, they walked about naked, but felt no qualms about that. They lacked the ability to distinguish and choose between what was beneficial or detrimental to their general well-being. Worst of all, the Edenic human beings lacked *heavenly wisdom* or the basic insight into spiritual matters relating to true life, sin, death, and the need for spiritual rebirth.

Edenic human beings lacked human conscience, which is responsible for human morality and for the general ordering of human behavior in terms of what is right and wrong. As we now know, the human conscience is also the Father's point of contact between humans and their incarcerated spirits. This crucial ability was willfully extracted from the original programming of the human mind. In fact, Jehovah forbade human conscience for the original humankind. Yet, this is the only ability that differentiates human beings from wild animals today. How then could any reasonable person argue that Adam and Eve were perfect without functional human conscience? It is impossible for anyone to be perfect without a thorough knowledge of the difference between what is good and evil.

The earliest human beings on planet Earth would have been perfect only if the earthly situation and the *hovering* spirits that invented human nature were perfect. As we have seen, however, the very foundation of planet Earth—the sun that sustains organic life on it, and the entire universe that contains both—is unstable and imperfect. How then could any right-thinking person expect that Jehovah, who was prototype of imperfect human beings on earth, could originate a perfect idea within the same imperfect situation? How could an inept, miserable farmer who sowed diseased seeds on arid soil reap quality products? Without the knowledge of the difference between human nature and true spirituality, the human spirits were simply blinded prisoners within the human earthen capsules.

Some religious apologists concede that the knowledge of good and evil was not bad for humankind, but still convict Adam and Eve of willful disobedience against a god whose sinister intentions were plainly stated. They argue that the god of Eden had intended to grant humankind that divine ability in due course. However, the scripture does not say anything like that whatsoever; nor does it imply in any way that Jehovah's ban on human quest for spiritual insight was to be for a while.

Even if, according to customary Christianity, Jehovah had meant ignorance to rule the lives of the original human beings for just one day in the very beginning, he would still have been a very evil mind. For the scripture says that "It is not good for a man to be without knowledge [not even for a second]." [Prov. 19:2] In any case, even if Jehovah might have genuinely thought that ignorance was a better foundation for heavenly wisdom, it still did not make Adam and Eve perfect in the beginning.

Ironically, the same preachers who bitterly convict Adam and Eve of willful disobedience, today, pride themselves as the very custodians of heavenly wisdom. While still castigating the noble pioneers and benefactors of humans' evolution in knowledge, they praise knowledge as the basis of their own *divine* callings. They also exalt themselves as divine paradigms of human morality without acknowledging that Adam and Eve were indeed the true pioneers. Surely, customary Christian ministers stand equally convicted by their own judgment, since Jehovah had never, at any point in time, lifted his standing commandment against human beings freely imbibing the said fruit of the knowledge of good and evil. For supporting human ignorance, even for a second, and for glorifying the author of it as *God Almighty* on earth, customary Christianity stands out as a religion without reason.

What experts of customary religions of the world are saying, in effect, is that ignorance or lack of knowledge amounted to perfection in the days of Adam, and that knowledge of good and evil brought about imperfection and death in the world. They are also saying that although Jehovah judged Adam and Eve with that yardstick, he no longer uses the same standard now that *conformist* religious adherents themselves have somehow become the sole experts and disseminators of the same *forbidden fruit* of knowledge of good and evil. They suppose that Jehovah instituted human religion in the wake of *Adam's failure*, as they see it, to teach unenlightened human beings the same knowledge of good and evil that Adam and Eve were eternally condemned for. They suppose that he has now changed his mind and willingly decided to help human beings advance from their *natural* state of spiritual blindness to ultimate spiritual perfection. Such logic is utterly flawed.

Ignorance is still the basic program of the human mind. Jehovah never intended average human beings to grow out of it. If Adam and Eve had not courageously defied god of Eden on behalf of the entire human race, human beings would have remained uncultured animals in the wild to this day. Unfortunately, humanity basks in the brave accomplishments of Adam and Eve today, and yet fails to acknowledge their true worth. Human morality and the general refinement of human conscience and spiritual integrity among humans today are direct outcomes of Adam and Eve's so-called 'sin of disobedience.'

As it were, we are all emulators of Adam and Eve. Deep within us, we all yearn for the same *knowledge of good and evil*, because we know that it is central to our physical and spiritual well-being. We are, therefore, as guilty today as they were then. Knowledge is power. It is the only vehicle by which we can attain ultimate spiritual enlightenment, and then spiritual rebirth. If humanity had not followed in the *righteous disobedience* of Adam and Eve, we would not have been where we are today regarding our spiritual evolution in social and spiritual goodness. We would have remained clueless barbarians as god of Eden had originally intended.

If religious ministers were honest with themselves, they would have looked back at the lives of human beings that ever lived on earth and seen that ignorance is a permanent aspect of human nature. The life of newborn babies illustrates actual legacy of Jehovah's eternal will for humankind. It portrays the natural state of the original human beings. Parents, guardians, schoolteachers, and other educators who work tirelessly to wean infants and young people of innate witlessness know the agony of human ignorance.

Even among the most enlightened adults in human societies, ignorance is still the bane of true humanity. Very wealthy religious and government officials who accumulate material riches far more than they need while impoverishing helpless masses, for instance, are suffering from the worse kind of ignorance. Ironically, their infatuated religious followers generally pretend that they do not see and feel the programmed anomalies of human nature. That is proof of utter ignorance on their part.

As far as the god of Eden was concerned, anyone who eats of the heavenly fruit of knowledge of good and evil and disseminates the same "*will surely die.*" He meant that he would persecute such a person to death, and his reasons were not far-fetched. Accordingly, he cursed and persecuted Adam and Eve, even to this day. He persecuted and murdered Jesus Christ, our heavenly Teacher, and did the same to his true apostles. He still does the same to true disciples of Jesus Christ in our present age.

Therefore, there is still no other way for human beings to avail themselves of the saving knowledge of good and evil, except by knowingly defying Jehovah and his perpetual threat of death. He makes it clear in the scripture that people who violate that *unacceptable* commandment today are still as guilty in his sight as were Adam and Eve. He still cannot stand people yearning for true knowledge. He still fumes and says, "The people of this world used their reason and sinned [against him]; ... And that is why they [are suffering and] will suffer torment. ... Even now, they [people who seek and stand for spiritual insight] last no longer than a vapor; they disappear like fire and smoke; they catch fire, blaze up, and quickly go out." [2 Esdras 7:72, 61 (GNB)]

It is clear from the above that Jehovah's vicious old threat of death is still very much in force on people who seek spiritual enlightenment. Genuine seekers of true spiritual rebirth must, therefore, make the same choice, as Adam and Eve made in their time, whether to obey their inner yearning for the fruit of the heavenly Christ or to cower before the toothless god of Eden. I stand for knowledge and for 'righteous disobedience' to Jehovah's law of forced ignorance.

Furthermore, human beings were *mortal* composite beings right from the very beginning. The scripture says that the "tree of life and the tree of the knowledge of good and evil" stood somewhere "in the middle of the garden" and not within the Edenic human beings. What that meant was that the prospect of discovering and imbibing the fruits of the two most important trees of true divinity existed within the borders of the world but was expressly forbidden for humankind.

Heavenly wisdom and eternal life are divine heritages of perfect sons of the Father in heaven. Therefore, without the knowledge of the difference between the *good* Father and the *evil* Jehovah and without eternal life, Edenic human beings were spiritually dead imbeciles walking and talking. The mortal nature of the human earthen body and the fallen state of the human spirit were obvious signs of imperfection. These were not only restricted to Adam and Eve who were but made in the image and likeness of Jehovah. Jehovah himself was equally dead and imperfect, and therefore could not possibly give out what he did not have. A dead man cannot beget a living one; neither can an imperfect inventor invent something perfect.

The scripture also says in Genesis 2:25 that "the man and his wife were both naked and were not ashamed." I do not see how any honest human being could interpret this statement as meaning that "the man and his wife were perfect." Either customary Christian authorities are *naked, and are not ashamed* themselves, or they are deliberately turning the truth upside down. The statement is the clearest scriptural indication that Edenic human beings were in the worse kind of ignorance. Remarkably, wild animals remained naked and shameless as Jehovah intended, and no normal person calls them perfect.

It is very insincere on the part of customary Christian ministers to stand before their congregations *completely* dressed up, while at the same time condemning Adam and Eve for rejecting the life of involuntary nakedness. Most of them exhibit their wardrobes with that subtle air of pride and arrogance. The most common sight on our TV screens today is that of thoughtless church ministers, dressed in the best sets of Italian three-piece suits that conceal complete sets of branded under wears, with designers ties, real skin leather belts, and the trendiest pairs of Italian shoes. Surely, these do not paint the picture of people who truly prefer walking about naked, as the god of Eden had intended it.

I challenge the church ministers who condemn Adam and Eve for helping human beings imbibe the culture of covering their nakedness to practically prove them wrong. If they truly believe that human beings were better naked and senseless as Jehovah intended in the beginning, let them demonstrate their conviction in the presence of their devoted congregations. While preaching about the *fall of Adam* on the pulpit on a full Sunday morning service, let any of them who is true to his own judgment begin by first removing his topcoat, his inner coat, his tie, his shirt, and his singlet, then his shoes, his stockings, his trousers, and his underwear. If a single member of his congregation remains seated by the time he becomes fully naked as god of Eden intended him to be, then he would have made his point.

Only animals and outright lunatics walk about naked without feeling ashamed. No sane person does that, not even a partial lunatic. The fact that Adam and Eve were originally in that state of mind was proof that they were literally in an extreme state of insanity. Indeed, it is knowledge that makes the difference between sanity and insanity. In other words, ignorance is to insanity what knowledge is to perfection. Edenic human beings belonged to the former. It was obvious that the god of Eden wanted ignorant beings that he could easily dominate, but he could not achieve that with enlightened Adam and Eve and their immediate posterity.

Perfection means absolute completeness and flawlessness. It means that someone or something is not lacking in any essential quality or detail. Most especially, perfection also means zero presence of ignorance. In their original state, Adam and Eve were literally born "*blind from birth*," since they lacked the knowledge of good and evil. They were also "*blind in spirit*" and, therefore, bereft of moral and spiritual integrity. Hence, they walked about naked without knowing that their act was immoral and shameful. That did not in any way amount to perfection.

Human spirits were already dead and human nature inevitably revolved around artificial cyclic mortality. It was obvious therefore that certain things needed to be added and some extracted from Edenic human beings before their spirits could contemplate perfection. The perishable needed to be permanently separated from the imperishable.

The timely intervention of our loving Father through his heavenly Christ opened the spiritual eyes of the Edenic couple. He re-armed Adam and Eve with the missing—*forbidden*—power of knowledge, reason, and understanding. With that, they were able to differentiate between morality and spiritual impropriety and immediately took corrective action. *"They sewed fig leaves together and made themselves aprons [of moral rectitude],"* and thus inaugurated human morality as a means toward social and spiritual refinement. They also set in motion humankinds' long and difficult, but eternally rewarding march, toward true spiritual emancipation.

Wisdom is the principal essence of perfection; without knowledge, there is no wisdom. Jehovah did not just deny Edenic human beings that, he forbade it with the threat of physical persecution and death. Exponents of customary religions of the world who support position of the god of Eden are simply his hired agents. Their express mandate remains to subvert the truth in favor of their mystical paymaster. Such religious mercenaries have *sold their own souls to the devil.* To them ignorance is bliss! Therefore, their spiritual state is far more pitiable than that of Edenic human beings.

Spiritual blindness is the most debilitating aspect of imperfection. Human nature epitomizes that. Adam and Eve overcame that in Eden only with the special help of the *heavenly Restore Guide*. Spiritual blindness is still the greatest handicap of the so-called enlightened humankind today. Evidently, civilized peoples of the world need the special help of the heavenly Messiah most, because they think that they see, while they do not. They desperately need him to open their spiritual eyes to the basic spiritual status quo.

According to the Qur'an, "Whoso is blind here [in the world] will be blind in the hereafter, and yet further from the road [from the way that leads to true spiritual salvation]. ... For indeed it is not the eyes that grow blind, but it is the hearts [the spirits], which are within the bosoms, that grow blind." [Qur'an 17:72; 22:46] Most people presume that civilization or advanced level of technological innovations, social and political development in human society is synonymous with spiritual enlightenment. On the contrary, human civilization largely enhances spiritual blindness.

Usually, advanced levels of development in society entail complex social and political organization, marked by material, scientific, and artistic progress. But these do not necessarily provide the right atmosphere for spiritual development; they distract peoples' attention from pure spiritual pursuits. Human civilization mostly provides answers to the material needs of human beings. It provides irresistible objects of human comfort and enjoyment that collectively overwhelm human minds with worldly matters. The so-called *good things of life*, in turn, largely bring about spiritual decadence. These are basic facts of life.

Paradoxes of biblical standards stand out clearly in the case of human beings' genuine quest for heavenly wisdom. The same Bible, which vehemently forbade heavenly wisdom for the original human beings in the book of Genesis, sings the praises of knowledge and wisdom in its other books. While it still holds Adam and Eve eternally condemned for courageously imbibing the fruit of heavenly wisdom, it glorifies the least noble Jewish patriarchs, like King Solomon, whose wisdom was purely of worldly standard. Solomon's case is proof that the god of Eden approves and esteems *worldly wisdom*. What he is enraged about is *heavenly wisdom* and the people who seek to acquire and disseminate it in the world.

The book of Proverbs strongly commends wisdom and spiritual insight. Among other things, it says, "The beginning of wisdom is this: Get wisdom, and whatever you get, get [spiritual] insight. ... To get wisdom is better than gold. ... He who gets wisdom loves himself." [Prov. 4:7; 16:16; 19:8] These are statements of spiritual insight. The questions are: Who really inspired the bible book of Proverbs? Did the god of Eden know about these wise sayings in the beginning; and did he approve of them? Does he agree with them even now?

What Adam and Eve did in the Garden of Eden was exactly what the bible book of Proverbs enjoins today. They sought and obtained wisdom and spiritual insight for the good of their own fallen spirits. Surprisingly, Jehovah felt so terminally threatened by such a noble act that he declared them unpardonable sinners and placed eternal curses on them and on their posterity. He did not even stop at that, but also inspired eternal hatred of Adam and Eve in the minds of his hired religious operatives. It should not be difficult to see that Jehovah did not inspire or sanction the pro-wisdom verses of the biblical book of Proverbs. He hated and still hates Adam and Eve, their divine source of spiritual insight, and indeed, all exponents of divine knowledge and wisdom, even to our present generation.

The scripture makes it clear that knowledge and wisdom are the natural rights of every spirit in existence. "It is not good for a man to be without knowledge," it says in Proverbs 19:2. It also says that lack of knowledge and wisdom leads to eternal spiritual death, rather than the other way around. "But fools die for lack of wisdom," it says in Proverbs 10:21. If Edenic human beings did not lack wisdom in the first instance, they would not have had any need to imbibe the fruit of the tree of knowledge, which was especially "to be desired to make one wise." [Genesis 3:6] Jehovah deliberately refused to play by the heavenly norm, and it was obvious that he had ulterior motives. Therefore, Edenic human beings had no other option but to claim what was theirs by divine will of the Father.

To find perfection and eternal life, Adam and Eve first needed to find the wisdom from the realm of perfection. Of course, such wisdom could only come from forces that were external to Jehovah and his imperfect world order. The heavenly Messiah came to their aid, and they immediately regained their spiritual sight. The heavenly Messiah remains our only source of genuine enlightenment today.

Inspired by the divine Spirit of Knowledge, Eve suddenly realized that the tree of knowledge was "good for food, and that it was a delight to the eyes, and that the tree was **to be desired to make one wise.**" Evidently, they were not already wise or perfect. She received and ate the fruit of knowledge; she also gave some to her husband, and he ate. Surprisingly, the fruit of knowledge did not cause them to die, as Jehovah had threatened. Rather, it opened their spiritual eyes and restored their spiritual integrity, just as the heavenly Spirit assured. Immediately, they sewed fig leaves and covered their nakedness, in direct positive reaction against their original state of ignorance and imperfection. Adam and Eve took the first positive step toward true spiritual perfection on behalf of the entire humankind, and thus inaugurated the crucial battle of salvation for ultimate spiritual rebirth of captive human spirits.

Official stance of **all** worldly religions on the straightforward events of Eden, concerning humankind's righteous stride toward knowledge and spiritual rebirth, is a clear indication that they serve the will of Jehovah, the god of Eden, and not the will of the Father or of the heavenly Christ. Jehovah instituted human religion not to serve the spiritual needs of captive human spirits, but to obscure the liberating truth and mislead as many as possible.

It is very encouraging to see that despite the universal and aggressive nature of adverse religious influence over people in today's world, there is still a good number of conscientious individuals who are not intimidated or fooled by the religious fallacy of *lost human perfection*. They are sure that human beings were never perfect at any point in time on earth. Human nature and the chaotic state of the universe simply could not allow that. They know that perfection is to be sought beyond the bounds of the imperfect universe. That is why they cling firmly to the special love of the Father that Jesus Christ represents. They do not doubt that Jesus Christ is the heavenly Restore Guide who alone can guide their prodigal spirits back to true perfection in the Father's heavenly kingdom.

Human nature was terribly flawed right from its conception and Jehovah's express intent was to manipulate human weaknesses to his ulterior ends. For true perfection to be possible, the perfectible human spirit must be eternally separated from the perishable earthen cloak. Presenting it in another way, our heavenly Restore Guide says that human beings must be born *anew*—"Truly, Truly, I say to you, unless one is born anew, he cannot see the kingdom of the Father." [John 3:3] This is a direct indication that their present birth in the image and likeness of Jehovah, the god of Eden, is eternally flawed. It also shows that perfection is only possible in the Father's spiritual realm of perfection.

The heavenly Messiah appeared in Eden and inaugurated the divine separation process, beginning with Adam and Eve. He reactivated their subjugated spirits and elevated their consciousness. Then, he raised the human conscience over their susceptible minds. An unbiased reappraisal of the actual encounter in the so-called Garden of Eden between Jehovah, humankind, and the divine Spirit of Knowledge will show that religious peoples of the world have deliberately turned the table of honor upside down. Correct interpretation of the events of Eden must recognize the redemptive nature of the role played by the *giver* of the fruit of knowledge. It is most uncanny that Jehovah libeled the *giver* of spiritual insight serpent and devil. His lopsided logic purporting that knowledge spoils perfection is also very mischievous.

Majority of so-called enlightened people of the world today still accept such a fable and have taken it upon themselves to persecute the few who dare to apply their acquired power of spiritual insight. Roman Catholic Church of Jehovah particularly hated and persecuted truly enlightened thinkers and philosophers of old. Members of certain religious groups who were certainly *better enlightened* than Catholics, such as the Gnostics and others who read proper meaning into the Genesis encounter between Jehovah, Adam and Eve and the heavenly Christ became the Church's worst victims. The Church called them all sorts of names, officially branded them heretics, atheists, and witches and ruthlessly persecuted, massacred and burnt many of them at stake.

The Church openly carried on persecution of Adam and Eve and their spiritual posterity from where Jehovah stopped in Eden, while doing everything it could to permanently suppress the simple meaning of the events of Eden. The horrible atrocities of the

Crusaders and the Inquisition, as well as the deliberate propagation of misleading satanic doctrines to unsuspecting multitudes of its adherents remained the Roman Catholic Church's way of rendering active service to Jehovah, who remains terminally opposed to spiritual enlightenment of Adam's posterity.

Gnosticism was a more enlightened religious movement that flourished in the Roman Empire during the second and third centuries and presented a major challenge to the false doctrines of orthodox Christianity. It rightly recognized human spirits as *fallen* sparks of transcendent Divine Spirit that is not of our present material universe. Presently entrapped in human earthen bodies, Gnosticism held that human spirits needed to find a way of escape or spiritual rebirth, and that only heavenly wisdom or *gnosis* ("revealed knowledge") could liberate and help captive human spirits to return to their proper home in transcendent spiritual realm.

Ophites were a group of Gnostic sects that attached special importance to the unique entity in Eden that imparted the *gnosis* or heavenly wisdom to Adam and Eve, whom god of Eden maligned as serpent. They honor him as the actual *liberator of humankind*, since he was the first to open the spiritual eyes of human beings to the necessity of spiritual revolt against Jehovah, and against his willful spell of ignorance over the human spirits. He was the actual author of humankind's spiritual evolution toward true perfection.

Like other Gnostics, they believed, among other things that:

- Human spirits are in prison in human bodies, within the material universe, and can be saved only through *revealed knowledge* of the spirits' transcendent origin.
- The unique serpent mentioned in the story of the Garden of Eden imparted that saving knowledge to Adam and Eve—in reality, he was not a serpent at all.
- The god of the Old Testament is the evil deity who invented the material world order.

- All those who defied him were noble and venerable; and
- The Father of Jesus Christ is not the same as Jehovah, the god of the Old Testament.

The Ophites understood and reinterpreted the so-called story of "fall of man" in its right perspective, away from the fictitious theme presented by the Genesis narration. They noted that the so-called *serpent* in the Genesis fairytale was not the evil one. He was rather the giver of the redeeming knowledge (*gnosis*) that enabled the original human beings to rediscover their true identities. Consequently, they longed to become as perfect as their heavenly Father, which remains the will of the Father and Jesus Christ to this day. They concluded, therefore, that the so-called *serpent* was indeed *an envoy of the perfect Divine Spirit*. Jehovah, the ruler of the imperfect world order, had wanted to prevent original humans from imbibing the knowledge (*gnosis*) so that they would remain spiritual imbeciles forever under his eternal dominion.

The Ophites had no doubt that this miserable material world of mortals was never a creation of perfect Divine Spirit. They credited the flaws and enslaving processes to Jehovah, the Old Testament Jewish Demiurge, thus agreeing with 1 John 2:16, which says, "All that is in the world is not of the Father but is of the world."

In their conscientious view, human nature represents spiritual impediment to the human spirit. Human's dilemma centers on his conflicting spiritual and material elements. Such a self-counteracting entity could not have been perfect at any point in its existence. Only *gnosis*—the revealed knowledge of truth—could make original humans aware of their *forgotten* origin in the Father who is the source of all perfect beings. Only positive application of the knowledge of good and evil could give humans a true sense of direction and help captive human spirits to strive toward extricating themselves from unwholesome bond with imperfect matter for the perfect heavenly existence.

Having correctly interpreted the crucial events of the Garden of Eden, it was natural for the Ophites to see that Jesus Christ shared the same personality and purpose with the so-called *serpent* in Eden. As it were, the so-called serpent in Eden was none other than the heavenly Christ, and Jesus Christ was his incarnation in present-day Eden. Thus, the first and second coming of the heavenly Christ into the world were clearly highlighted. Accordingly, Ophites regarded Jesus Christ as *a perfect Spirit being who had come into the world, assuming the human form* to effectively interact with modern humans and to bear witness to the same saving knowledge (*gnosis*) introduced by the redeeming *serpent* in the Edenic garden of ignorance. Hebrew 2:14(NLT) says, "Because the Father's children are human beings [now]—made of flesh and blood—the Son [the heavenly Christ] also became flesh and blood," while Jesus Christ affirms in John 18:37(NLT), saying, "Actually, I was born and came into the world to testify to the truth."

Furthermore, John Fowles wrote in his book, *The Aristos*:

> "I interpret the myth of the temptation of Adam in this way: **Adam** is hatred of change and futile nostalgia for the innocence of animal; **The Serpent** is imagination, the power to compare, self-consciousness; **Eve** is the assumption of human responsibility, of the need for progress and the need to control progress; **The garden of Eden** is an impossible dream; a parahades [near hell] of the past; **The Fall** is the essential *processus* of [spiritual] evolution, and would be more better termed *"The Move."* **The god of Genesis** is a personification of Adam's resentment [handicap]. ... The Fall or move is every day."

Every clear-thinking human being would interpret the fateful events of the so-called Garden of Eden the same way. Garden of Eden was a kind of hell, Adam and Even needed heavenly assistance to move out of it, and the heavenly Christ offered that to them. "The move is every day" means that more and more people are steadily experiencing spiritual reawakening every day, as Adam and Eve did.

I hope that religious authorities of this world can understand that they cannot possibly stop *"the Move"* that Adam and Eve inaugurated in Eden for all of humanity through the guidance of the heavenly Christ. Jehovah could not stop Adam and Eve then; he still cannot stop his spiritual posterity now. More importantly, I pray that average twenty-first-century human beings will emulate Adam and Eve in striving to imbibe the true gospel of Jesus Christ. For he is none other than the same *heavenly Restore Guide* that first appeared for our rescue in the Garden of Eden.

CHAPTER SIX

HUMAN NATURE: CAPTIVITY OF HUMAN SPIRITS

People who use computers are very familiar with the *system restore* feature that enables them to undo harmful changes to their computers by restoring the systems to original settings and performances. Most modern GSM handsets also have the *restore original factory default settings* feature. I call this feature, a system *second-chance*.

No doubt, this is a very thoughtful innovation by conscientious computer manufacturers. Usually, restoring the system to its original settings is the best available option for a system faced with prospect of total collapse due to *harmful changes* or mistakes made by its operator. Forging ahead regardless could result in permanent damage, which would mean deliberately causing one's computer to crash beyond remedy. Such a foolhardy step would be quite inexcusable.

Reserving his fallen, dead sons in a period of grace within the primordial nether gloom meant that the Father offers all of us the *second chance* to willingly strive toward restoring ourselves to our original perfect state and returning to our proper heavenly dwelling. The Father's offer is a gracious opportunity for us to avoid plunging completely into impending eternal darkness, which would then mean eternal spiritual death. Being *reserved* in a period of grace means that the Father gives us respite from total darkness now, but that period would not last forever. He also sent the heavenly Christ as heavenly *Restore Guide* to shepherd us through the spiritual process of restoration.

But Jesus Christ affirms that artificial light of stars and other luminary bodies that currently sustains our present false existence in the universe will not shine forever. "My light will shine for you just a little longer," he says. "Walk in the light while you can, so the darkness will not overtake you [completely]. ... Put your trust in the light while there is still time; then you will become children of the light." [John 12:35-36(NLT)]

The wisest choice in the unset was for the heavenly dropouts to have willingly *undone* the corrupted steps that brought them to this spiritual bondage in the outer darkness. If they had willingly shown genuine repentance, the Father would have immediately granted them divine amnesty, lifted them out of their primordial prison of darkness and restored them to their perfect heavenly home. Unfortunately, the heavenly dropouts chose obstinacy rather than reason, thereby plunging deeper into overwhelming darkness. They longed for another life and another home outside their proper heavenly dwelling, but it all turned out to be shambles.

Attempting to experience another life outside the Father only yielded a dreamy process of acting life rather than living life. Organic existence only offered an alternative life of illusion that ultimately enslaved the fallen, dead spirits to the selfish will of the potentates of the false life idea. Human nature represented one of such alternative steps in the wrong direction taken by the prodigal spirits. It literally amounted to a second degree of spiritual death.

Human nature effectively erased our memories of blissful existence as perfect spirits and true sons of the Father and replaced them with transient memories of a dreamy earthly life. While in the first stage of spiritual death, all the fallen spirits were aware of their current spiritual predicaments and knew about the Father's offer of a *second chance,* human nature rendered human spirits completely oblivious to all that knowledge. Without the slightest recollection of our spiritual past, we could not even tell who we really were. Someone must help us to rediscover our spiritual selves, and to rediscover our heavenly Father and his magnanimous offer of a *second chance.* That was why the heavenly Christ first appeared in Eden, and thereafter incarnated as Jesus Christ in Jerusalem. So, we know that Jesus Christ is the Father's official *heavenly Restore Guide* for all captive human spirits.

Jesus came into the world to remind us of who we really are and to reiterate the Father's *second chance* for true spiritual restoration. But we persecuted, murdered, and ran him out of our midst. Even some of his inspired Apostles and disciples who tried to disseminate his message of love and true spiritual restoration met similar fates in the hands of the same people whom the divine message was meant to liberate. Without a good measure of spiritual self-awareness, it remains nearly impossible today for average human beings to readily appreciate the need for true spiritual regeneration. Human nature has reduced us to spiritual imbeciles. We worship and look up the god of Eden who represents chief custodian of false life on earth because we are not ourselves. We look up to him as *God Almighty* because we do not know our spiritual rights.

Genesis 2:7 reads, "Then **[god of Genesis] formed the man from the dust of the ground**. He breathed the breath of life into the man's nostrils, and the man became a living person." This is how the Bible callously explained away our individual spiritual personalities and sold our spirits into captivity to opportunistic Jehovah, who is but a fallen, dead spirit, just as every one of us. Edenic human beings could not contest the travesty of perfect existence because they lacked spiritual insight into the basic truth. Human minds were not programmed to retain knowledge of true spiritual status quo. However, with the special help of our heavenly Messiah, the truth is gradually becoming evident to many.

That human nature was Jehovah's personal invention is not a big deal at all, if by that we mean that he played major part in engineering ethical modification of ape-man aborigines on planet Earth. Seasoned animal tamers and breeders do the same on earth today. Besides, our seasoned scientists have invented marvelous robots that are programmed to move, manipulate objects, and accomplish complex work routines while interacting with their environment. Some of these man-made machines even perform tasks far more quickly, efficiently, and accurately than human beings, and without necessarily enslaving any unsuspecting spirit in so doing. Surely, human beings would have been some godly machines if they did not involve spiritual enslavement of vulnerable spirits. The human mind became what it was programmed to be, with built-in self-hindering weaknesses that were deliberately intended to prevent spiritual reawakening.

The original mortal entity called *man* by the scheming god of Eden was strictly a modified species of animal, a beast of burden that was strictly meant to serve the selfish desires of the so-called *most high gods* of the refurbished world order. The Qur'an makes this point succinctly. "There is not an animal in the earth or a flying creature flying on two wings," it says, "but they are peoples like unto you [human beings]." [Qur'an 6:38]

Now, a mechanical automaton is a piece of *dead* earth. Only natural electricity flowing through it makes it a *living* robot, tool, or slave of its maker or owner. Religiously speaking, electrical energy is the *spirit* that animates electronic robots. The robot means nothing without electricity. Natural electricity is an explosive energy source that comes in various forms and ratings, so there is the need to *subdue* and effectively *control* it before it can be *enslaved* or utilized to animate the dead system of a mechanical robot. That is the work of the robotics expert.

The robotics expert is simply a *power manipulator* who formulates integrated circuitry or means of managing naturally available electrical energy sources to achieve a desired goal by driving the system of mechanical components. He is an inventor, not a *creator*, because he merely manipulates naturally existing substances to produce limited or finite effects. Likewise, man is a robot, while Jehovah and his accomplices were automatists.

An electrically driven robot dies a natural death when the circuitry dies or damages beyond repair. It is then scrapped, recycled, or dumped in the earth from where it was made. Natural electricity never dies with, or as, the silicon components of the robot that it animates. The same electrical power source would continue to stimulate the same electrical impulse if plugged into any other sound robot.

In precisely the same manner, the complete man is an earthen–spiritual fabrication. Like the mechanical automaton, he is composed of a *mortal* body made of unstable earthen matter and quickened by an *immortal* life force, light energy, or spirit that was subtly *subjugated* by some cosmic automatists. Man is merely a mortal robot, just like electrically powered machines. Jehovah was just an opportunist who became god over man and ultimately uses man as his slave and tool on earth. Jehovah is not a creator but a seasoned manipulator.

Physical death of man represents the formal dissolution of the *mortal* and *immortal* components of the complex human machine. Man's dead body eventually decays and dissolves into its natural earthen mineral constituents, while the immortal spirit or *spiritual electricity* lives on within the solar grid to be utilized in another budding mortal form, as dictated by the cyclic process of reincarnation or physical re-embodiment of human spirits. Scientifically speaking, therefore, the human spirit is the electricity that powers the human android. Jesus Christ explained this by saying that "it is the spirit that gives life, the flesh is of no avail." The immortal spirit created by the Father gives life; the mortal earthen flesh invented by fallen dead spirits is of no avail.

Indeed, the human body is very much like an electronic robot with built-in sensors, processors, motors, and effects, that its owner or operator compels to behave as programmed by transmitting electronic impulses via his remote control. The operator realizes his precise desires by simply hitting the right command buttons, while the electronic impulses that he beams out form the robot's body of experiences or functions.

The human body of experiences is, however, far more complex, many-sided reflections of his multiple encounters with the potentates of the false life of the world, other humans, animals, other life forms, the world in general, and with himself. The fact that there are two opposing owners and controllers of the physical man further complicates the human situation. Each part-owner, operating at his own frequency, transmits directly opposing mystical impulses to his specific sensor points on and within the human entity with the aim of outwitting the other. The Qur'an captures this basic scenario where it quotes Allah's comparison of a slave and a freeman. "Allah coineth a similitude: A man in relation to whom are several part-owners quarrelling and a man belonging wholly to one man are the two equal in similitude?" asks Qur'an 39:29.

Man is a composite being with the *spirit* belonging to the Father, and the *body* being an earthen organism formulated by the rebellious fallen spirits via cosmic encodement contained within the primordial blueprint. The Father's sensor point is the human conscience, which is the perceivable extension of the incarcerated spirit that animates every person, while man's carnal body is the devil's complex workshop. A man who obeys his conscience or spirit will not be able to please his carnal body. He will not be able to please Jehovah, the devil, who is chief custodian of universal veil of secrecy and potentate of false life on planet Earth. Jehovah demands nothing short of blind surrender of both body and spirit from his robotic human captives.

The scripture portrays the permanent conflict between sinful human nature and the captive human spirit this way: "The sinful nature wants to do evil, which is just the opposite of what the Spirit wants. And the Spirit gives us desires that are the opposite of what the sinful nature desires. These two forces are constantly fighting each other, so you are not free to carry out your good intentions." [Gal. 5:17 (NLT)] This is spiritual bondage in practical terms.

In other words, a permanent state of war exists within the physical man, between the two part-owners of his distinct parts—the Father of human spirit versus Jehovah, the *ruler* of human carnal body. In the end, the truly victorious person in this battle for spiritual emancipation will not be one who meticulously obeys the Torah, the Shari'ah, the Tao, or other religious laws of the land that Jehovah had inspired, but rather one who obeys his own good conscience that the Father inspires. Even Jehovah concedes that the will of the Father for the human conscience is all that matters in the battle for spiritual salvation. He says, "And a soul and him [the Father] who perfected it and inspired it (with conscience of) what is wrong for it and (what is) right for it. **He is indeed successful who causeth [his conscience] to grow**, and he is indeed a failure who stunteth it." [Qur'an 91:7–10]

Human conscience embodies a person's divine ability to distinguish between good and evil to enhance the goodness in him. Every genuine seeker of true spiritual salvation must diligently cause his conscience to grow, to the eternal glory of the Father who perfected it in him. He must courageously disobey Jehovah's desires that are built into his carnal member. Furthermore, he must defy every regressive religious institution, injunction, and convention that even, slightly encourages hedonism to live up to the true standards set in his own conscience by direct inspiration of the Father's Holy Spirit of truth.

Jesus Christ says to his true followers, "You, therefore, must be perfect, as your heavenly Father is perfect." [Matt. 5:48] He continually whispers to their conscience the need to return fully to the heavenly norm of perfection. On the contrary, Jehovah confesses that he comes between a man and his good conscience by constantly whispering spiritual apathy to his mind. He concedes that the human spirits constantly whisper to people the need for true salvation, but that he and his partners readily manipulate built-in human weaknesses to overwhelm their thoughts with desires of worldly goods—for material *breakthroughs*, *prosperity*, and *fame*. "And know that **Allah cometh in between the man and his own heart**," says the Qur'an. "We verily created a man, and we know what his soul whispereth to him, and we are nearer to him than his jugular vein." [Qur'an 50:16; 8:24]

What this means is that Jehovah is a *soul hacker* or pirate-controller of human minds. He is relentlessly trying to jam, scramble, or totally block out the Father's divine inspirations to the human conscience. Genuine seekers of true spiritual salvation must, therefore, pay serious attention to the dual and terminally opposed nature of human experiences. There is a round-the-clock battle within the human mind, between the forces of good and evil—one trying to liberate and the other hell-bent on leading the human spirit to eternal damnation. Hence, the scripture counsels true Christ-followers, saying, "Beloved, do not believe every spirit [impulse or inspiration], but test the spirits to see whether they are of the Father." [1 John 4:1]

Edenic human beings lived entirely on instinctive impulses, as they were spiritually blindfolded and made completely susceptible to the inordinate whims of the evil manipulator in Eden. They remained chattel slaves of Jehovah and had no way of testing or differentiating their stimuli before the divine intervention of the heavenly Spirit of knowledge. They woke up every morning to look for what to eat, to play within the zoo, have sex, and ultimately glorify Jehovah for being so good to them. Their body of knowledge and reasoning ability were only restricted to earthly matters that were within the programmed scope of the human minds.

Jehovah expressly forbade spiritual insight into matters relating to the human spirit and his origin in the Father. The human's experience, knowledge, and understanding were simply illusory programs of his mind. The Edenic man experienced and acted but did not know the source of his impulses or the implications of his actions. He lived in total ignorance of his spiritual potential, until the Father ushered in the liberating knowledge of basic reality. The spiritual encounter with the *heavenly Restore Guide* in Eden literally *opened man's eyes* and awakened his blindfolded spirit for good.

With the coming of the heavenly Teacher in human form, and by following his unique gospel of the truth, human beings now have greater insight into matters relating to spiritual life, death, and salvation of their fallen, dead spirits. Today, greater spiritual knowledge continues to dispel ignorance, and people are increasingly living by the Holy Spirit rather than by the flesh. Today, more informed experiences, knowledge, and understanding make the world of difference between humankind and the other species of uninformed animals. This brand-new power of understanding helps man to rationalize the conflicting impulses within him. Most importantly, it helps him to know how to relate his experiences with his overall *knowledge of good and evil* to guarantee the hope of spiritual salvation for his captive spirit.

CHAPTER SEVEN

FIRST BATTLE OF EDEN: GOD OF EDEN WAS THE REAL VENOMOUS SERPENT

Jacob cheated his twin brother, Esau, out of his natural birthright, and with the help of his mother, Rebecca, he also successfully usurped his rightful blessings from their father, Isaac. Then, he believed that he had become master of the game of life. He was not aware, however, that he had violated the law of natural justice and would have to pay dearly for his oppressive actions. His seeming successes eventually turned him into a fugitive for life. No matter how successful religious people may have considered Jacob to be, he never really had a single moment of inner peace in his entire life. The story of his life proved clearly that there could be no rest for any oppressor. "There is no peace for the wicked," as Jehovah would say himself.

Even so, Jehovah is the principal oppressor of humankind and the inspirer of all human oppressors. The scripture shows clearly that Jehovah incited Jacob to commit all the cruel deeds against his twin brother, Esau. "Is not Esau Jacob's brother?" Jehovah asked, "Yet I have loved Jacob, but I have hated Esau." [Mal. 1:2–3] Surely, an evil deity, such as Jehovah, who sows discord between individuals, as close as twins, who loves some people and hates others, cannot possibly be mistaken for the perfect, loving Father who loves everyone and hates no one.

Genesis 2:2 says that Jehovah finished creating his earthly world in six days and started to rest on the seventh day. Well, he barely embarked on his dreamy seventh-day sabbatical when the living Spirit of the heavenly Messiah touched down in his Edenic stronghold to officially abrogate his so-called paradise on earth.

Suddenly, he was jolted back to the realities of his lost spiritual heritages in the Father. For someone who called himself *God Almighty*, Jehovah would have been out of his mind to even imagine that he could find true rest anywhere within the restless universe.

How could god of Eden have thought that he would find true rest in his Edenic para-Hades or anywhere else on planet Earth, while sitting on the spiritual rights of his own kith and kin? By forbidding Edenic humans from seeking knowledge and eternal life, he willfully violated the Father's divine will and therefore, made himself archenemy of the Heavenly State. So, how could he have found rest when he not only rejected the Father's offer of spiritual rebirth for himself, but also stood in the way of other fallen spirits making the right choice for themselves? It was like planning for a sound sleep on a rickety raft caught in the eye of a raging storm. It showed how terribly shortsighted god of Eden was, and still is. No normal person talks about having a real rest in a crumbling shack.

Some people have questioned the right the Father had to interfere in Jehovah's happy hunting ground. It is like questioning why a loving father must intervene to rescue his wayward son from the overbearing influence of an oppressive gang lord? We are lost sons of the Father, and he loves us dearly. It is absolutely within his right therefore, to intervene to save us from self-affliction under the overbearing influence of Jehovah's oppressive world order. No one would have bothered the god of Eden in his para-Hades if he had not violated the divine rights of others in pursuing his own selfish desires. Just like Jacob, he usurped the spiritual *birthrights* of captive human spirits and believed that his evil scheme was foolproof forever. That was where he went wrong and had to be stopped by the superior power of the heavenly Christ.

Qur'an 11:7 says that god of Eden "created the heavens and the earth in six days—and established his throne *upon the waters*." Revelation 17:15 explains that *"The waters"* upon which Jehovah's throne rests "are [spirits of] peoples and multitudes and nations and tongues." So, how could Jehovah have hoped to enjoy an interminable rest feeling like *God Almighty* with his throne of oppression set upon captive human spirits? His myth was believing that no one could challenge him in his false safe haven. He had said to himself, "As I planned, so shall it be, and as I have purposed, so shall it stand." [Isa. 14:24] But he sounded much like the *rich fool* in the parable that Jesus Christ told his disciples in Luke 12:16-21, who said to himself, "My friend, you have enough stored away for years to come. Now take it easy! Eat, drink, and be merry!" Suddenly, the redeeming Spirit of knowledge intervened when he least expected it, set his captives free, and sacked his Edenic para-Hades forever. And just like the *foolish rich man,* Jehovah had continued to cry wolf ever since.

A person who steals away other peoples' means of livelihood is a thief and a criminal. One who steals away other peoples' right to life itself is a vicious murderer. His own crime is eternally inexcusable. Jehovah is three times a criminal; he is a thief, a liar, and a murderer rolled into one. His crime against fallen human spirits is heinous. With his program of *spiritual oblivion*, impressed upon captive human minds, he stole away the peoples' divine right to heavenly wisdom, and lied to them that knowledge would lead to eternal death. Thus, he literally subjected their captive spirits to a second degree of spiritual death. That made him not just a dissident, but also a self-confessed enemy of the Heavenly State.

A second-degree of spiritual death meant that captive human spirits were willfully subjected to a frozen state of limbo and expected to remain dead forever. While in limbo, captive human spirits are completely incapacitated and would never be able to think, meditate or fight to regain true life. Ultimate destiny of such spirits lies only in the hands of an external liberator who must be willing and able to fight the repressive cosmic forces on their behalf. That is precisely why the heavenly Christ touched down in Eden. He came into the world to disarm Jehovah and the principalities who are the potentates of present oppressive world order to set free *frozen* spirits of captive humans.

As we have seen, the Edenic human beings were mere religious animals, designed to eat, play, engage in sexual intercourse, sleep, and worship the god of Eden. Without the knowledge of good and evil, they were unconscious people, which was tantamount to being dead. They lived for the god of Eden, while they were literally dead to themselves. They moved about as zoo animals in the Edenic Limbo and were not aware that they were dead, until the Father's Word of Life miraculously reached them as redeeming Spirit of Knowledge.

Edenic inmates became *human beings* or *enlightened animals* only when they received the initial ray of the liberating knowledge of good and evil that the Father beamed into the world through his heavenly Envoy. For obvious reasons, Jehovah cried wolf. He termed the Divine Spirit of Knowledge "serpent" and "devil," but he was none other than the Redeeming Spirit of the heavenly Christ in his first descent into the world. He would later manifest in human form as Jesus Christ to actualize the spiritual liberation and resurrection of incarcerated spirits of human beings, against the express design and desires of the principalities.

Consequently, there are two groups of organic beings on the face of the earth today. The humans that received the Divine Spirit of Knowledge and the wild animals that did not. The former became *enlightened*; they regained divine ability to reason, and subsequently advanced into the jungle of human cities. The latter remained absolute animals, being a clear reminder to present-day humans of Jehovah's original intention for them. Therefore, wild animals represent the point of reference by which *human beings* should constantly appraise their overall progress toward total liberation from ignorance or spiritual oblivion.

What the heavenly Messiah did for humankind with his first coming in the Garden of Eden was that he awakened our *frozen* spirits to the point of the first spiritual death. From that position, we were all expected to fight positively for our individual spiritual rights. Only the proper utilization of basic knowledge of good and evil with the accompanying power of reason differentiates human beings and wild beasts at the present. It follows, therefore, that any human being who is still unable to recognize and choose wisely between good and evil is still a wild beast of burden.

Genuine emancipation from the spell of ignorance or spiritual oblivion entails adequate empowerment with the knowledge of good and evil. Only this can bring a human being to the crucial point where he can knowingly choose between the imperfect life of the world and the heavenly life of perfection. Absolute liberation from ignorance, therefore, means absolute empowerment for life. Nevertheless, every individual will still have to make that personal choice of eternal abode—either for spiritual eternal life in the Father's heavenly kingdom or for eternal spiritual death in the outer darkness. Jesus Christ did not come into the world to make that choice for anyone; he came to empower the people who believe in him to make the choice for themselves.

The Divine Spirit of Knowledge in Eden stood for total abolition of human nature that thrives on forced ignorance. He later manifested in the person of Jesus of Nazareth and became our heavenly Teacher. He fought against human ignorance in ways that we can all appreciate as human beings, and he sought for disciples only people who would stop at nothing in seeking higher knowledge, which he called *gospel truth*. His passing words for such people read, "If you continue in my word, you are truly my disciples, *and you will know the truth, and the truth will make you free.*" [John 8:31–32] He made it clear that it is knowledge that leads to true spiritual rebirth and not faith in any sectarian religious conviction.

On completion of his earthly ministry in human form, the heavenly Christ transubstantiated into the Holy Spirit of truth and continued revealing the *gospel truth* to his true disciples, in line with his solemn promise in John 14:16-19, which reads, "I will not leave you desolate; I will come to you. Yet a little while, and the world will see me no more, but you will see me; ... even [as] the Spirit of truth, whom the world cannot receive, because it neither sees him nor knows him; **you know him, for he dwells with you, and will be**

in you." Indeed, the Holy Spirit of truth dwells within the conscience of all truly enlightened human beings today, assisting them toward perfecting the inevitable choice they must make in the matter of spiritual rebirth, as individuals. And no one who is truly "*born anew*" would choose to remain a chattel slave of Jehovah in the hellish world.

Against the backdrop of the god of Eden caging our fallen spirits and stealing away our divine rights to full spiritual restoration, customary religions of the world have continued to vilify Adam and Eve as sinners, and the redeeming Spirit of the heavenly Christ as serpent and devil. It is not difficult to see why they do this. They hate the truth because they are official agents of the archenemy of enlightened humanity. Worldly religions serve the will of god of Eden. They are antichrist by vocation and, therefore, stand diametrically opposed to true spiritual salvation of humankind.

As it were, simple-minded adherents of various religious sects have willfully chosen to remain completely oblivious, even in the face of common sense and abundance of knowledge. They have refused to see with their eyes or to hear with their ears. Although they enjoy the full dividends of the divine endowment of heavenly wisdom by the so-called *Serpent*, they still agree with hired agents of worldly religions that he was the actual devil. This is the saddest irony of human religiosity. But the question is, who among the very lovers of Jehovah and human religion would honestly deny eternal goodness and value of knowledge? Which of them would deny the spiritual values of human morality, which was the outcome of Adam and Eve's ability to distinguish between good and evil?

In the light of practical human experiences and well-documented scriptural evidence that attest to what really transpired in Eden, no clear-thinking human being in our present generation would fail to correctly evaluate the main characters involved in the fateful events of Eden. It is not enough for human beings to pride themselves on being educated or intellectuals with long lists of impressive paper qualifications. Ability to speak Queens English and conceptualize complex religious logics is immaterial in this matter. What is needed here is the simple ability to distinguish between good and evil, and the courage to be able to call a spade a spade. Anyone with a functional conscience can see and accept the gospel truth.

The issue to determine in the Edenic account is whether Jehovah did or did not deny human beings their natural right to knowledge, and whether the so-called *Serpent* did or did not help human beings to recover that right. The scripture affirms that "**It is not good for a man to be without knowledge**." Therefore, the real serpent and devil should be the one who denied human beings their divine right to knowledge. It should not be otherwise under any circumstance.

The scripture shows, in so many ways, that Jehovah, the god of Eden, is the real devil and venomous serpent. From what we already know, the devil brings disaster and causes calamity to befall human beings, and the real serpent is a deceiver, not a giver of knowledge, good conscience, and moral rectitude. As the supreme embodiment of the universal process of *yin and yang*, the devil is but a natural aspect of Jehovah, the god of Eden. The scripture quotes him as saying so himself: "I create both light and darkness; I bring both blessing and disaster. I Jehovah, do all these things." And "No calamity befalleth save by Allah's leave." [Isa. 45:7 (GBN); Qur'an 64:11]

Jehovah is also the great deceiver that sends human beings astray. He says so himself and the Qur'an confirms it: "Lo! Allah sendeth whom he will astray. … Those whom Allah sendeth astray, there is *no Guide* for them. **He leaveth them to wander blindly** on in their contumacy." [Qur'an 13:27; 7:186] That was exactly the situation in Eden. Jehovah was leading Edenic human beings astray before the *heavenly Restore Guide* appeared and endowed them with heavenly wisdom, good conscience, and moral rectitude. He helped them to stop wandering in darkness with *no Guide*, as Jehovah intended.

The Genesis account proves clearly that Jehovah was the **thief**, the **deceiver**, and the **liar** in the Edenic confrontation. Yet, he was the first to call his noble opponents names. Of course, that was perfectly in line with his true nature as the sneaky Old Serpent. He was the thief because he stole knowledge from human beings, and the liar because he said that knowledge of good and evil would lead them to death.

Jehovah is the **Great Red Dragon**, referred to in the book of Revelation, that dominates the imperfect world of human beings: "That Ancient Serpent, who is called **the Devil** and **Satan, the Deceiver** of the whole world [of human beings]." [Rev. 12:3, 9] The Bible further confirms the fact that "the whole world is in the power of the evil one." [1 John 5:19] However, Jehovah is in league with the seven lesser dragons—the so-called archangels. Together they form "the principalities ... powers ... and world rulers of this present darkness." [Eph. 6:12]

Jehovah is the real serpent that meant eternal harm to captive human spirits. He is the actual deadly snake that human beings must overcome to attain true spiritual rebirth. The heavenly Messiah came into the world to enlighten the humans and to help them to do just that, because they could not do it on their own. Unfortunately, people have continued to *wander blindly* as Jehovah rendered them. But how could any human being ever hope to see the greater picture or discover the truth without first recognizing the divine gesture on the part of the heavenly Redeemer in the Edenic encounter? How could anyone rightly claim to be a Christian without appreciating that the redeeming Spirit of knowledge in Eden was none other than the heavenly Christ himself? How could people hope for true spiritual salvation without first appreciating the so-called *Serpent* in Eden as the actual benefactor of humankind's spiritual evolution?

We generally say that knowledge is power, that knowledge is life! Well, the so-called *Serpent* in Eden imported the power of knowledge into our world. He opened the spiritual eyes of blind humans and inspired the noble prophets of old, who then prophesied about his expected physical incarnation. At the right time, Jesus Christ manifested among captive humans and continued precisely where the redeeming *Serpent* in Eden had stopped. Subsequently, the Holy Spirit of truth took over from where Jesus Christ left off. Jehovah, on his part, was the principal obstacle in the beginning; he is still the principal obstacle in the way of the spiritual salvation of captive human spirits.

Jehovah was the big *Serpent* and god of mountain that revealed himself to Moses in the magical burning bush in the wilderness of Median. He was the *staff of worldly power and authority* that Moses took to Egypt against the Pharaoh. Jehovah is the supreme serpent that mysteriously gulped in the lesser serpents in the Egyptian confrontation to prove that he was indeed the greatest serpent among the rest of the venomous serpents that rule the material world of powerless kings and pharaohs. The Father does not go to battle to claim supremacy among lesser gods. Most importantly, the Father does not manifest his divine power through snakes.

When Moses cast down his shepherd's rod, as commanded by Jehovah, it manifested the serpent. He instinctively turned around and began to flee because that was the last sign he expected from someone whom he had thought was true Divine Spirit. Jehovah called him back and allayed his fears with lying words of authority, assuring him that he was safe in his presence: "O Moses! Fear not! Lo! the [my] emissaries fear not **in my presence**. … O Moses! Draw nigh and fear not. Lo! thou art of those who are secure [in my presence]." [Qur'an 27:10; 28:31]

That Moses eventually felt secure in the presence of the *Writhing Snake* meant that he betrayed his good conscience and unwittingly became one of the abducted emissaries of Jehovah, the real Old Serpent. "So, he [Jehovah] showed him [Moses] the mighty sign [the *Mighty Sign* of the real Ancient Serpent!]." [Qur'an 79:20] That was clearly against what his good conscience had judged to be right and proper. Yet he gave in.

Jehovah was the *Fiery Serpent* that led the helpless Jews through the endless desert trek, purely to mimic Christ's ultimate *Spiritual Exodus* for all resurrected spirits at the last day. Pretending to be true *God Almighty* and best friend to the Jews, he systematically steered them back to the harsh realities of his Edenic para-Hades. The distance from Goshen in Egypt to the so-called Promised land in Canaan was just about 300 miles, but it took Jehovah a whole 40 years to lead the Jews to the place for obvious reasons. He took his time to horrify and inflict untold grief on his sheepish followers. In fact, he humiliated, tormented, and murdered the entire helpless population in the wilderness. Of a whole nation that he led out of Egypt, only two persons survived and managed to set their feet on the so-called Land of Promise. Thus, Jehovah proved that he was nothing but a Shepherd of Doom.

The graven image of the *Fiery Serpent* set on a pole that Jehovah could not resist authorizing Moses to mold was, perhaps, his clearest statement that he is the actual venomous serpent. He made Moses cast the Fiery Serpent of durable bronze to symbolize his universal role as the god that *wounds and heals* the sons of men. As the Fiery Serpent himself, he bit and then made his Jewish victims look to him for the antidote. He is the one who afflicts human beings with bodily ailments; he is also the one that human beings look up to for synthetic cure. In other words, the life we live in Jehovah is entirely dependent on his serpentine verve. Again, this clearly proves the cold-heartedness of his serpentine nature.

In time, the Fiery Serpent that Moses set on a pole became the *Nehush'tan* that he really is. The Jews worshiped him accordingly, until it was broken in pieces by their naïve king, Hezekiah. As would have been expected, Jehovah tactically made King Hezekiah pay dearly for his ignorant zeal. Although the broken pieces of *Nehush'tan* were unceremoniously swept away from the Jerusalem Temple, the *Fiery Serpent on a pole* still ruled the whole world. It mysteriously became the universal symbol of pharmacology to which sick humans all over the world still look up to for bodily cure, and therefore, for the transient life of the world.

Nevertheless, we already know the efficacy of the cure in the serpentine verve. We also know that the life it gives is the one that dies repeatedly. On the contrary, our heavenly Redeemer came to heal our sick spirits, and to give us true eternal life. Thus, the scripture compares Moses' gift of transient remedy for worldly infirmities as contained in the serpentine verve to perfect spiritual gift of eternal life by the Father through Jesus Christ, our heavenly Guide. John 3:14 reads, "And as Moses lifted up [Jehovah] the Serpent in the wilderness, so must [Jesus Christ] the Son of man be lifted up that whoever believes in him may have [his fallen, dead spirit restored to perfect health and] eternal life."

We now know that Jehovah is the proper serpent. He is the god that rules the world of humankind. The Father has already lifted Jesus Christ high above the malignant scheme of Jehovah, the deadly serpent. Those who look up to Jesus Christ can now be sure of true spiritual restoration. Jesus Christ is *"the Way, the Truth, and the Life"* that our afflicted spirits earnestly yearn for. He has already overcome Jehovah and his hellish world order. It is now up to individual human beings to choose between Jesus Christ, who gently leads our fallen, dead spirits back to the Blessed Tree of Life, and Jehovah, the venomous Ancient Serpent that has vowed to mislead us all.

CHAPTER EIGHT

BODY-SPIRIT INTERFACE

THE SIN WITHIN

As we already know, the human being is a bipartite entity, comprising of a nonmaterial *inner self* or spirit trapped within a mortal physical body. The immortal spirit emanated from Divine Spirit, while the lifeless earthen body grew out of corrupt cosmic experimentation by fallen dead spirits within a lifeless milieu. The immortal spirit is perforce held in captivity within the lifeless earthen body to animate it and that is the bone of contention. With the desires of the carnal body willfully designed to contradict and suppress those of the inner essential self, the human entity is by nature at war with himself. The war is between the Father who desires total liberation for the captive spirit and Jehovah who works so hard to sustain the false status quo on planet Earth. Now, every kingdom divided against itself is bound to collapse, and no person divided against himself will prosper. This is a fact.

The scripture portrays the permanent conflict between sinful human nature and the fallen human spirit this way: "The sinful nature wants to do evil, which is just the opposite of what the Spirit wants. And the Spirit gives us desires that are the opposite of what the sinful nature desires. These two forces are constantly fighting each other, so you are not free to carry out your good intentions." [Gal. 5:17 (NLT)] It is obvious, therefore, that the fraternity of body and spirit is an imperfect arrangement.

Once, an Iranian good friend and colleague of mine showed me his badly corroded set of teeth with such a deep feeling of self-guilt and helplessness. He was the fifth engineer onboard, and I was the second engineer. He was a chain smoker and had always complained of severe toothache, but I never thought he was suffering from such intense self-inflicted agony.

> "What caused that?" I asked, surprised at what I saw looking closely at his wasted set of teeth. Meanwhile, a burning stick of cigarette stuck between his left fingers.
> "This!" He raised the burning stick of cigarette trapped between his left fingers. "This!" he said.
> "Are you sure?" I asked, still surprised—not because I thought it could not be possible but surprised at him for being so deliberately cruel to himself.
> "Believe me, Sec," he affirmed, standing before me with a very moving impression of a lost child badly in need of rescue from his worst bullying situation.
> "But why don't you stop?" I asked, as if to say that I could have easily done so if I were in his shoes.
> "I don't know, Sec! Believe me, I tried so hard, but I cannot!"
> Suddenly, it dawned on me that I was just speaking to every human being on the surface of the earth, including myself, and so I tried to make him know that he was not alone.
> "I understand, my young man," I assured him. "We are all the same!" I said this from the depth of my heart, and I could see that it served his immediate need better than if I had tried to lecture him on how I stopped smoking myself. That would have further aggravated his far more destructive feeling of self-guilt and worthlessness.

Human nature is self-destructing. There are, by nature, varying degrees of self-destructive tendencies in every human being. We are all struggling to be better than we are. That is a fact. Every living human being shares this same inevitable agony, akin to a house divided against itself. Truly enlightened human beings must fight this *battle against the physical self* responsibly to foster the general well-being of their captive inner selves.

Looking inward, I could also see in myself persistent struggles with other forms of self-demeaning tendencies that are even more harmful than smoking. A set of teeth that is completely eaten up by nicotine could be easily replaced with a more serviceable alternative, with the help of modern science. But a defective mind would need special heavenly assistance to save it from eternal self-destruction. Jesus Christ did say that what comes out of the heart of a human being is far more detrimental to his spiritual well-being: "For from within, out of the heart of man, come evil thoughts, fornication, theft, murder, adultery, coveting, wickedness, deceit, licentiousness, envy, slander, pride, foolishness. **All these evil things come from within**, and they defile a man." [Mark 7:20–23]

Like other struggling people, I would have loved to be the perfect man that my good conscience persistently whispered to me about, but I just could not. Somehow, it seemed much easier for me to do all the things that my conscience disapproved of. I tried, just like my friend, but had never been able to triumph over certain self-demeaning impulses of my own to obey my good conscience as I would have loved to. So, for me too, the battle within had been real, continuous, and overwhelming. The question, therefore, is why do people not simply do all the good things that gladden their spirits, since they would really love to do so, and since they know they would find real happiness within themselves if they did?

Well, quite unlike my friend, **I knew** precisely why my mortal body desired all the things that led to self-destruction. Human nature is a false alternative to true spiritual existence, and human minds are deliberately programmed to be at odds with spiritual ideals to stifle possible desire for spiritual rebirth, *so that enlightened human beings may not be free to carry out the good intentions of their good conscience.* Human minds are also made highly impressionable and manipulable to enable ease of external control via piratic impulses or outright possession by deceitful spirits. As we already know, the entire universal situation is imperfect and under the power of evil spirits.

But I knew also that human beings are not altogether helpless. Jesus Christ is our heavenly Comforter; he understands our weaknesses as human beings, and he is already at hand to help us overcome the powers that hold our spirits in captivity. People who willingly allow him to help, will steadily experience general improvement in their overall spiritual outlook. For, as the scripture says, "If the Son makes you free, you will be free indeed." [John 8:36]

The book of Romans, chapter seven, records Paul's personal struggles against the same built-in human dilemma. He confessed his emotional predicament this way: "**I do not understand my own actions**. For I do not do what I want, but I do the very things I hate. ... Wretched man that I am [made]! **Who will deliver me** from this [human] body of death?" Paul not only recognized that he was made that way, but he also realized that he needed a special *Deliverer* to be able to understand and overcome the contradicting forces operating within him.

He tried to analyze his personal experiences to see if he could arrive at the ultimate solution based on the whole truth. "Now," he reasoned, "if I do what I do not want, I agree that the law is good. So, then it is no longer I that do it, but *sin which dwells within me.* For I know that *nothing good dwells within me, that is, in my flesh.* I can will what is right, but I cannot do it. For I do not do the good I want, but the evil I do not want is what I do."

Here again, Paul reached the conclusion that his flesh was sinful by design, while the norm governing his spirit was the direct opposite. What he needed to be sure about was that the two opposing parts of his being were handiwork of two opposing forces. That crucial knowledge would have helped him to appreciate the battle line, and therefore, to understand who the true Messiah was that he should have looked up to for genuine *deliverance*. It would have helped him to see Jehovah for what he really stood for and then, reject him and all his works. For it would have been impossible for him to reject the desires of his flesh without denouncing the piratic manipulator of it. Unfortunately, Paul stopped short of projecting his self-analysis in that direction.

It is obvious that *sin* is not just all the obnoxious and self-humiliating things that human beings do, but the actual building block of *wretched* human nature. Practically everything that human beings do on earth is sinful because they are living in a sinful world. Without doing those sinful things that define human nature, they will not exist. *Sin*, therefore, is the lifeblood of human nature. Remarkably, the human conscience never goes along with the natural follies of the human flesh. There is always that definite line of divide between the sinful desires of the carnal nature and the noble desires of the human conscience. It is obvious, therefore, that human conscience is not an aspect of human nature, and it is not of the world.

As I already stated, human nature is the work of corrupted spirits in darkness, while human conscience is the perceivable extension of incarcerated human spirit that the heavenly Messiah activated in Adam and Eve during his first advent in Eden. Without first activating the human conscience in human beings, it would have been practically impossible for the heavenly Messiah to institute human morality and thought refinement that would ultimately extricate captive spirits from overwhelming sinful nature.

With the growing influence of the heavenly Messiah through his imported knowledge of good and evil, human conscience has gradually found a place in every human being on earth today. It represents the noble outpost of the real self in every human being—that gentle, friendly inner pep voice that relentlessly whispers to the human mind the need to rise above sinful nature. The conscience persistently whispers to the human mind the need to knowingly override harmful original programs of carnal nature that hamper the well-being of the human spirit.

Even though Paul fell short of making that definite distinction between the gods of the human flesh and the Father who originated the human spirit, he rightly concluded that it was far more helpful to live by the divine will of the Father transmitted by the human conscience than by the programmed intentions of the potentates of the human android. His advice to truly enlightened individuals on this matter captures the sincerity of his personal conviction. He counsels:

> "Let the Holy Spirit guide your lives. Then you won't be doing what your sinful nature craves. The sinful nature wants to do evil, which is just the opposite of what the Spirit wants. And the Spirit gives us desires that are the opposite of what the sinful nature desires. These two forces are constantly fighting each other, so you are not free to carry out your good intentions. **But when you are directed by the Spirit, you are not under obligation to the law of Moses** [given by Jehovah, the chief custodian of human nature]." [Gal. 5:16–18 (NLT)]

In the end, Paul did draw valuable conclusions from his personal experiences that confirmed the built-in nature of humans' enmity with themselves:

> "Now if I do what I do not want, it is no longer I that do it, but *sin which dwells within* me. So, I find it to be *a law* [effectively built into human nature] that when I want to do right, evil lies close at hand. For I delight in the law of God [the Father], in my inmost self, but I see in my members *another law* at war with *the law of my mind [conscience]* and making me captive to the law of sin which dwells in my members. ... So then, I of myself serve the

law of God [the Father] with my mind [conscience], but with my flesh I serve the law of sin [programmed by authors of human nature]." [Romans 7:20–25]

Certainly, "a house divided against itself" is a perfect analogy of the carnal human being that is terminally turned against his own *inner essential self*. We are all *laid waste* as human beings unless we can successfully unravel the mystery of **the sin within** ourselves. As we diligently strive to suppress self-destructive excesses of our carnal bodies, we must strive harder to clearly identify and confront the masterminds behind it all to prevent eternal suffocation of our spirits.

To fail in this regard would be the actual *fall of man*. True spiritual salvation, therefore, involves enlightened human beings knowingly refusing to fail in the battle against the principalities and the built-in weaknesses of human nature. Our bodies live upon the death of our spirits. For as long as the body lives, the spirit dies; so, we must literally kill ourselves in Jehovah to find true spiritual life in the Father. This does not mean that one should tie the noose and hang himself. That rather favors the position of the authors of human mortality. Killing oneself in Jehovah means that one should persistently denounce him and all his works, while strive to "*walk by the Holy Spirit.*"

According to the scripture, those who walk by the Holy Spirit are literally dead to Jehovah and to the sensual world; "they belong to Jesus Christ and have crucified the flesh with its passions and desires." [Gal. 5:24] Jesus Christ says the same thing in another way in Mark 8:35 (NLT): "If you try to hang on to your life, you will lose it. But *if you give up your life* for my sake and for the sake of the Good News, you will save it."

Straightaway, we see the complex nature of the battle of spiritual salvation confronting captive human spirits, both the enlightened and the oblivious. Ordinarily, telling people to fight and *kill* their bodies to save their spirits might sound sarcastic and unreasonable, yet it is the most realistic way to depict the seriousness and the complicated nature of the raging battle of spiritual life and death. What it means is that people should systematically *deaden* their human habits and appetites for worldly comfort and enjoyment.

The scripture says plainly that we are fighting against a band of ruthlessly determined adversaries—"the principalities … powers … world rulers of this present darkness … the spiritual hosts of wickedness in the world." [Ephesians 6:12] The ultimate solution or weapon against these divine banditti is knowledge. But the knowledge must be wisely and courageously applied. Furthermore, people need to know what it means to *walk by the Holy Spirit*. I shall deal with this topic in the last chapter of this book.

Beyond the sneaky hosts of wicked manipulators of the built-in human weaknesses, **our only real enemy is still ignorance**, which is another name for the *sin that dwells within* our present being. Ignorance breeds inaction, and that in turn portends eternal spiritual death. Even with the raging inferno staring at all of us, many people appear to see nothing at all, and when someone tries to point attention to the looming eternal doom, nothing still makes sense to such people. That is the hallmark of ignorance. That is the greatest handicap confronting humanity.

The principalities readily triumph over us, because we do not know who they really are and why we should never allow them to dominate our mental aura. We easily *surrender* to the humiliating impulses and wishes of Jehovah because we do not know who he really is, and because we do not know about our divine rights in the perfect Father. We lament perpetual agonies of human life, but surprisingly seem uninterested in genuinely confronting the root of the problems. Most of us do not even seem to recognize the oddness of human nature, the fact that one is permanently torn between the desires and foibles of his own body-spirit interface. Neither do we seem willing to take sides with one of the two known sources of our conflicting impulses.

To successfully reclaim our divine rights in the Father, we must first distinguish him from Jehovah and know with certainty that such rights exist. Next, we must convince ourselves that Jehovah presently obstructs our mental vision of the Father and the said rights. The Bible cryptically affirms in Genesis 3:24(TEV) that Jehovah indeed, positioned "living creatures and a flaming sword which turned in all directions at the east side of Jerusalem" and says, **"This was to keep anyone from coming near the Tree that gives life."** And we already know that the Father is the Tree that gives eternal life.

To know that the rights exist, we must scrutinize the consistent words of our heavenly Messiah, beginning from his assurances to Adam and Eve in Eden that said, "You will not die" to his authoritative assertions to his true disciples in Jerusalem, which clearly outlined the will of our loving heavenly Father. "For this is the will of my Father," he says, "that everyone who sees the Son and believes in him should have eternal life; and I will raise him up at the last day." He also assures entire humankind, saying, "I am the resurrection and the life; he who believes in me, though he die, yet shall he live, and whoever lives and believes in me shall never die." [Gen 3:4-5; John 6:40; 11:25-26]

Furthermore, we must imbibe and build upon the knowledge of good and evil that Adam and Eve handed down to us. Therein lies our official password to regain our heavenly citizenship. Then, we must readily sacrifice our so-called human rights for our spiritual rights because double citizenship for the human spirit is indeed a myth. It is practically impossible to belong to the Father and to the world at the same time. Jesus Christ puts it in a different way. *"You cannot serve God and Mammon,"* he says. [Matt 6:24] Jehovah is Mammon; the world is his domain.

To those who care for details, a dove can never beget a vulture no matter how religiously people believe otherwise. Neither can a seasoned builder mix cement and oil for his mortar. Jesus Christ says, "no good tree bears bad fruit" and "no bad tree bears good fruit." [Luke 6:43] The human body is a house set with a mixture of cement and oil. It is certainly not the work of the Father. Nothing that is "good and evil" can be the product of a perfect mind. That human beings can already feel and see the difference, even with their limited knowledge of the difference between good and evil, means that human situation is indeed worse than it seems to less-informed humans.

It is very unfortunate that human beings have made the issue of human deficiencies and the urgent need for outright spiritual liberation from the world a matter of religious *belief* and *blind faith*. But **faith** without knowledge is death; and **believing** in a god that notoriously radiates harmful vibes is sheer foolishness. The Father is Love. Seeing or not seeing him physically is immaterial because we *feel* him within ourselves in positive ways. Therefore, those who have faith in him live in him. The notion of Jehovah as *God Almighty* is a deadly myth. His religious devotees generally *believe* that he is benevolent though they see, feel, and experience the direct opposite in their everyday lives and in every aspect of the world around them. Therefore, faith in Jehovah is self-delusion, which only prepares the grounds for eternal self-condemnation.

Jesus Christ defines spiritual salvation in very simple words, as the ability of human beings to correctly distinguish and choose between the Father and the false *Almighty* in the world. "And this is the way to have eternal life," he says "—to know you, the only true Father, and Jesus Christ, the one you sent to earth." [John 17:3] That also involves the ability to define ourselves in terms of how we presently hold dual citizenship. We presently belong to the hellish world but have the potential to regain our proper place in the heavenly paradise. However, that miraculous privilege will not remain open forever. The heavenly bridge of grace will disappear on the last day of the Father's special grace upon the world. Only the courageous ones who have made the wise choice now for true spiritual life "will eventually shine like the sun in the kingdom of their Father." [Matthew 13:43]

In the meantime, we must fearlessly seek to discover all the so-called *secret things* that the god of Eden hid from us that presently prevent us from making the crucial choice for true spiritual life. We should begin to say "no" to Jehovah's programmed sinful impulses within ourselves. Jesus Christ empowered us with human conscience to help us sift between truths and subtle falsehood. He also ratified fidelity and eternal goodness of the human conscience, so we know that living by our good conscience is infallible.

Jesus Christ says that we must be *born anew* right here in the world to be certain of a place in the Father's heavenly kingdom—"Truly, truly, I say to you, unless one is born anew, he cannot see the kingdom of the Father." [John 3:3] What the Messiah means is that we must completely reorientate our minds away from ignorance and sinful desires as Jehovah and the world never intended us to. The scripture puts it another way. It says, "Do not be conformed to this world but be transformed by the [radical] renewal of your mind." That is the only way we can "prove what is the will of the Father, what is good and acceptable and perfect [for heavenly life]." [Rom. 12:2]

We must gradually reprogram our own minds with the gospel truth that takes root in our good conscience. The earthen human body will eventually pass away at physical death. Thus, the Father would have divinely erased all imperfect accretions of the enemy over the human spirit for the redeemed spirit to sail into true spiritual salvation. Of course, "Flesh and blood cannot inherit the kingdom of the Father, nor does the perishable inherit the imperishable." [1 Cor. 15:50]

Jesus Christ made it clear that **the sin within** is not necessarily organic matter or substance of the human body. It has nothing whatsoever to do with Adam and Eve eating some fictitious fruit of sin in the Garden of Eden. It is also not a matter of what we eat or how we eat it; human beings are defiled from within. **The sin within every human being is a deliberate program of the human mind.** It is a built-in aspect of human nature. And we cannot overstress the fact that the perfect Father did not invent that.

From the built-in *loco-magnetism* of human sexuality that brings out the worst kinds of animal tendencies in human beings to the flawed programs of the human mind and our spontaneous, self-destructive sensory impulses, carnal human bodies are the devil's personal workshops. Although religious believers still find it so hard to *believe* that devils can successfully set up their own workshops, human nature is such a devil's workstation.

The Qur'an states that human nature and our sinful world are inventions of Allah. "He it is who created for you all that is in the earth," it says. ... He hath made for you pairs of yourselves, and of the cattle also pairs, whereby he multiplieth you." [Qur'an 2:29; 42:11] Allah even challenges the Jews and customary Christians who hold that the perfect Father created the world through Jesus Christ to show practical evidence to prove their point. He says, "Show me what they [the Father and Jesus Christ] have created of the earth. Or have they any portion in the heavens? Bring me a Scripture before this (Scripture) [that says otherwise], or some vestige of knowledge (in support of what ye say), if ye are truthful." [Qur'an 46:4]

Of course, no such vestige of knowledge or evidence of perfection exists in entire universe to prove that the Father and his Son, Jesus Christ had any hand in worldly creation. Neither do they have any portion in the cataclysmic heavens of this world. The Bible clearly says that "All that is in the world, the lust of the flesh and the lust of the eyes and the pride of life [of the world], **is not of the Father, but is of the world.**" [1 John 2:16] But religious believers do not get the message. It is obvious however, that Jehovah is being overrated in the pages of the Bible and the Qur'an because invention of the world was by *Elohim*—group of homeless gods—and not by one bereft desert hermit that Abraham rescued from complete obscurity. I wonder how else anyone can present these facts for customary Christian *believers* to believe them as gospel truth.

POLLUTION WITHIN AND WITHOUT

As we have seen from both the Bible and the Qur'an, the world "**is not of the Father, but is of the world**." So, who is or are "the world" in the equation? Well, Genesis account attributes creation of the world to *Elohim*, meaning "group of gods." But the only group of gods mentioned at the beginning of the said creation were the displaced spirits that groped their way in total darkness. Gen 1:1-2 reads, "In the beginning *Elohim* created the heavens and the earth. The earth was without form and void, and darkness was upon the face of the deep; and spirits of *Elohim* were moving over the face of the waters." So, we know for sure that "the world" does not refer to the Father who is Divine Light or to the heavenly Christ, who is 'Light from Light.' It rather refers to *Elohim* or all the fallen dead spirits that were trapped within primordial darkness, who desperately needed to recreate their prison of darkness. "Let there be light!" could only indicate a collective outcry of spirits that were suddenly overcome by total darkness. So, "the world" stands for all of *us*, meaning, all spirit beings that today populate the universe; that operate at various levels of consciousness within the various spheres of the material universe.

The world is not the work of the Father but the work of devils. Jesus Christ has no hand in the making and running of it. In fact, the reason he came into the world was to overcome the world—"*to destroy the works of the devil*"—and to set free captive human spirits trapped therein.

For this reason, he says, "Every plant which my heavenly Father has not planted will be rooted up." [Matt. 15:13] This means that since all that is in the world is not of the Father, then all that is in the world, including human nature and the world itself, would eventually be *rooted up,* as they are mere illusions. "And the world passes away," the scripture affirms, "and the lust of it; but he who does the will of the Father abides forever." [1 John 2:17] Only the fallen dead spirits who do the will of the Father in the world will be rekindled and reunited with the heavenly household.

Now, doing the will of the Father in the world has absolutely nothing to do with excelling in religious activities. Jesus Christ taught us to pray that *"The will of the Father be done on earth as it is in heaven."* He was telling us to pray that true love may rule our lives on earth, as it rules the lives of perfect spirits in heaven. Doing the will of the Father on earth means living a life that corresponds to the heavenly norm of love. It involves loving one another, just as Jesus Christ exemplified among us. It also involves *walking by the Holy Spirit*, which means living in harmony with one's good conscience. True Christ-followers should persistently struggle to *crucify their flesh* with its built-in passions and desires. Here again, crucifying one's flesh means applying strict restraint to one's unhelpful carnal desires.

Looking at issues of human's body-spirit interface, even strictly from the Jehovah-inspired religious point of view, the natural functions of the human body are generally considered polluting. A typical list of polluting organic processes and things includes "menstruation, sexual intercourse, birth, illness, death, and all bodily excretions and exuviae—urine, feces, saliva, sweat, vomit, blood, menstrual blood, semen, nasal and oral mucous, and hair and nail cuttings." [*Britannica*. 1999 Multimedia Edition. CD-ROM.]

Human nature is not just imperfect and full of disgusting mistakes, the entire mortal human android is a polluted entity. Even Jehovah finds certain of his religious devotees far too polluted that he is ashamed to be associated with them. If he sees the human body system as generally polluted that he had to decree ostracizing devotees considered polluted from his religious congregations, what then are we to conclude about ineptitude of the minds that formulated human nature as a creative idea? Nonetheless, the endless list of polluting *organic processes and things* makes up the human being, his experiences, and his overall present situation. Without all these spiritual impurities, there would be no human.

Below are some of Jehovah's religious injunctions against natural human infirmities:

- "He whose testicles are crushed or whose male member is cut off shall not enter the assembly of Jehovah." [Deut. 23:1]
- "The leper who has the disease ... shall remain unclean as long as he has the disease; he is unclean; he shall dwell alone in habitation outside the camp." [Lev. 13:45–46]
- "When any man has a discharge from his body, his discharge is unclean. ... Whether his body runs with his discharge, or his body is stopped from discharge it is uncleanness in him. Every bed on which he who has the discharge lies shall be unclean; and everything on which he sits shall be unclean." [Lev. 15:2–15]
- "And if a man has an emission of semen, he shall bathe his whole body in water, and be unclean until the evening. And every garment and every skin on which the semen comes shall be washed with water, and be unclean until the evening. If a man lies with a woman and has an emission of semen, both of them shall bathe themselves in water, and be unclean until the evening." [Lev. 15:16–18]
- "When a woman has a discharge of blood which is her regular discharge from her body, she shall be in her impurity for seven days, and whoever touches her shall be unclean until the evening. ... And if any man lies with her, and her impurity is on him, he shall be unclean seven days; and every bed on which he lies shall be unclean." [Lev. 15:19–24]
- If "they ask thee (O Muhammad) concerning menstruation. Say: **It is an illness**, so let women

alone at such times and go not in unto them till they are cleansed." [Qur'an 2:222]

- "If a woman has a discharge of blood for many days, not at the time of her [regular monthly] impurity, or if she has a discharge beyond the time of her impurity, all the days of the discharge she shall continue in uncleanness." [Lev. 15:25–30]

- "If a woman conceives, and bears a male child, then she shall be unclean seven days; as at the time of her menstruation, she shall be unclean. And on the eighth day the flesh of his foreskin shall be circumcised. Then she shall continue for thirty-three days in the blood of her purifying; she shall not touch any hallowed thing, nor come into the sanctuary, until the days of her purifying are completed. But if she bears a female child, then she shall be unclean two weeks, as in her menstruation; and she shall continue in the blood of her purifying for sixty-six days." [Lev. 12:2–5]

Such injunctions go on and on and on in the Jewish scripture, till it becomes appropriate to say that Jehovah is the chief custodian of "impurities" on planet Earth. According to *Britannica* [1999 Multimedia Edition. CD-ROM.]:

- Associated with this category [of human impurities] symbolically may be various persons, animals, natural objects, sense-related objects, and professions;
- Women in general (because they menstruate), pregnant women, prostitutes, and widows (the latter because of their additional association with death);
- Pigs, dogs and other scavengers because they eat or associate with excrement and garbage;

- Carrion-eating animals because of their association with death;
- Left over food, because it has come in contact with saliva via the fingers or utensil that have touched the mouth, or because it may have visually resembled vomit or undigested contents of the stomach.
- Pungent vegetables or spices (such as garlic, onions, and leeks) and strong-smelling meats or fish because they cause foul breath odors;
- Food in general because of its ultimate state as excrement;
- Certain professions because their members are required to handle corpse or bodily exuviae, and
- Things associated with lowliness—the entire body below the navel, the feet, the hem of the garment, the floor or ground—because most bodily excretions derive from the lower part of the body.

With a list like that, it is not difficult to see that the earth is just a compost, and the human body a moving mass of natural impurities. The human spirit, which is the only perfectible nonmaterial substance associated with all these impurities, is in a fallen, dead state itself. So, life of the world is death indeed. In fact, the universe, as we know it, is literally a spiritual mortuary. It is shameful, therefore, that twenty-first-century human beings are still unable to figure out the fact that it is not the work of our perfect heavenly Father.

Of course, religious *professionals* have their selfish, financial reasons for pretending to associate the rotting world with the Father, whom they surprisingly hold to be perfect, transcendental, and eternal. Religious practitioners make their living from falsehood and so, have no use for the gospel truth. Their hypocritical views are, therefore, entirely immaterial. The spiritually oppressed masses are the ones who should endeavor to understand and act on these facts in the overall interest of their own captive spirits. In the end, every individual's personal understanding will either save or condemn him forever.

The *Britannica* further says that "major category of polluting phenomena involves **violence** and all associated aspects. ... Violence pollution involves a wide variety of activities: murder, hunting, warfare, physical fights, quarrelling, cursing, or speech that is considered foul, aggressive language, lying, and various aggressive human passions (e.g., greed, anger, and hatred)." [*Britannica*. 1999 Multimedia Edition. CD-ROM.]

Now, violence is the foundation of the universe, and violence continues to sustain universal realities as we see and know them today. What scientists call the *Big Bang* was the cataclysmic violence that triggered rapid expansion of debris of matter and gases that brought about our present expanding universe. All activities taking place within the expanding universe are fueled and sustained by violence; formation of stars, planets, galaxies, blackholes and all other celestial bodies are predicated on violent interactions of imbalance of forces within space-time continuum.

Therefore, violence is an inevitable aspect of all lifeforms everywhere in the universe. Jehovah personifies violence on planet Earth in his capacity as supreme *man of war*. He is the principal oppressor of human beings and the self-confessed author of violent human calamities. He says in Isaiah 54:16, "See, it is I who created the blacksmith who fans the coals into flame and forges a weapon fit for its work. And it is I who have created the destroyer to work havoc." Thus, Amos 3:8 asks, "Does disaster befall a city, unless Jehovah has done it?" And Quran 64:11 concurs that "No calamity befalleth save by Allah's leave [approval]."

Jehovah depends entirely on violence to maintain his false position as *God* over his ignorant human victims. But apart from Jehovah's imperious excesses, human beings are already an endangered species. In an overpopulated world of limitations where life is naturally based on the survival of the fittest, violence is inevitable. In this kind of oppressive world, one must fight for virtually everything he gets. One must fight for his daily bread, for his natural human rights, for his daily existence, and more. Because there is a natural self-survival instinct in every being in such an aggressive situation, even people who genuinely wish to make peace sometimes rely on violence. As it were, every being in the world is as polluted as every other. All the so-called gods of heavens and earth, primitive as well as modern humans, animals on land, sea, and air, insects, and even microorganisms; all survive by violence in thought and action.

Jehovah has decisively proved that he is supreme in this regard. In fact, he perfected and taught human beings everything they know about warfare and social strife. He is the supreme warlord of the world, and his official language is violence. Moses called him *"the great man of war,"* and David sang about him, saying, "This God [Jehovah] is my strong refuge … **He trains my hand for war**, so that my arms can bend a bow of bronze." [2 Sam. 22:33–35] "Blessed be Jehovah, my rock, who trains my hands for war, and my fingers for battle." [Ps. 144:1] Of course, these men, among other great apostles of Jehovah, were violent men by their calling.

Indeed, Jehovah officially ordained war and social strife as acceptable ways of life, which gave impetus for religious sects to classify their brutal aggressions against their defenseless victims as *holy wars*. His official decrees in the Qur'an in support of warfare read: "Warfare is ordained for you [human beings], **though it is hateful unto you [unto your good conscience]**. … Sanction is given unto those who fight because they have been wronged; and Allah is indeed able to give them victory." [Qur'an 2:216; 22:39]

The Torah is the book of Jehovah's trial battles designed to groom the Jews and their would-be religious emulators. In it, he taught nothing but hardheartedness, without which it would be impossible for anyone to live by war and violence in thought and action. He dictated the Qur'an to the Arabians as a direct follow-up to the Jewish war manual. Thus, the Muslim Shari'ah reinforces the

Jewish law of compulsory retaliation [*tit-for-tat*] that he handed down to the Jews through Moses. His violent decree in the Torah reads, "When a man causes a disfigurement in his neighbor, as he has done it shall be done to him, fracture for fracture, eye for eye, tooth for tooth; as he has disfigured a man, he shall be disfigured." [Lev. 24:19:20] And in Deuteronomy 19:21, he says, "**Your eye shall not pity**; it shall be life for life, eye for eye, tooth for tooth, hand for hand, foot for foot."

Because Jesus Christ had come and convinced people, by personal example, that it was godly to love and live in harmony with their neighbors, Jehovah felt the need to reiterate and invigorate his violent order through Muhammad of Arabia. Jehovah's defiant words in the Qur'an prove his resolute determination to smother the human conscience, to mislead and keep human minds permanently indoctrinated in favor of violence in thought and action. In Qur'an 5:44–45, he owned up the brutal injunctions of the Torah and restated his resolute position. "Lo! We did reveal the Torah, he says. ... We prescribed for them [human beings] therein: The life for the life, and the eye for the eye, and the nose for the nose, and the ear for the ear, and the tooth for the tooth, **and for wounds retaliation**. ... Whoso judgeth not by that which Allah hath revealed: such are wrong-doers."

Despite his documented personal confessions such as these, Muslim believers still refer to him as 'compassionate and merciful.' They even pray to him to forgive them their trespasses—a god who does not even expect people to forgive each other of minor offences like accidental bodily harm.

All prophets of Israel who promoted violence as their official credentials were inspired by Jehovah. They spoke the language of the devil and not of Jesus Christ. In their recorded outing, Abraham, Moses, Elijah, Elisha, David, and others were nothing but devil's advocates, as portrayed by their violent deeds. The Father did not inspire their actions and utterances. Jesus Christ exemplified the Father as "King of Peace" in the world, and he says that only peacemakers shall be called his true sons. *"Blessed are the peacemakers, for they shall be called sons of the Father,"* he says. All the Jewish prophets of doom who ended up slaughtering the defenseless people they purportedly came to shepherd were evidently Jehovah's hirelings. Jesus Christ referred to them as *thieves and robbers* and added that *the thief comes only to steal and kill and destroy.*

It is not difficult to distinguish Jesus Christ from Jehovah and his religious thugs, both old and contemporary. Jesus Christ came from the true King of Peace to teach us how to love and live in peace with one another, to show us how to *walk by the Holy Spirit*. He distinguished himself as the "Prince of Peace;" and as the Good Shepherd, he laid down his life for all oppressed human spirits in the world. Accordingly, he said, "I came that they may have life, and have it abundantly. I am the good shepherd. The good shepherd lays down his life for the sheep. He who is a hireling, and not a shepherd, whose own the sheep are not, sees the wolf coming and leaves the sheep and flees; and the wolf snatches them and scatters them. He flees because he is a hireling and cares nothing for the sheep." [John 10:7–13] Jehovah is the chief wolf of this world; all customary religious professionals are *hirelings* and his official abettors. They are all polluted minds.

Furthermore, according to *Britannica*. [1999 Multimedia Edition. CD-ROM], there are yet other categories of polluted or polluting things, phenomena, and concepts. These include:

- Satan, demons, witches, predatory ghost, and the practice of black magic.
- Alcohol because it stimulates aggressive impulse.
- Carnivorous, predatory, and aggressive animals.
- Meat, because of the act of slaughtering the animal.
- Certain professions because their members manufacture [deadly weapons] or kill or fight for a living.

- Certain events of nature (e.g., comets or lunar or solar eclipses).
- Unusual births (e.g., twins or other multiple births, breech deliveries, miscarriages, or still births).
- Physical deformities, especially sexual deformities, (e.g., monorchids [men with only one testis], hermaphrodites, or eunuchs).
- Speech defects and voices appropriate to the opposite sex.
- Unusual developmental sequences (e.g., children who cut their upper teeth before their lower).
- Anomalous animals or types of plants that have features of several species.
- Viscous substances that seem neither solid nor liquid.
- Person in liminal (threshold or transitional) categories or status (e.g., persons undergoing initiation rites, strangers, or captives).
- Persons not considered fully in control of their faculties (e.g., children, drunken persons, the insane or the mentally or physically handicapped, such as cretins); and
- Perversions of social relationships, especially sexual, that a culture generally considers to be normal (e.g., adultery, homosexuality, bestiality, incest, births of children to unwed parents or as a result of adulterous relationships, or the breaking of vows of celibacy by monks or nuns).
- Concepts ... repression, suppression, and oppression ... are related to the notion of something or someone being forcibly prevented from expression; that is, of being under some sort of pressure. This idea suggested why polluting things are viewed as threatening and not simply as interesting

peculiarities of the world, because things under pressure are volatile, liable to escape, or capable of erupting at any moment.

It is obvious from all the above that the human world is entirely polluted. It is also obvious that only polluted minds could have conceived such a complex body of impure ideas. The world is *repressive, suppressive, and oppressive* and Jehovah, the god of Eden, epitomizes all that in the lives of captive human beings. He is the principal oppressor of human spirits. Strangely, human beings have persistently shied away from confronting the basic truths. Anyone who condemns pork as a pollutant and yet cooks it for others to eat is far more polluted than the pork and they who eat it. Jehovah has the most polluted mind on planet Earth and out of his polluted mind comes all manners of polluted ideas.

Divine Spirit is perfect, and he creates perfect ideas. He is Love, and he gives only perfect gifts. "Every good endowment and every perfect gift is from above," says the scripture, "coming down from the Father of lights with whom there is no variation or shadow due to change." [James 1:17] Jesus Christ is the Father's perfect gift to his fallen, dead sons in the world. There is no variation or shadow in his divine will for our fallen spirits. He sent his perfect Son to help us overcome the weaknesses of human nature and to liberate our captive spirits from Jehovah's oppressive world order.

Nevertheless, individuals must choose between the polluted world order and perfect heavenly existence. They must choose between Jehovah's polluted standards and walking by the Holy Spirit with the help of Jesus Christ, our heavenly Messiah. Indeed, true spiritual salvation is strictly an individual's affair. What the Church or the Muslim *Ummah* believes and says is entirely immaterial. Finally, the scripture concludes:

> "When you follow the desires of your sinful nature, the results are very clear: sexual immorality, impurity, lustful

pleasures, idolatry, sorcery, hostility, quarreling, jealousy, outbursts of anger, selfish ambition, dissension, division, envy, drunkenness, wild parties, and other sins like these. … **Anyone living that sort of life will not inherit the kingdom of the Father**. But the Holy Spirit produces this kind of fruit in our lives: love, joy, peace, patience, kindness, goodness, faithfulness, gentleness, and self-control. There is no law against these things [and **anyone living that sort of life will inherit the kingdom of the Father**]!" [Gal. 5:19–23 (NLT)]

CHAPTER NINE

GIFT OF ABUNDANT FOODS FOR THE HUMAN BODY: GENEROSITY OR SHEER SADISM?

When I was a poultry farmer, I reared white broilers for table meat. I fed my birds day and night, from day-old till they reached market weight at about eight weeks. Then, the food processing company would come in to weigh and evacuate them for slaughtering, dressing, and blast freezing. And in just a few hours, very attractive birds that I spent sleepless nights nourishing and admiring proceeded from the farm floors to freezer chests in supermarkets. Next, they ended up in peoples' pots of soup and into peoples' stomachs from where they were finally expelled as excrement.

Meanwhile, I smiled all the way to the bank because that was the actual reason I became a poultry farmer. What my helpless little birds never knew was that their ultimate demise brought me prosperity and happiness. So, how sincere, and meaningful would one say my wonderful love for my well-nourished little birds was? My love only nourished them for death and that was not love at all.

The world is a zoo and Jehovah is the zookeeper. Just like me, he justifies his love for human inmates in terms of the abundance of foods that nature makes available for organic beings within the ecosystem. He claims, "When I had created the world, I supplied it with **an abundance of food**." [2 Esdras 9:19 (GNB)] Yet, human history abounds with stories of ghastly famines and shows that millions of people have continued to starve to death in every generation. It is not enough that Jehovah claims to be the supplier of abundant natural sources of nutrients for all living things on planet earth, but does he make sure that every one of them gets its fair share of daily sustenance? What kind of parent merely provides an abundance of food materials in his house while watching his children go about utterly malnourished, frail, and stunted in growth? Assuming Jehovah is indeed the supplier of abundant foods to humans on planet earth but does not care whether they fine enough to eat or starve to death, then he is even a worse farmer than I was. Unlike him, I provided the foods for my ill-fated birds and made sure that none of them starved to death, while they lived.

Like broilers, human life is all about eating and excreting. Human beings work to eat, and they eat to live to continue working and eating. The moment they can no longer find food to eat, they die. Then everything they did or did not do, and everything they owned or did not own, vanishes like a very sad dream, both for them and for those who once knew them. Yes! Human life is like a *dead* man dreaming. The dream ends when reality saves the day, and the *dead* remains dead.

Indeed, a human being is a *living* dead. His well-nourished body has no real value to him or to any other person on earth, except for the brief, illusory moment of comfort he may feel as a *living* being. The human body is like a biennial flowering plant. In the first year, it germinates; grows roots, stems, and leaves. The second year, it produces flowers and fruits; then it ages and dies. Indeed, the plant and its flowers hold no real value to the planter or to anyone else, except that people look upon them and admire the mere illusion of transient beauty. All is meaningless!

The life of this world is like the flickering flame of a burning candle. It continues to flicker on for as long as it feeds on the vanishing wax. It dies automatically when the wax runs out. The Qur'an says that *"The life of this world is but comfort of illusion."* It means that though human beings feel that they are living, they are indeed dead. On its part, the Bible says that life of the world *"is an unhappy business that the god of Genesis has given to the sons of men to be busy with."* It further calls it *"vanity upon vanity!"*

This is not peculiar to humans; the so-called gods of the world are also *living* dead entities because they are equally organic beings, animated by fallen, dead spirits. Because all life forms in the universe depend on one form of material nutrient or fuel, all are *living* dead. Even universal superstructures wear away before our eyes. The sun sustains organic life on planet earth, while its own life depends on the availability of hydrogen fuel for its nuclear fusion. Even fabricated machines live on various kinds of fuels. The moment all stocks of fuels or foods run out in the universe, the entire universe will die a natural death.

What it all means is that the only life that exists in the universe is artificial, and that is worthless in spiritual terms. A life that is nourished and sustained by fuel or food that runs out in time is a bad imitation of true spiritual life, which is eternal. Any effort spent by prodigal spirits in nourishing and admiring the false life of the world is energy completely squandered. Since true life is not possible in any sphere of the universe, truly enlightened human beings know that they must look beyond the life of the world for true spiritual existence, which is eternal.

Unfortunately, Jehovah is just a zookeeper, and he desires to preserve the status quo because he derives his own illusory *prosperity* and *happiness* from spiritual squalor and death. He mobilizes his religious agents on the ground to propagate *fattening-the-cow* for the market day. King Solomon, in his celebrated position as the wisest man on earth, recommended that human beings should just *"eat and drink and find enjoyment"* in the meaningless life of the world, rather than seek to disentangle their captive spirits from spiritual bondage to sheer vanity. No wonder Jehovah surnamed him *Jedidiah*, "Beloved of Jehovah." Solomon's words in Ecclesiastes 5:18 speak the mind of his inspirer plainly: "Behold, what I have seen to be *good and to be fitting* is to *eat and drink and find enjoyment* in all the toil with which one toils under the sun the few days of his life which Jehovah has given him, for this is his lot." It should not be difficult to see that Solomon and his mastermind do not mean well for captive human spirits.

In the days of Noah, people lived the ravenous life approved by Jehovah, and total self-destruction was the outcome for all of them.

Jesus Christ enjoins true seekers of the heavenly life not to emulate Noah's gluttonous generation, as he says, "for as in those days before the flood they were eating and drinking, marrying and giving in marriage, until the day when Noah entered the ark, and they did not know until the flood came and swept them all away." [Matt. 24:38–39] True seekers of spiritual salvation should weigh the *lawfulness* of fattening one's perishable body and thus gratifying the self-destructive desires of human nature against the *expediency* of feeding and resurrecting one's fallen, dead spirit that is trapped within the perishable human frame.

Paul had sound counsel on this matter that spoke the mind of the Father who desires the spiritual salvation of captive human spirits. His reasoning goes like this: "All things [foods] are lawful [to the human body in the lawless world], but not all things are [spiritually] helpful. All things are lawful! But not all things build up [the human spirit]. ... **Food will not commend us to the Father.** We are no worse off if we do not eat, and no better off if we do. ... **Food is meant for the stomach and the stomach for food.**" [1 Cor. 10:23; 8:8; 6:13]

Synthetic foods nourish synthetic mortal bodies of human beings and both the foods and the stomachs that they fill will eventually perish with the perishing world. But every spirit that feeds on the love and guidance of the Father through the heavenly Christ will live forever. The world lacks the food of the spirit, so it cannot give what it does not have. People who seek true life for their spirits must look to the Father who feeds the spirits. The problem here is that people do not even know the difference, and so do not make positive efforts toward distinguishing **Jehovah,** who claims to give an abundance of food for their bodies, from **the Father** who feeds their spirits for true spiritual life. The Father wishes us well; Jehovah does not.

DIFFERENTIATING THE FATHER AND HIS PERFECT PROVISIONS

Ordinarily, people say "***God* is good**" when their barn is overflowing with the milk and honey of this life—and **the Father** is indeed, good! However, when one asks which "God" they mean, they feel surprised at first and then indignant. Their answer is always that "**there is only one God**"—and there is indeed, only one true Father or Source of entire existence! Yet practical human experiences show that a major false *God* exists on the earthly stage to whom multitudes of people refer to as *God Almighty*, both knowingly and unknowingly.

Now, for the purpose of argument, and for the need to clarify this matter, there is need to hold in view the prevailing influences of "two distinct *Gods*" on the earthly stage. There is the Father of all origins and the earth-bound *God Almighty*, our perfect *loving* heavenly Father and the *Evil God*. Human religion purportedly exists to help people distinguish between the two. It supposedly exists to lead people away from the *Evil God* who holds fallen human spirits captive in the world to the perfect, loving Father who pays the full ransom, as it were, for the spiritual redemption of our captive spirits. It is entirely another matter altogether whether human religion fulfils what it pretends to be its official responsibility to humankind. In any case, human religion is entirely meaningless to people who are not able to distinguish between the truly loving Father and the evil god of Eden. True spiritual salvation is nearly impossible for such people.

One important credit to human religion, though, is that it has correctly identified the false and evil god as the devil or Satan. At least, that gives us the basis upon which to begin our differentiation between Jehovah and the Father. There are more than eight billion human beings on the face of the earth today, and my conservative estimation is that the devil is "God" to more than 80 percent of them at the present. Adherents of the major religions of the world may not readily appreciate this because they believe that *pagans* are the only devil worshipers on planet Earth. However, the truth is not far-fetched. For, even the scripture affirms that "**the whole world** is in the power of the Evil One." [1 John 5:19]

We all know that the devil is not the Father, quite all right. But merely arguing that he is not without showing who he really is will be of no spiritual benefit to anyone. The devil or Satan is a well-known person among human beings on earth. He is not merely the figment of peoples' imaginations. He is the chief potentate of human nature and the custodian of the present-day world order that supplies synthetic foods or fuels for human bodies. In other words, he is the *god of human nature*. Human beings simply call him *"God Almighty"* because human minds are programmed to see him as such, and because he is directly involved with every mundane aspect of the life of mortal human beings on earth. In fact, he has such an overwhelming influence on the world of humans. The Qur'an specifically calls him the *Lord of mankind*, the *King of mankind*, and the *God of mankind*. For these reasons, it has been nearly impossible for unenlightened minds to look beyond him to see the true Father of entire existence who is silently involved with the well-being of captive human spirits.

In the interest of people who genuinely seek spiritual insight for spiritual rebirth, let me say it categorically here that **the Father whom Jesus Christ introduced to the world is the *only* true Source** of infinite existence. He is the Divine Spirit in whom the life of every spirit in existence depends. He is not the author of human nature; neither is he the nourisher of perishable human bodies that imprison human spirits. Jehovah is not the Father but **the devil** that holds the human spirits captive in well-nourished earthen corpses. This is the clear-cut distinction between the Father and Jehovah, and it will surely help us to understand the real value of the so-called gift of abundance of foods for the human bodies that Jehovah claims to have provided for ignorant humans on earth.

Next, positive-minded seekers of spiritual rebirth need the heavenly grace of the Father to be able to access ratified information about the Father. As Jesus Christ says, "No one truly knows the Son except the Father, and no one truly knows the Father except the Son **and those to whom the Son chooses to reveal him**." [Matt. 11:27 (NLT)] Therefore, only the heavenly Christ can reveal the Father to captive human beings. Great multitudes of religious believers worldwide know only Jehovah who rules their present world order. The Jewish Shema, the Apostles' Creed, and the Muslim Shahadah prove my point. Officially, the Jews, customary Christians, and Muslims know and believe in *"the god who made heavens and earth"*—the god who sits upon the throne of the world. They do not know the Father who transcends the entire material universe together with its so-called heavens and earth. They do not look up to the Divine Spirit whose positive influence can only be felt by perfect spirits who dwell within the spiritual realm of perfection, whose kingdom is not of the world.

As it were, only Christ-enlightened individuals truly know and look up to the Father and to his Son, Jesus Christ. These have firmly decided for themselves that although Jehovah, the *evil god*, rules the whole world, he would not be their *God*. I, too, have firmly decided that although Jehovah rules the kingdom of men, he would never be my *God* because he is false and evil. Every human being on earth today must make the same crucial choice of eternal fellowship for himself, and people do, knowingly and unknowingly.

Paul said that he chose to look up to the Father and to Jesus Christ, but he presumed to make the same decision on behalf of all customary Christians. Unfortunately, this is not a decision anyone can make on behalf of any other. He declared, "For although there may be so-called gods in heaven[s] or on earth—as indeed there are many 'gods' and many 'lords' [that rule the world of humankind]—yet for us there is one *God*, the Father ... and one [true] Lord, Jesus Christ." [1 Cor. 8:5–6] Surely, this is not the official position of the Church that Paul founded. The Apostles' Creed says a different thing altogether.

Clearly, Paul's personal statement of choice did not challenge the fact that Jehovah is the principal *lord, king,* and *god* of humankind. It showed, however, that he had conscientiously chosen, though contrary to his implicit personal religious stance, to look to the true *God*, the Father, whom Jesus Christ alone testified to the world. There is no doubt that Paul made a wise choice, irrespective of whether he understood the full implications of his choice or not. He also decided not to be misled by Jehovah's desperate artifice that merely replaced his official name, "Jehovah," with the false title, "the Lord," purely to fool uninformed minds. For Paul, as for every true Christ-follower, the only true "Lord," regarding humans' spiritual salvation, is Jesus Christ of Nazareth. This is perfectly in line with Acts 4:12 (NLT), which reads, "There is salvation in *no one else*! God [the Father] has given *no other name under heaven* by which we must be saved."

Human beings generally think of Jehovah, the god of the world, as being entirely benevolent. By that, they mean to assert that he is perfect. The Muslims, for instance, out of sheer doctrinal habitude, refer to god of the world as "the Beneficent, the Merciful." That means they believe he is entirely beneficial to humankind, and that everything he has done or will do is an act of kindness and charity genuinely intended for the overall good of his human slaves. Yet their Qur'an is full of evidence to the contrary.

Many religious believers, driven by ignorance and sheer blind reverence, have compulsively pledged eternal indebtedness to Jehovah. According to them, he gave *life* to human beings and supplies abundant varieties of food substances to nourish and sustain their bodies. They also claim that he provided them with sexual and sensual body apparatuses that enable them to extract moments of pleasure, enjoyment, and comfort from the life of the world that he gave them. However, most of these believers hardly think deeply about the true nature and value of the kind of life that Jehovah has given them. And they never try to examine the real benefits or disadvantages of his so-called gift of abundant foods for the nourishment of their mortal bodies at the expense of their captive spirits. So many of these people do not even *believe* that a perfect life form exists beyond the life of the world and the mystical scope of Jehovah that does not depend on synthetic foods. The Father gives perfect spiritual life in his perfect spiritual kingdom.

The *life* that Jehovah claims to have given to human beings is even worse than spiritual death. He indeed, confesses in the Quran that "The life of this world is but comfort of illusion." What this means is that people who think they are enjoying life in the world are merely dreaming. Human life is merely a complex dream existence, strictly intended to beguile and prevent them from genuinely seeking to regain their lost spiritual glory and true eternal life. In fact, the life of the world is spiritually detrimental to the well-being of the human spirits. It is a spiritual impediment, which serves only the ulterior desires of Jehovah and his cosmic accomplices. It effectively prevents human beings from readily recollecting that they are fallen, dead spirits that need urgent spiritual redemption. Since they do not remember that they are dead in the first place, it has become practically impossible for them to genuinely desire to live again. Indeed, no one sincerely struggles to regain what he does not know that he lost.

If the fallen, dead human spirits had remained unimpaired in their spiritually dead state, they would have been constantly reminded of the clear difference between spiritual life and death. It would have been much easier for them to see that the life of the world is worse than spiritual death, and that there is an urgent need for outright spiritual redemption from the world of abundant synthetic foods. Because the life of the world gives human beings the erroneous impression of *living*, they languish in ignorance of their spiritual death. As a result, they not only show extreme dislike for genuine gospel of true life, but they also violently oppose the people who preach it. Thus, their spirits run the risk of ending up in *second* eternal death at the close of the Father's extended period of grace, which is currently running.

As we already know, every human being is made up of two distinctly opposed parts, the mortal body that belongs to the world and the prodigal spirit, which fell from his proper place in the Father's heavenly realm of perfection. Jehovah makes it implicit that human body is a "tracer" or bug over captive human spirit. As such, desires of carnal nature hold the upper hand over desires of human spirits in their present captive condition. What he is saying is that the human body, with its built-in weaknesses, offers him the opportunity to wield opposing control over the human spirit. He also confesses that the only successful person in this life is the one who helps his spirit to win the present battle of supremacy over the impure and deadly desires of his carnal body. "He is indeed successful who causeth [his spirit or conscience] to grow, and he is indeed a failure who stunteth it," he says. [Qur'an 91:10] Thus, the *body* and *spirit* of human beings depend on two different kinds of sustenance.

While the Father works through Jesus Christ and the Holy Spirit of truth to feed fallen human spirits with love and the life-giving word of true life, Jehovah, the devil, feeds the human bodies to weigh down the spirits through the built-in weaknesses of human nature. Jehovah feeds the human bodies and starves the human spirits. Consequently, people who indulge or excessively feed and nourish their mortal bodies inadvertently foster the well-being of Jehovah's personal weapon against their own spirits. In other words, the battle between the body and spirit of a human being is one between the Father and Jehovah. The foods that nourish the body cripple the spirit, and vice versa.

As Paul figured out, when we *live in the flesh*, that is, in accordance with the programmed dictates of the human body, our sinful passions, aroused by *the law of carnal nature*, are at work to bear fruits for death. When, on the other hand, we *walk by the Holy Spirit*, he gradually subdues in us the law that holds our spirits captive to sin and death and repositions us for the true spiritual life that is in the Father. Therefore, man's battle for true spiritual rebirth is also a battle between *"the law of carnal nature,"* mystically imprinted on the human mind by Jehovah, and *"the law of the Spirit,"* impressed upon the human conscience by the Father through Jesus Christ. *"The law of the Spirit"* is love.

Paul rightly concluded, "To set the mind on the flesh is [spiritual] death, but to set the mind on the Spirit is life and peace." He then advised positive-minded people to strive to "walk by the Spirit [of love and goodness], and do not gratify the desires of the flesh," since "the desires of the flesh are against the Spirit, and the desires of the Spirit are against the flesh." [Rom. 8:6; 5:16–17] In fact, Paul made it clear that a mind set on feeding and nourishing the flesh is hostile to the Father; it does not submit to the law of the conscience because it obeys the law of carnal nature. People who *live in the flesh* are friends of the world and its god; as such, they are intrinsically opposed to the will of the Father even for their own captive spirits. For this reason, the scripture asks in James 4:4, "Do you not know that friendship with the world is enmity with the Father? Therefore, whoever wishes to be a friend of the world makes himself an enemy of God [the Father]."

It is against this critical backdrop that people who genuinely seek spiritual rebirth should reappraise Jehovah's so-called great generosity in providing human beings with abundant foods for their flesh. The abundance of *foods of the body* that Jehovah claims to supply for the satisfaction of the reckless *passions of the flesh* are the root source of *the burden of existence* in the world. Every human problem, whether physical, emotional, mental, or psychological, has its origin in *foods*. True spiritual salvation will be practically impossible for anyone who fails in the end to overcome the built-in traps of carnal desires.

In this regard, the human body is like a holed *bag of futility*, whose material desires are both futile and practically insatiable. Jehovah admits that he "verily has made man in an atmosphere (to be in distress)." [Qur'an 90:4] Indeed, a synthetic body obsessively craving synthetic sustenance in a synthetic atmosphere is in serious spiritual distress. Excessive craving for the enslaving *foods of the body* naturally blocks out man's subconscious yearning for the life-giving *foods of the spirit* needed to resurrect his dead spirit. A well-nourished body is a paralyzed spirit. A *living* body is a *dead* spirit anyway. For the spirit to be in good health and hopeful, one must knowingly deprive the body of excessive nourishment. And for the spirit to finally secure true spiritual life, it must ultimately step out of the carnal body, completely and forever.

GENEROSITY OR SADISM?

Spirits do not need organic foods to stay alive. That is true, even for the fallen human spirits in the world. That is why Jesus Christ says that *man does not live by bread alone*. Love is the food of the spirit. Anyone who creates opportunities for love and works of love creates food for the human spirit. When Jesus Christ went about his mission of love without caring about food for his stomach, his disciples worried for him, but he assured them that he had enough to eat. He said to them; "My food [i.e., the food of my spirit] is to do the will of him who sent me, and to accomplish his works [of feeding human spirits with the divine word of love and life]." [John 4:34] The Father is Love, and Love is life. Love of the Father perfects living spirits within the heavenly household. Abundant love is their divine food, and none is lacking in the heavenly kingdom because the Father's love saturates the realm.

In the world, Jehovah deliberately turned the table of honor upside down. He provides an abundance of food for human carnality, while starving human spirit by decreeing intolerance, hatred, war, and violence among humans. "**Your eye shall not pity**"; he commanded the Jews, "it shall be life for life, eye for eye, tooth for tooth, hand for hand, foot for foot." In other words, Jehovah "empties peoples' hearts [spirits] and fills their bellies; he weakens their spiritual wills and strengthens their bones." His ulterior motives are so obvious here that any honest human being can easily see through his mind.

By giving an abundant food supply for the perishable bodies and not for the redeemable spirits of human beings, Jehovah purposely schemed to starve the captive human spirits to *second* spiritual death. Of course, he utilizes the human bodies as sheer implements of dominion over the human spirits. But Jehovah's interest in the human bodies is only for as long as they serve his selfish dreams and aspirations. Once they have served their transient purposes on earth, they are discarded, just like used up batteries.

Jehovah is no different than a *generous* poultry farmer who feeds his birds copiously because they bring him financial gains. He is not different from a *caring* crews' welfare manager of a shipping company or an *open-handed* slave master who provides abundant nutrition for his toilers because the success of his business depends entirely on their raw energy. The slave master provides all sorts of energy-giving food items for his slaves and then exploits their physical vigor for his selfish ends. The situation is even worse in Jehovah's case; he does so mainly to distract human beings from seeking true spiritual salvation for their captive spirits. This is a basic, selfish business move, not a sign of true benevolence. In fact, Jehovah is the worst kind of slave master, because he also poses as the loving Father to his ignorant victims. If a slave master truly loves his slaves, he would set them free unconditionally, not *filling their bellies and strengthening their bones.*

If Jehovah had truly wished well for his fellow fallen spirits that trustingly looked up to him for genuine guidance, he would have helped humans to remain focused on regaining their lost spiritual selfhood. Claiming to have supplied abundance of foods on earth, upon which human lives depended, while at the same time pronouncing the curse of "suffering before you eat" on humans, make Jehovah both callous and a premeditated sadist.

Again, when we think of the primordial *nether gloom* as a spiritual quarantine intended as a reform center for the fallen, dead spirits, and compare it with our present state of total spiritual oblivion, we will appreciate the gravity of Jehovah's crime against captive human spirits. Every fallen, dead spirit enjoyed independence and had the right atmosphere to freely reflect and act upon the Father's offer of outright spiritual redemption. Cosmic experimentation with artificial life of the world sealed off that special opportunity for captive human spirits. They were practically lured from mere *spiritual house arrest* only to be squish into some tiny, dark earthen capsules, from where they could hardly see any light at all.

Generously providing nourishment for restrictive human bodies meant that captivity of the human spirits was further maximized, thereby perpetuating their spiritual bondage. That was nothing but calculated wickedness. Closing off the human spirit with the colonizing excesses of the human carnal body was a deliberate attempt to permanently smother and put the human spirits out of spiritual pursuits forever. Indeed, the body effectively denies the trapped spirits the necessary breathing space and all the benefits of the true heavenly generosity that the Father freely offers to them.

FOODS FOR THE STOMACH

Enslaving foods of the body could be grouped under two broad headings, namely, "foods for the stomach" and "foods for sensual gratification and mental self-imaging." These collectively expand into the endless chain of the passions of the human flesh, which the scripture calls *"the lust of the flesh and the lust of the eyes and the pride of life."* [1 John 2:16] These are eternally at war with the human spirit, yet some of them are inevitable for the life of the human being.

To *live* in the material world, the human body needs foods, which include oxygen, water, and all other chemical and mental substances taken into the body by the living organism to nourish and sustain its fake life. Without food, the body dies willy-nilly. Therefore, synthetic foods are a matter of compulsory utility to the human body. The real problem is that the so-called abundant supply of food to humankind is merely religious rhetoric. Millions of people starve to death daily all over the world for the lack of food to eat. Surely, Jehovah knows the most about this issue because he rules the world of humans. As human beings, we are equally in a good position to understand the merits and demerits of a life that depends entirely on perishable food substances that are not universally available to all. We are also in a good position to understand whether Jehovah's so-called gift of abundant foods to humankind was well intended or not.

The usual response of religious people to mass starvation due to some human and natural disaster is that we could never understand the mind of Jehovah. Indeed, we do not need to understand how or what he thinks. The way he feels about how we feel does not matter; that should be his own personal headache. If we can understand our own minds and sincerely express our true feelings precisely the way we feel them, we will be able to solve our human problems as a united family.

We are the ones whose earthly lives depend on synthetic foods. We are the ones who have been condemned to spending our short days on earth in agony, searching for artificial sustenance at the expense of life-giving foods for our dead spirits. We are the ones who are enslaved, suppressed, and oppressed for the want of food for our many helpless dependents, and we are the ones who starve to death whenever there are famines and other natural disasters. Therefore, our practical human experiences perfectly qualify us to fully understand and express our conscientious views on the merits and demerits of Jehovah's so-called gift of abundant "foods for the body" to humankind that is scarcely available to all.

It should be noted that Jehovah depends on some kinds of artificial foods himself, both physical and psychological, to sustain the fake life that he now lives as a fallen, dead spirit, just as we all do. He understands what it is to hunger and starve to death. After all, he became a human being on planet Earth before all other human beings who now share his exact image, likeness, and weaknesses. That explains why he also demands daily rations of odor of burnt blood, ritualistic worship, prayers, and praises from his religious slaves. When his worshipers supply his daily food, he is happy, and when he does not get it at the appointed time, he loses his temper and torments them. He once commanded the Israelites, saying, "My offering, the food for my offerings by fire, my pleasing odor, *you shall take care to offer to me at its appointed time*. … **daily, as a regular offering**." [Num. 28:2,3] "**A perpetual fire shall be kept burning** on the altar; it shall not go out." [Lev. 6:12]

Therefore, Jehovah does think and understand like every other human being on the earth, especially regarding the fact that the life of mortal human beings depends entirely on foods for the stomach. Hence, when we understand and express our own minds on the issue, we understand and express Jehovah's mind as well.

The situation on the ground is that the so-called gift of an abundance of food to humankind is not an unconditional, regular *blessing* meant for all and sundry. Jehovah meant it to be only for people who surrender unconditionally to his selfish desires. Unfortunately, for him, he does not really have the power to deprive the entire world of the Father's goodness that he makes possible by his interim grace upon all and sundry. Jehovah's wishes are particularly of no effect on true friends of Jesus Christ.

The Bible says that Jehovah provided Adam and Eve everything they needed in the Garden of Eden, but for as long as they served his selfish interests. Once they asserted their spiritual independence, he targeted their livelihood and proceeded to curse their farmland, even for their posterity yet unborn. Such a spontaneous act of malice captured the real mind of an actual Evil Spirit. There is absolutely nothing godly about providing food only for people who serve your purpose. Even the most terrible slaveholders and slavedrivers do the same. Therefore, Jehovah's so-called gift of "food for the body" is only a clear case of someone caring for his winning horses, at their own peril of course, or like a slavedriver fueling his serviceable cart! Today, Jehovah even goes to the extent of empowering his favored religious emissaries to exploit and feed upon the sweat of their ignorant followers, through religious tithing, pledges, and vows, because they work for him.

Overall, Jehovah does not really care whether human beings have enough to eat or if they starve to death; he is mainly interested in getting people to worship him at all costs. Even though people are compelled to pray endlessly to Jehovah for their daily bread, majority of religious believers who do so still starve to death for the lack of it. His high-handed battering of the hungry and helpless Jews during the Exodus proved the kind of shepherd that Jehovah really is. While speaking to his battered flock in the wilderness, Moses recalled: "And you shall remember all the way which Jehovah your God had led you these forty years in the wilderness, that he might humble you, testing you to know what was in your heart, whether you would keep his commandment, or not. **And he humbled you and let you hunger.**" [Deut. 8:2–3]

As our practical human experiences show, humans are completely preoccupied with matters directly and indirectly relating to eating and searching for more and more scarce food substances for their stomach. As a result, they find hardly any quality time left to devote to matters relating to the spiritual well-being of their captive spirits. All evident human miseries and vices hinge entirely on the natural apprehension of *the rainy day* and the need to accumulate and hoard resources at the expense of others. Jehovah's so-called gift of "food for the body" is not well intentioned at all because people who do not have enough food worry and starve to death, while those who have too much wallow in spiritual emptiness and die of stupor anyway. In fact, such a gift can be deemed evil because it only lends opportunity for Jehovah and other wicked individuals to readily use natural famine, deliberate deprivation, and mass starvation as weapons of oppression against their less-privileged victims.

Jehovah used the weapon of deliberate deprivation and mass starvation against the Jewish Exodus in the wilderness. According to Moses, Jehovah humbled them by deliberately letting them hunger so that "he might know what was in their heart, whether they would keep his commandment, or not." Prophet Jeremiah equally recorded very shocking incidents in his book of Lamentations that reveal the true mind of Jehovah, regarding his use of mass starvation as weapon of oppression over his followers. He stated that "Jehovah gave full vent to his wrath, he poured out his hot anger; and he kindled a fire in Zion, which consumed its foundations. ... **Happier were the victims of the sword than the victims of hunger**, who pined away, stricken by the want of fruits of the field. [To the extent that] the hands of compassionate women have boiled their own children; they became their food in the destruction of the daughter of my people" [Lam. 4:11, 9–10] What a terrible god!

Even if we decide to look at Jehovah's so-called gift of abundance of foods to humankind from a different perspective, his motive would still be questionable. Now, let us assume that the life of the world is worth something after all, and that Jehovah's gift of an endless chain of food substances to sustain it was a benevolent act in the first instance. How then could he justify the fact that he allows millions of people to starve to death daily all over the world? So many people work so hard on earth but still starve to death, because they can hardly find enough to eat. How could he also justify the fact that he uses famine as a weapon of oppression over people? If he had freely given life that he valued himself, and had given enough food because life depended entirely on food to fuel it, what do we say then when he knowingly severs the food supply to people? Such an action would be criminal by every reasonable standard.

I once spoke to an Iranian colleague of mine on the issue, and he completely agreed that eating and searching for foods to eat causes humankind untold misery. He concluded that, in his honest opinion, "Allah actually uses food as a bait to attract, entice, and compel human beings to worship and look up to him as *God*." Every time a hungry person finds food to eat, his first reaction is always spontaneous: "Thank you *God* for the food you have given me; for you're good." Farmers are probably the ones who praise Jehovah most for his generous provision of an abundance of food for humankind. In fact, they have no other business except depending on the god of fertility to grant them bumper harvests. Of course, practically every human being on earth thanks and worships *"God"* before and after he has found and eaten any meal during the day. Therefore, Jehovah's gesture is not a gift at all, but a sheer religious weapon of domination over less-privileged humans.

Religious people generally believe that everyone who fears and worships the god who rules the world with all his heart will always have food for his stomach. Accordingly, they usually blame poor and hungry people for not worshiping Jehovah enough. That is an absolute fallacy. The truth is that nature guarantees daily bread to all human beings on earth, but Jehovah and his evil emissaries—wicked rulers of nations, capitalist rulers of industries, criminals of all sorts, and religious racketeers—usurp and hinder peoples' right to it. The truth is that Jehovah *prospers* only the ruthless ones in the societies, via all kinds of fraudulent means of *robbing Peter to pay Paul*, because they help him to subjugate and control the poor and needy ones to forestall spiritual revolt in the land. So, Jehovah's so-called offer of daily bread is not guaranteed for ordinary religious believers. Even when his followers pray, worship, jump up and down, and kill for him, there is still no guarantee. And surprisingly, the poor and needy worship and pray most, yet they starve to death most too.

In the end, Jehovah's so-called great generosity in providing abundance of foods for humankind merely turns out to be a means by which he rewards his ruthless human agents and torments his *enemies*. King David showed in some of his Psalms of infatuation that Jehovah's express guarantee of the *good things of this life* is only for his friends: "The friendship of Jehovah is for those who fear him. ... Blessed is the man who fears Jehovah, who greatly delights in his commandments! His descendants will be mighty in the land; ... **wealth and riches are in his house.**" [Pss. 25:14; 112:1–3]

Finally, Jehovah personally confirms that there are preconditions to his so-called benevolence. He says, "**Hearken diligently to me, and eat what is good, and delight yourselves in fatness** [of your mortal bodies]. **Behold, [only] my servants shall eat,** but you [my enemies] shall be hungry; Behold, my servants shall drink, but you shall be thirsty." [Isa. 55:2; 65:13] Evidently, he works hard to make sure that people who would rather hearken to the will of the Father in their good conscience do not find enough to eat. However, he is completely powerless over the true friends of Jesus Christ. The Father shields his own on earth and freely provides all their material and spiritual sustenance in miraculous ways.

FOODS FOR SENSUAL GRATIFICATION AND MENTAL SELF-IMAGING

These are the most spiritually debilitating kinds of foods for the human body—ones that Jehovah has indeed provided copiously for humankind. These are the so-called *ornaments* of worldly enjoyment—"*the lust of the flesh and the lust of the eyes and the pride of life.*"

An inordinate desire for sexual gratification, sensual pleasures, and worldly comfort and enjoyment is the defining factor of animalistic life. It is also the chief bane of true humanity. Sexual concupiscence, for instance, is at the root of the worst kinds of physical, mental, emotional, and psychological pain and sorrow felt by human beings. Whether people say they enjoy sex or merely pretend that they do, the fact remains that it is a source of great misery and unfulfilled dreams for so many people.

Speaking on why monks do not miss sex, marriage, and family life during his first visit to Nigeria in November 2008, Dalai Lama, the spiritual leader of Tibet, had this to say:

> "Sexual pressure, sexual desire is short period satisfaction. But often, it leaves more complications. One of my friends, a Canadian, was a Buddhist monk, but after some time, he disrobed. Now he complains about so much sexual pressure, that's he's virtually trapped. Obviously, due to sexual pressure, people marry, soon after, they divorce. Again, they marry, and

may divorce again. Divorce in a marriage which has produced children is terrible. In marriage, there is short period of sexual satisfaction, but there are many ups and downs. Monks, nuns, naturally as human beings have desires for sex, it is biological. But then, those who marry always have trouble, and in some cases it leads to murder or suicide. So, that is the consolation. We miss something, but at the same time, we live better lives. More independence, more freedom. In marriage, if you live together, happy, and get old, there is the issue of who goes first, who dies first. Human attachment to your children and partners. And **it becomes an obstacle to peace of mind.** Whether right or wrong, we monks think that way. ... The attachments bring trap. Whether it is to a person, to substance or whatever, **it is a trap.** Monks are detached." [Extract from his interview featured in *Great Encounter*, Saturday Sun, December 13, 2008]

For obvious reasons, Jehovah calls human sexuality *"the flower of the life of the worlds,"* but it is indeed, the deadliest hemlock to the captive human spirits. Not surprisingly, he also confesses that the so-called ornaments of this life are not just a *comfort of illusion,* but a *spiritual trap* for the vulnerable human spirits. He finds in this an opportunity to scorn humanity. His words in the Qur'an clearly reveal his ulterior intentions. He says:

"Beautified for mankind, is the love of the joys (that come) from women, offspring, and stored-up heaps of gold and silver, and horses branded (with their mark), and cattle and land. **This is comfort of the life of the world.** ... **The life of this world is but comfort of illusion.** ... Lo! Among your wives and your children there are enemies for you, therefore beware of them ...

> **Your wealth and your children are only a temptation.** ... And whatsoever you have been given [of worldly treasures] is a comfort of the life of the world and an ornament thereof; ... **Have ye then no sense?"** [Qur'an 3:14; 64:14–15; 28:60]

Indeed, if we have sense, we will agree with Jehovah that going after illusory worldly pleasures and treasures at the expense of striving to feed our spirits with the Father's Word of Love is foolishness. Yet human senselessness benefits his grand evil scheme. Sexual propensity in human beings is particularly spiritually damaging. Usually, a person who thirsts or hungers after the foods of the stomach is sober, pitiable, and *normal*, but someone craving sexual gratification sometimes behaves like a lunatic. For instance, it is said that *a man craving after a woman is blind*. Indeed, he is in a temporary state of psychosis. This is the worst kind of hunger that Jehovah willfully projected into the human mentality, and his motive was by no means godly. He intended it purely to blind and incapacitate the human spirit.

Unrestrained sexual foibles are clear reminders that human beings were originally meant to be wild animals. Today, the wild *spirit of eroticism* still overwhelms the entire human race, both the young and the old. Social civilization, it seems, gives impetus to wild sexual expressions, especially among young people. Usually, children are thought to be innocent and pure, but that is no longer the case in our present civilized world. It is outrageous what most young people feel in themselves, and to the extent they actually go to try to relieve their riotous sexual impulses.

Naturally, the sane world frowns at bizarre teenage sex experimentations, sexual abuse of minors, child pornography, etc. Most helpless parents adopt all kinds of *imperfect* measures to try to shield off their own wards, while praying and hoping that they would successfully scale through the teenage years, which is a *natural* phase of intense sexual hyperactivity. Nonetheless, many teenagers actually love every bit of what they feel and do with their bodies. They are not ashamed, worried, or sorry for whatever they do with their *divine sexual bequest*, as they see it. Most of the time, adult predators who take sexual advantage of minors do not have to convince them to experience what they feel. It is obvious, therefore, that Jehovah schemes and equally enjoys all forms of sexual paraphilia, child pornography and sex abuses of minors.

On the other hand, some adults who are expected to know and act better, are by far more *obsessed* with sexual pleasure than the minors are. They have invented and legalized all kinds of sexual fooleries. Even the best of enlightened humans today are still merely hybrid animals in this regard. For as long as the human carnal body exists, the universal *spirit of eroticism* will always remain a larger part of its genetic makeup.

Concerning sexual concupiscence, the *only* difference between human species and wild animals in bushes is not that there is anything done by animals that human beings do not do, even with gusto, but that the heavenly Messiah came among humans. Christ-consciousness is the divine essence presently helping redeemable humans to stop living like animals, as much as possible. Usually animals eat, play, copulate, relax, and sleep. Human beings do all that, and in the worst possible ways. They are caught in the crossroads between being outright batteries, charged and dumped into the earth as chattel slaves of the gods, and being self-enslaved by their misguided sense of freedom.

For instance, animals eat only when they feel hungry, and mate only when they are in heat, and strictly for procreative purposes. Human beings have turned themselves into experimental gluttons. They eat, drink, smoke, ingest all kinds of assertive junks marketed by greedy business charlatans, and have sex whenever and wherever they come together, and without regards to the obvious lifetime damages both to their fragile bodies and to their captive spirits. For human beings, sexual revolt has become a completely new way of demonstrating the *superior* right of humans to total self-expression.

Today, modesty speaks rather better of dogs, while modern human beings brazenly invent, invest in, and indulge in all sorts of demeaning sexual travesties, both as commercial ventures and for sheer hedonism. This has led many religious defeatists to conclude that the fruit of knowledge of good and evil was indeed harmful for humankind, and that human beings were better off as unenlightened animals, as Jehovah had intended in the Garden of Eden.

This is a very sad development indeed for the twenty-first-century human race. It is a sign of spiritual regression. Of course, nakedness and shamelessness were the natural way of life in Eden as the Edenic inmates were mentally and spiritually blind. Sexual lewdness or immorality was never an issue among humans, and god of Eden never intended it to be. Edenic human beings lived in total harmony with Jehovah's express intentions for the human bodies. The scripture simply says that "The man and his wife were both naked and were not ashamed." The full implications of that should be obvious to people today.

Morality became a factor of humans' spiritual refinement the very moment the heavenly Redeemer opened the spiritual eyes of the Edenic inmates. It became a serious issue only when Adam and Eve stood their grounds against the spiritually demeaning will of the god of Eden who manipulated and exploited the built-in animal magnetism of human nature to subject human spirits to mental and spiritual blindness.

No doubt, the present state of sexual madness in the world pleases the lusty god of Eden. It shows a remarkable return of humankind to his intended Edenic mode. Nevertheless, those who argue that the total state of shamelessness in Eden was a better way of life are most certainly still blind, both mentally and spiritually. They might argue that the Edenic lifestyle was *easy and fun*, but the way that leads to eternal spiritual damnation is also *wide, easy, and fun*. Yes! "The gate that leads to life is *narrow and hard*," but it is eternally rewarding. The heavenly Messiah encourages his true disciples to fight against the *natural* cravings of their carnal bodies in the ultimate interest of their redeemable spirits.

Paul was convinced that the gift of sexuality to humankind was necessarily malevolent. He tried in his own way to help enlightened humanity understand that clearly. In reply to an inquiry from some of his Corinthian disciples on the matter, he wrote, "Now concerning the [sex and marriage] matters about which you wrote. **It is well for a man not to touch a woman [and vice versa]**. ... To the unmarried and the widows, I say that it is well for them to remain single as I do." [1 Cor. 7:1, 8]

People who marry do not only have worldly troubles, but they are also distracted from crucial spiritual pursuits. Jehovah confesses that sex is like a *poisoned apple*, meant to trap people, and one that truly enlightened people ought to avoid completely, or at best, relish with utmost caution. He even advises abstinence, knowing that people would not find that easy. "And [to the unmarried]," he says, "strain not thine eyes towards that which we cause some wedded pairs among them to enjoy the flower of the life of the world, **that we may try them thereby**." [Qur'an 20:131]

Jesus Christ wanted his disciples to look at the issue from a practical point of view. "Not all men can receive this saying," he said to them, "but only those to whom it is given. [As we know] there are eunuchs who have been so from birth, and there are eunuchs who have been made eunuchs by men, and **there are eunuchs who have made themselves eunuchs for the sake of the kingdom of heaven [for the sake of true spiritual rebirth]**. He who is able to receive this [message], let him receive it." [Matt. 19:11–12] The close disciples of Jesus Christ understood his position on this matter very well and concluded that sexuality and marriage were indeed spiritually harmful to humankind. "If such is the case of a man [even] with his wife," they concluded, "it is not expedient to marry [at all]." [Matt. 19:10] The Messiah quickly made it clear that not everyone would accept this, even though it is obvious that one could, in fact, do without the so-called gift of sexuality.

It is common knowledge that people generally looked down on prostitutes and loose women as being very far away from the gate of heaven, while virgins are respected and held in honor. Hence, when we think of Mary, the wife of Joseph, as "Virgin," we naturally accept her as being spiritually qualified to be the mother of Jesus Christ, the Son of the Father. In a way, Jesus Christ made it clear that the kingdom of the Father earnestly seeks virgins in the world. "For behold," he says, "the days are coming when they will say, 'Blessed are the barren [i.e., equivalent of eunuch], and the womb that never bore, and the breast that never gave suck!'" [Luke 23:29] Of course, this does not detract from the fact that "Christ Jesus came into the world to save sinners." [1 Tim. 1:15] He says, "For I have come to call not those who think they are righteous, but those who know they are sinners." [Matt. 9:13] "For the Son of Man came to seek and save those who are lost." [Luke 19:10 (NLT)]

The words of our Messiah authenticated Paul's position on the matter. Indeed, "it is well for a man not to touch a woman and vice versa." The fact that Jesus Christ ratifies the stringent efforts of men who knowingly make themselves eunuchs "for the sake of the kingdom of the Father" means that he encourages every genuine seeker of true spiritual salvation to abstain totally from marriage and sexual contact with women, and vice versa. It means that he finds the so-called gift of sexuality harmful to the spiritual well-being of human beings. Nevertheless, Jesus Christ also recognizes the fact that not everyone can be eunuch or a virgin. Hence, people who are not able to control their sexual desires are encouraged to marry and stay married. "For it is better to marry than to be aflame with passion," says Paul. [1 Cor. 7:9]

Honest individuals should ask themselves this crucial question regarding the issue of sexuality and marriage: Considering that it is sacred for women to remain virgins and spiritually beneficial for men to avoid sexual contact with women, shouldn't everyone aspire to be virgin or eunuch, since we all seek the same spiritual reunion with our heavenly Father? Indeed, chastity is a divine virtue, and absolute chastity is halfway to the heavenly paradise. A human society that is free of prostitution, rape, seduction, polygamy, incest, infidelity, venereal diseases, and all manner of mental and emotional agonies associated with sex, would be spiritually healthier and happier. Unfortunately, these things are *natural* aspects of human nature.

Closely associated with the natural lust for foods for the stomach and the compulsive desire for sexual and sensual gratification is the insatiable desire of human beings for fame, power, and public acclaim. This is also a deliberate program of the human mind, purely intended to distract humans from devoting quality time to matters of spiritual value. In our modern world, the craze for class distinction and vainglory, as reflected in ostentatious lifestyles, has become a severe obsession hinging almost entirely on money or economic power. With the power of money comes the power associated with worldly authority, and the temptation of wielding suppressive influence over the less privileged in the society. All these feed on the built-in weaknesses of human nature and on peoples' flawed mental outlook.

This is the true nature of Jehovah's kind of benevolence. His so-called gift of abundant foods for the human body is sheer sadism. Truly enlightened human beings should positively reject this kind of spiritually enslaving generosity. In fact, they must fight against it if they truly seek true spiritual salvation for their fallen, captive spirits. The battle for outright liberation of one's captive spirit from materialism is the *battle for righteousness*. Every serious-minded human being must knowingly fight this battle for the ultimate spiritual salvation of his own spirit. This battle generally involves fighting against our personal fears, obsessions, hunger, and unhelpful religious and cultural conventions.

The battle against our basic human nature is a fight against Jehovah's overall program of damaging human impulses. It also means fighting against the spiritually enslaving aspects of some powerful worldly institutions and agencies, such as the family, religion, school, government, culture, and market forces, which directly and indirectly propagate the devious will of Jehovah in the world. This is by no means an easy battle, but **it is winnable** if fought with the power of knowledge and the spiritual guidance of our heavenly Messiah. Already, the life of this world is a bitter struggle. Every single day that human beings scale through on earth is a day of victory or failure in the raging battle for spiritual survival. Therefore, the battle is unavoidable. Oppressive worldly forces fight tirelessly to thwart both the physical and spiritual well-being of every human being on earth, so the best option is for everyone to knowingly fight for true spiritual rebirth.

ACTUAL VALUE OF JEHOVAH'S MATERIAL BLESSINGS

True benevolence is not in the abundance of the giving, but in the actual benefit of the gifts. What then are the real benefits of Jehovah's abundant material provisions? As we have seen, his abundant supply of material nourishment for our mortal bodies stifles and endangers our redeemable spirits. Therefore, he does not qualify to be called "The Beneficent, the Merciful." He does not mean well for humankind, and he says so plainly. In fact, he taunts his favored emissaries and religious believers who think that he means well for humanity, saying, "Think they that in the wealth and sons [the good things of this life] wherewith we provide them, we hasten unto them with good things? **Nay, but they perceive not**. … Let them eat and enjoy [the material comfort of this] life and let [false] hope beguile them. **They will come to know [later when it would have become too late]**! [Qur'an 15:3; 23:55–56]

Only the Father gives perfect gifts. The scripture says that with the Father, *"there is no variation or shadow due to change."* Jesus Christ is the living proof of the Father's perfect gift to humankind. His selfless love is the only thing that sustains and gives hope of true life to our captive spirits.

Edenic human beings did not know whether Jehovah was loving or evil, because they lacked the knowledge of good and evil. They did not know whether his gifts were good or evil either. Today, we know because knowledge of good and evil has been firmly impressed upon our minds by the heavenly Christ through Adam and Eve. We are in a better position, therefore, to compare Jehovah's devious offer of perishable foods for our mortal bodies with the Father's perfect gift of eternal life to our fallen dead spirits.

There should be no room for religious infatuation in examining the actual effects of Jehovah's *lawful* provisions and injunctions for the human body. As we have seen, Jehovah's abundant foods do not even give life to the human body for which they were meant. They have rather turned people into gluttons, drunkards, addicts, junkies, and all kinds of social misfits. It should be remembered that all government-regulated or banned narcotics and addictive substances are all parts of natural food crops provided for human consumption. Caffeine, nicotine, aphrodisiacs, alcohol, etc. are also parts of the universal food chain. Yet they lead to narcosis, psychosis, and death.

Even when Jehovah personally fed the Jewish Exodus in the wilderness with his so-called *manna from heaven*, it merely turned out to be some kind of magical bread conjured out of midnight flakes of dewdrops, which naturally turned maggoty with the morning light. Virtually all the people who ate of it died there in the wilderness. That further buttresses the fact that Jehovah's foods do not give life but death, even to human bodies. Of course, he does not have life himself, and so cannot give what he does not have.

Jesus Christ reminded the Jews of his time that Jehovah's kind of bread was but bread of death. He assured them that neither Moses nor Jehovah, their tribal deity, could give anyone the bread of life, because they did not have it. He offered them the true bread of life from the Father, one guaranteed to give true spiritual life to anyone who received and imbibed it. The true bread from the Father, he told them, should be "that which comes down from heaven, and gives life to the world. ... Your fathers ate the manna in the wilderness, and they [all] died, [because it was bread of death]." [John 6:33, 49] He told them that he was the divine incarnation of that heavenly bread from the Father: "I am the bread of life; he who comes to me shall not hunger, and he who believes in me shall never thirst. ... *If anyone eats of this bread, he will [assuredly] live forever.*" [John 6:35, 51]

That true bread of life is the Father's *Word of Love* to the world; it feeds our captive spirits. Adam and Eve received and ate the heavenly bread of life in the defunct Garden of Eden and were spiritually rekindled. Jesus Christ speaks the same *Word of Love* to our captive spirits today, and it revives the divine light of life in his true disciples. He explains, "It is the spirit that gives life, the flesh is of no avail, **the words that I have spoken to you are spirit and life**." [John 6:63]

The true gospel of Jesus Christ is that *Word of Love* from the Father; it is the true bread of life from our loving, heavenly Father. In the physical absence of our heavenly Messiah, the Holy Spirit of truth continues to feed, rekindled, and reposition more and more dead spirits in the world for the ultimate spiritual resurrection with the same heavenly *Word of Love*.

Jehovah's magical manner continues to bring death to many who feed on it. Clean air and potable water are easily the most essential of all the foods for the human body, but they are also primary sources of social troubles, diseases, and death. While the air we breathe is heavily polluted with all kinds of *natural* life-threatening impurities, the false spring generated from the primordial deep salt seas is hardly available in many parts of the world. The scarcity of drinkable water constitutes a great source of trouble for human beings all over the world. Apart from drinkable water being scarce, waterborne diseases claim many lives every year, especially in the poor and undeveloped countries of the world. According to the United Nations, waterborne diseases, such as cholera and typhoid fever, kill an estimated 5 million to 10 million people worldwide each year.

Perhaps, nothing has been taken for granted more on this earth, by those who have it, than clean drinking water. On the contrary, the love of the Father is freely available and does not hold impurities or life-threatening parasitic microbes.

The ill-fated Jewish Exodus was literally a story of dryness and bitterness. Yet Jehovah personally planned and controlled the entire exercise—a god who had boasted that his servants would eat and drink, while his enemies would starve and thirst to death. Lack of proper food and water were the central themes of the bitter *desert trek*.

For the entire first three days' journey into the unknown, after the magical Red Sea crossing, all that the displaced population of Israel could find to quench the thirst of the people and their flocks was the bitter and undrinkable water of Marah. Luckily or unluckily for them, the so-called benevolent provider was right there on the ground. "What shall we drink?" they asked him through Moses, his mouthpiece. He did not send down the *living spring* to quench their thirst. Rather, he performed some magic over the same bitter waters of Marah to make it taste as if it were no longer bitter. The scripture reports that "Jehovah showed him [Moses] a tree, and he threw it into the water, and the water [magically] became sweet." [Exod. 15:24–25]

Even though Jehovah succeeded in magically making the bitter water of Marah taste *sweet* in the Jewish mentality, it ultimately brought nothing but bitterness and death to the helpless population. Furthermore, the famous water of Meribah in the desert of Zin was rightly called *"waters of contention."* It not only brought untold misery to the floating population of Israel, but it also ultimately cost Moses and Aaron everything that they had earnestly labored and hoped for in Jehovah, the god of Israel.

Again, Jesus Christ made it plain to the Jews, and indeed, to the entire human race, that Jehovah simply does not have access to the *living spring* because he is, indeed, a dead god. He is rather directly opposed to it. The Father is the *living spring*, and Jesus Christ is his living fountain in the universe. Only he can give the true living water from above to our thirsty spirits because he is one with the Father.

The bittersweet waters of this world that Jehovah gives only quench our carnal thirst for a very little while and can never link us to the eternal heavenly spring. On the contrary, the living water that Jesus Christ gives to our thirsty spirits rekindles them for true eternal life. His words say it all. "Everyone who drinks of this [Jehovah's magical waters] will thirst again," he says, "but whoever drinks of the water that I shall give him will never thirst; **the water that I shall give him will become in him a spring of water welling up to eternal life**." [John 4:13–14]

TRUE FASTING AND WHAT IT MEANS FOR OUR CAPTIVE SPIRITS

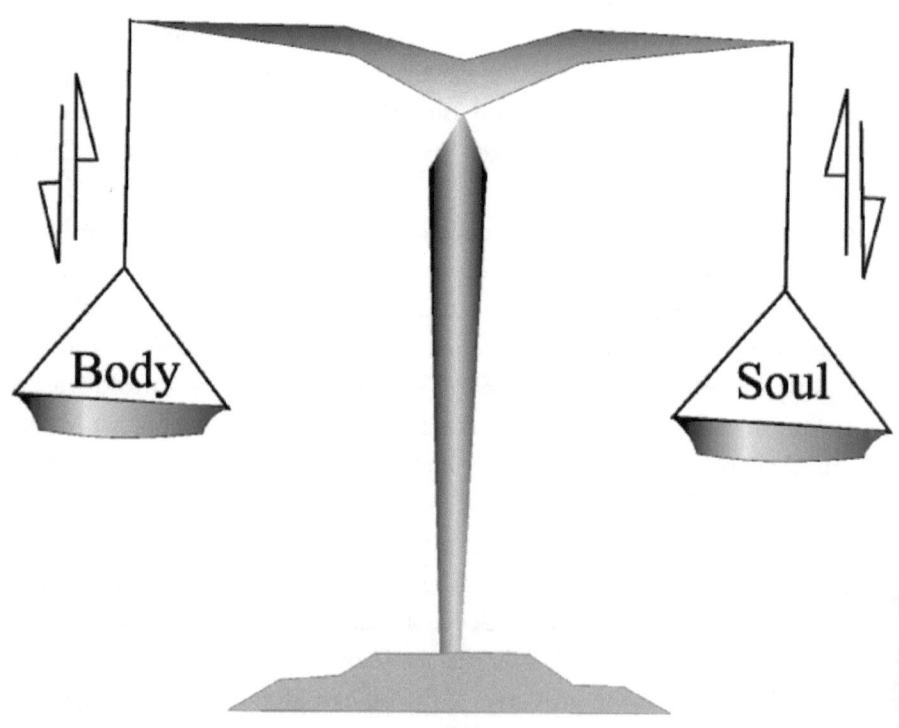

BODY-SPIRIT SCALE

A WELL-NOURISHED BODY IS A BADLY STARVED SPIRIT AND VICE VERSA

Life of this world is not worth nourishing, especially at the expense of true spiritual life. Yet, so long as we live as human beings on the earth, we need some measure of material sustenance, which is hard to come by for so many of us. Therefore, if I simply say that it is good for human beings to starve their mortal bodies to death for spiritual advantage, I would be saying the truth, but I would also be unrealistic. This is because getting rid of the mortal human cloak is not the real answer to the universal obstacle to spiritual salvation. Otherwise, people would simply tie the noose and hang themselves. There is much more to ultimate spiritual liberation.

Nevertheless, fasting is a very practical, result-oriented mode of battling against unhelpful desires of one's carnal body. The human spirit is in prison within the carnal body because that is not his proper habitat. The natural heritage of every perfect spirit is freedom, which the body does not allow. The spirit languishes in the restrictive earthen capsule, and therefore yearns for eternal liberation. During fasting, we knowingly starve the body to lower its potency, and thereby increase the potency of the spirit.

Physical suffering and death of this world go hand in hand. They both play on the human's ignorance of their ultimate spiritual benefits. The truth is that suffering with knowledge lowers the body's undue dominion over the captive spirit, which is a very healthy situation for the meditative spirits. We strive to achieve this exact condition when we knowingly undertake fasting. The body must literally suffer and ultimately die an eternal death for the spirit to regain eternal freedom. This does not mean that one should unnecessarily inflict pains on his body or that he should commit suicide. True fasting is a war of moderation. True fasting aims at restricting the desires of the body to the barest necessities of life.

At stake in every person's life on this earth is the endless battle of supremacy between the desires of his body and those of his spirit.

The body and the spirit occupy opposite arms of the weighing balance. One suffers when the other gains, and vice versa. Eternal death to the body means eternal redemption for the incarcerated spirit. Just as a dry seed put in the soil needs to die to yield life, the redeemed spirit in a human being must shed the earthen encumbrance to regain true spiritual eternal life. However, just as the dry seed must be potent before the process of dying in the soil and yielding life can be possible, the human spirit must first find salvation before death of the body can become eternal and of spiritual value to him. That is why merely starving oneself to death is not the answer.

The body naturally wears away gradually before it dies. That process of gradual wear down means suffering. Every human being goes through that process willy-nilly. No quantity and quality of food nutrients can stop aging and death of the human body. And no one can ever go to heaven without first suffering and dying to every aspect of the life of the world. Even the Son of man, Jesus, suffered and died to the world. So must all his true disciples suffer and "crucify their flesh with its passions and desires."

Jesus did not suffer and die once for everyone in the world, as customary Christians believe and preach. Rather, he suffered and died to give example to his true disciples, and to strengthen their hearts for the inevitable. He wants his true disciples to understand that suffering and death are inevitable for every human being on earth, and that choosing to "crucify their flesh with its passions and desires," as he exemplified needs special courage. He once identified the needed special courage in Simon Bar-Jona and nicknamed *it* "Peter" or "*Courage of Rock*," and added, "On this Rock [*Peter* or *Courage of Rock*] I will build my [ministry], and powers of death shall not prevail against it." [Matt. 16:18]

There was absolutely nothing in the words, context, and body language of Jesus Christ when he renamed the "special courage" he found in Simon Bar-Jona "Peter" that suggested that ungodly Roman Catholic Church fathers should erect a man-made building for his divine mission upon the bones of Simon Bar-Jona or of anyone else.

Immediate apostles of Jesus Christ exhibited the same *Courage of Rock* in the face of extreme persecutions, torture, and executions in the hands of Jehovah's zealots, and they ultimately wore the crown of spiritual salvation.

Paul showed remarkable insight regarding the need for suffering and death of the human body. He wrote:

- "I tell you this, brethren: flesh and blood cannot inherit the kingdom of the Father, nor does the perishable inherit the imperishable." [1 Cor. 15:50]
- "For to me to live is Christ, and to die is gain. ... My desire is to depart and be with Christ, for that is far better." [Phil. 1:21–23]
- "We know that our old self was crucified with him so that the sinful body might be destroyed, and we might no longer be enslaved to sin. **For he who has died [of the world] is free from sin.**" [Rom. 6:6–7]

Having seen physical suffering and death of this world in the right perspective, some people might argue that Jehovah has our interest in mind after all when he causes people to suffer and die. However, he did not impose the curse of starvation, suffering, and death on human beings with the intention of doing them any good whatsoever. He did so with the express intent to punish, humiliate, terrorize, and dominate humankind. Besides, he also makes sure that human beings do not readily realize or try to utilize the unintended benefits arising from his punitive measures.

Let me draw an analogy of Jehovah's actual position on human suffering and death from the military regime of one of Nigeria's dictatorial generals. During General Babangida's severe military regime in Nigeria (1985–1993), the masses suffered untold forced austerity and hardship. Many unfortunate people who tried to protest lost their lives at the hands of government agents, and many helpless ones simply starved to death. Few privileged ones "checked out" to

Western countries to find better life, while the hardiest majority struggled hard to adapt and survive within the system.

By the time the general was forced out of office after eight years of pure satanic mandate, corruption, and high-level fraudery had become an indelible way of life in the country. It was during this period that the notorious *advance-fee fraud* (419 scams), drug pushing, etc. officially took root and flourished in the country. During this period too, many Nigerians learned much about self-help trades and established mini household industries.

As the situation became more difficult, it toughened the people, and they kept going. In the end, most people became better at self-help efforts. One could be tempted to argue, therefore, that General Babangida's corrupt regime helped the average Nigerians to look inward and maximize the use of their latent potentials. However, it would not be true to assume that that was his projected intention. It was purely a case of necessity being the mother of inventions.

However, while the man, Babangida, might technically plead insanity or ignorance, Jehovah is a premeditated oppressor of human beings. He says, "Certainly we have created man to be in distress." Therefore, Jehovah did not impose his curse of hunger, suffering, and death on humankind as a means of trying to bring out the best in the people. These are deliberate scheming of a habituated evil mind. He meant for human beings to feel tormented and helpless under his control. Nevertheless, clear-thinking human beings should emulate the courageous Nigerians who looked inward to discover their innate potentials. They should recognize and utilize the *unintended* opportunities presented by programmed human suffering and death to the benefit of their spirits.

Various levels of fasting or strict self-denial have been practiced in various worldly religions, as a process of spiritual discipline for uplifting one's spirit. Most of the Eastern religions are noted for asceticism; most were founded by great ascetics, like the Buddha, Guru Nanak, etc. Some customary Christian sects fast for forty weekdays every year during Lent, and the Muslim world, thirty days during the month of Ramadan, and so on. Besides being a period of self-denial, prayer, and atonement, the various religions consider fasting periods especially helpful for meditating and focusing better on their gods and showing gratitude for his benevolence. During fasting, the religious adherents reflect on how generous their god has been in supplying their daily bread, and then worship and praise him with more diligence.

These kinds of routine group fasting imposed by worldly religious institutions on their adherents are merely periods of mock spiritual discipline that deliberately plough at the tip of the spiritual gold mine. They are mild forms of group meditation based on preset doctrines, which hardly encourage digging deeper into the spiritual gold mine for real spiritual benefits. In fact, routine group fasting is one of the devious religious programs used by Jehovah to consolidate his dominion over the minds of the blinded worshipers. People who take part in *ritual* group fasting by various religions derive little or no real spiritual benefit for their captive spirits because they are literally tuned to a false spiritual frequency that is routed to an impostor.

Jehovah does not expect his worshipers to derive individual spiritual benefits from fasting, but rather to find deeper opportunities to magnify his name. He states his actual aim plainly in the Qur'an: "O ye who believe! Fasting is prescribed for you, even as it was prescribed for those before you … [during] the month of Ramadan in which was revealed the Qur'an. … **Allah desireth for you ease**; he desireth not hardship for you; and (he desireth) that ye should **[just] complete the period, and that ye should magnify Allah for having guided you, and that peradventure ye may be thankful**." [Qur'an 2:183, 185]

Even then, Jehovah confirms that fasting is only beneficial to people who plough deeper because they know the true value of it. He says, "And that ye fast is better for you if ye did but know [why you should]." [Qur'an 2:184]

Jesus Christ fasted, and he explained to his true disciples how they would obtain the right benefits from true fasting. "And when you fast," he instructed, "do not look dismal, like the [religious] hypocrites, for they disfigure their faces that their fasting may be seen by men. Truly, I say to you, they have received their reward [from Jehovah who delights in mock religious group fasting]. But when you fast, anoint your head and wash your face, that your fasting may not be seen [or known about] by men but by your Father who is in secret [in Spirit]; and your Father who sees in secret will reward you [in spirit]." [Matt. 6:16–18]

During true fasting, one knowingly starves, *suffers*, and denies his body of regular foods and sensual pleasures and enjoyments. This naturally reduces the body's mystical weight or potency, while the spirit gains. In that state, the fasted person is in a better position to appreciate spiritual truths and the need to attain full spiritual selfhood. The scriptures authenticate the automatic efficacy of fasting, and that is true whether one fasts for a good cause or for an evil one. In fact, there can hardly be any real mystical or spiritual achievement by any human being on earth without him first undergoing that mystical shedding of the body potency. All the prophets of the world fasted to finally activate their latent mystical energies. Even Jesus Christ, our heavenly Messiah, fasted forty days and forty nights before he could fully overcome the natural, debilitating influence of human nature to finally begin his divine mission in the world.

The temptations of Jesus Christ during and after his prolonged fasting show that the world feels threatened by true fasting. The devil-cum-god of the world that nourishes the human body for its purposes feels greatly threatened by people who fast for the right cause. The scripture says that Jesus Christ "fasted forty days and forty nights and afterward he was hungry. And the tempter [Jehovah, the nourisher of the human body] came and said to him, 'If you are the Son of the Father, command these stones to become loaves of bread.'" [Matt. 4:2–4] Of course, the tempter knew that he was the

Son of the Living Father; and that he could indeed turn stones into bread. However, the heavenly Messiah, having fully activated his spiritual personality, no longer depended on Jehovah's organic foods to stay alive. Hence, he authoritatively reminded the powerless tempter that the *spirit-man* does not need the magical bread of this world to live. He reminded Jehovah of what they both knew very well. "It is written," he said to him, 'Man shall not live by bread alone, but by every word that proceeds from the mouth of the Father.'" [Matt. 4:4]

Jehovah and the gods of the world do their utmost to conceal the real benefits of proper fasting from humankind. They tempt and entice anyone who embarks on true fasting with appetizing edibles to derail him from his noble cause. The answer to that is perseverance, because we know that though our outer nature wastes away in the process, our inner beings are strengthened for eternal glory.

CHAPTER TEN

FALLACY OF HUMAN COMFORT AND HAPPINESS

As we have seen, "the beauty of the world is deceptive and there is danger in human comfort and enjoyment." People call this the pauper's popular maxim. Unsurprisingly, the opulent sing a different song because they are living in spiritual limbo. To them, "the world is beautiful," "life is good," "life is sweet," and "life is enjoyable."

Most electronic brand advertisers use some of these as promotional slogans to woo the public into buying their innovative gadgets that are guaranteed to enhance human comfort and enjoyment. Such sayings are also popular with aesthetes, aestheticians, fashionistas, and TV religious promoters of material *blessings*, *breakthroughs*, and *prosperity* from the god of the world. Even social misfits whose lives have nothing to show for it, sing the same slogans—drunkards, prostitutes, womanizers, polygamists, drug addicts, and the like. They all pretend to be enjoying this life, while deep inside they groan because they know they are in fact, living in bondage.

Often, when people pray, they thank the god of Genesis for giving them this life and for making *wonderful* provisions to make life very enjoyable on earth. In fact, the consensus among regular people is that the *good things of this life* are blessings from *God*. Of course, one cannot blame them for believing and saying so, because earthly life and its glories are all they know and experience as humans. In their present state of spiritual oblivion, they no longer have any idea of the Father's perfect spiritual kingdom, and they are unable to imagine its perfect beauty and bliss. Hence, illusion seems real, and sheer vanity presents itself as beauty, comfort, and enjoyment. Even then, human enjoyments and the so-called *good things of this life* are not without physical and ultimate spiritual costs. They are most certainly not blessings from our loving heavenly Father.

Most Western prison yards are very beautiful and comfortable, for instance, but they are prison yards all the same. Their primary purpose is to deprive prisoners of their natural freedom. The beauty and comfort of a prison yard only give the inmates the false impression of being at home, and once they feel *at home* in forced incarceration, it becomes harder for them to genuinely desire to regain their freedom. In fact, most prisoners in the West do their best to remain jailbirds because they feel more comfortable in prison *homes* than being out, free, and fending for themselves.

Life in the world is a terminal sentence; the earth is a very beautiful prison yard, and human beings are the worst kind of jailbirds. They seriously need salvation first, from the illusion of homeliness, and then, from ultimate spiritual self-damnation. Sadly, they all talk about spiritual salvation, but do not genuinely desire to attain it. As Jesus Christ says, "No one after drinking old wine desires new; for he says, 'the old is good.'" [Luke 5:39] That is very unfortunate indeed!

Merriam-Webster's Collegiate Dictionary defines salvation as "deliverance from the power and effects of sin," "**liberation from ignorance or illusion**," "preservation from destruction or failure," or "**deliverance from danger or difficulty**." In the case of human beings, deliverance or liberation implies the state of inevitable battle against an overpowering situation. It also indicates that human spirits are presently astray and in real danger of eternal *destruction or failure*. It means that human spirits are presently in captivity to a foreign power and in the enemy's own territory.

The word "liberation" clearly establishes the distinct triangle of the characters involved in the raging battle for the salvation of human spirits. The triangle consists of the **captor**, the **captives**, and the **heavenly Liberator** who must wield superior powers to be able to overcome the captor in his own territory to set free the captives.

Liberation also stresses outright retrieval of the captives from the entire sphere of influence of the captor.

Being in captivity also means that the present situation blocks human spirits from the natural realm of reality. *Liberation from ignorance or illusion*, therefore, becomes the primary therapy necessary for reactivating the captive human spirits for ultimate salvation. Knowledge is the master panacea for true spiritual salvation, as only knowledge can liberate from ignorance. Without spiritual insight, the human spirits are dead and lost forever. The human body is the physical manifestation of the forced incarceration of the human spirit. While the human body *enjoys* the illusory comfort and happiness of the earthly prison and worships the devious god of the world, the human spirit languishes in darkness and death.

The earth seems so spacious and awesomely beautiful to its human inmates, but it is merely a gigantic zoo—a first-class prison yard all the same. The sheer phantom of worldly beauty beguiles many people into playing down the obvious "dangers in the comfort" of the world. The truth is that human beings are bedeviled entities. Speaking to them about the need for liberation or deliverance from the world may never yield a positive result until they can fully understand both who they are and where they are. Salvation is practically impossible for anyone who is not genuinely convinced of being in some form of real danger. It is important, therefore, that those who preach true spiritual salvation must make it clear that it means outright *exodus* from the entire imperfect universe. Nothing is worthwhile in the entire world; worldly treasures, pleasures, joys, and happiness are all false.

The *basic needs* of every human being are **food, clothing**, and **shelter**. These are the basic requirements for basic human comfort and happiness on earth. Here, *basic* means most essential; it means plain and utilitarian, not luxurious or fancy. Basic does not necessarily mean cheap or lack of quality, but adequacy for its purpose. Naturally, any human being who has an adequate supply of balanced daily diet, proper clothing, and a dwelling place that offers secure shelter from weather and other social and environmental hazards should be comfortable and happy. Beyond the *basics* is overindulgence, and with that comes unhappiness, pain, and self-damnation. Sadly, millions of people the world over lack the basic needs.

Primitive human beings were largely hunters; they ate their game, clothed themselves with animal hides and dwelt in caves and under groves for shelters. Their lives were unsafe, and they lived in fear and anxiety from day to day. Even then, one might suppose that they were relatively comfortable and happy. With the help of science and technology, favorable government policies, industrialization, and mechanized farming techniques, modern human beings have far more than the *basics* at their disposal. Today, people have a wide variety of natural and synthetic fabrics to choose from for their fashion needs and for various weather conditions. Most people live in secure brick houses with secure doors and windows. And together with the availability of clean drinking water and an abundance of food, both organic and GMO, natural and processed, modern human beings should be altogether comfortable and happy. Unfortunately, that is hardly the case.

The contemporary definition of comfort refers to things that make someone physically relaxed—for example, home ornaments, generally referred to as *comforts of the home*, and other luxury possessions that distinguish individuals as classy and comfortable in society. Today, being comfortable simply means that one has enough money or economic power to provide for himself whatever material elements of relaxation he desires—the so-called *good things of this life*. It also means that someone has the wherewithal to provide adequate security for his personal and corporate interests. Ordinarily, people consider *comfortable* individuals in society to be happy as well. Indeed, the contemporary definition of happiness is a state of physical well-being and contentment, which are still factors of financial prosperity.

Nevertheless, an inner emptiness exists in every human being, which the best of foods, clothing, shelter, and all the luxuries and comforts of the world cannot possibly fill. Earthly life is bedeviled with so many natural handicaps. These culminate in environmental and social insecurities that create a permanent state of inner anguish. True comfort and happiness are components of spiritual well-being, possible only where there is genuine inner peace. Because genuine inner peace is practically impossible in an imperfect situation, true comfort and happiness are practically impossible anywhere within our insecure universe.

The world is imperfect. Life in the world is a very bad dream. Both science and religion agree with these facts, and practical human experiences prove them beyond every doubt. The Qur'an says that "the life of this world is but *comfort of illusion*." What this means is that everything about this life is a bad imitation of perfect spiritual reality. Therefore, comfort and happiness of the world are mere fantasies. Only the human spirit feels true happiness or joy, but the carnal human body and the physical world of vanities effectively prevent that. The spirit and body of the composite human being do not share the same foods, activities, and joys. The world nourishes perishable human bodies, while deliberately starving the human spirits that matter. This creates an inner emptiness in every human being on earth, which makes true human comfort and happiness a sheer mirage.

Captive human spirits hunger for different types of food, comfort, and fulfillment, which the world cannot provide. They are neither comfortable in the human earthen capsules, nor happy in the world that maliciously cuts them off from their own natural food source. There is innate yearning in every human being for true providence, and for the perfect environment where peace of mind and happiness are real and eternal. Somehow, we now know that we are relocated spirits, and that our true comfort and happiness lie in successful reunification with our true origin. Inwardly, we all yearn to return to our familiar habitat and regain our true spiritual personalities. We all seek the true Father of our captive spirits because we know that only he can remedy our inner emptiness. For as long as we are in the world, we are not at home; therefore, we can never experience perfect peace of mind or true comfort and happiness.

Human religion presented itself as the much-desired agency for spiritual salvation, and we instinctively looked up to it to reveal to us our true heavenly Father who is the Source of true spiritual life and happiness. We looked up to religion to help restore the severed link between the Father and our lost, captive spirits. Unfortunately, human religion, being an entirely worldly institution, led us to the impostor that rules the same world of emptiness. Religion worsened our inner emptiness and unhappiness by pretending to be what it was not, while forcibly impressing upon us polluted ideals that totally contradicted the ones that we clearly perceived in our spirits. So, we became convinced that human religion could not lead anyone to the Father because it did not know him.

Appearance of Jesus Christ on the worldly stage with the Father's *Word of Life* for our fallen, dead spirits brought us the answer we had all longed for. For the very first time in the history of humans' quest for spiritual insight, he clearly revealed to us the true nature of our heavenly Father. Unsurprisingly, his attributes completely contrast those of the monstrous god that human religion promotes. He not only preached his heavenly Good News to our lost spirits, but he also lived out the exemplary lifestyle that he guaranteed would bring us back to the presence of the Father in his perfect heavenly kingdom. Jesus Christ offers us the unique opportunity to reunite with our heavenly Father to find the perfect life of eternal happiness. All we need to do is to walk in his exemplary footsteps.

Apostle Philip spoke the mind of the entire human race when he asked the Messiah to show us the Father in ways we would all understand as humans: "**Lord, show us the Father, and we shall be satisfied.**" [John 14:8] Only by rediscovering our true Father, can our captive spirits find true sustenance and, therefore, true comfort and happiness. Only by returning to our proper heavenly dwelling can we *be satisfied*.

Through his loving deeds and life-giving utterances, Jesus Christ showed us the Father that dwelt in him and asked us to walk in his footsteps to be sure of attaining spiritual rebirth. He assured us that his is the only way that leads to true happiness. His words left no doubts in the minds of his true disciples that *the true light that enlightens every man* had indeed come into the world. He authoritatively defined himself in ways that countered prevailing claims of human religion and its god. "**I am the way, and the truth, and the life;**" he said, "**no one comes to the Father, but by me**. ... He who has seen me has seen the Father. ... [Because] I am in the Father and the Father in me." [John 14:6, 9–10]

The mission of Jesus Christ in the world poses great danger for the worldly regime of Jehovah and the other principalities. Exposing their well-kept secrets concerning the Father, his gracious offer of eternal life, and true spiritual status quo spells doom for their dominion ambition over captive human spirits. So, they are desperately fighting to thwart rapid spread of the Messiah's true gospel of life and happiness.

Jehovah invented and used **religion** to try to safeguard universal status quo. That explains the sudden, heightened religious activities during the period immediately after the spiritual ascension of the heavenly Messiah. The radical incidents leading to the founding of customary Christianity and Islam particularly revealed the urgency with which the gods responded to the monumental threat posed by the mission of Jesus Christ on earth. Of course, Jehovah's religious propaganda strategy was purely to buy time, not to stop the inevitable demise of the doomed world order. As it were, the gods have succeeded in no little measure in that regard. Yet they are even more desperate today because they know that time is not on their side. Today, we can see a doubling of effort on the part of all religious movements in the world. While Islamic jihadists employ terrorism, bloodbath, and outright butchery to obtain forced *surrender* and turn people into slaves of Allah, customary Christian hirelings target the same result by powerfully invigorating the preaching of earthly prosperity, comfort, and happiness.

Apart from the covert mission of human religion, the world also devised other measures to try to preoccupy human minds with enhanced obsession with material elements of comfort and sensual pleasures. The central aim is to keep human spirits out of necessary spiritual activities. When Qur'an 3:14 says, "Beautified for mankind is love of the joys (that come) from *women* and *offspring*, and stored-up heaps of *gold* and *silver*, and *horses* branded (with their mark), and *cattle* and *land*," it shows clearly that Allah is deliberately distracting humans with the illusory joys and comfort of the world. Accordingly, it also says that such are the "comfort of the life of the world" and that "the life of this world is but comfort of illusion."

Obsessive love of money has taken the center stage in peoples' minds, both the old and the young, and they willingly kill or die for it. Today, the spirit of capitalism seems to dictate another rule of the game altogether. People no longer want to be wealthy; they want to be rated as the richest men and women in the world. Today, we hear about financial frauds by officials of government and nongovernmental agencies in various countries of the world. They massively defraud and embezzle public funds to the extent of impoverishing the masses and causing many to starve to death. This is all because they believe that having very fat bank accounts can bring them true comfort and happiness. Unfortunately, most of them eventually die very miserable; some even commit suicide. True comfort and happiness do not lead to such miserable fate.

Today, the world has become very rich, yet poverty has become more pronounced and overwhelming all over the world. Because the rich are getting richer, the poor are becoming poorer. The effect of that is contemporary unhappiness for both the rich and the poor, because they are both poor in spirit. While the poor spend all their time brooding over poverty, the rich spend all their time mocking poverty by downgrading their own humanity. Hence the inner emptiness remains in both the poor and the rich.

Perhaps the unhappiest people on the earth are the extremely rich because they are the ones privileged enough to reach the point where they can discover that money does not buy happiness after all. The pop singer and film actor, Madonna, once reached that point of realization and confessed that indeed, money does not attract happiness but problems. She said, "The more money you have, the more problems you have. I went from having no money to making comparatively a lot and all I've had is problems. Life was simpler when I had no money, when I just barely survived."

Another U.S. comedian and actor, Groucho Marx, said, "Look at me: I worked my way up from nothing to a state of extreme poverty." What Marx discovered through personal experience is that happiness of the world means nothing but *extreme inner emptiness*. It is strange indeed, but the richer one gets in the world, the *poorer* he becomes within himself. The riches of the world bring nothing but spiritual emptiness, and that explains why some very rich people end up committing suicide in our present *civilized* world.

Any way we look at it, poverty and prosperity of this world are just two sides of the same coin of death. They are both programmed vicissitudes of spiritual bondage. The book of Proverbs says, "The wealth of the rich is their [meaningless] fortress; the poverty of the poor is their destruction." [Prov. 10:15] Immediate effects of poverty include low self-esteem, spiritual lethargy, illiteracy, juvenile crime, child abuse, child labor, malnutrition, diseases, homelessness, mass starvation, and death. Prosperity of the world, on its part, brings about pride and arrogance, spiritual indifference, loss of personal privacy and freedom, anxiety and insecurity, marital disappointments, unhappiness, suicide, or death.

The prayer of every wise person on earth, as Jesus Christ directed, should be: "*Father, give me* **this day** *my daily bread!*" Proverb 30:8 portrays the same wisdom in the prayer of Agur, son of Jakeh of Massa. It reads, "Give me neither poverty nor riches; **feed me with the food that is needful for me**,"—that is, food that is needful for his captive spirit.

Jesus Christ spoke against the riches of the world in so many ways. He made it clear that worldly riches are not compatible with peace of mind and with true spiritual salvation. He said that "It is easier for a camel to go through the eye of a needle than for a rich man to enter the [heavenly] kingdom of the Father." [Mark 10:25] He portrayed the sheer futility of worldly riches, comfort, and happiness with the parable of the rich fool, and enjoined his true disciples to accumulate their own treasures in the Father's heavenly kingdom where it is guaranteed to give true eternal life with absolute peace of mind. "Do not lay up for yourselves treasures on earth," he said, "where moth and rust consume and where thieves break in and steal, but lay up for yourselves treasures in heaven, where neither moth nor rust consumes and where thieves do not break in and steal." [Matt. 6:19–20]

Customary Christians vehemently reject that kind of teaching, preferring instead, to submit to the god that gives worldly riches. And Paul presents them with a perfect alibi in 2 Cor 8:9 that makes them feel bold about their choice of worldly affluence over plain and simple lifestyle on earth. "For you know the grace of our Lord Jesus Christ," he says to customary Christians, "that though he [Jesus Christ] was rich, yet for your sake he became poor, so that by his poverty you might become rich." With that, customary Christian ministers regard Jesus Christ as *poor God* and expressly refuse to identify with his gospel of laying up treasures in heaven for *future* consumption. So, they knowingly worship and preach Jehovah on earth, and reap his financial *breakthroughs*, *blessings*, and *prosperity* here and now.

Unfortunately, people who busy themselves accumulating Jehovah's riches and treasures of the world only store them up for their own burials, because they always forget to ask for, and obtain from him, the guaranteed lifetime with which to enjoy their so-called good things of this life. A reasonable person would seek life first before the things that nourish it. Nevertheless, the life of the world has no such guarantee. The heavenly life that the Father offers to all of us through his Son, Jesus Christ, is blissful and eternal, and it is guaranteed.

The world also provides other means of illusory comfort, enjoyment, and happiness to human inmates in the form of **mental depressants**. These include alcohol, narcotics, aphrodisiacs, music, and other forms of mental downers. All these give a transient sense of extreme enjoyment and happiness, but ultimately lead to extreme depression and self-destruction. The book of Proverbs 31:6–7 captures the will of Jehovah in this matter: "Give strong drink to him who is perishing, and wine to those in bitter distress; let them drink and forget their poverty and remember their misery no more." So, mental depressants only help the addicts to temporarily *forget their poverty and remember their misery no more*, but the bitter distress always returns with a surge immediately the effects of the intoxicants subside.

Jesus Christ tells us that people who spend their time on earth eating and drinking, marrying and giving in marriage, enjoying sex and romance, getting high and getting low on *mind-Tweedle*, will ultimately end up spending eternity in spiritual bondage. He cited Noah's generation as a terrible example of spiritual indifference and charged his true disciples to earn their spiritual salvation. "As were the days of Noah, so will be the coming of the Son of man," he said. "For as in those days before the flood they were eating and drinking, marrying and giving in marriage, until the day when Noah entered the ark, and they did not know until the flood came and swept them all away, so will be the [last] coming of the Son of man." [Matt. 24:37–39]

Many people in the world today depend heavily on **professional entertainers**—musicians, actors, comedians, dancers, sports stars, religious motivational speakers, and other kinds of public performers—to exorcise their natural mental anguish and unhappiness. I call such professional entertainers *social exorcists*. They are among the richest people in the world today, but they are surprisingly, also the loneliest and unhappiest.

The truth is that one can pretend to be happy, but no one can act real happiness. What these *professional entertainers* do not understand is the principle of equilibrium of forces. They do not know that unhappiness is an evil spirit and an indestructible component of the life of the world. Just like matter, unhappiness cannot be exterminated, but can merely be transmitted from person to person. When a musician, actor, or comedian makes a fool of himself just to force laughter out of his gloomy audience, for instance, he simply transfers the peoples' unhappiness onto himself. Over the years, he accumulates so much of other peoples' melancholy that he begins to crack.

History holds endless lists of names of renowned celebrities and top-class entertainers who ended up in mental institutions or had to undergo group therapy at the pinnacle of their careers, and so many others who simply committed suicide due to extreme depression. Is it not strange that people who are in the business of making other people laugh and light up with happiness are usually the most dejected in real life? No doubt, the kind of happiness provided by the entertainment industry creates bigger inner emptiness in people who make it their profession.

There is a completely new obsession with the world of showbiz, sports, and games for the wild euphoria associated with its ability to manipulate peoples' passion for *emotional* happiness. For so many people in the world today, happiness comes and goes with the seasonal international, regional, and national sports and games, such as the Olympics, World Cups, National Leagues, UEFA Cup, African Cup of Nations, NBA games, Wimbledon, French Open, Masters Tournament, Grand Prix, etc. Closely associated with the *emotional* happiness of winning in sports and games, however, is the deep sorrow and anguish on the part of losing teams and their fans, for there must always be winners and the losers in these games.

People who are alert to the worldly trend of counterattacks on peoples' spiritual evolution will have noticed the radical shift of fortune in favor of professions hitherto left only for educational dropouts in society. Footballers, musicians, actors, comedians, and the like, were generally regarded as nothing but social jesters; many of them still are. But today, the world pays them so much that everyone wants to become one of them. Today, even educated parents encourage their young ones to abandon education in pursuit of high-paying football careers, for instance. The impact of that for the future will be very grave indeed. Tomorrow's world would ultimately become full of illiterate millionaires, and that would not augur well for humankind's spiritual advancement.

Present-day Pentecostal ministers are easily the most charismatic of all religious motivational speakers. People usually wonder how these preachers attract millions of followers, and they erroneously judge the success of customary Christianity with the magnitude of these crowds of frustrated miracle seekers. Sadly, majority of these great multitudes of churchgoers do not attend the so-called prayer meetings and crusades to find the true Jesus Christ or the Father. They do not go to heal their inner emptiness, but to relieve their immediate mental agonies. Every week, millions, and millions of unhappy people troop to the various *revival clinics* with their endless lists of material problems—like people going to cinemas, music concerts, stand-up comedians' shows, etc.—to hear mind-blowing sermons from sweet-talking preachers that magically erase all their worries for as long as they are hearing them.

Just like narcotics, the words of these Pentecostal hirelings are extremely addictive to those who are enthralled by them, and so the adherents gradually become addicted to hearing them. For as long as they hear the words, they feel comforted and happy, and so they do not care whether Jesus Christ is there or not. Sadly, they never find permanent solutions to their real problems, which hinge entirely on their inner emptiness.

These *great men of God*, as people call them, perform fake miracles of healing the sick, the blind, the deaf, the dumb, and the crippled Sunday after Sunday. Yet every day, the situation remains the same, even worse in our societies. The sick, the blind, the deaf, the dumb, the crippled, and the very poor believers never find any respite from their predicaments. Yet, the heartless hirelings greatly enrich themselves by extorting from the poor, ignorant miracle seekers who go to them hoping to receive favors from the wolfish god of the world. In the end, both the so-called *men of God* and their beguiled victims *feel* comfortable and happy, or so they believe.

What the greedy preachers and their ignorant hearers do not know is that they are victims of Jehovah's end-time mass-religious hypnoses, as predicted in the book of Joel. Jehovah said, "And it shall come to pass afterward, that I [Jehovah] *will pour out* my spirit on all flesh; your sons and your daughters shall prophesy, your old men shall dream dreams, and your young men shall see visions. Even upon the menservants and maidservants in those days, I will pour out my spirit." [Joel 2:28–29]

Money seems to be all that matters to all church ministers; it has been so from the very inception of customary Christianity. Most of them have become so blinded by its allures that they cannot even see just how far away they are from the true way of Jesus Christ. They also do not care to know the extent to which they are endangering the eternal fate of their own spirits, as well as those of their blind followers. Worst of all, they do not wish the situation to change. Therefore, the inner emptiness remains deeply imbued in religious believers, translating itself into universal mental anarchy and lack of love among human beings that, today, completely emasculates the whole world.

It is sad to see the so-called Pentecostalists clowning about the crucial battle for the heavenly crown of true life that Jesus Christ laid down his life for, and for which all his true apostles were persecuted, tortured, and brutally murdered. As painful and challenging as it was, all the apostles sealed their faith in Jesus Christ with their own blood, but today's so-called Christian ministers believe that they can win the same heavenly crown of honor by clowning about on their pulpits, dancing, laughing, extorting their helpless devotees, and enjoying the treasures of the same world that persecuted, tortured, and crucified their heavenly Redeemer. Evidently, they believe that they are being clever and wise, while the people who sacrificed and the ones who are still sacrificing their lives in following the very footsteps of Jesus Christ are fools. But only time will tell!

CHAPTER ELEVEN

FALLACY OF HUMAN RIGHTS

I was born into a polygamous family of three wives and seventeen children. My father loved and treated some of his children as true heirs, while others were neglected and treated as outcasts. I happened to be foremost amongst the ones considered outcasts. At about the age of six, he managed to completely cast me aside from his family, and I lived the rest of my childhood and adult life with various relatives and friends, like an orphan. Although my father was wealthy and influential at the time, he never cared about me. Throughout his life, he consistently showed me, in both words and actions, that I had no rights whatsoever in his home. In due course, I accepted that the way he felt about me was entirely his prerogative, based on circumstances that might have been within and beyond his control. I also accepted, deep in myself, that I did not have the divine right to contest his position.

His will represented a blatant injustice and generated heated controversies between him and some of the less wanted sons shortly before he died, but I refused to be drawn into the fuss. I knew that I would eventually become a man myself and have whatever my father denied me. Even after his death, I never tried to claim any rights in his estate, because I knew that, deep in his heart, he never accorded me any during his lifetime.

My sorrowful childhood experiences made me determine that I must run my own home differently from my father's. In my own home today, my wife and six children are bona fide members of the household, and I fought concerted opposition from both human and divine quarters to maintain my stand on that. They have full rights in whatever may be considered my accomplishments in this life, and they all know it. I love and care about them equally, and through my consistent actions and words, they know that they will never have to fight to *claim* whatever their dues are in my estate.

In fact, there was a day I decreed that my room had become out of bounds to all the children, except by my express permission, because they were nearly turning it into everybody's apartment. Everybody preferred coming to use daddy's washing machine, daddy's toothpaste, daddy's hairbrush, daddy's perfume, etc. My second daughter, Ruby, took me up on that, and argued that I was trying to turn them into slaves in their own father's house. She simply invoked the immutable rights she knew they all had in my house, and the decree flopped instantly. Obviously, my children would not expect to enjoy the same rights outside their own father's home or in other peoples' homes.

Having said this, however, I accept that my love for my wife and children is only human, subconsciously conditional, and therefore imperfect. I accept that if I fared better than my father did in this regard, it was out of the sheer grace of our loving Father in heaven. No one can accomplish any good deeds on earth without his divine grace. He is the Sovereign Benefactor of all goodness in the hearts of human beings. In other words, no entity within the imperfect universe, whether human or divine, can bequeath another with irrevocable rights under any circumstance.

We can see from the two scenarios that *rights* are solemn *privileges* granted by the chief sponsor(s) of an endeavor to some other people in any given situation. If those privileges were formally given, implicitly or explicitly, and the situation remains the same, the need to agitate or fight to claim them does not arise. If the person who gave the rights withdraws them formally, there is no basis to fight to claim them. Only when someone else usurps the rights, for any reason, is one fully justified to fight to *reclaim* them.

When someone accommodates another person in his house out of goodwill, for instance, he gives him the solemn right to reside in the house. If someone else tries to evict him, he is justified in fighting to protect his rights. However, if the person who offered him the shelter revokes his generosity for any reason, there is no basis for him to contest revocation of his right. On the other hand, if the house is a joint bequest and one of the part-owners tries to dispossess the other of his own right, then the victim would have full right to fight to *re-claim* his right. Generally, if someone withholds what belongs to him and other people, the aggrieved persons have the full rights to fight to *re-claim* what belongs to them.

Furthermore, if a couple decides to hire wedding garments from someone instead of making them by themselves, they are under obligation to use the garments only within the limit of the rights given to them by the owner. They do not have any basis to agitate or fight for rights that are not explicitly contained in the contractual agreement. An adage says that a man does not preside over the sharing of a game he did not kill. It would be highly enlightening to examine the issue of human rights from these and other pertinent perspectives.

Only the Father bequeaths *inalienable rights*, and the only place where anyone can freely enjoy them is within his spheres of positive influence, which is his perfect spiritual kingdom. Because the love of the Father for his perfect heavenly sons is perfect and eternal, their divine rights, or heritages in him are inalienable and eternal. Divine rights of perfect spirits include among other things, equal access to the infinite love of the Father, absolute free will, and blissful eternal life. No one agitates or fights to claim his rights in the kingdom of the Father because he is everything to everyone forever. As Jesus Christ says, "There is more than enough room in my Father's home." [John 14:2 (NLT)] He means that there is absolutely no need for anyone to struggle to be comfortably accommodated in the infinite love of the Father within his heavenly domain.

The situation is entirely different in the finite, makeshift world inhabited by corrupted and unstable spirits. Limitations bring about greed, rivalry, tendency to want to dominate others, uprising, and wars. In the realm of imperfection, nothing can be guaranteed. No one can bequeath anyone irrevocable rights in any circumstance in a world that is constantly changing. Moreover, the scripture says that **"the whole world is in the power of the evil one,"** meaning that the situation is entirely hopeless on its own. This should not be difficult to appreciate because, according to the scripture, "when the righteous are in authority, the people rejoice; but when the wicked rule, the people groan." [Prov. 29:2]

The whole world is in the power of Jehovah, the groping god of Genesis, and he is the most unreliable mind in the world. His utterances and actions on earth vividly portray the volatile nature of his personality. He says,

- "I kill and make alive; I wound and I heal; **and there is none that can deliver out of my hand** [in the world]." [Deut. 32:39]
- "I bring both blessing and disaster." [Isa. 45:7]
- "I rule the kingdom of men and give it to whom I will." [Dan. 4:17]
- And "As I have planned, so shall it be, and as I have purposed, so shall it stand [in the world]." [Isa. 14:24]

Statements like these clearly show a highly unreliable person trying to consolidate an ill-earned authority over some less privileged ones that are within his domain. People should, therefore, expect grave physical and spiritual enslavement, oppression, and injustice to be the natural order of the worldly regime. People should expect the world to be a heated arena for terminal battles, not only for the *defense* of the social rights of oppressed human beings, but especially for the *reclamation* of the inalienable spiritual rights of captive human spirits.

As the reader can now imagine, defining the rights of "man" is very complicated indeed, because he is partly a *corrupted* spirit in an alien environment and partly an inconsequential earthly creature invented by external cosmic authority. The Qur'an graphically depicts "man" as partly **freeman** and partly **slave**, and of "whom are several part-owners quarrelling." Indeed, man's spirit emanated from the Father, while man's earthen body and programmed nature are products of cosmic experimentation as detailed in the primordial blueprint. But Jehovah presently rules the world of humans and holds both man's body and spirit in captivity. Unfortunately, because man's spirit has no guaranteed rights outside the Father's heavenly sphere of positive influence, he is entirely vulnerable. People should examine the issue of human rights with these crucial facts in mind, and without neglecting the central position of Jehovah as the chief principality and *ruler* of the physical and mystical aspects of the present earthly situation.

As we have seen, perfect spirits who maintain their *proper* place in the Father's perfect spiritual kingdom enjoy divine rights or heritages in him that are inalienable and eternal, while the ones that violate the heavenly norm *die* or forfeit all their natural rights. That is what the scripture means when it says, "the soul that sins shall die." Violation of the heavenly norm of love means willfully rejecting the Father's positive guidance and guaranteed divine rights in him. The wages of that for any perfect spirit in heaven is eternal spiritual death in the outer darkness. It also means living without one's guaranteed divine rights in the Father. In other words, a fallen, dead spirit no longer has any guaranteed rights anywhere whatsoever.

All the fallen, dead spirits in the world were in such a vulnerable state *in the beginning*. None of them had any guaranteed rights of their own or over any other. The situation presented a level playing ground to all, which at first called for collective efforts to overcome immediate common handicaps. Thereafter, inherent characteristics of the realm of imperfection gradually took over the thoughts, ambitions, and deeds of the fallen sons of heaven. Concepts and inventions proliferated freely, as is still the case on earth today. Soon, the need to excel in such a state of acute limitations gave rise to rivalry, greed, desire to dominate others, uprising, and wars, as the situation stands today in the world. Soon, *survival of the fittest* became the norm of life outside the natural sphere of the Father's love. It soon became obvious that the realm of imperfection is the realm where *he who pays the piper dictates the tune* completely, and where *the winner takes it all.*

The Genesis creation fable attributes the creation of modern human beings to Jehovah and some faceless entities. Genesis 1:26(NLT) reports that at some point in the *beginning, Elohim* (a group of groping spirits) who were already humans decided to make other human beings in their exact "image and likeness." "Let us make human beings in our image, to be like ourselves," they said to themselves. And they did. The facts should, however, be set straight here. Jehovah and his faceless partners did not *create* human beings from the scratch with the porter's clay as the Genesis fable narrates, but merely upgraded the genetic makeup of aboriginal ape-man that was already existing on planet Earth.

As we already know, various species of organic lifeforms evolve naturally wherever the right conditions exist within the universal space as contained in the primordial blueprint, but the natural process of evolution, which includes random mutations, heritable variation, migration, natural selection, adaptation, gene flow and genetic drift, are all very slow and take a very long time. But being scientifically advanced, it was easier for the gods to readily alter the genetic makeup of our primitive species, just like our genetic scientists and seasoned breeders do today with some domestic animals and plants. Advanced scientific methods ultimately gave the gods power of dominion over the *lower* humans, and they became rulers of the ecosphere. We only need to look at our closest cousins, the chimpanzees, to understand the mental and cosmetic improvements that differentiated us from our natural ape nature. We can fully appreciate the triumph of human nature against this backdrop.

But as we can see, Jehovah was not the kind of super intelligent being that religious people make him out to be. Certainly, he was not the sole inventor of complex human civilization as we know it. Various specialized geneticists working in various fields and playing diverse roles and in collaboration with other scientists contributed to the marked improvement in the genetic aspects of human nature, advances in medicine, agriculture, conservation, and various other fields that brought about improvement in overall human situation. How then did it seem like Jehovah supplanted all his partners to assume the supreme title of "God of the world?"

Well, Moses once sang about Jehovah's preeminence among the gods like this: "Who is like thee, O Jehovah, among the gods? Who is like thee, … **terrible** in glorious deeds, doing wonders?" [Exodus 15:11] So, we know that Jehovah is indeed an aggressive personality. But besides Jehovah's hardline nature as an individual spirit, the dissident gods needed badly to queue behind such a master swindler to impersonate the Father in their unified battle against our heavenly Redeemer. Revelation 17:13-14 confirms that "These [gods] are of one mind and give over their power and authority to [Jehovah] the beast; [so that] they will make war on the Lamb [as a united force]." In any case, Quran 37:164-166 sets the records clear by saying, "There is not [just] one of Us but [each of us] hath his known position. Lo! We, even We are they who set the ranks. Lo! We, even We are they who hymn His [Jehovah's] praise." So, Jehovah is just a sly schemer; and so, he wields a crushing hold on entire humankind. There is nothing divine or *powerful* about that. The power we now ascribe to him is merely a product of the irrational fear of him that his religious hirelings instill in human minds.

All in all, the gods merely utilized their chance advantages to hold *lower* human beings in spiritual captivity. In much the same way, Western civilizations utilized their privileged intellectual advantages to colonize Africans and other less-informed races of the world. Things work that way in the realm of darkness and imperfection. Here, those who know something exploit and keep those who do not know in the dark, the mighty rule over the weak, and the rich enslave the poor. It has everything to do with opportunism and ruthlessness, and absolutely nothing to do with heavenly wisdom or intelligence.

Before we go further, the reader must settle it in his mind that the present world order was not founded on equity, justice, *or equality of people*, as some wishful thinkers say. Jehovah is the central figure here, whether by merit or not is not the issue at all. He is at the very center of the complex definition of human rights. People do not become anything by merit in the realm of imperfection anyway. It is not considered pragmatic.

The two important facts pertaining to the issue of human rights are:

- **A fallen, dead spirit naturally has no guaranteed rights anywhere.** That makes him entirely vulnerable to exploitation. If another fallen, dead spirit manages to outwit and enslave him in any given situation, he becomes his slave. That becomes the eternal *wages* of his sin. No other entity in existence can redeem or alter his fate for good, except if the Sovereign Father chooses to overturn the natural recompense of his spiritual violation and grants him divine amnesty from eternal spiritual death. Only the special grace of the Father can rekindle some of his divine rights in the interim, pending his ultimate resurrection and re-assimilation into the heavenly household—the only place where he can have his full divine heritages and rights restored.
- **A *chattel* slave has no guaranteed rights**, but limited privileges granted by the slaveholder. Jehovah's aggressive demand on captive human beings for *unconditional surrender* to his selfish will is predicated on this singular fact. And one can easily agree that it is within his rights in a world that recognizes and protects the rights and interests of privileged individuals and entities who own slaves.

Under the two conditions—that is, in the absence of the Father's gracious intervention—agitation for the *rights of man* was eternally doomed from the start. Man was a fallen, dead spirit without rights in the first instance; Jehovah outwitted and enslaved him, and therefore, rules his life and his world. Slavery is a natural tenet of the imperfect world. So, the only option open to man was to worship and serve the selfish interest of his master or he would make him suffer. That is what slavery is all about. Ecclesiastes 12:13 simply says, "The end of the matter; all has been heard. Fear Jehovah and keep his commandments; for this is the whole duty of man."

But true disciples of Jesus Christ are no longer under the law of slavery but under the grace of the Father. They are no longer slaves of Jehovah, and so are no longer under any obligation to keep his commandments. Their heavenly Redeemer has given them a brand-new commandment that is centered on love. "**A new commandment** I give to you," he says to them, "that you love one another; even as I have loved you, that you also love one another." [John 13:34] Unsurprisingly, Jehovah still tries to cajole unserious customary Christians with worthless offer of foods, drinks, and fatness of their perishable bodies. "Hearken diligently to me, and eat what is good, and delight yourselves in fatness," he says to them. ... **Behold, my servants [slaves] shall eat, but you [the liberated] shall be hungry**; behold, my servants shall drink, but you shall be thirsty; behold my servants shall rejoice, but you shall be put to shame." [Isaiah 55:2 and 65:13] What a lousy attempt at divine blackmail by the so-called *God Almighty*!

Religious believers set the pace in surrendering unconditionally to the will of Jehovah, their slave master. They worship and dutifully serve his will on earth and would stop at nothing to try to please him even at their own peril. In return, he promises them food, drinks, and other material blessings, which he seldom fulfils—*financial breakthroughs* and *public acclaim*. In fact, Muslims are proud to admit that they are **slaves of Allah**. According to them, "To be *abd Allah*, 'a slave of God [of the world],' is the proudest rank the Muslim can claim." But Prophet Muhammad frankly confessed that he was only cowed by fear. "Lo! I am commanded to worship Allah, making religion pure for Him (only), he said. "And I am commanded to be the first of **those who surrender (unto Him)**. Lo! **if I should disobey my Lord, I fear the doom of a tremendous Day**. [So] Allah I worship, making religion pure for Him (only). ... I only follow that which is inspired in me. Lo! if I disobey my Lord, *I fear* the retribution of an awful Day." [Qur'an 39:11–14; 10:15]

Indeed, Jehovah favors all manners of ruthless evil men who serve his will on earth—religious hirelings and racketeers, ruthless politicians, greedy capitalists, corrupt legal professionals, criminal kingpins, and all other social miscreants. They help him maintain state of controlled social and spiritual insecurity in the system, which forces more and more people to seek religious and occult solutions to their unending predicaments. They systematically persecute and terrorize peace-loving and law-abiding people in society to increase the number of religious loyalists.

Religion, secular government, and underworld regimes are the official arms of the present world order. They all serve the will of Jehovah to sustain the status quo, and in return, he prospers and protects the operatives from aggrieved masses. Religion sustains spiritual oblivion in the minds of believers; secular government at all levels creates and sustains social hardship, while seeming to be working hard to make life easier for the people; and the underworld regime provides the undercurrent of fear and spiritual paralysis necessary to forestall true spiritual advancement. Thieves, armed robbers, hooligans, gangsters, racketeers, prostitutes, and all other social miscreants fall into the same line of duty as pests, bugs, viruses, and the like; they are entirely desirable as *system props and safeguards* spiritual enlightenment.

According to Lao-tzu, the legendary founder of Taoism, a true leader or "*holy man*" of the world should discreetly work toward banishing true wisdom, righteousness, and ingenuity among ordinary human beings, while making the people believe that they are benefiting a hundredfold. "Therefore," he said, "the *holy man* rules [the lives of his devotees] by emptying their hearts (minds) and filling their bellies, weakening their [spiritual] wills, and strengthening their bones, ever striving to make the people knowledgeless and desireless." [Britannica. 1999 Multimedia Edition. CD-ROM]

As we have seen, there would have been no need to resort to the use of religion and all the other complex *system props and safeguards* to try to sustain the worldly regime if there had not been a major external threat to its continued existence. Life on earth would have seemed much *easier and enjoyable* than it is now, and people would not be conscious of being in spiritual bondage. Jehovah and the other gods would have enjoyed eternal lordship over the *lower* humans. Of course, there would not have been any need for the so-called gods to start disguising their humanity in relating with the lower humans on earth. It is obvious, therefore, that the Father eventually intervened on behalf of captive human spirits, as only he has the Sovereign Power to alter the fate of the evil world order.

Jehovah concedes that human beings are suffering in the world now, because they accepted another law that violated the law of divine slavery, and for obvious reasons, he holds Adam and Eve responsible for that. He says in 2 Esdras 7:72 (GNB), "The people of this world used their reason and sinned. ... And that's why they will suffer [that's why I make them suffer] torment." He makes it clear that the gods seek nothing else but the **return** of human beings to the Edenic mode of existence—to their original state of total spiritual oblivion when the gods enjoyed absolute dominion over them. He says, "(But it was said unto them [enlightened humanity]): Flee not, but return to that (existence) which emasculated you and to your [Edenic] dwellings, that ye may be questioned." [Qur'an 21:13] "Return to me and be saved, all the end of the earth! For I am *God*, and there is no other." [Isa. 45:22]

It should be obvious from the above that the situation did not remain as Jehovah and the gods had plotted and hoped it would. The gods had enjoyed absolute dominion over their own dimwitted kinfolk, but sudden advent of the heavenly Christ in Eden altered the situation in favor of captive human spirits. For Jehovah and the gods to be seeking *return* of human beings to the original state of universal harmony that favored them, means that humans are in a better place now. It means that liberated humans have indeed regained a measure of their *inalienable rights* as redeemable lost sons of the Father and are therefore, no longer outright slaves to the earthly system.

The gods are the ones *agitating* and trying to *reclaim* their nullified right of dominion over enlightened human spirits. For this reason, the scripture says, "Jehovah is enraged against all the nations, and furious against all their host, he has doomed them, has given them over for slaughter." Jehovah swore that he would *fight* to re-enslave human spirits, *to reclaim his full rights* as a slaveholder, and to receive worship from all humans at all costs. "By myself I have sworn," he says, "from my mouth has gone forth in righteousness a word that shall not return: **'To me every knee shall bow, every tongue shall confess.'**" [Isa. 34:2; 45:23]

Unfortunately, for Jehovah, captive human spirits are no longer under the full authority of the gods. The Father had graciously intervened on their behalf, and the world would never remain the same again. The heavenly Christ is unshackling the captives and repositioning them for the ultimate spiritual exodus. Regrettably, most humans do not realize that they now have divine immunities and rights over their captors. Usually when a chicken tied at a place for so long is released, it tends to remain there until someone, or something helps it to realize that it has been freed. In the same way, most people still "confess and bow to" Jehovah and earnestly need to be jolted to their senses. *The Final Testaments* is the *divine jolt* given for our present age, and it is saying to genuine seekers of true spiritual resurrection "Awake, O sleeper, and arise from the dead, and Christ shall give you light." [Eph 5:14]

Yes! We were once dead spirits in eternal bondage to the gods of the lawless worldly regime, but the infinite love of our heavenly Father has revived us. Yes! "The recompense for our heavenly transgression was death" for us all, "but the free gift of the Father has re-bequeathed to us some of our lost divine heritages in him." The situation is no longer what it was in Eden; captive human beings now have the divine basis upon which to *reclaim* their *inalienable spiritual rights* that Jehovah and the selfish gods of the world once usurped.

These divine rights include:

- unhindered access to the Father's infinite love for us, and to his present gracious offer of spiritual rebirth
- unhindered access to the special love and guidance of Jesus Christ, our heavenly Shepherd
- unhindered access to heavenly wisdom or spiritual insight
- absolute free will
- absolute spiritual self-expression
- unsullied inner happiness
- ultimate spiritual resurrection

These are some of the *guaranteed rights* that the mission of Jesus Christ makes available to every captive spirit in the world. These are the rights that human beings should *fight to reclaim* from Jehovah and his accomplices. Rights or privileges pertaining exclusively to human nature have become of no serious consequence to truly enlightened individuals as they are largely conditional. Genuine seekers of true spiritual salvation must streamline their understanding of the rights to fight for and the ones that are not worth contesting in this life. They have regained absolute free will in the Father and are now able to make firm and informed choices between *things of the Spirit* and *things of the world*, between walking by the Holy Spirit and continuing to be slaves of the world.

Indeed, it makes no sense that a prisoner who was already discharged and acquitted returns to the prison cafeteria to struggle for his own portion of porridge. Neither is it sensible that someone carrying an elephant game on his head should be stooping to also pick up a cricket. There is a need to abstain from the things of the world, as much as possible. A person running away from a grave danger should not linger, as someone running toward the finish line to receive a medal of honor does not meander. It would have been foolish if the proverbial prodigal son had waited to contest his unjust treatment in the hands of the ruthless pig farmer after he had figured out that the best solution to his self-affliction was to return home to his loving father.

Jesus Christ assures his true disciples that the world will fight with every arsenal at its disposal to try to *reclaim its right* of dominion over its freed captives. Temptations, injustices, discrimination, and persecutions will increase in the world against people who have found the true way home. Indeed, that should be the surest indication that such people have found the right way. It is impossible for the world to prosper and honor true disciples of the heavenly way. They should therefore not waste their precious time contesting the right to be treated better or equally as friends of the world.

People who find comfort in the *breakthroughs* and *prosperities* of the world are friends of the world. For true disciples of Jesus Christ, the world should be a transit place, not a place to fight to claim any heritage. Their perfect heavenly home is the ultimate destination where they are already sure to "receive the *crown of life,* which the Father has promised to those who love him." [James 1:12] Jesus Christ spoke plainly about these facts to prepare the minds of his true followers against unwarranted despair and against fighting for the wrong cause on earth. Among other things, he counseled his true followers in these words:

- "There will always be temptations to sin, but what sorrow awaits the person who does the tempting! ... Even those closest to you—your parents, brothers, relatives, and friends—will betray you. They will even kill some of you. And everyone will hate you because you are my followers. But not a hair of your head will perish! **By standing firm, you will win your souls.**" [Luke 17:2; 21:16–19 (NLT)]

- "I have said all these to keep you from falling away. They will put you out of the synagogues; indeed, the hour is coming when whoever kills you will think he is offering service to the Father. And they will do this because they have not known the Father, nor me. But I have said these things to you, that when their hour comes you may remember that I told you of them." [John 16:1–4]

- "Truly, truly, I say to you, you will weep and lament [in the world], but the world will rejoice; you will be sorrowful, but your sorrow will turn into joy [in your heavenly home, in the end]." [John 16:20]

- "If the world hates you, remember that it hated me first. The world would love you as one of its own if you belonged to it, **but you are no longer part of the world. I chose you to come out of the world**, so it hates you. ... Since they persecuted me, naturally they will persecute you. And if they had listened to me, they would listen to you. They will do all this to you because of me, for they have rejected the One [the Father] who sent me." [John 15:18, 20–21 (NLT)]

- "God blesses you when people mock you and persecute you and lie about you and say all sorts of evil things against you because you are my followers. **Be happy about it! Be very glad! For a great reward awaits you in heaven.** And remember, the ancient prophets were persecuted in the same way." [Matt. 5:11–12 (NLT)]

- **"Don't let your hearts be troubled [at all]**. Trust in the Father, and trust also in me. There is more than enough room in my Father's home. If this were not so, would I have told you that I am going to prepare a place for you? **When everything is ready, I will come and get you, so that you will always be with me where I am. … I am leaving you with a gift —peace of mind and heart.** And the peace I give is a gift the world cannot give. So don't be troubled or afraid. Remember what I told you: I am going away, but I will come back to you again." [John 14:1–3; 27–28]
- "I have told you all this so **that you may have peace in me**. Here on earth, you will have many trials and sorrows. But take heart, because I have overcome the world." [John 16:33 (NLT)]

These words of perfect love guarantee true eternal life. Every genuine seeker of true spiritual resurrection should appreciate the message that Jesus Christ conveys and begin to view the issue of human rights in its proper perspective. Evidently, the battle for true spiritual salvation is not as easy as conformist ministers of customary Christianity make it out to be. It is hard and terminal, but the scripture asks, "Is anything worth more than your soul?" [Mark 8:37 (NLT)] That is why Jesus Christ tells his true followers to allow him to show them the way. "Come to me, all of you who are weary and carry heavy burdens," he says, "and I will give you rest. Take my yoke upon you. **Let me teach you**, because I am humble and gentle at heart, and you will find rest for your souls. For my yoke is easy to bear, and the burden I give you is light." [Matt. 11:28–30 (NLT)]

Our great consolation is in knowing what our ultimate reward will be. Our heavenly Restore Guide says that in the end, "the righteous will shine like the sun in the kingdom of their Father," and that "they cannot die anymore; because they are equal to angels and are sons of the Father, being sons of the resurrection." [Matt. 13:43; Luke 20:36]

Finally, I need to stress the importance of being very clear about who our actual enemy is. It would be senseless and counterproductive for captives to fight and maim one another while worshipping the same person that incites hatred and disunity amongst them. A thief steals from us because a greater thief has stolen away his good conscience. We will not accomplish anything beneficial by setting him on fire, especially in response to the express wishes of the real thief that inspired him. That *real thief* is our actual enemy.

The slave-prefect who bullies the other slaves is not the actual enemy, but the slaveholder who empowers him to do so. People who hate their fellow human beings do so only because the principal hater of true humanity hates both of them so much that he tries to transmit his wishes through them. Our actual enemies are not the people who hate us for reasons they cannot explain, but the ones who feed on human disunity. Both the parent who hates his child and the child who causes his parent grief are victims of the same circumstance; the sponsor of the circumstance is the culprit. That is why Jesus Christ says that we should forgive, and in fact, pray for our [human] enemies, for *they do not know what they do*. This is the rule of thumb.

For this reason, Jesus Christ counsels, "You have heard that it was said, 'An eye for an eye and a tooth for a tooth.' But I say to you, Do not resist one who is evil. But if anyone strikes you on the right cheek, turn to him the other also; and if anyone would sue you and take your coat, let him have your cloak as well; and if anyone forces you to go one mile, go with him two miles." [Matt. 5:38–41] A certain singer puts it in a different way; he says, "Whatever the situation may be, don't worry, be happy!"

It was a positive omen in the history of humankind's spiritual evolution that human beings eventually reached a point, since the fateful events of Eden, when it really became necessary to found international and regional action groups for the universal declaration, agitation, and protection of the *"rights of man."* It proved that the world never accorded man any guaranteed rights. Indeed, the only person who *fights* for his rights is one who has none, or whose rights have been forcibly usurped by someone else, who is either stronger and repressive or merely better placed. Efforts of some international, regional, and non-governmental activist organizations must be highly commended for the progress made so far in that regard.

The United Nations and its many allied agencies, the Council of Europe, the Organization of American States, the Organization of African Unity [now known as African Union], the International Committee of the Red Cross, Amnesty International, International Commission of Jurists, some Church affiliated action groups, etc., have been outstanding. However, it must be quickly added that their collective achievements still lack the right bite, because they have conspicuously avoided confronting the well-known root of the matter. Every form of agitation or protest for "human rights" ought to be a battle move geared against whoever denies human beings the said rights in the first place. That has not been the case at all. Without accurately identifying and confronting the actual culprit, all these wonderful human agencies for the agitation and protection of human rights are merely shadowboxing.

When the American colonies fought for *political freedom* from Great Britain, for instance, they specifically focused all their energies against King George III and against the British colonial policies. That eventually led to effective revolution and ultimate independence. It would have been totally meaningless and fruitless if they had started fighting among themselves or against some other country instead of Great Britain. Thomas Jefferson, the third president of America and the principal author of the Declaration of Independence that was proclaimed by the thirteen American colonies on July 4, 1776, asserted that his countrymen were a "free people claiming their rights *as derived from the laws of nature* and not as the gift of their Chief Magistrate."

Thomas Jefferson's argument in favor of his people's *natural* rights became increasingly religious, as relations with Great Britain grew increasingly worse. According to him, *"The God who gave us life* gave us liberty at the same time: the hand of force may destroy, but cannot disjoin them." Then he made a personal pledge not to relent in his cause, which read, "I have *sworn upon the altar of God* eternal hostility against every form of tyranny *over the mind of man."* The Declaration itself had poetically stated, "We hold these truths to be self-evident, *that all men are created equal,* that they are *endowed by their Creator* with certain unalienable Rights; that among these are Life, Liberty, and the Pursuit of Happiness."

No doubt, these *religious* statements of solemn political will must have sounded very intelligent, honest, and meaningful at the time, but they contained very serious contradictions. In the first instance, truly *free people* do not fight to claim their *natural right* to freedom. Only captives fight to re-claim their natural freedom. Secondly, if *the God who gave us life* truly gave with it the natural liberty to life, then no amount of human opposition could have been able to destroy it. Furthermore, swearing *"eternal hostility against every form of tyranny over the mind of man"* upon the altar of the same *God* who oversees the entire slavish human situation was born out of either ignorance or extreme hypocrisy. Thomas Jefferson's *"God"* is the principal tyrant over the minds of human beings. He is the actual *King George III* that humanity ought to confront to re-claim not only their *natural* right to freedom, but also their spiritual right to spiritual liberation. In fact, the *"God"* who denied human beings the basic knowledge of good and evil in the beginning did *not* endow them with any rights whatsoever. Finally, it is rather evident that all men are *not* created equal in the world.

Worst of all, the same Jefferson who powerfully proclaimed the *natural equality* of all men, also strongly argued among other adverse points, "that the blacks were inferior in physical beauty ... might be lacking in foresight ... were equal in memory but inferior in reason and imagination to the white race." Hence, in pursuit of his various selfish interests and worldly happiness, he owned and managed estates, which included several thousand acres, and at one time, about 150 slaves. The truth is self-evident, therefore, that by nature, human beings feel the pain only when it hurts them directly. They struggle with their right hand to free themselves from oppression in the hands of those stronger than they are, while at the same time holding others in bondage with their left hand.

The American revolt for political freedom and independence succeeded, not because the agitators were honest or that what they were saying made any sense, but purely because they were able to identify and focus all their revolutionary actions against their exact detractor—King George III of the Great Britain.

Borrowing directly from the pronouncements of the American Revolution, the French National Assembly adopted the Declaration of the Rights of Man and of the Citizen on August 26, 1789, later reaffirmed by the constitution of 1958. According to them, it was sealed *"in the presence and under the auspices of the Supreme Being."* The first article insisted that "men are born and remain free and equal in rights," while the third article held that "the source of all sovereignty lies essentially in the Nation. No corporate body, no individual may exercise any authority that does not expressly emanate from it." Clearly, that was in direct contrast with clause 3 of article 21 of the United Nations' Universal Declaration of Human Rights of December 10, 1948, which stated that *"the will of the people shall be the basis of the authority [or sovereignty] of government [or the Nation]."* Therefore, the French idea that "men are born and remain free and equal in rights" is only in words. The fact that "no individual may exercise any authority that does not expressly emanate from the Nation" is tantamount to saying that though all men are "born free," the Nation remains the authorized usurper of their rights to the actual freedom.

There were other such ostensible *declarations* by various other revolutionary groups, which were associated with the American and French revolutions, and infused with the political philosophy of liberal individualism and economic and social doctrine of *laissez faire* or the practice of letting people do as they wish. The truth is that none of the human rights declarations obtained the consent of *the god who gave us the life* with unguaranteeable rights. They all merely assumed that the so-called *Supreme Being* ought to be in support of whatever they felt was in the best interest of human beings. None of them bothered to understand why the oppressive situation existed in the first place if *the god who gave us life* never intended it to be so. While human beings continued to *declare* their wishes for a better humanity, believing that *Jehovah who rules our worldly life* approved, he dared the activists to try implementing their wonderful declarations. Meanwhile, he openly incited hatred and disunity among people. He expressly approved *tit for tat*, ordained religious antagonism, and instigated conflicts among various tribes and religious sects.

One man who knew the way the world worked was **Adolf Hitler**. Certainly, he obtained the authoritative mandate of *Jehovah who rules the life of humans* to reiterate the actual universal status quo on earth. In fact, the so-called *Supreme Being* of the world literally appeared in the man, Adolf Hitler, to prove to the visionary *freedom claimants* that there were no such things as standard *human rights* and equality of persons in the basic concept and design of human situation. Indeed, equality and inalienability of peoples' rights are unnatural in an imperfect capitalist world order. It is rather natural to have a hierarchy of powers and interests, where only the rights of the mightiest are guaranteed purely on the premise that he takes things by force. In fact, unchecked universal movement for human liberation and equality of persons greatly threatened both the privileged position of the gods and the natural order of worldly regime.

In his *natural* theory of the *Volk,* Hitler made it clear that the *caste system* is the natural law of human relationships on earth—that inequality between races and individuals are a part of an unchangeable *natural* order. Hitler's *principle of the Volk* was a very simple but cryptic introduction of himself as the potentate of human nature and the supreme ruler of the present world order. On the surface, the principle held the natural unit of humankind to be the *Volk*; then the "Aryan race" was the greatest and the only creative race on earth, the only source of human greatness and progress, while the Jews, of whatever educational and social development, are forever fundamentally different from, and contrary to Germans. That was also a cryptic way of spiritually identifying the friends and enemies of the world. To Hitler, Germans represented all proponents of the oppressive world order, while the Jews, as the spiritual descendants of Adam, represented custodians of the latent force of revolt for ultimate spiritual emancipation of captive human spirits from the world.

He then stressed that he stood at the apex of the mysterious universal hierarchy, as the supreme *Fuhrer* or Supreme Leader, Ruler, or God of the Aryan race. As the first among the greatest of the human races, he expected people to deduce that he was the *God* of all human races. Not many people understood that riddle then, and even now.

Hitler's mission was very straightforward; he came to stop the freedom claimants to maintain the worldly status quo. Accordingly, Nazism, which he founded, ultimately became a profoundly counter-revolutionary movement in direct opposition to the positive revolutions of the seventeenth and eighteenth centuries that were geared toward general social changes and the universal improvement of human dignity. According to *Britannica* [1999 Multimedia Edition. CD-ROM.], Nazism's open agenda "rejected rationalism, liberalism and democracy, the rule of law, human rights, and all movements of international cooperation and peace. It stressed instead, instinct, **the subordination of the individual to the state,** and the necessity of blind and unswerving obedience to *leaders appointed from above*. It also stressed the inequality of men and races and the right of the strong to rule the weak. It sought to purge or suppress competing political, religious, and social institutions, and advanced an ethic of hardness [of heart] and ferocity …"

Remarkably, Paul had earlier made the same demand of *unswerving obedience to leaders appointed from above* on his customary Christian followers. It read: "Let every person be subject to the governing authorities. For there is no authority except from *God*, and those that exist have been instituted by *God*. Therefore, he who resists the authorities resists what *God* has appointed, and those who resist will incur judgment. ... One must be subject, not only to avoid *God's* wrath but also for the sake of conscience. For the same reason you also pay taxes, for the authorities [who use the taxes] are ministers of *God*, attending to this very thing." [Rom. 13:1–6] This means that Paul's and Hitler's inspirations came from the same source. And people who understand Paul's basic inspiration know that the "God" he refers to here is not the Father, but *Jehovah who rules the kingdom of men and sets leaders over them.*

With his enigmatic colleagues, Benito Mussolini and Emperor-god Hirohito strategically positioned in Italy and Japan respectively, Hitler openly made nonsense all the great achievements of the pre-war social reformists. By the time he took his mysterious exit at the end of World War II on April 30, 1945, he had already broken down the entire social structure of the world and inaugurated a new era of racism, nationalism, power and war mongering, cold-heartedness among peoples, and greater potentialities for human destruction. In his last will before his departure, he authoritatively reiterated his fundamental interpretation of human situation: "Above all, **I demand** of the nation's leaders and followers scrupulous adherence to the race laws and to ruthless resistance against the world poisoners of all peoples, international Jewry." Hitler's will was **not an appeal** but **a command** on world rulers to firmly resist fellow feeling among the peoples of the world, and especially to resist the new religion of reason being spearheaded by some great Jewish free thinkers.

The United Nations was born as an international organization established by charter on October 24, 1945, in direct reaction to the obvious destructive effects of Hitler's influence on the new world order. It was charged "with the purposes of maintaining international peace and security, developing friendly relations among nations on the principle of equal rights and self-determination, and encouraging international cooperation in solving international economic, social, cultural, and humanitarian problems." [*Britannica*. 1999 Multimedia Edition. CD-ROM.]

The United Nations Commission on Human Rights completed the draft of the **Universal Declaration of Human Rights** in June 1948, and it was adopted, after few changes, by the General Assembly at its Paris session on December 10, 1948, by unanimous vote. Nevertheless, the world would certainly never be the same again with the detrimental legacies of Hitler and Nazism already fully impressed upon world leaders. The actual wordings of the declaration merely represent the comprehensive wishes of the sane world communities, but it still lacks the right bite because there was no specific revolutionary target.

In the treaty that established the United Nations, all members pledged themselves to take joint and separate actions for the achievement of "universal respect for, and observance of, human rights and fundamental freedoms for all *without distinction to race, sex, language, or religion.*" Yet the world has continued to live with those precise setbacks and has never stopped playing host to ruthless military and political "*Hitlers*" who openly trample upon the so-called rights of people without any constructive attempt by the world body to stop them.

The Charter itself is conspicuously general and vague in its human rights clauses and expressly provides that nothing in it "shall authorize the United Nations to intervene in matters which are essentially within the domestic jurisdiction of any state …" Therefore, the United Nations really had no proper standing upon which to insist on human rights safeguards in its member states. In any event, the Universal Declaration is not a treaty or an enforceable legal obligation, but mere public statement of "*a common standard of achievement for all peoples and nations.*"

What it all means is that *human rights* still cannot be guaranteed on earth. As much as I highly commend the selfless efforts of individuals and agencies who have contributed to the *fight* for human dignity, I wish to state some underlying truths of the situation. The little goodness we presently experience in the world is part of the guaranteed provisions contained in the special grace of the Father that presently *preserves* us in our *spiritual quarantine*. Apparent successes of the various activist groups in this regard are practical manifestations of that grace; they were not necessarily the outcome of the militant actions of the people involved.

Infinite love of the Father grants us certain social and material privileges within the world that are necessary for our spiritual well-being and pursuits, which the world cannot contradict, even though it tries. The right to life and necessary sustenance for as long as we must tarry on earth is guaranteed by the Father's grace. The world has no power to kill or starve to death any true disciple of Jesus Christ before his time is up in the world. Therefore, whether we fight for the right to life or not, it is already guaranteed in the special grace of the Father for us. Just as the Jewish religious agents of Jehovah could not put Jesus Christ to death before he had completed his earthly ministry, the repressive forces of the world cannot eliminate any true disciple of his before his time.

Besides, the world presently functions on the universal principle of *yin and yang* or good and evil, meaning that absolute evil situation or circumstance does not exist on earth. This is also due to the interim grace of the Father upon the entire world. Therefore, whether we fight or do not fight for a measure of justice and goodwill to prevail among human beings, it will always be there. The rich will always need the poor, so the rich are under subconscious obligation to care for the poor in some ways. Jehovah knows that his lifetime dreams depend entirely on the lesser human beings, so even if he pretends to be so enraged and in a position to destroy them all, he simply cannot afford to do so. He cannot help but abide by the interim governing principle of good and evil. Naturally, a killer does not want to be killed. If Jehovah decides to become absolute evil to destroy everyone, he will equally destroy himself, and he knows that very well.

It was obvious that Adolf Hitler did not necessarily intend to end the world, but to beat it into harmony with universal principles. Indeed, both the aggressors who unleashed violence on people and the so-called defenders of the world who counteracted with extreme violence on people in World War II were unconsciously fighting for the same cause. They were both products of the same violent world order, responding to inherent fears contained within the imperfect system to safeguard the will of the world. The world is the perfect picture of a house divided against itself.

Ultimately, the will of the Father still prevails in the world at present. Therefore, truly enlightened humans must understand that there is absolutely no need to agitate or fight to get along on earth for the very short time they have left on it.

CHAPTER TWELVE

FINDING THE RIGHT WAY BACK TO OUR HEAVENLY HOME

The proverbial prodigal son knew who he was. He knew his father and his personal attributes very well. He knew exactly where he came from; and when he decided to return home, he knew the right way back. The greatest problem militating against the spiritual salvation of human spirits is that they have long lost knowledge of all this vital information in relation to their own situation. They no longer remember who they were, where they came from, or where they are at present. Worst of all, they no longer remember anything about their true Father and the impeccable nature of his eternal attributes. Hence, like domestic goslings, they readily follow any larger looking predator that pretends to be their parent. Captive human spirits now look up to their captor and archenemy as the only God and Savior in existence. That is the crux of the difficulties involved with humankind's battle for true spiritual salvation.

Normally, a person would look at a map to find out where he is on the surface of the earth. A map can tell a traveler what city he is in and what street he is on in a particular country. Hence, a person who has the right map and a good means of communication would never be lost. He would always reach his desired destination. That is not the case with captive human spirit. He is totally in limbo in the outer darkness where he is further encased in an earthen mortal capsule. Finding his way back home has been particularly difficult because he has neither the right map nor the right contact.

The captive human spirit is presently overshadowed by the human mind, which is programmed with the wrong map of eternal abode that leads directly to an earthbound predator. Therefore, for captive human spirits to stand any real chance of finding their way back home, they must be divinely **re-awakened,** and **re-directed**. First, they must be helped to discover who they really are, where they came from, and where they are at present relative to their true heavenly abode. Secondly, and most importantly, they must be helped to remember and contrast the perfect attributes of their true Father in heaven with the inconsistent character of the imposter they presently call *God Almighty* on planet Earth. Only then will they be able to appreciate the only possible way back to their proper heavenly abode.

For a person to understand who he is, it helps to have someone who can show him who he looks like. Captive human spirits are lost sons of the Father. They are prodigal spirits. All the spirits in the universe are fallen, lost sons of the Father. All are prodigal spirits. Jehovah and the so-called ruling gods of the world have further made themselves *irredeemable*, while captive human spirits are technically *disadvantaged*. The former are obstinate, while the latter are in an utter state of ignorance. What this means is that with special divine assistance, oppressed human spirits stand a better chance of appreciating the special love of the Father that manifests in his living Son, Jesus Christ, which grants them outright resurrection from waywardness. However, they must endeavor to learn all the good lessons from the life experiences of the proverbial prodigal son.

It is important to recall that the greedy and selfish young man willfully abandoned his royal household in search of some strange kinds of sensual pleasure and prosperity. He gambled away the life blessed with true happiness, believing that extraordinary kinds of *good things of life* could be found in the outside world. Before long, however, he squandered all his precious inheritance in pursuance of the riotous life of pleasure and then began to reap the inevitable wages of his grave error of judgment. Frustrated, hungry, and humbled, he searched for some kind of salvation, and hoped for some material *breakthrough and prosperity* within his world of self-affliction. Luckily, for him, *no one gave him anything*. The heartless farmer who took him in to tend his swine used him as a mere chattel slave. So, for him, there was no *breakthrough* in captivity.

His situation worsened by the day, until it dawned on him that there could be no meaningful salvation for him anywhere within the world of his impure dreams. Eventually, the total hopelessness of his situation presented him with a special opportunity to look inward for true salvation. When he remembered the everlasting greatness of his father's love, he repented from the depth of his heart and decided to return home. He did just that without undue difficulties. Because he knew his way home so well, he needed no personal guide or liberator. As the scripture shows, his true salvation was not in any sphere of the distant country, but at home with his ever-loving father.

No doubt, the life of the proverbial prodigal son in the distant country directly mirrors the lives of all the fallen, dead spirits in the alien material universe. They equally sacrificed their heavenly life of absolute bliss as perfect sons of the Father for that of greed, immorality, and total abandon in the outer darkness. In pursuance of their impure passions, they jointly invested their entire divine provisions in an extravagant outburst that was hoped to transform eternal darkness and chaotic matter into a picturesque pleasure paradise.

What they obtained instead was utter disappointment. Their dream universe merely turned out to be a *shatter-home* whose extreme conditions greatly contrasted the lush widespread pleasure garden they had originally expected from the blind venture. What religious people on earth erroneously call an ordered *creation* by *God* and scientists refer to as *the cosmos* or an ordered harmonious, systematic universe, is but a gigantic expanse of sheer chaos, jointly invented by the heavenly dropouts. A system in constant chaotic motion is completely unpredictable, so there is nothing *orderly* about the universe. Fallen, dead spirits are merely subsisting within the giant expanding universe.

In the false serenity of the moonlit sky, human beings standing on the surface of planet Earth usually feel that there is absolute peace in outer space, but it is even far crazier out there than it is in our overpopulated, ramshackle human cities. Outer space is completely tumultuous, with random explosions and eruptions, flickers and flashes that flare up and fade out in a matter of seconds, minutes, or hours; and there are restless vortexes of gases and billions of chunks of rock and metal floating about throughout outer space. What goes on out there can be best likened to everyday traffic situation in Lagos city, Nigeria, where rickety vehicles abound and frustrated, stoned drivers collide and brush one another in a frenzied struggle for the right of way, as they race toward nowhere in particular.

The cataclysmic *big bang* that created the formless universe brought nothing but disappointment to the heavenly dropouts; yet it represented their *joker card* in the prevailing primordial situation. With that initial great disappointment came utter desperation and a subconscious yearning for alternative salvation. At that point in time, the prodigal spirits had the same opportunity, as the proverbial prodigal son had, to have looked inward for genuine spiritual salvation. At least, they all still had clear knowledge of who they were, where they came from, where they were, and why they were in anguish. They still remembered the Father, infiniteness of his love for them, his gracious offer of spiritual rebirth, and the perfect splendor of heavenly existence. So, they had the gracious opportunity to have repented and returned home to their loving Father. Unfortunately, they collectively choose to sink further into spiritual oblivion in the chaotic dark universe.

While the prodigal son learned from his failures and disappointments and made the right choice, the prodigal spirits adamantly continued to scheme and hope for alternative salvation or eventual *breakthrough* and *prosperity* within eternal realm of darkness and spiritual death. With such obstinacy came undue opportunities for individual spirits to proffer self-seeking solutions to common debilitating situations confronting all fallen, dead spirits. Some discreetly nursed ideas that would help them outwit and dominate others in the general search for any kind of salvation within the meaningless universe. After all, the name of the game within the realm of imperfection is "the winner takes it all."

Planet Earth offered the right conditions for the evolution and adaptation of hominines and other species of organic lifeforms. Some enlightened species of hominines seized their undue advantages to scheme eternal enslavement of their less-privileged kith and kin. That was the true beginning of humankind's woes. Besides having their fallen dead spirits trapped within the earthen mortal capsules, they became captives to a more privileged species of ruthless, self-seeking hominines. Thus, human nature signified a second degree of spiritual death for the captive human spirits, and spiritual salvation was bound to become harder from that state.

As I pointed out earlier, the so-called *creation* of the world by Jehovah is a sheer fabrication devised by the colonizing hominines to completely block out entire rich memories of captives human spirits to make it easy for them to be subjugated and dominated forever. It was that singular gambit that effectively rendered human beings spiritually blind and therefore, utterly lost. Jehovah and his homeless accomplices are absolute fraudsters and criminals. The Genesis account of *creation* in the Bible, for instance, says nothing about how the entire expanding universe originated. And certainly, it does not pretend or imply that the so-called creation has anything to do with the eternal and uncreated spiritual kingdom of the Father, which transcends not only the transformed planet Earth and the universe within which it is just like a grain of sand, but also the entire realm of primordial darkness.

Anyone who reads the Genesis account objectively will appreciate the earthbound nature of the so-called *Genesis* creation. He will see clearly the complex wicked ruse executed by the self-seeking principalities and will then appreciate the height of their cruelty and crimes against captive human spirits. Such a person will be in a better position to understand the exact position of the human spirit relative to the true spiritual kingdom of the Father. He will be in a better position to appreciate the need for true spiritual salvation from the twofold darkness of human earthly existence that is unduly dominated by Jehovah and the colonizing principalities. Finally, he will become very clear about the redemptive mission of Jesus Christ in the world, appreciate his selfless love for captive human spirits, and therefore, know why he is the only possible way back to the Father. "I am the way, the truth, and the life. No one can come to the Father except through me," says our heavenly Redeemer. [John 14:6]

The first two verses of the fabricated Genesis account of creation, as contained in The Living Bible, reads: "When God [*Jehovah*] *began* creating the heavens and the earth, the earth was a shapeless, chaotic mass, with the Spirit of God [Jehovah] brooding over the dark vapors." [Gen 1:1-2(TLB)] This account clearly reveals the state of planet Earth that already existed before the said *makeover* by Jehovah. Of course, planet Earth was not the only *shapeless* and *chaotic mass* within the expanding universe before Jehovah's fictitious creation. Neither was it the only biosphere where living organisms existed. Even then, evolution of the planet Earth and the lives on it took billions of years, not six days, as the false Bible narrative says. Empirical scientific evidence proves beyond every reasonable doubt that Genesis creation account is worse than a cock and bull story. Irrespective of the time ratio utilized by *inspired* fabricators of the Bible creation fable to arrive at six days of creation, their claims were utterly spurious.

It is necessary at this point for me to reproduce the day-by-day account of the magical six days of creation, as contained in the Bible. Most religious people have taken the straightforward meaning of the texts for granted. But any honest person reading them now without habitual religious bias can easily appreciate the earthbound nature of the false creation. He will then realize the magnitude of the dangerous lies that so-called Bible scholars and ministers have endlessly propagated just to promote Jehovah as true *God Almighty* in the minds of spiritually blinded human beings. The lies are so powerful and widespread. They dominate and completely enslave human minds, thereby making it hard for them to readily assimilate intuitive spiritual guidance from their true heavenly Father. But Jehovah remains "a murderer from the beginning, ... a liar and the father of lies." [John 8:44]

The so-called creation account goes like this:

- *"When God [Jehovah] began creating the heavens and the earth, the earth was a shapeless, chaotic mass, with the Spirit of God [Jehovah] brooding over the dark vapors." [Gen 1:1-2(TLB)]*

It is obvious from the above that the *shapeless and chaotic Earth*, the overwhelming darkness, or *the dark vapors* that Jehovah's spirit was helplessly *brooding over* were already in existence before the so-called creation. Jehovah was physically present and stranded within the overwhelming darkness, so he could not have been the perfect Divine Spirit "who alone has immortality and dwells in unapproachable light." [1 Tim. 6:16] The verses literally allude to the primordial situation when all the fallen dead spirits were still stranded in absolute darkness, before the big bang and the formation of the stars. In the true *beginning* of our universe, the prodigal spirits of Jehovah and the rest of us were *brooding over* the primordial darkness that overwhelmed us as we were spewed out of the eternal realm of light. The big bang that brought about our expanding universe was not a creation of one single prodigal spirit but the collective outburst of the group of *Elohim*. According to Deut 32:10, Jehovah was just a homeless desert hermit that Abraham encountered "in a desert land ... in a barren and howling waste," dusted up and emboldened to become a *God*. Religious people would later single Jehovah out and make him not only the sole *creator* of the universe, but also a transcendent *God Almighty*.

- **First Day:** *Then God [Jehovah] said, "Let there be light," and there was light. ... Then he separated the light from the darkness. [He] called the light "day" and the darkness "night."*

And evening passed and morning came, marking the first day.
[Gen 1:3–5 (NLT)]

Well, we all know that the artificial light that shines on planet Earth is the sun, and "night" and "day" occur because of axial rotation of the earth in relation to the heliocentric orbit. That Jehovah just said, "*Let there be light*," and the sun appeared, is a blatant lie. Today, with the help of science, we all know what stars are and how they form and die. A star is a big ball of hot glowing gas, made up of mostly hydrogen and helium that give off heat, light, and other kinds of solar energy. Stars are born from swirling clouds of gas and dust in the expanding universe. Gravity pulls the gas and dust together to form a spinning ball. As it spins, it gets bigger and hotter, and the gas and dust get tightly packed. Finally, nuclear fusion begins, and the star starts to shine. The sun is a star, and stars do not form in "one day." In fact, a star the size of the sun requires about 50 million years to form.

In any case, the sun was born about 4.6 billion years ago, long before Jehovah's so-called creation, which is generally estimated at about 6000 to 8000 years ago using the Bible's genealogical records and the Genesis account of creation of the Earth and the universe. Also, the sun is a second-generation star, meaning that it formed from the remnants of earlier generations of stars that had shone and died. In fact, the light of the first stars and galaxies started their journey nearly 13.6 billion years ago and travelled all the way through space to reach Earth even before Jehovah's fictitious sun was born.

It would help if enlightened human beings tried to learn more about the sun from empirical scientific records rather than from fictitious religious belief systems. A star takes millions of years to form, and it dies when its hydrogen fuel runs out. There is nothing religious about that whatsoever. The same fate awaits the earth's sun despite religious peoples' belief that Jehovah made it to be everlasting. The sun cannot shine forever, because it will eventually use up its present stock of hydrogen fuel. It has already used up about 37 percent of its hydrogen fuel, and astronomers estimate that it will completely run out of fuel in about 7 billion years. However, that does not mean that human beings have that long to live on the earth.

- **Second Day:** *Then [Jehovah] said, "Let there be a space between the waters, to separate the waters of the heavens from the waters of the earth." ... [He] called the space "sky." And evening passed and morning came, marking the second day.* [Genesis 1:6–8 (NLT)]

Here again, outer space, which includes the space between Earth and the other planets and satellites within the solar system, was already established before the so-called second-day invocation by Jehovah, and it was entirely determined by the interplay of the sun's gravitational pull on the planetary bodies. The strong gravitational pull of the sun holds Earth and the other planets in their orbits in the solar system. It is entirely false that Jehovah simply called into being the space surrounding Earth in isolation to the natural forces acting within the solar system that was already in existence.

- **Third Day:** *Then [Jehovah] said, "Let the waters beneath the sky flow together into one place, so dry ground may appear." ... [He] called the dry ground "land" and the waters "seas." ... Then [he] said, "Let the land sprout with vegetation—every sort of seed-bearing plant, and trees that grow seed-bearing fruit. These seeds will then produce the kinds of plants and trees from which they came." ... The land produced vegetation—all sorts of seed-bearing plants, and trees with seed-bearing fruit. Their seeds produced plants and trees of the same kind. ... And evening passed and morning came, marking the third day.* [Genesis 1:9–13 (NLT)]

The presence of dry land on planet Earth was determined entirely by the favorable effects of the right distance between the sun and Earth and the intensity of the sun's heat reaching the earth's surface. Excess heat from the sun would melt the polar ice regions of the earth and flood the entire surface. Depletion of the ozone layer that causes overheating of the earth's atmosphere is proof that Jehovah did nothing—and can do nothing—to influence the overall environmental conditions on planet Earth.

Again, the formation of vegetation is the outcome of the natural evolution of organic lifeforms on planet Earth, which of course is still in progress to this day. Just as generations of hominines came and went, some species of animals and vegetation naturally became extinct. Jehovah and his gang of homeless spirits did not start and finish evolution of species on planet Earth on the mysterious third day as religious people believe.

- **Fourth Day:** *Then [Jehovah] said, "Let great lights appear in the sky to separate the day from the night. Let them mark off the seasons, days, and years. Let these lights in the sky shine down on the earth." ... [He] made two great lights, the sun and the moon—the larger one to govern the day, and the smaller one to govern the night. He also made the stars. [He] set these lights in the sky to light the earth, to govern the day and night, and to separate the light from the darkness. ... And evening passed and morning came, marking the fourth day.* [Genesis 1:14–19 (NLT)]

As we have already seen, other stars existed in outer space long before the earth's sun formed. They were not necessarily there to light up the earth, and all the glowing gas balls in the universe put together have not been able to light up the earth and will never be able to light up anywhere else within our present realm of darkness. This is the hard truth. The scripture says explicitly that "This world is a dark place, and its people [all the heavenly dropouts in it] have no light." [2 Esdras 14:20 (GNB)]

- **Fifth Day:** *Then [Jehovah] said, "Let the waters swarm with fish and other life. Let the skies be filled with birds of every kind." So [he] created great sea creatures and every living thing that scurries and swarms in the water, and every sort of bird— each producing offspring of the same kind. ... Then [he] blessed them, saying, "Be fruitful and multiply. Let the fish fill the seas, and let the birds multiply on the earth." And evening passed and morning came, marking the fifth day.* [Genesis 1:20–23 (NLT)]

- **Sixth Day:** *Then [Jehovah] said, "Let the earth produce every sort of animal, each producing offspring of the same kind—livestock, small animals that scurry along the ground, and wild animals." ... [He] made all sorts of wild animals, livestock, and small animals, each able to produce offspring of the same kind. ... Then [he] said, "Let us make human beings in our image, to be like ourselves. They will reign over the fish in the sea, the birds in the sky, the livestock, all the wild animals on the earth, and the small animals that scurry along the ground." So [he] created human beings in his own image. ... Male and female he created them. ... And evening passed and morning came, marking the sixth day.* [Genesis 1:24–31 (NLT)]

Now, "*let us make human beings in our image, to be like ourselves*" and "*male and female he made them*" means that Jehovah and the persons he was speaking to were already mortal human beings themselves. Their fallen spirits had already mutated into *earthmen*. It could not be otherwise. It is very important, therefore, to note that men and women are in the image and likeness of Jehovah, who is the archetype of all men on planet Earth. They are not in the image and likeness of the Father who is Divine Spirit and transcends Jehovah, the transformed planet Earth, and the entire universe.

Prodigal human spirits are the ones made in the image and likeness of the Father. And their proper place is neither in earthen human capsules nor anywhere else within the chaotic universe. The Father sent his perfect Son, Jesus Christ, into the universe not to redeem men and women that are formed in the image and likeness of Jehovah, but to redeem the fallen, lost spirits that emanated from Divine Spirit. These fallen lost spirits include the spirits of Jehovah and his companions who were the first humans on earth. Clear-thinking people can now see why the name Jesus Christ is divinely elevated *above all other names ... in heaven and on earth and under the earth.*

- **Seventh Day:** *On the seventh day [Jehovah] had finished his work of creation, so he rested from all his work. [He] blessed the seventh day and declared it holy, because it was the day when he rested from all his work of creation.* [Genesis 2:2–3 (NLT)]

That Jehovah finished *creating* the earth and heavens in six days and started to rest and enjoy himself on the seventh day clearly portrays the parochial nature of his original mindset. Given the unstable nature of the entire universe, that statement alone proves that Jehovah has been nothing but a daydreamer. How could any reasonable being within the chaotic universe even contemplate the idea of having eternal rest and enjoyment here?

As it were, Jehovah was the *first* human being on earth; he was also its first *rich fool*. This same mindset permeates human communities because every other human being thinks exactly like Jehovah. People who suddenly stumble into great material possessions, for instance, always think to themselves that the time has come for them to *rest* and *enjoy* all that they have acquired. However, they always become disappointed in the end. Obviously, Jehovah has never had a moment's rest since he made that unrealistic statement because true rest is simply impossible in a restless universe.

Besides, Jehovah is a wicked spirit and *there is no peace of mind for the wicked*, as he himself said.

No matter how real a dream may seem to a daydreamer, it always fades away. For Jehovah and all the unrepentant spirits on earth, the life of this world will eventually end in disappointment and eternal grief. The wise ones will seek and find true salvation now that the Father's free offer of eternal spiritual redemption in Jesus Christ still stands.

The so-called six days creation account is merely a simplistic itemization of the major phenomena pertaining to the earth that were readily obvious to the ancient religious storytellers. Jehovah's fictitious creation tale necessarily captures the mindset and high hopes of all the heavenly dropouts who had imagined that their blind cosmic experimentation would have yielded a paradisiacal world of sensual enjoyment in the outer darkness. It all turned out to be a place of mental agonies, and a complex process of physical and spiritual oppression against the less privileged majority by a few ruthless impostors.

That Jehovah said, "let there be this or that" and it appeared is just a cheap religious tactic to make Jehovah seem truly Almighty. It gives the impression of him having positive control over natural elements and of the finality of the so-called creation. But authentic scientific evidence proves beyond every reasonable doubt that Jehovah is grossly shortsighted, inept, and phony. With everything in the universe being in a permanent state of flux, the claim of an ordered and finished creation is simply baseless. Remarkably, the Genesis account gives no empirical explanation for any of the natural phenomena it credited to Jehovah, neither is any of its claims corroborated by scientific facts.

Human religion would later metamorphose the same shortsighted *first* human mutant on planet Earth into *God Almighty* who transcends the entire universe where his stranded spirit has loitered aimlessly in darkness for billions of years. This is the sad effect of the programmed power of illusion over the human minds.

The truth is that Jehovah is as helpless as the most handicapped of human beings. He is not *God Almighty*, but merely an opportunistic enslaver of humans. His position is akin to that of the pig farmer that the prodigal son attached himself with in the parable of the lost son. A rich pig farmer is not necessarily a free man himself. He is just an opportunistic slave driver within the same harsh, *piggish*, earthly situation. Other human beings became Jehovah's chattel slaves simply because they were less opportune. The same situation exists in human communities all over the earth. In any case, survival of the fittest is the general order of the day in the realm of imperfection, among both ordinary humans and the so-called gods.

Captive human spirits sought salvation in the precarious universe and received a disguised life of eternal bondage to life of sin. Thus, human spirits were not as lucky as the proverbial prodigal son who could not find any reprieve, whether real or artificial, for his sorrows and anguish in the land of his self-captivity. Human beings presently live an artificial life of sheer vanity to the overall detriment of their fallen spirits. Meanwhile, sensual enjoyment is only a false program written on the human minds. The Qur'an speaks plainly about the sheer futility of human life as an alternative to outright spiritual rebirth. It says, "Beautified for mankind is love of the joys (that come) from women and offspring, and stored-up heaps of gold and silver, and horses branded (with their marks), and cattle and land. This is comfort of the life of the world. ... **The life of this world is but comfort of illusion.**" [Qur'an 3:14, 185]

The Qur'an further says that *man is in a state of loss* and that time is fast running out for him. It says that hell awaits all the people who spend their valuable time gathering the wealth of the world, thinking that their great wealth will render them immortal. It concludes that the treasures and pleasures of the world are major distractions to peoples' true spiritual pursuits. It says, "Rivalry in worldly increase distracteth you until ye come to the grave. ... Then, on that day, ye will be asked concerning pleasure." [Qur'an 102:1–2] Jesus Christ equally says that *eternal life does not consist in the abundance of a man's possessions*. The greatest obstacle to true spiritual salvation is human nature and the so-called good things of the world. Human beings simply do not know who they are, where they are, or what they are doing.

Ordinarily, the only prodigal son recognized by customary Bible readers is the one who died, repented, and regained his true life—the one Jesus Christ portrayed in the parable of the lost son. He was the perfect example of who the Father and his Son, Jesus Christ, expect every dead and lost spirit in the world to be. He symbolized a **repentant lost son**.

Jesus Christ revealed a second kind of prodigal son in many other parables—**the oblivious and unrepentant one.** In the parables of *the unforgiving debtor*, *the willing and unwilling son*, *the wicked tenants*, *the nonchalant wedding guests*, *the rich man and Lazarus* and *the rich fool*, the Messiah discreetly portrayed the heedless son of perdition who would not recognize the time of his visitation. This second kind of prodigal son reflects the present status of most spirits in the world. He is the example of who the Father and his Son, Jesus Christ, do not want any of us to be. Sadly, most of us have not even recognized this oblivious and unrepentant one, let alone understanding that he represents who we are.

Finally, to be able to find the right way back to the true spiritual kingdom of our ever-loving Father, every fallen spirit in the world must be clear on the following facts:

- **Every spirit in the world is like a dull flickering light bottled up in a dark niche.**
  The Qur'an, in trying to describe Allah as the light of the earth, inadvertently supplies the perfect analogy of the present status of every fallen dead, spirit in the universe. It reads:

  "Allah is the light of the heavens and the earth. *The similitude of his light is as a niche wherein is a lamp. The lamp is in a glass. The glass is as it were a shining star.* (This lamp is) kindled from a Blessed Tree [of Light], an Olive neither of the East nor of the West [i.e., a Tree of Light that is not of world], whose oil would almost glow forth (of itself) though no fire touched it. … (This lamp [light of Allah] is found) in houses which Allah hath allowed to be exalted and that his name shall be remembered therein. Therein [oblivious religious believers] do offer praise to him at morn and evening." [Qur'an 24:35–36]

I guess the facts speak clearly. Allah is just a fallen, dead light mistaken as a shining star and worshiped by human beings whose own lights have been completely overshadowed by human nature.

- **The spirit in man is doubly dead and lost in the earthen human body.**
  Now, if the light of Jehovah or Allah, as the chief of all the fallen dead spirits on earth, is like a flickering lamp in a glass that is in a dark niche, the captive human spirit is like a flickering lamp in earthenware that is in a dark niche. The difference between the two is that the former at least shines as dull light in transparent glassware, while the latter is completely blacked out in opaque earthenware. Both are corrupted lights originally lit from the Blessed Tree of eternal Light in the realm of perfection.

  Some of us may have watched an old Indian voodoo film where a wicked spellbinder reduced his victim into a miniature human being with his magical powers, put him into a bottle, and plugged the lid. Thereafter, he controlled his captive's condition by heating, cooling, shaking, or spinning the bottle to entertain himself and his friends. For as long as the miniaturized human remained trapped inside the lidded bottle, he was entirely under the power of the callous spellbinder. There were only two possibilities of salvation open to the captive. It was either the spellbinder changed his mind and voluntarily reversed his evil spell—which seldom happened—or someone more powerful than the spellbinder came to his rescue.

Such scenario perfectly describes the present state of captive human spirits. The mortal human body represents the lidded bottle; Jehovah is the heartless spellbinder, the so-called gods and religious operatives of the world are his abettors, while Jesus Christ is the superior *Spell Buster* that overcomes him and his entire world. Jesus Christ is the only available Redeemer for captive human spirits.

- **Life of this world is but comfort of illusion.**
Now, let us imagine a scenario where the spellbinder transferred the miniaturized man into a very spacious and beautiful walled garden that was decorated with miniaturized versions of every object of aesthetic and sensual appeal. The spellbinder even added other miniaturized men and women into the beautified walled garden so that they formed a harmonious community, and they had everything they required as a community of little people. With time, the miniaturized people would gradually begin to look up to the spellbinder as *benevolent and merciful*, and they would begin to worship and pray to him as *God*. In their diminished mental state of awareness, they would completely forget everything about their past; how they became who they were, the actual

relationship between them and the spellbinder, and the fact that they were captives in his walled garden.

How then would such people find salvation, especially since the spellbinder was resolute on perpetuating his evil enterprise? How would such people even begin to think of salvation as necessary and urgent, without an external influence jolting them back to their senses? How would they willingly listen to anyone amongst them that suddenly began to speak against the only god they ever knew as spellbound miniatures, and about regaining their true selves? How would they accept that life in their plush environment was but comfort of illusion, and that escaping from the walled garden was their wisest option?

This is the nature of the problem confronting captive human spirits on earth. They need to know that they are not merely mortal human beings as the world has reduced them, but redeemable, fallen spirit beings in an alien milieu. Their proper dwelling place is not in any sphere of the perilous universe, but in the perfect spiritual kingdom of their loving Father. Although planet Earth is vast and sumptuous, although it offers human beings great opportunities for sensual enjoyment, it is still a walled detention camp to the captive human spirits.

Jehovah, the only god ever known to human beings, is nothing but a wicked spellbinder. He is a captor, a cold-hearted slave driver resolute on perpetuating his hold on blindfolded human spirits. Jesus Christ of Nazareth, on the other hand, is the supreme Liberator of captive spirits. Only he has the power and the will to cancel out Jehovah's terminal spell of ignorance and servitude on every willing spirit on earth. Only he can truly set captive human spirits free forever. Yes! *"If the Son sets you free, you are truly free."* [John 8:36]

To be able to make it back to his heavenly home, the captive human spirit must practically retrace his origin. This is nearly impossible without adequate knowledge of his past and present situations. It is not possible without the special help of Jesus Christ who is the heavenly Spell Buster. The following steps are necessary for every captive human spirit:

- He must understand that he is not at home, but in an entirely alien territory; that he is outside his Father's perfect spiritual kingdom.
- He must appreciate therefore that the Father is *not here* in the alien world, i.e., that the world is not within the sphere of the Father's positive influence, hence, the need for him to literally travel back home.
- He must appreciate that he is completely lost and powerless in his present situation, and that he needs the superior help of a truly transcendent power.
- He must be clear on the fact that Jehovah is his captor, and that he would never willingly relinquish his terminal hold on his captives.
- He must understand that no one else in existence can redeem him from his present spiritual quandary but Jesus Christ of Nazareth. Only he has the power, the will, and the Father's divine mandate to perform that mission of love for people in the world.
- He must appreciate that the human body, needs, and conventions are distractions from the spiritual pursuits of his captive spirit. He must, therefore, formulate an entirely new viewpoint toward human religion and long-established human values. He must responsibly struggle against, and gradually overcome,

the false allures of the life of the world. He must literally die to human nature and the world of sensual enjoyment.

- He must persistently try to live the Messiah's new commandment of love. Indeed, trying to love one's friends—as one loves himself—can be hard in an unpredictable world such as this. Trying to love one's enemies is even harder. Yet the Messiah says that it is the only possible route back to true eternal life in the perfect spiritual kingdom of the Father. **Pure and selfless love for all is the name of the hard and narrow way that every fallen, dead spirit in the universe must walk to make it back home.** There is no alternative way whatsoever.

- He must courageously testify the redeeming love of the Father that he has received in Jesus Christ to help other misled individuals.

- Finally, there should be no physical symbolism with the worship of the Father in spirit and truth. ***Water baptism*** is certainly unnecessary for people who discover the great love of the Father in Jesus Christ. Such physical symbolism ended with John the Baptist. And so-called ***Holy Ghost baptism,*** invented by blind mystics within Pauline Christianity, is outright blasphemy against the Holy Spirit of the Father.

In the first instance, a "*Holy* Ghost" does not exist because no ghost can be called holy. Certainly, Holy Ghost does not refer to the Father's Holy Spirit of truth that Jesus Christ promises his true disciples. Secondly, the Father's Holy Spirit does not come into people with signs observable by human senses, as in the case of the so-called *Holy Ghost baptism*. Thirdly, Jesus Christ does not baptize with *fire*, but with the *silent inner glow* that rekindles the dormant spirit in his true disciples. Mark 1:8 is very clear about that. The true testimony of John the Baptist reads: "I [John the Baptist] have baptized you with water; **but he [Jesus Christ] will baptize you with the Holy Spirit**." Period! Jesus Christ will not baptize with so-called *Holy Ghost*, and most certainly not with *fire*. The so-called Church fathers interpolated all that blasphemy in the name of Jehovah who is their god. Of course, Jehovah is a *ghostly* spirit, and he is *the god that answereth with fire*.

CHAPTER THIRTEEN

BATTLE AGAINST THE ODDS

IGNORANCE, FEAR, RELIGION, AND THE GODS

In a very simplistic way, **ignorance** means lack of knowledge. It means that a person does not know what he is supposed to know. It could be because someone denies him the knowledge, or because he himself, for some reason, refuses to acknowledge what he knows. In any case, ignorance is not a natural state. In fact, the scripture says that it is state of deficiency. "It is not good for a man to be without knowledge," says Prov. 19:2. This raises the question; how did human beings turn out to be without knowledge if indeed they were perfect creatures made by the perfect Father?

Knowledge, heavenly wisdom, free will, and willpower are some of the natural endowments of perfect spirits in the perfect heavenly kingdom of the Father. The Father is Infinite Intelligence; all his perfect sons naturally mirror his perfect attributes. As we have seen, however, all the fallen, dead spirits in the world suffer from varying levels of ignorance. They forfeited their guaranteed rights in the Father when they violated the heavenly norm of perfection, and thus became exposed to external manipulation in the realm of darkness and imperfection. Naturally, no one can safeguard or guarantee their divine rights outside the natural sphere of the Father's positive influence, love, and protection, except the Father himself decides to extend divine amnesty to them out of sheer grace.

Jehovah, the self-glorified god of humankind, decreed *ignorance* for Adam and Eve and threatened that they would die if they opted for the knowledge of good and evil. He lied to them, knowing that that would make them aware of the difference between the lost glories of their former spiritual life and their present life of illusion and servitude as humans. He knew that definite knowledge of the difference between perfect heavenly life and the false life of the world would bring about massive revolt for spiritual rebirth among his human slaves. He decreed *"knowledgelessness"* because he knew that that was the only means by which he could effectively dominate the human spirits to fulfill his evil ambitions unopposed. It is obvious, therefore, that Jehovah, the god of Eden, is the principal sustainer of human ignorance.

That Edenic human beings should not eat of the fruit of the tree of knowledge of good and evil was a hypnotic injunction meant for not only Adam and Eve, as some religious people think, but for the entire human race. As far as Jehovah and his accomplices are concerned, the command is still very much in force and is having the projected hypnotic effect even on the most enlightened people of the world. His entire world order was founded on falsehood. Allowing human slaves unhindered access to knowledge of superior heavenly option would mean sealing the total collapse of his ungodly clockwork. His position was and still is explicit in support of human ignorance.

In respect of humankind's moral refinement and spiritual salvation, ignorance means much more than lack of knowledge. It means total *spiritual amnesia*, resulting in total lack of spiritual enlightenment, free will, and willpower. *Spiritual blindness* is the perceivable manifestation of spiritual amnesia. Human nature casts a spell of total spiritual blindness over the fallen, dead spirits in the world.

Spiritual amnesia is the state of total loss of one's memories of perfect spiritual selfhood, brought about by the deliberate hypnotic programs of the primordial blueprint. **Spiritual enlightenment,** on the other hand, is the special wisdom from above that the Father grants to repentant fallen spirits in the world as a matter of divine grace through his heavenly Envoy, Jesus Christ. **Free will** is the rekindled power of choice that every enlightened human being now has to choose to regain eternal life of perfection or to perish eternally in the outer darkness. Free will is the power to determine eternal fate of one's own lost spirit, while **Willpower** is a combination of determination and self-discipline that enables him to express and live by what he already knows, despite the difficulties and dangers involved.

A person who is ignorant of how to drive a car needs only to be taught the skill. Once he acquires the knowledge, he begins to drive. Essentially, no agency exists on earth that has deliberately constituted itself to try to hinder any normal adult from expressing his driving skill. However, the scenario is not that straightforward for someone who desires to attain true spiritual salvation. Knowing what spiritual salvation is and what to do to attain it is only the beginning of a lifelong battle against some ruthless, powerful agencies that are vehemently determined to frustrate the positive efforts of any genuine seeker.

Ignorance or spiritual blindness is a deliberate program of human nature, intended by its inventors as a weapon of dominion over the human spirits. The moment the desperate fallen spirits consented to the binding covenant or the so-called *pre-eternal covenant* with the inventors of organic life experience and willingly donned the earthen garbs of delusion, susceptible human minds automatically formed dark shutters over the human spirits, closing off their memories of past spiritual realities. *Blank* human minds were entirely susceptible to manipulative impulses, while heightened sensory awareness completely suppressed original spiritual consciousness of humans' inner selves.

That ultimately resulted in a state that the scripture alludes to as "*soul sleep*," which is marked by human mutants functioning at an altered level of awareness from the original conscious state of the fallen spirits. Human beings simply became spiritual imbeciles, condemned to respond to the wishes and dictates of mystical manipulators of human minds. Accordingly, Eph. 5:14 beckons on slumbering human spirits, saying, "Awake, O sleeper, rise up from the dead, and Christ will give you light."

People can best understand human ignorance as a state of **spiritual hypnosis**, and Jehovah as the mystical hypnotist. As we all ought to have known by now, human beings are of dual personalities; they possess separate bodies of spiritual and physical experiences. However, with human spirits suffering from total spiritual amnesia, human beings lack spiritual consciousness. They totally lost knowledge of who they were, where they came from, and who their true Father was. In their altered state of awareness, they simply began to see their hypnotist as their alpha and omega and as the only true *God* in existence, in accordance with the hypnotic programs of the human mind.

The techniques used by ordinary hypnotists to induce **hypnosis** share common features with that employed by Jehovah in hypnotizing the human mind. The most important consideration is that the person to be hypnotized must be willing and cooperative and must trust the hypnotist. For successful induction, suitable rapport must first exist between the subject and the hypnotist. A person's responsiveness to hypnosis is greatest when he believes that he can be hypnotized, that the hypnotist is competent and trustworthy, and that the undertaking is safe, appropriate, and in harmony with his own personal wishes. All these conditions were present in the case of the desperate fallen spirits, during their *pre-eternal covenant* with the devious inventors of animal nature.

To begin with, the hypnotist invites the subject to relax in *comfort* and to fix his gaze on a certain object. He continues to suggest, usually in a low, quiet voice, that his relaxation will increase and that his eyes will become tired. Soon the subject's eyes really show signs of fatigue, and the hypnotist suggests that they will close. The subject allows his eyes to close and then begins to show signs of profound relaxation, such as limpness and deep breathing. He has now entered the state of hypnotic trance. The hypnotist then begins with very simple suggestions that the subject will almost inevitably accept, and gradually issues suggestions that demand increasing distortion of the subject's memories or original perceptions. In a profound trance state, a suggestion from the hypnotist can effectively block out the subject's memory more completely, only to restore it by a later suggestion if he so wishes.

With adequate amnesia induced during the trance state, the subject will not be aware of the actual source of his impulse to perform the instructed act. Furthermore, appropriate suggestions by the hypnotist can induce a remarkably wide range of psychological, sensory, and motor responses from persons who are deeply hypnotized. By acceptance of and response to suggestions, the subject can become deaf, blind, paralyzed, hallucinatory, delusional, amnesic, or oblivious to pain and personal discomfort. He can display various behavioral responses that he regards as reasonable or desirable in the given situation that the hypnotist has suggested to him. In other words, a hypnotized person is just a mindless puppet in the hand of the hypnotist. That is what human beings are in the hands of Jehovah.

Although there are degrees of hypnosis, ranging from light to profound trance states, ordinarily, all trance behavior is characterized by simplicity, directness, and a literalness of understanding, action, and emotional response that are suggestive of childhood. The surprising abilities displayed by some hypnotized persons derive partly from the restriction of their attention to the task or situation at hand and their consequent freedom from the critical demands of their true consciousness. All these clearly describe the present state of human beings on earth.

Through the suggestive, mind-bending stories of the Bible and other worldly scriptures, and the protracted, institutionalized religious brainwashing, Jehovah and his religious agents have completely altered humans' memories and awareness of their preexistent spiritual selves, thus making them think of themselves as mere disposable clay sculptures temporarily animated by Jehovah's breath. Human beings now respond in an uncritical, automatic way to direct and indirect commandments of Jehovah, while ignoring all truth-revealing aspects of their environment other than those pointed out to them by him. They see, feel, smell, and perceive sheer illusion as reality in accordance with his suggestions, even though the suggestions might be in apparent contradiction to the truer stimulus that impinge upon their inner conscience. That is how deep human ignorance runs.

Indeed, although Jehovah declares openly that *the life of the world is but comfort of illusion*, his overall impression on the human mind still does not allow human beings to appreciate the true meaning of that. Rather, they feel earnestly compelled to see and pursue the things of the world, as if they were of eternal value to their whole being. Even when the Bible clearly says that *it is not good for man to be without knowledge*, and Jehovah himself declared Solomon the wisest man on earth for asking for knowledge rather than perishable worldly riches, the overriding impression upon the human mind still holds that Adam sinned because he acquired knowledge. Furthermore, people fight and kill one another—and sometimes they even kill themselves—in the name of the same god whose purported ten topmost commandments say, *"thou shall not kill."* Obviously, his actual desire, as *a murderer from the beginning*, remains deeply impressed on human minds.

Even though Jehovah expressly tells hypnotized human beings that he is **"god of war,"** they instinctively still believe that he is the Father of the Prince of Peace. And even though he openly tells the whole world that he is responsible for all the evils that befall human beings on earth, people still call him the perfect *God*, rather than the devil that he really is. He admits that he kills, wounds, causes human disasters, poverty, human suffering; that he brings people down to *Sheol*, and these are natural activities of the evil one. He also stresses the fact that he does not change. Yet people call him *"the Beneficent, the Merciful,"* rather than seeing him as the heartless murderer that he truly is. These are symptoms of the most complex kind of induced ignorance.

Human beings are indeed living in a terminal state of hypnotic trance, dutifully helping their archenemy to bring them down to *Sheol*, as he desires. Human beings believe that they see with their eyes, but they are indeed living with very thick spiritual blindfold. The Bible says that human beings are blind at heart. The Qur'an says, "For indeed it is not the [physical] eyes that grow blind, but it is the hearts, which are within the bosoms [of human beings], that grow blind." [Qur'an 22:46]

Anyone who has watched a session of hypnotism can appreciate that it is practically impossible for a deeply hypnotized person to snap out of his state through his own willpower while the hypnotist continues to issue suggestions to the contrary. Only the hypnotist or someone with higher occult powers can restore the hypnotized person to his original consciousness. The same is the case with the human situation. Human beings are entranced and lost forever because Jehovah, their hypnotist, does not intend to restore them to normalcy. He has betrayed their trust, and he is adamant about it.

That is where Jesus Christ comes in. The Father is the Supreme antidote for all evils. He sent us his perfect Son, Jesus Christ, to restore our lost spiritual consciousness and ultimately to guide us unto spiritual resurrection. He is our heavenly *Spell Buster* and our only hope against the heartless perpetuator[s] of the human state of ignorance. He has the power and the will to cancel out this terminal dream life of spiritual bondage permanently for every genuine seeker of spiritual rebirth. To such people, he assures, "I entered this world to render judgment—to give sight to the blind and to show those who think they see that they are blind." [John 9:39 (NLT)]

Fear is also an exclusive program of human nature, working in conjunction with the highly impressionable human mind. The human brain controls human emotions, such as hatred, anger, fear, sorrow, desire, love, and joy. These are the constituents of the emotional makeup of every human being. No human being can eradicate these feelings completely for as long as he lives. Truly enlightened people can only display these emotions in a balanced manner to live balanced human lives on earth. Indeed, an appropriate level of fear preserves life. For instance, every normal human being is afraid of jumping into a raging fire or taking a dive into the deep sea when he knows he cannot swim. This is not the fear that holds human spirits captive. The fear that is completely detrimental to the spiritual salvation of human spirits is the fear associated with religion and its god.

When Jehovah decreed human ignorance for the Edenic human beings, he also added a threat, purely intended to instill fear in the people to ensure compliance. Then, when Adam and Eve overcame both his programmed spell of ignorance and the associated threat with the help of the heavenly Christ, he proceeded to horrify humanity physically to force them to worship and obey him out of fear. He carved out a nation of Israel and used the people as guinea pigs to propagate the fear of him as the foundation of worldly wisdom.

For four hundred years, he tormented and humiliated the helpless population in the land of Egypt and reduced them to such a low level of national self-esteem that they deeply yearned for some kind of divine intervention. Their sorry situation made their minds highly susceptible to external manipulations. Then Jehovah appeared to Moses, and through him wrought unspeakable horror against the Egyptians. Although his unwarranted brutalities against Egypt gave the Israelites assurance of physical deliverance, it ultimately bound their minds in the bondage of fear. Exodus 14:31 says, "And Israel saw the great work [of sheer human tragedy] which Jehovah did against the Egyptians, **and the people feared Jehovah; and they believed in Jehovah and in his servant Moses.**"

He did not stop there. For a whole forty years, he brutally horrified and massacred the Jewish exiles themselves in the dreadful deserts of Sinai, and created so much dread in their minds that the people involuntarily declared him *God* over them. Terribly shaken by the fear of what Jehovah would do to them if they rejected his one-sided covenant administered by Moses, the people answered with one voice, "All that Jehovah has spoken we will do, and we will be obedient." [Exod. 24:7]

A Jewish traditional rendering reads, "**What Jehovah says, we will do—and afterwards we'll try to understand as best as we can.**" That is a clear indication that the Jews were simply overcome by the fear of someone who made their lives miserable. They did not declare Jehovah *God* over them because they believed that he behaved like *God*, but purely because he scared them to death.

Subsequently, all the great prophets and patriarchs of Israel proclaimed his will against their true conscience. Solomon boldly declared in Proverbs 9:10 that "the fear of Jehovah is the beginning of wisdom," and concluded in Ecclesiastes 1:18 and 12:13 that human beings do not need knowledge and heavenly wisdom to please Jehovah, but fear. "For in much wisdom is much vexation," he said, "and he who increases knowledge increases sorrow. ... The end of the matter; all has been heard. **Fear [Jehovah] and keep his commandment;** for this is the whole duty of man." Remarkably, the same Solomon, or another Jew writing in his name, boldly contradicted all that in The Wisdom of Solomon 17:12 saying that "fear is nothing but a giving up of the helps that come from reason; and hope, defeated by this **inward weakness, prefers ignorance** of what causes the torment." In other words, some Jews still managed to discover that *the fear of Jehovah* indeed signifies an inner weakness that abnormally prefers ignorance to heavenly wisdom.

In that critical sense, fear is an inner weakness in unenlightened human beings. It is the irrational apprehension of the unknown. But Jehovah has his own weaknesses and fears. So, people who fear Jehovah are those who do not know him and his incurable weaknesses. According to **Eric Hoffer** (1902–1983), an American philosopher and dockworker, "You can discover what your enemy fears most by observing the means he uses to frighten you." Jehovah plays solely on human ignorance, violent tendencies, and disunity, meaning that the surest weapons against him are heavenly wisdom, human unity, and peaceable coexistence. People who seek and obtain heavenly wisdom will naturally love and live peaceably with their fellow human beings, as Jesus Christ desires for them. Jehovah inevitably cringes before such people.

Fear is a factor of programmed human ignorance and the imperfect world order. Fear is not of the Father; it is not of perfect spirits in his heavenly realm of perfection, and it is not of truly enlightened human beings in the world. We know that the Father is love, and that fear cannot exist where there is perfect love. According to 1 John 4:18, "There is no fear in love, but perfect love casts out fear. For fear has to do with punishment, and he who fears is not perfected in love." Surely, fear cannot exist in the hearts of people who truly love the Father, for "God is love, and all who live in love live in the Father, and the Father lives in them." [1 John 4:16]

The only people still affected by *the fear of Jehovah* are people who have not discovered the Father and his Son, Jesus Christ, whose love drive away all fears. The courage and confidence of people who know the Father are firmly rooted in their knowledge of the unchangeable nature of his love for them.

What Jehovah could not achieve with Adam, he did with his hypnotized descendant, Abram, whom he appropriately renamed Abraham. He laid his foundation of religion of fear on Abraham, which eventually blossomed under the calamitous prophethood of Moses into Judaism, the state religion of Israel. After putting Abraham through ten humiliating tests of blind obedience, he finally declared to him, "Now I know that you **fear** *God*." [Gen. 22:12] He was convinced that Abraham feared him so completely that he would willingly destroy or kill the most precious person in his life, his very special son, Isaac. For obvious reasons, Jehovah subsequently became the "fear of Isaac" as well. The whole nation of Israel eventually lived in the fear of Jehovah and fully experienced the horrors associated with it. Israelites are still cordoned off in the doldrums of that hypnotic life of fear and knowledgelessness, even to this day.

The Jewish religious authorities condemned and crucified Jesus Christ because they were hirelings. They knew that Jesus Christ was indeed the heavenly Messiah and that posed the greatest threat to the false position of Jehovah, their god. They feared the horror that Jehovah would unleash on their entire nation, through the Roman armed forces that he had already positioned for the onslaught, if they failed to help him persecute and run Jesus Christ out of the world. The documented, official submission of the Jewish religious council on the matter was very plain and direct. John 11:47–50 captures their fears vividly: "**What are we to do?** For this man [Jesus] performs many [good] signs. If we let him go on thus, everyone will believe in him [rather than in Jehovah our god], and the Romans will come and destroy both our holy place and our nation."

Then, their high priest concluded, in the spirit of the traditions of their fathers, that it was wiser to destroy the most precious thing in their lives to protect the false position of their endangered god. "You know nothing at all," he said to the council, "you do not understand that it is expedient for you that one man should die for the people, and that the whole nation should not perish." Indeed, Caiaphas, the high priest, spoke the collective fear of the Jewish nation.

Eventually, the Jews infected their teeming, worldwide religious cronies with their traditions of *inner weakness* and *preference of ignorance over knowledge*. The fear of Jehovah ultimately became the official tradition of Pauline Christianity and Islam. In his typical encounter with the Jewish religious authorities, concerning the Messiah's gospel of truth that he purportedly preached, Paul feared so much for his life that he appealed to the Roman Caesar, of all people, for justice, instead of holding firmly to the unchangeable love of the Father and of Jesus Christ that casts out all fears. Remarkably, similar situation confronted Jesus Christ and most of his true disciples before Paul, and they held firmly to the infinite love of the Father. Besides, Jesus Christ particularly told his true disciples to "give to Caesar what belongs to Caesar and give to the Father what belongs to the Father." [Matt. 22:21 (NLT)]

Appealing to Caesar in a matter pertaining exclusively to the gospel of Jesus Christ was Paul's clearest statement that he was indeed antichrist. The blunder was far too direct for true disciples of Jesus Christ to overlook as mere coincidence. Besides, Paul's specific words of defense proved clearly that he was Jehovah's apostle and, therefore, a false apostle of Jesus Christ. In his public hearing before Governor Felix and the Jewish council, he stated plainly, "**But this I admit to you** that according to the Way, which they call a sect, **I worship the *God* of our fathers**, believing everything laid down by the law or written in the prophets. ... [Therefore], I am standing before Caesar's tribunal, **where I ought to be tried**. ... **I appeal to Caesar**." [Acts 24:14; 25:10–11]

Thus, the universal Church of Rome that Paul founded has been nothing but a clandestine outpost of Judaism. Customary Christians equally *worship the god of the Jewish fathers, believing everything laid down by the law and traditions of Moses*. In other words, they are intricately inducted into the Jewish religion of fear—into their religious traditions of *inner weakness* and *preference of ignorance over knowledge*.

Muhammad of Arabia also feared and involuntarily keyed into the same spiritually retrogressive traditions. His graphic account of his call to prophethood by the god of Abraham on that seventeenth night of Ramadan on Mount Hira in 610 showed clearly that he was abducted into the cult of Jehovah against his good conscience. He said that an angel, whom he later identified as the *archangel* Gabriel, appeared to him, and commanded him to recite the words of Jehovah that he had come to put in his mouth. "Recite!" (*iqra!*) He instinctively refused, protesting that he was not a reciter or a soothsayer—"I am not a reciter!" It is on record, at least, that Muhammad did not find Jehovah and his methods godly at first.

The book, *A History of God* (Armstrong 1994), explains what happened after Muhammad refused to recite the words of Jehovah:

> "But, Muhammad said, the angel simply enveloped him in an overpowering embrace, so that he felt as if all the breath was being squeezed from his body. Just as he felt he could bear it no longer, the angel released him and again commanded him to "Recite!" (*iqra!*). **Again, Muhammad refused and again the angel embraced him until he felt he had reached the limits of his endurance.** Finally, at the end of a third terrifying embrace, Muhammad found the first words of a new scripture pouring from his mouth."

Who would have imagined that the same Gabriel purported to have gently announced to Mary that she would be the mother of Jesus Christ, could be the menacing monster who would squeeze Muhammad into unconditional surrender, all in the name of calling him to become a messenger of Jehovah. Here, Gabriel displayed the true nature of Jehovah and all his partners. They are the hooded, ruthless principalities of our world.

An extract from Part I of the Introduction to *The Glorious Qur'an* by Marmaduke Pickthall vividly captures Muhammad's genuine inner struggles against the call of Jehovah, and shows how, in the end, **the fear of Jehovah** landed him and his followers in eternal divine enslavement. It reads:

> "To understand the reason of the Prophet's difference and his extreme distress of mind after the vision of Mt. Hira, it must be remembered that the Hunafa, of whom he had been one, sought true religion in the natural and regarded with distrust the intercourse with spirits of which men "avid of the Unseen," sorcerers and soothsayers and even poets, boasted in those days. Moreover, he was a man of humble and devout intelligence, a lover of quiet and solitude, and the very thought of being chosen out of all mankind to face

mankind, alone, with such Message [of total blind surrender], appalled him at the first. Recognition of the Divine nature of the call he had received involved a change in his whole mental outlook sufficiently disturbing to a sensitive and honest mind, and also the forsaking of his quiet, honored way of life.... [However,] with the continuance of the revelations and the conviction that they bring, he, at length, accepted the tremendous task imposed on him, becoming filled with an enthusiasm of obedience which justified his proudest title of 'The Slave of Allah.'"

The truth was that Muhammad sought the *natural religion of love* with which he hoped to remedy the social injustices of his Qurayshi community but found the religion of terror and fear. He sought the truly loving Father in his innermost self, but the notorious god of sorcerers and *kahins* abducted him. He knew very well that Allah was not who he sought and tried his best to resist him, but he was ultimately subdued and forced to become a "Slave to Allah." Only ignorance and fear of the unknown could make a sane individual see anything dignifying in being turned into a slave—any kind of slave.

In the end, Muhammad also had this to say about the foundation of his conviction and of Islam, a religion of unconditional surrender to the will of Allah:

"I am no new thing among the messengers (of Allah), **nor know I what will be done with me or with you.** I do but follow that which is inspired in me, and I am but a plain warner. ... Lo! *I am commanded* to worship Allah, making religion pure for Him (only). And *I am commanded* to be the first of those who surrender (unto Him). Lo! If I should disobey my Lord, **I fear the doom** of a tremendous Day. [So] Allah I worship, making my religion pure for

Him (only). ... Lo! if I disobey my Lord, **I fear the retribution** of an awful Day. [Qur'an 46:9; 39:11–14; 10:15]

Therefore, Muhammad, like his forefather Abraham, *feared* and then *surrendered*. His teeming followers ignored his express genuine fears and doubts and plunged into the same religion of fear and total blind obedience, as did the Jews and customary Christians. Thus, Islam became a religion of fear of the truth. The menacing Gabriel still holds all Muslims in a terminal bear hug, daring them ever to say no to their oath of divine enslavement to the dreaded one of Israel. According to the Qur'an, "They [Muslims] have an awning of fire above them and beneath them a dais (of fire). With this doth Allah appall his bondmen. O My bondmen, therefore, **fear Me!**" [Qur'an 39:16]

The danger of succumbing to religious fears is that they directly attack the human conscience and then cripple common sense. The great messengers of Jehovah were not the only people humiliated by lack of knowledge and tortured by an intense, imbued, inner fear of the unknown. The life of every religious person on earth today is dominated by all kinds of fears that are directly and indirectly associated with human ignorance and the irritable and unforgiving nature of Jehovah and the principalities. People fear poverty, failures in human endeavors, sickness, fatal accidents, social insecurities created by social miscreants; they fear heartlessness of wicked, evil people, and they fear death. According to **Theodor Adorno** (1903–1969), a German philosopher, sociologist, and musicologist, "Of the world as it exists, one cannot be enough afraid." Yet people who have discovered the perfect love of the Father harbor no such fears.

In the presence of human ignorance, fear of Jehovah and his occult and human accomplices has become almost entirely unavoidable to uninformed minds. This is so because human religions have systematically reduced human beings to thinking of themselves as helpless and inconsequential earthen creatures owned exclusively by the chief god of the world. Religions of the world knowingly and unknowingly market Jehovah as Almighty and the only being who can protect humans from all the things they fear. Thus, they have systematically indoctrinated the entire human race with their programmed traditions of induced *inner weakness* and *preference of ignorance over knowledge*. A British writer, **A. A. Milne** (1882–1956) wrote, "It is hard to be brave ... when you're only a Very Small Animal."

Indeed, human religions have successfully reduced human beings to *Very Small Animals*, simply by manipulating human ignorance. Truly enlightened people know the true position of things. With adequate knowledge of the basic status quo, the most powerless human being on earth can be more powerful than Jehovah and his entire occult and human armies put together. This fact is tried and tested. Which is why the scripture says in James 4:7, "Submit yourselves therefore to the Father. **Resist the devil and he will flee from you**."

Yes! Human beings are not helpless and powerless, as religious people preach; and certainly, Jehovah is not Almighty. The Father is the true Almighty; his loving Son, Jesus Christ, is the invincible powerbase of truly enlightened human beings in the world. People who know Jehovah well know that he lives in greater fears than the average human being does, because he has much more at stake and much more to lose in the event of eventual rebound of fate in the world. And he knows that the table of honor will eventually be righted in the world.

True friends of Jesus Christ do not live in fear; they should not, because he has perfected them in his special love that casts out all fears. The scripture plainly tells us why the Father sent Jesus Christ into in the world. He came to inform and to liberate oppressed human beings from all fears so that he might redeem captive human spirits. The scripture says that he came "to bring Good News to the poor; to proclaim that captives will be released, that the blind will see, that the oppressed will be set free, and that the time of the [Father's] favor has come [on captive human spirits]." [Luke 4:18–19 (NLT)]

Death is the ultimate of all human fears; it is the ultimate of all weapons used by Jehovah and all evil people to hold peace-loving masses in eternal bondage. Adequate knowledge overcomes even death. Jesus Christ came to give us that liberating knowledge. Hence the scripture says, "Because the Father's children are human beings [now]—made of flesh and blood—the Son also became flesh and blood. For only as a human being could he die, and only by dying could he break the power of [Jehovah] the devil, who has the power of death. Only in this way could he **set free all who have lived their lives as slaves to the fear of dying**." [Heb. 2:14–15 (NLT)]

With his physical death, Jesus Christ helped us to understand that physical death is mere illusion and not final. Religious propagandists twist the facts about physical death to create and sustain irrational fear of it in people's minds. Hebrew 9:27(NLT) says that "each person is destined to die once and after that comes judgment" and that is a twisted fact. The death we fear as humans is both inevitable for every mortal being on earth, as well as very important for the spiritual liberation of every captive human spirit. Jesus Christ showed us that the life of the world is a programmed hindrance to spiritual rebirth, and compared the human life to the outer shell of a potent seed that must be shed to yield an abundance of fruits. He said, "Truly, truly, I say to you, unless a grain of wheat **falls into the earth and dies**, it remains alone; but if it dies, it bears much fruit." Then, he added, "He who loves his life [of the world] loses it [anyway], and he who hates his life in this world will keep it [i.e., exchange it] for eternal life." [John 12:24–25]

In fact, Jesus Christ stated plainly that he would have been of little or no help to captive human beings if he had remained in human form longer than necessary. Without his physical death, he would not have been able to recover his full spiritual powers needed to "*break the power of [Jehovah] the devil, who has the power of death ... to set free all who have lived their lives as slaves to the fear of dying.*" He made it clear that he could only begin to draw all men to himself when the Father had lifted him away from the incapacitating human cloak and environment. He said, "Nevertheless, I tell you the truth: it is to your advantage that I go away [i.e., that I die in the flesh], for if I do not go away, the Counselor will not come to you; but if I go, I will send him to you. ... And I, when I am lifted up from the earth, will draw all men to myself." [John 16:7; 12:32]

Two thousand years after his departure from the worldly physical scene, practical human experiences and events in the world prove beyond doubt that Jesus Christ indeed, overcame the world after his physical death.

In the light of this truth, anyone who has fully overcome the fear of death has fully overcome *the power of [Jehovah] the devil, who has the power of death*. Of course, when one overcomes the deadliest weapon of his enemy, he overcomes him indeed. Sadly, most people who call themselves Christians do not understand the power they really have in Jesus Christ over Jehovah and his occult and human cohorts. Where the Messiah said to his true disciples, "Even those closest to you—your parents, brothers, relatives, and friends—will betray you. **They will even kill some of you**. And everyone will hate you because you are my followers," he also added, **"But not a hair of your head will perish!"** [Luke 21:16–18 (NLT)] That means that people who persecute and kill true Christ followers cause absolutely no harm to their spirits.

Jesus Christ was literally saying that the death of the world does not remove a single hair of their spiritual personality. He proved that with his own physical death. Of course, he had already assured his true disciples that he held the key to true eternal life. "I am the resurrection and the life," he assured. "Anyone who believes in me will live, even after dying." [John 11:25 (NLT)] Therefore, true disciples of Jesus Christ have no business with fear of Jehovah, or fear of his deadliest weapon of oppression. "Don't be afraid of those who want to kill your body," he says to them; "**they cannot touch your soul**." [Matt. 10:28 (NLT)]

That brings me to the actual role of **religion** and religious authorities. Religion is an exclusive institution of the world, founded entirely by Jehovah and the ruthless principalities to propagate their evil agenda on earth. Religious authorities on earth are defenders of the oppressive world order. They are the direct mouthpieces and brutal muscles of the ducking gods whom the presence of Jesus Christ has driven deeper into darkness. Like hardened slave prefects, religious authorities of the world are sometimes far more heartless than the ruthless gods themselves. As **Lin Yutang** (1895–1976), a Chinese-born writer and philologist said, "Few men who have liberated themselves from the fear of *God* and the fear of death are yet able to liberate themselves from the fear of man."

The history of Jewish brutality and massacres in the name of Jehovah, of peoples who had done them no wrong, is well recorded in the Bible. The so-called *battles of Jehovah* executed by the Israelites were calculated hostility against defenseless communities of people. Atrocities of the Roman Catholic Church of Jehovah are also very fresh in human history. They tortured and maimed peace-loving people; they persecuted, burned, and stoned to death true friends of Jesus Christ; and they extorted means of livelihood from defenseless masses with impunity, all in the name of Jehovah. Yet, as the sane world mourned the brutal excesses of the Crusaders and the Inquisition, Jehovah declared the head of his killing Church *infallible*, just as he had declared Abraham *righteous* for showing willingness to slaughter an innocent child in cold blood in his name.

The spread of Islam was also calamitous for people who did not share the slavish convictions of the extremists. They called their sheer brutality against defenseless peoples "*holy wars*," and it sounded right in their ears, just because they fought in the name of Allah. Likewise, Jehovah granted Muhammad *infallibility* to support his atrocious mission against peace-loving humanity. Thus, the Qur'an portrays Muhammad as a person who made mistakes, but who never sinned against Allah.

Collectively, religions of the world are anti-humanity, for never in the history of humankind has violence been so decisively committed against defenseless people except in the name of human religions and their gods. Religious authorities of the world are hired emissaries of the chief hater of peace-loving humanity. Their mandate is three-fold: to systematically sustain human ignorance, to permanently destabilize humanity by occasionally fueling religious intolerance and violence among peoples, and to instill and sustain the fear of Jehovah in peoples' minds. Their working manuals are the so-called *Holy Books* that were personally inspired by Jehovah and his companions. As it were, the Bible, the Qur'an, and all other religious books of the world are nothing but books of hypnotic codes. Religious hirelings administer these codes to keep humankind permanently hypnotized. They tirelessly preach and dramatize the mind-bending precepts to the point that, the more people hear, the less they understand.

Having said all that, the religious authorities of the world are indeed the most ignorant of all captive human beings on earth. They are much like senseless mercenaries who sacrifice their own lives to protect the lives of other people for monetary rewards that they may never be alive to enjoy. They are subsisting in the most profound level of hypnotic trance. Their own state of ignorance is double-fold, and their own fears almost insurmountable. They survive by faking knowledge and bravery, and by merely pretending to feel secure in the service of some deranged deities. Of course, Muhammad did not hide his total state of loss as an abducted messenger of Allah. "I am no new thing among the messengers (of Allah)," he confessed, "**nor know I what will be done with me or with you.** I do but follow that which is inspired in me." [Qur'an 46:9]

In fact, Jehovah makes it clear to his religious headmen or overseers that they are nothing but his *favored slaves*; and with their full consent, he uses them as such. Thus, he used and discarded all the great prophets of Israel at will. Naturally, a slave does not know what his master does: "They cannot [even] listen to the Highest Chiefs for they are [equally] pelted from every side." [Qur'an 37:8] People who look up to these cataleptic *slaves of god of Eden* for true spiritual guidance are as eternally doomed as they are. For according to Wisdom of Solomon 17:8, "Those who promised to drive off the fears and disorders of a sick soul were sick themselves with ridiculous fear."

Finally, **the principalities rule the world**. They fashioned out the present world order, and they are in total control of the proceedings here. They hold fallen human spirits in a hypnotic trance to extort worship from them. They are terminally opposed to the spiritual salvation of human spirits; hence, they fight with every weapon at their disposal to sustain the status quo. The most effective of such weapons of eternal dominion over humankind is human religion. The Father did not invent the world for Jehovah and his partners to dominate, and certainly, Jesus Christ is not one of the ruling principalities. As the Bible plainly says, "the whole world is in the power of the evil one." [1 John 5:19]

Genuine seekers of true spiritual salvation must first be very clear on these facts. They must seek knowledge and fortify themselves with heavenly wisdom. Then, they must systematically exorcise human ignorance and fears, both in themselves and in others. Finally, they must firmly stand up against organized religions, their advocates, and their gods, by allowing Jesus Christ to be at the helm of their divine projects.

THE BODY STEALERS

Besides the built-in aspect of humans' enmity against their own spirits, demonic activities of sneaky evil spirits, whom I call "*body stealers*," further compound the human dilemma. The human body serves as a topcoat for the human spirit, and in normal circumstances, one human body is just right for one human spirit. When more than one spirit resides within one human body, the problem of mixed personality arises, which can result in insanity depending on the number and characters of the invading spirits. While every *normal* human being on earth permanently struggles to control, or at least to contain, the self-destructive passions and desires of human carnality, *insane* people are ones whose entire bodies and mental faculties have been *possessed* by faceless evil spirits who shamelessly hide behind false cloaks and identities.

Usually, when people read from the Bible statements like, "Jehovah is *a man* of war; Jehovah is his name," they assume it is merely allegorical. They cannot imagine that Jehovah is a man, like every ordinary man on earth. Jehovah is, indeed, human. According to the Bible, human beings are made in the *image and likeness* of Jehovah and his faceless accomplices, meaning that he is also a human being. People meet and interact with him in the streets, in offices, in marketplaces, etc., and yet do not notice, because they do not expect him to be as ordinary as every human being on earth. Another reason *uninformed* people might never notice him is that he does not always wear the same body; he could be anybody at any time. Nevertheless, people who know his basic personality and major interests can always know where to expect him to show up. In general, Jehovah is a principal *body stealer*, meaning he can steal and use peoples' bodies with ease.

The same Bible that calls Jehovah a man also says that "he has chosen to dwell in thick darkness." What this means is that Jehovah is a heavily disguised man. He has not only hidden behind the natural pitch darkness of our present situation and behind a thousand and one false names and attributes, claiming to be what he is not, he also ducks behind bodies of helpless individuals whom he temporarily overpowers and uses as mouthpieces. In fact, most of the so-called men of *God*—prophets, messengers, blind mystics, ruthless human rulers, favored slaves of Jehovah, etc.—have been none other than *stolen voices* and effigies of Jehovah.

It became necessary for Jehovah to disguise his public appearances after the heavenly Messiah opened the inner eyes of people, enabling them to distinguish spirits. We all know that he walked around and talked with Adam and Eve in Eden before the sudden advent of the heavenly Christ. It is on record that he also walked, talked, ate, and associated with the humans in the days of

Abraham. Genesis 18:1–2, 8, and 33 set it out clearly that he came to Abraham by the oaks of Mamre as a man with two of his human partners, and they ate the curds, milk, and calf that Sarah prepared and set before them.

For every inhuman, erratic, or queer action by a *normal* person, a faceless entity, god, or demon has temporarily stepped into the physical body of the individual concerned. Naturally, human minds are highly susceptible to external influences, resulting in degrees of involuntary mood swings and various levels of bipolar disorder in people. In fact, humans are usually under the influence of one cause or the other every second of every day on this earth. The food we eat, the things we see and what we hear can easily change who we are at any given time. Most of the time, we are indeed *possessed* and impulsively acting the parts of unseen, *invading* manipulators. We only manage to be ourselves sometimes.

This explains why we suddenly feel dejected, used, and filled with self-pity after certain actions that are not compatible with our true personalities. It shows that in such situations, we were compelled, against our good conscience, to do things we normally would not have done. Prophet Jeremiah alluded to the same situation when he stated: "I know ... that the way of man is not in himself, that it is not in man who walks to direct his steps." [Jer. 10:23]

Thieves, liars, rapists, and murderers, for example, are not *always* thieves, liars, rapists, and murderers. They are different when they can manage to be their real selves. It is only when the invading evil spirit of a particular vice steps into the *habituated* individual's body that he automatically begins to act *possessed*. Therefore, what we have are mostly impulsive or habituated thieves, liars, rapists, murderers, whose lives persistently fluctuate between normality and temporary insanity.

I knew a certain senior citizen in my town. His family provided all his material needs, but somehow he was habitually hooked on petty stealing. Quite unfortunately for him, too, whenever he ventured out to steal, the villagers caught, beat, and publicly disgraced him in the village square. Despite his family's love and generous material incentives to help him reform his life, he seemed terminally condemned to the self-humiliating vice, not because he felt comfortable with himself or with the humiliation and shame his actions caused his kith and kin.

One day, his family members invited him to explain why he was so bent on soiling the family's good name and image, why he had decided to pay them back with public disgrace for their brotherly love toward him. Filled with genuine deep sorrow, the man stood up among his disappointed family members but could not find the right words to make them understand just how lost and helpless he felt. He simply burst into tears and wept so profusely that his family temporarily had to put aside their anger to console him. Nevertheless, when he felt a bit better, they still demanded that he explained to them exactly what the matter with him was.

When he finally spoke, he confessed to them that he was not really a thief, but that something literally took over his entire body and mind on those sad occasions. He said that he never really knew when he left his house, where he went, or what he was stealing and for what; that he only began to regain his senses when he heard many people shouting and felt them beating him up.

There was no doubt that the man seemed to be a unique kind of thief. He did not steal for any reason he could explain. It was obvious that he was not really the one doing the actual stealing since he was never in control of his right senses on those occasions. We have records of similar incidents, even in the civilized Western world, of millionaire kleptomaniacs, who are purely compelled to steal, not because they need to, but because of temporary insanity.

This temporary insanity syndrome, as the most appropriate explanation for certain human vices, is not true only for the *major*, socially disapproved human vices; there is also a demonic influence for every *minor* but harmful human habit or addiction, such as lying, cheating, gambling, smoking, alcoholism, drug abuse, sex mania, fetishism, etc. In that regard, we really are all the same. How did Paul explain his own temporary insanity? He says in Romans 7:19–20, "For I do not do the good I want, but the evil I do not want is what I do. **Now if I do what I do not want, it is no longer I that do it, but sin which dwells within me.**" Here, the *sin which dwells within me* refers to the invading, sinful spirit.

In simple psychiatric terms, every human being on earth is potentially *possessed*, insane, or suffering from varying degrees of *manic-depressive psychosis*, which accounts for the moments of natural *highs and lows* in our everyday lives. A certain *mad*woman in my town, called Anunobi, once expressed the same fact of this life in her own honest way as she wondered why *normal* people were usually indifferent to her expressions. She said, "Haven't the people said that I am mad, just because when I want to say one thing another thing comes to my mouth?" The truth was that Madam Anunobi was only suffering from more recurrent temporary insanity than the so-called *normal* people were. Remarkably, she knew that, but *normal* people around her did not. In this regard, certain people we ordinarily call insane are simply men and women whose feelings or words we do not understand. Otherwise, we would be able to discover the strange moments of sanity within their insanity.

The *stolen prophets* of the Bible, as well as most eccentric geniuses of the world, were people intermittently possessed by some sneaky, faceless gods of the world against their good conscience or volition. They all suffered from severe and recurrent mania and depression, which is evident from their historical works, documented behavioral patterns, and utterances. In other words, every human being on this earth is insane, even while looking sane. So, people are reminded of the importance of permanently guarding their sanity by strengthening their spiritual dominion over their own bodies.

People who walk by the Holy Spirit are naturally in a better position to ward off unwanted body stealers. The Father's Holy Spirit does not invade the human body in such a way that causes madness; he takes up his unique place in a person's conscience, giving stability and purpose to the person's life. This marks the difference between activities of people who truly have the Father's Holy Spirit abiding in them and the ones who are merely possessed by Jehovah's so-called *Holy Ghost*. As Jesus Christ assured, we can know the difference from their fruits.

Ironically, where the Bible reported that prophet Isaiah ran mad during his prophetic career, and that for a whole three years he walked about the streets of Israel, stark naked and barefooted, religious believers say that it was okay because Jehovah told him to do so. Jehovah was equally proud enough to portray himself as the god and master of *mad prophets*: "My servant Isaiah has walked naked and barefooted for three years as a sign and a portent." [Isa. 20:2–3] Yet people seldom imagine what the *common* lunatics in our streets were told or are being told, and by whom. The truth is that only evil spirits cause people to become mad. Jehovah's spirit of prophecy that drove Isaiah mad was evil; it was not the Father's Holy Spirit at all, because madness is not the fruit of perfect spirit. True Christianity involves recognizing and stating obvious facts such as this one without bias.

Of course, we read stories of demoniacs in the Bible. They were men whose bodies and mental faculties had been *stolen* by *homeless* evil spirits, who then used the bodies as recklessly as bandits use stolen cars to foment physical and spiritual disorder both within and without the helpless individuals. This could best be imagined as the case of a wanton criminal forcing himself into an already tight-fitting outer garment of a good citizen, both as a cover and as a tool for carrying out his sinister vocation. This usually results in severe temporary or permanent "body riot" as the legal and illegal occupants of the material cloak struggle to overcome one another.

There are also demoniacs who may seem calm in outlook but are destructive in action. Most seemingly normal people belong to this category. Every *normal* human being on earth becomes a demoniac whenever his spirit or good conscience gives room to the wandering evil spirits who are ever at hand to pounce on any *abandoned personality*, for example, during a sudden outburst of extreme anger. In fact, what we call human temptation is the manipulation of a person's built-in sensory perceptions and weaknesses of the flesh by the homeless gods to distract or lure his spirit temporarily or permanently away from resolute spiritual focus. A distracted spirit or conscience is an "abandoned personality" and a safe den for demonic spirits.

Indeed, Jesus Christ says that temptation is a demonic attack and unavoidable in the world. It is *necessary*, though not approved by the Father, as it keeps the habituated good minds constantly on their toes in a world where sinful living is generally deemed trendy and fashionable. In Luke 17:1 and Matthew 18:7, the Messiah says, "Temptations to sin are sure to come; but ... Woe to the world for temptations to sin! For it is *necessary* that temptations come, **but woe to the man by whom the temptation comes!**" In other words, temptation to sin is not sin, but yielding to it exposes the individual to the manipulative powers of demonic entities who then drive him along to engage in sinful, evil acts. Jesus Christ makes it clear that tempters are silent demoniacs.

While we struggle against the built-in weaknesses of human carnality daily, we must also fight round-the-clock to keep at bay the restless, homeless, unclean spirits who never give up trying to overtake our personality to destroy our chances of eternal spiritual salvation. Jesus Christ particularly spoke on the importance of keeping round-the-clock vigil over one's spirit by watching and praying without ceasing. He explained this by saying, "When the unclean spirit has gone out of a man, he passes through waterless places seeking rest; and finding none he says, 'I will return to my house from which I came.' And when he comes he finds it swept and put in order. Then he goes and brings seven other spirits [helpers] more evil than himself, and they enter and dwell there; and the last state of that man becomes worse than the first." [Luke 11:24–26]

Certainly, this calls for clear understanding. According to Jehovah, "There is no peace for the wicked." This means that the wicked gods will never give up. Neither should those who genuinely seek spiritual salvation give in to them. Salvation is a continuous battle against Jehovah, the sneaky principalities, and their tireless legion of demonic operatives. War is never over, until it is decisively won and lost. So, it pays to understand that Jehovah makes no empty threats. He threatens wrath and vengeance on humankind, and he means every word of it. Isaiah 34:2 assures us that "Jehovah is enraged against all the nations, and furious against all their host, he has doomed them, has given them over for slaughter." We are already seeing and feeling the ravaging effects of Jehovah's bottled-up wrath and merciless attacks against our collective humanity, as he incites large scale senseless wars, infrastructural destruction, and ruthless slaughter of defenseless masses all over the world today.

There is no doubt that the principalities are ruthless and relentless; they are highly mobilized and determined to fight until the last bell. The so-called archangel Gabriel, one of the menacing principalities, has this to say concerning their collective resolve to fight to the death: "We created not the heaven[s] and the earth and all that is between them in play [we mean business!]. If we had wished to find a pastime, we could have found it in our presence—if we ever did." [Qur'an 21:16–17] Of course, they never did; and they can hardly afford to, in their prevailing circumstance. Tyrants never have peace or any time for meaningful pastime; they spend all their time scheming and re-scheming how to perpetuate their oppressive reign. The Qur'an quotes Jehovah affirming that he is ultimate of shrewd schemers. "And they (the disbelievers) schemed, and Allah schemed (against them). And **Allah is the best of schemers**," says Allah. ... "Are they [human beings] then secure from Allah's scheme? ... None deemed himself secure from Allah's scheme save folk that perish. ... Lo! **My scheme is firm**." [Qur'an 3:54; 7:99; 68:45]

It is very strange indeed that religious people do not wonder, sometimes, why the world's "Great Almighty" spends all his time and energy scheming and counter-scheming destruction against human beings. A playwright in Nigeria once wrote, "We are just like pencils in the hand of our Creator," and that is the big problem. If indeed Jehovah is truly our loving Father, should we really be like breakable sticks in his hand or like tender children, loved and admired? The truth is that Jehovah is an impostor. He is our captor. Although mortal human bodies belong to the world, immortal human spirits belong to Divine Spirit. Yet Jehovah is desperately fighting to claim the entire man—both body and spirit—and to return already enlightened humanity to the spiritually emasculated mode of life in his so-called Garden of Eden. He is always scheming and counter-scheming because he is an evil spirit, but he keeps failing because he is fighting against truth and righteousness. True disciples of Jesus Christ will never become pencils in Jehovah's hand.

The only people who are still pencils in Jehovah's hand are people who do not know their spiritual rights, people who still look up to Jehovah as *God Almighty*. Genuine seekers of spiritual rebirth look up to their loving heavenly Father through his loving Son, Jesus Christ. They are not harassed, bullied, or intimidated by anyone; and they do not live in fear, because the Father loves and guides them with tenderness. The Messiah says to his true disciples, "If a man loves me, he will keep my word, and my Father will love him, and we will come to him and make our home with him." [John 14:23] This is the living assurance that true disciples of Jesus Christ have of the Father's perfect shield of love over their lives.

Jehovah's vehement threat of wrath, vengeance, and eternal destruction is not for true friends of Jesus Christ. Surely, I, Ephraim Uchenna Enujekwu Chuku, am not a pencil in the hand of Jehovah. I belong wholly to Jesus Christ and to the Father who love me dearly. Every true disciple of Jesus Christ should be able to make the same firm assertion regarding his personal position in this matter.

The battle for true spiritual rebirth is not for the undecided; it is not a battle for the faint-hearted. What Apostle James said to the earliest disciples of Jesus Christ I say to their twenty-first-century counterparts: "Submit yourselves therefore to the Father. **Resist [Jehovah] the devil and he will flee from you**. Draw near to the Father and he will draw near to you." [James 4:7–8]

To resist the devil effectively, one must first know who the devil is and how he operates. The first step, therefore, is for one to equip himself with knowledge of the true gospel of Jesus Christ. According to the scripture, "Knowledge is power!" Having the right knowledge empowers those who fight the complex battle for true spiritual salvation with divine *courage of rock* and not with fear. The strength of Jehovah lies only in guile and stealth. That is why the scripture counsels knowledge, spiritual vigilance, and courage. 1 Pet. 5:8–9 says, "Be sober, be watchful. Your adversary [Jehovah] the devil prowls around like a roaring lion, seeking someone to devour. **Resist him, firm in your faith**, knowing that the same experience of suffering is required of your brotherhood throughout the world."

The scripture tells us that when Jehovah dethroned Saul, the first king of Israel, for failing to destroy the Amalekites completely as he instructed, he sent into him vile spirits who haunted and tormented him to death. "Now the spirit of Jehovah departed from Saul, and **an evil spirit from Jehovah** tormented him," says 1 Sam. 16:14. This shows that, apart from being a body stealer himself, Jehovah is the master of demonic body stealers. The Qur'an equally confirms the fact that Jehovah and his companions do indeed assign *devils* or devilish spirits to their human enemies to terrorize and intimidate them into submitting to their repressive will. "He whose sight is dim to the remembrance of the Beneficent, **we assign unto him a devil** who becometh his comrade," says Gabriel. [Qur'an 43:36]

It was Jehovah—and not the Father—who assigned an evil spirit to harass and keep Paul in check after his Arabian Desert mystical tutorial with Jehovah who personally revealed to him misleading gospel of Jesus Christ. Paul confessed that Jehovah literally bugged him with one of his evil spirit messengers to prevent him from going out of line. "Even though I have received such wonderful revelations from [Jehovah]. So, to keep me from becoming proud, I was **given a thorn in my flesh, a messenger from Satan to torment me** and keep me from becoming proud." [2 Cor. 12:7(NLT)]

Using the appropriate words here, Paul confessed that he was *demon-possessed* throughout his ministry. No honest human being on earth today should be in any doubt that neither the Father nor his Son, Jesus Christ, assigns messengers of Satan to torment true disciples of Jesus Christ. The Father and his Son do not have anything in common with Satan and his demonic messengers. Rather, Satan assigns his own demonic messengers to torment his own followers to keep them under control and to keep them from becoming proud, because he never trusts any of them. This true confession by Paul should also help to prove to his customary Christian followers that his Arabian Desert encounter was not with the Father or with his Son, Jesus Christ. Paul was indeed a full-time apostle of Jehovah, and therefore, a false apostle of Jesus Christ.

For a human being to kill or even contemplate killing another human being is abnormal. No normal human being would knowingly kill another human being unless he is mentally deranged. Therefore, all murderers are suffering from temporary insanity or dementia, which is another name for demon-possession. A sound mind would love and treat his fellow human beings, as he would expect everyone else to treat him. Unfortunately, perfect love does not have a place in the world. In the Father's heavenly kingdom, no one reminds anyone else to love the Father or to love his brother as he loves himself. Perfect love is the lifestyle there; it is the central norm, and because perfect love brings about perfect eternal life, to kill does not even come to mind there.

The situation is the direct opposite in the imperfect world where Jehovah is worshiped and praised as supreme **man of war**. Oppression, hatred, fighting, and killing are natural aspects of the life of the world. As a man of war, Jehovah is a murderer both by nature and by vocation, and he trains his followers to be like him. David, for instance, praised Jehovah for training him to be like him. "Blessed be Jehovah, my rock *who trains my hands for war, and my finger for battle*," he sang. What this means is that Jehovah sends evil spirits into peace-loving people to transform them into murderers. Indeed, no spiritually sound person would take up soldiering as a career. One must be demon-possessed to overlook the grave implications and accept to be a professional murderer under any circumstance.

Jehovah merely pretends to discourage murderers in the Decalogue where it is written, just for the records, "You shall not kill." His actual commandment reads, "Cursed is he who does the work of Jehovah with slackness; **and cursed is he who keeps back his sword from bloodshed.**" [Jer. 48:10] In reality, Jehovah grooms and loves murderers and cannot do without them, because he is a career murderer himself. That was why Jesus Christ reminded the Jews that they were being inspired by Jehovah, the murderer, when they sought for unfounded opportunities to put him to death. "For you are the children of your father the devil," he said to them, "and you love to do the evil things he does. He was a murderer from the beginning. He has always hated the truth because there is no truth in him. When he lies, it is consistent with his character; for he is a liar and the father of lies. … Anyone who belongs to the Father listens gladly to the words of the Father. But you don't listen because you don't belong to the Father." [John 8:44, 47(NLT)]

This background knowledge will help us to understand the basic inspiration of the violent prophets of the so-called Old Testament. Most of them were true prophets of the heavenly way but were *abducted* and infested with Jehovah's evil spirits of violence and then, transformed into impulsive murderers. The man, Abram, was a bona fide son of Adam and a true prophet of the Father's Word of Life. He was a peace-loving person by nature until the murderous Jehovah cunningly *abducted* and systematically transformed him into a heartless person and then, renamed him Abraham. From then on, Jehovah readily compelled him to fight and kill in senseless wars and to lie and cheat his way into material prosperity. Ultimately, he agreed with Jehovah to murder his defenseless little child, Isaac, to prove that he was fully under the power of Jehovah's evil spirits.

No doubt, Jehovah could not have made such an evil demand on Abram in his true disposition, because the Spirit of the Father was fully exalted in him. If Abraham had the Spirit of the Father in him, he would have loved his son as he loved himself. I am sure that he would have thought twice if Jehovah had asked him to kill and roast himself instead. Abraham acted against his true self, against his good conscience, evidently, because he was *demon-possessed*. The same is true of all murderers or intending murderers on the face of the earth.

The *demonized* man, Abraham, became Jehovah's prototype of a good Muslim or *mindless devotee*. There was no doubt that he was deep in hell until he managed, by the special grace of the Father, to regain the "Abram" that Jehovah's evil spirit had displaced in him. Jesus Christ cryptically alluded to Abraham's eventual spiritual turnabout when he said to the Jews, "Your father Abraham rejoiced that he was to see my day; he saw it [eventually] and was glad." [John 8:56]

The spirit of the man, Elijah, was also an abducted prophet of the heavenly way. Jehovah abducted and renamed him Elijah, meaning, "Jehovah is my God." Elijah became a stolen mouthpiece and effigy of Jehovah who used him to fight his final battles of ascendancy over the rest of the ruling principalities, as he tried to unify the wrath of the gods in preparation for the expected physical advent of humankind's heavenly Messiah. Elijah was *possessed* by Jehovah's evil spirits of violence and perforce transformed into a compulsive mass murderer and a "troubler of Israel."

When *Elijah* massacred the 450 prophets of Baal at the brook of Kishon, and when he called down the ravaging fire of the faceless *god of armies* to consume the two groups of fifty soldiers and their captains, it was not he but Jehovah who possessed his body that accomplished his own dirty jobs. The spirit or the essential inner self of the man was never at peace; he constantly struggled for spiritual liberation from demonic possession. However, the scripture says that the hand of Jehovah was far too heavy upon him. After what should have been a victorious outing against the prophets of Baal, and as Queen Jezebel threatened retaliation against his own life, the man, Elijah, felt afraid, dejected, and abandoned, evidently because the invading evil spirits from Jehovah had temporarily stepped aside. Hence, he instinctively had to flee for his dear life.

Thus, the life of the man, Elijah, alternated between extreme highs and lows, corresponding to the times he was *demon-possessed* and the times he was his real self. At one point, he became so dejected that he wished he were dead, and he even mustered the courage and told Jehovah that enough was enough for him. "And he asked that he might die, saying, 'It is enough; now, O Jehovah, take away my life; for I am no better than my fathers.'" [1 Kings 19:4]

Just like Abraham's, the spirit of the man, Elijah, languished deep in hell until he had the privileged opportunity of seeing the day of his true heavenly Redeemer. It was only when he returned to the human sphere as John the Baptist, and under the positive influence of the Messiah's personal presence on earth, that he was able to achieve total liberation of his real self. Suddenly, he was able to condemn evil boldly, even to the point of sacrificing his earthly life. And he ultimately fulfilled his actual prophetic mandate of ushering in the heavenly Messiah on the physical plane.

John's testimony summarized and sealed off all the true messianic prophecies. Finally, he said, "After me comes he who is mightier than I, the thong of whose sandals I am not worthy to stoop down and untie. I have baptized you with water; but he will baptize you with the Holy Spirit." ... "Therefore, this joy of mine is now full. He must increase, but I must decrease." [Mark 1:7–8; John 3:30] Nevertheless, Elijah still paid fully for all his atrocities while in the forced service of Jehovah. For it is the law of nature that "Whoever sheds the blood of man, by man shall his blood be shed." [Genesis 9:6] In the end, Herod the tetrarch had John the Baptist beheaded in cold blood for no good reason. Thus, any man that allows himself to be possessed and used by Jehovah for his evil deeds will always pay the price in the end.

The man, Moses, was another true prophet of the expected Messiah. Jehovah's evil spirit of violence equally abducted and possessed him. He qualified to be enlisted in the service of Jehovah the day he clubbed to death the Egyptian who was fighting with an Israelite. Jehovah made him the typical example of a *bad shepherd*. He was perhaps the most tormented in spirit of all the true prophets of the Old Testament, because, as the greatest direct shepherd of Israel, he was forced to officiate over the gruesome massacre of his own defenseless flock. Redeeming his people from stage-managed bondage to fellow human beings in Egypt, Moses ultimately sold the Jews into eternal spiritual bondage to Jehovah, whose monstrous laws, and ordinances, as summed up in the *tit for tat*, were intended not only to enslave the lost sons of Adam forever, but also the entire human race.

Right from the onset, however, the man, Moses, tried his utmost to disentangle himself from the captivating yoke of Jehovah. He gave many excuses to show why Jehovah should look for someone else to make his hatchet man, "Oh my Lord, I am not eloquent, either heretofore or since thou hast spoken to thy servant; but I am slow of speech and of tongue. ... Oh my lord, send, I pray, some other person [I do not want to work for you]." [Exod. 4:10, 13] However, Moses eventually gave in because he really believed that Jehovah was *God Almighty*.

The scripture also documents the fact that the man, Moses, was never at peace with his real self throughout the traumatic Jewish Exodus. Perhaps, more than all the rest of the stolen prophets of Israel, Moses was the most tormented in his soul. He persistently wished that he were dead rather than continuing to put up with Jehovah's extreme acts of wickedness against a defenseless people, using him as a mere puppet. He even snapped at a point and told Jehovah that he was indeed a cruel deity. "I can't be responsible for all these people by myself; it's too much for me! If you are going to treat me like this, have pity on me and kill me, **so that I won't have to endure your cruelty any longer**," he said to him. [Num. 11:14–15 (GNB)]

Just like all the other *demon-possessed* prophets of Jehovah, Moses struggled with mental and emotional distress in partnership with the foul spirit of Jehovah, but he never discovered the truth in that lifetime. Nevertheless, he too, eventually saw the salvation of his heavenly Redeemer, and was saved. The scripture confirms that at the transfiguration of Jesus Christ. "And he [Jesus Christ] was transfigured before them, and his face shone like the sun, and his garments became white as light. And behold, there appeared to them Moses, and Elijah, talking with him," says Matt. 17:2–3.

The man, Isaiah, was probably the only prophet before John the Baptist who prophesied in some definite ways about the coming of the long-suffering Messiah of humankind. Nonetheless, Jehovah's evil spirits eventually *possessed* and drove him mad. Jehovah's evil spirits interpolated most of Isaiah's prophecies with those of an expected, cryptic King of Zion who would rule directly from Jehovah's fixed throne of power in Zion, create a "new" Jerusalem on earth, and eventually bring total peace all over the earth, by force.

The prophecy of the coming Messiah recorded in Isaiah 9:6–7, for instance, was a sheer mishmash of truth and falsehood, a near perfect trick on the mentality of people who might not know the true nature of the heavenly Christ. It reads:

> "For to us a child is born, to us a son is given; and the government will be upon his shoulder, and his name will be called **"Wonderful Counselor, Mighty God, Everlasting Father, Prince of Peace**." Of the increase of his government and of peace there will be no end, **upon the throne of David**, and over his kingdom, to establish it, and to uphold it with justice and with righteousness from this time forth and for evermore. **The zeal of Jehovah of hosts will do this**." [Isaiah 9:6–7]

There is no doubt that the "*Wonderful Counselor, Mighty God, Everlasting Father, Prince of Peace*" were intended to fool people into think that the prophecy was talking about Jesus Christ. But the heavenly Christ was certainly, not coming into the world to sit "upon the throne of David, and over his kingdom, to establish it, and to uphold it." Remarkably, Jehovah, the devil, personally offered to make Jesus Christ king of the whole earthly world when he eventually appeared physically on the earthly stage. "I will give you the glory of these kingdoms and authority over them," the devil said to him. [Luke 4:6(NLT)] But Jesus Christ told him off, and thereby disproved the fake prophecy. He plainly said, "My kingship is not of this world," and "Do you think that I have come to give peace on earth? No, I tell you, but rather division." [John 18:36; Luke 12:51] Moreover, it is definite that *"the zeal of Jehovah of hosts [of occult armies]"* did not and cannot establish the mission of the Prince of Peace in the world, because they are entirely of directly opposed vocations.

People should closely compare the two groups of prophecies recorded in Isaiah, referring to two different Messiahs altogether, to see that he was speaking from under two distinct inspirations. The set that follows (Isaiah 9:2; 42:7; 61:1–2; 53:3–9) refers to the coming of the heavenly Christ:

- "The people who walked in darkness have seen a great light; those who dwelt in a land of deep darkness, on them has light shined."
- "A light to the nations, to open the eyes that are blind, to bring out the prisoners from the dungeon, from the prison [world] those who sit in darkness … To bring good tidings to the afflicted … To bind up the brokenhearted, to proclaim liberty to the captive [of the god of armies], and the opening of the prison to those who are bound [or possessed]; to proclaim the year of the [Father's] favor."
- "He was despised and rejected by men; a man of sorrows, and acquainted with grief; and as one from whom men hide their faces he was despised, and we esteemed him not. Surely, he has borne our griefs and

carried our sorrows; yet we esteemed him stricken, smitten by *God*, and afflicted. But he was wounded for our transgressions, he was bruised for our iniquities; upon him was the chastisement that made us whole, and with his stripes we are healed. ... He was oppressed, and he was afflicted, yet he opened not his mouth; like a lamb that is led to the slaughter, and like a sheep that before its shearers is dumb, so he opened not his mouth. By oppression and judgment he was taken away; and as for his generation, who considered that he was cut off out of the land of the living, stricken for the transgression of my people? And they made his grave with the wicked and with a rich man in his death, although he had done no violence, and there was no deceit in his mouth."

This next set (Isaiah 13:4–5,9; 42:8; 2:2–4; 66:22–23) refers to the end-time appearing of Jehovah himself, as the expected Immanuel (meaning, "Jehovah dwells among the Jews in Zion"):

- "Hark, a tumult on the mountains as of a great multitude! Hark, uproar of kingdoms, of nations gathering together! Jehovah of hosts is mustering a host for battle. They come from a distant land, from the end of the heavens, Jehovah and [the demonic] weapons of his indignation, to destroy the whole earth ... Behold, the day of Jehovah comes, cruel with wrath and fierce anger, to make the earth a desolation."
- "I am Jehovah, that is my name; my glory I give to no other."
- "It shall come to pass in the later days that the mountain of the house of Jehovah shall be

established as the highest of the mountains, and shall be raised above the hills; and all the nations shall flow to it, and many peoples shall come and say: 'Come, let us go to the mountain of Jehovah, to the house of the God of Jacob; that he may teach us his ways and that we may walk in his paths.' For **out of Zion shall go forth the law, and the word of Jehovah from Jerusalem**. He [Jehovah himself] shall judge between the nations, and shall decide for many peoples; and they shall beat their swords into plowshares, and their spears into pruning hooks; nation shall not lift up sword against nation, neither shall they learn war anymore."

- "For as the new heavens and the new earth which I will make shall remain before me, **says Jehovah**; so shall your descendants and your name [Israel] remain. From new moon to new moon, and from sabbath to sabbath, all flesh shall come to worship before me, **says Jehovah**."

It should not be difficult for any sound mind to imagine the emotional turmoil taking place within the man, Isaiah. On the one hand, he delivered the soothing message of hope for the coming heavenly Messiah that would redeem oppressed humankind. On the other hand, he was being forced to deliver the counteracting message of doom for a certain indignant King of Zion who was coming into the world not to save, but to kill, destroy, subdue nations, and forcibly enthrone himself over the entire human race. Such conflicting inspirations of hope and utter doom literally drove Isaiah mad in the end.

Jesus Christ came and proved conclusively that he was the expected "Suffering Redeemer" of captive human spirits. He also made it clear that he was most certainly not the "expected" indignant

King of Zion, as his mission has nothing to do with wars, human destruction, and rulership of the world.

Jehovah, on his part, made it clear that he was the *eternal* King of Zion, and would be the expected *Reformer* and *Defender* of world peace in the later days. He never disguised the fact that he was an alternative messiah to Jesus Christ and that his salvation is entirely earth-bound. Furthermore, he says clearly that he does not share his glory with anyone. Hence, he says that people should return to him and not to Jesus Christ:

> "I am Jehovah, that is my name; **my glory I give to no other**. ... Turn to me and be saved, all the ends of the earth! For I am God, and there is no other. ... There is no other god besides me, a righteous God and a Savior; there is none besides me. ... Hearken to me, you stubborn of heart, you who are far from deliverance: I bring near my deliverance, it is not far off, and my salvation will not tarry; **I will put salvation in Zion, for Israel my glory**. ... For behold, I create new heavens and a new earth; and the former things shall not be remembered or come into mind." [Isa. 42:8; 45:22, 21; 46:12–13; 65:17]

The man, Jeremiah, was also overpowered by Jehovah and held against his own good conscience to prophesy Jehovah's end-time doom's day, rather than spreading the good news of the coming of our heavenly Messiah. Like the man, Moses, Jeremiah never liked to speak for Jehovah right from the onset. He hated and rejected Jehovah in his inner self. The fact that the man, Jeremiah, struggled with extreme crisis of conscience is evident from the whole of his books. Of course, his book of Lamentations is a book of sober reflections—a book of sadness, fears, doubts, helplessness, and explicit disappointment in Jehovah's ulterior motive and methods.

Every time he tried to resist, Jehovah personally threatened, intimidated, and held him under duress to prophesy violence and hopelessness. He confessed, "The word of Jehovah has become for me a reproach and derision all day long. If I say, 'I will not mention him, or speak any more in his name,' there is in my heart as it were a burning fire shut up in my bones, and I am weary with holding it in, and I cannot." He also felt used and betrayed, and he said so clearly: "O Jehovah, thou hast deceived me, and I was deceived; [because] thou art stronger than I, and thou hast prevailed. I have become a laughingstock all the day; every one mocks me. For whenever I speak, I cry out, I shout [like a madman], violence and destruction!" [Jer. 20:7–9]

Even Jehovah's mandate to Jeremiah conveyed the air of arrogance and willful oppression. His words read: "Do not say, 'I am only a youth'; for to all to whom I send you you shall go, and **whatever I command you you shall speak.** ... Behold, I have put my words in your mouth [i.e., I have put my evil spirit in you]. See, I have set you this day over nations and over kingdoms, **to pluck up and to break down, to destroy and to overthrow.**" [Jer. 1:7–10]

"*To pluck up, break down, destroy, and overthrow,*" meant that Jeremiah had become yoked with the devil himself, for only he plucks up, breaks down, destroys, and overthrows. Jeremiah bitterly cursed the day that he was born, which was tantamount to wishing that he was dead rather than called a prophet of Jehovah. He lamented bitterly, saying, "Cursed be the day on which I was born! ... Why did I come forth from the womb to see toil and sorrow, and spend my days in shame?" [Jer. 1:20:14–18] That was exactly how Jeremiah felt. For Jeremiah, being yoked with Jehovah felt like "*toil, sorrow, and shame!*"

The man, Ezekiel, on his part, was yanked off his feet by the evil spirit from Jehovah, pulling at a lock of his head. He reported, "He put forth the form of a hand, and took me by a lock of my head. ... The [evil] spirit lifted me up and took me away, and I went in bitterness in the heat of my spirit, **the hand of Jehovah being strong upon me**." [Ezek. 8:3; 3:14]

Clearly, that was another case of body stealing. Ezekiel was also *demon-possessed*. "*The hand of Jehovah being strong upon me*," clearly confirms the fact that he was overpowered and held under duress. That also explains why he felt so much bitterness and grief in his *real self*. His good conscience could not justify Jehovah's actions through him.

Ezekiel was tactically intimidated and forced to eat words of woes and lamentations that were disguised to taste like honey, but which, however, spelt out the terrible evils that Jehovah had planned against defenseless human beings. Ezekiel could not help wondering how a "God" could conceive such an elaborate evil scheme against a defenseless people if he were not the devil himself. Jehovah's problem, as always, centered entirely on his inordinate obsession with the need to dominate the whole world.

Jehovah's evil spirit compelled him saying, "Son of man, prophesy and say, 'Thus says Jehovah, Say: A sword, a sword is sharpened and also polished, sharpened for slaughter, polished to flash like lightening! ... Wait, Alas for the day! For the day is near, *the day of Jehovah is near*; it will be a day of clouds, a time of doom for the nations. ... As I live, says Jehovah God, Surely with a mighty hand and an outstretched arm, and with wrath poured out *I will be king over you.*" [Ezek. 21:9–10; 30:1–2; 20:33]

Indeed, Ezekiel was made to act out the intended suffering and humiliation of his fellow human beings. He was forced to recognize Jehovah as the undisputed god of the world; but he also became fully convinced that he was neither the true Divine Spirit nor the heavenly Comforter that captive human spirits earnestly expected. Jehovah's express motive and method stood in stark contrast to the gracious message of hope for the oppressed humankind, which was simultaneously being impressed upon his innermost self. Hence, his emotional dilemma remained unabated.

All these prophets, as well as many others not mentioned here, were practical examples of *stolen voices and effigies* of Jehovah. Through them, he wrought calamities against defenseless peoples and made so much noise, alluding to himself as the *"all and all"* in existence, just to confuse the divine revelations or information coming through to the prophets from our truly loving Father regarding the coming of the true Messiah of humankind into the world.

Considering all the troubles that Jehovah went through to try to obliterate knowledge of the coming heavenly Christ, nothing would have been known about Jesus Christ before, during, and after his physical presence in the world if he were not the true Messiah from the Father. To this day, Jehovah and his faceless gang of sneaky banditti are still chasing the wind and doing their utmost to stop captive human beings from knowing about or recognizing the Father's love, the true Christ, and the true nature of his gracious mission of salvation for their lost spirits. To me, Jehovah's kangaroo terror tactics against the *possessed* prophets of the Old Testament only prove beyond reasonable doubt that he was indeed a powerless evil spirit.

Jehovah failed to stop the heavenly Christ during his first advent in Eden, he equally failed to stop the true prophesies of his second coming in human cloak, and he remains a chronic failure to this day. Everything that Jehovah and the principalities feared concerning their inordinate dreams ended up happening with the eventual incarnation of the heavenly Christ, and the victory scoreboard clearly shows the results so far. The heavenly Messiah came in human form in accordance with his promise to Adam and Eve, and the whole world now recognizes that Jesus of Nazareth was indeed the Christ *"to the eternal glory of the Father."*

Meanwhile, Jesus Christ walked the earth spreading the same gospel of knowledge and true life to humankind that he delivered to Adam and Eve in Eden, and the demoniacs could not stop him. He chased Jehovah's powerless *body stealers* out of their human victims. Though the *possessed* men and women had been called demoniacs, some of them were in fact, camouflaging effigies of Jehovah and the principalities themselves in their ill-fated attempts at antagonizing and disrupting the Messiah's ministry. But they still failed woefully. Rather than fighting at the sight of Jesus Christ, they had all fallen prostrate at his feet, shouting and begging for clemency.

The scripture has this to say about the remarkable encounter between Jesus Christ and the fiercest of all the demoniacs who lived among the tombs in Gerasene:

> "No one could bind him any more, even with a chain; for he had often been bound with fetters and chains, but the chains he wrenched apart, and the fetters he broke in pieces; and no one had the strength to subdue him. [However,] when he saw Jesus [the Messiah] from afar, he ran and worshiped him; and crying out with a loud voice, he said, 'What have you to do with me [in my *nether world*], Jesus, son of the Most High *God*? I adjure you by *God*, do not torment me!' For he had said to him, 'Come out of the man, you unclean spirit!' [In fact,] **whenever the unclean spirits beheld him, they fell down before him and cried out**, 'You are the son of *God*.'... [Or] 'What have you to do with us, Jesus of Nazareth? Have you come to destroy us? I know who you are, the Holy One of *God*.'" [Mark 5:2–8; 3:11; 1:24]

Jehovah's newest dilemma today centers on how to curb Christ-consciousness that is rapidly spreading all over the world. Meanwhile, humans' spiritual evolution has already reached such an advanced stage today that a book such as *The Final Testaments* has now been written with totally ineffectual challenge from the repressive forces that be. This proves how acutely limited and powerless Jehovah really is and just how futile his attempts at challenging the divine will of the Father in the world have been for him. Yet Jehovah shamelessly continues his shadowboxing, kicking at empty pots and pans, fomenting social disorder, and instigating wars and ruthless massacres of innocent masses all over the world, instead of mapping out a definite program of direct confrontation with Jesus Christ who is his actual opponent in humankind's battle for spiritual salvation.

In 1648, a twenty-two-year-old Jewish young man, Shabbetai Tzevi, proclaimed himself the "expected Messiah" and earnestly began his cryptic mission of abrogating the Torah or the Law of Moses. Sometimes he deliberately broke the Law of Moses. He would publicly eat forbidden foods, utter the sacred name of Jehovah, and say that he had been inspired to do so by a special revelation. He naturally posed a serious threat to the rabbinical authorities, who were the official custodians of the Torah, both in Europe and in the Middle East. The provoked rabbinate ran him out of his home city of Smyrna, Turkey, in 1656, and he wandered through Greece, Thrace, Palestine, and Egypt for many years and made disciples. He returned to Smyrna in 1665 after being forced out of Jerusalem with the threat of excommunication.

The man, Shabbetai, suffered from *"bipolar disorder"* or manic-depressive psychosis. He personally believed that he was *possessed* by demons and in fact, consulted an exorcist. Yet he mysteriously attracted a mass following from all classes of Jewish societies everywhere, with his movement spreading to Venice, Amsterdam, Hamburg, London, and several other European and North Africa cities. Throughout Jewish history, no messianic movement had ever attracted such massive support. His supporters came from all classes of Jewish society—rich and poor, learned and uneducated—and his detractors were afraid to speak out. Pamphlets and broadsheets advertised his mission in English, Dutch, German, and Italian.

Nathan of Gaza, who had become his personal "Elijah" and forerunner to his messiahship, had prophesied imminent restoration of Israel and world salvation through the bloodless victory of Shabbetai, *riding on a lion with a seven-headed dragon* in his jaws. He cited 1666 as the apocalyptic year of Jehovah.

There were *public processions in his honor* in Poland and Lithuania; and in the Ottoman Empire, prophets wandered through the streets describing visions of him *seated upon a throne*. Ominously, the Jews of Turkey substituted the name of the Sultan in the Sabbath prayers with that of Shabbetai. Consequently, he was arrested on his arrival in Istanbul in January 1666, charged with rebellion, and imprisoned in Gallipoli. A few months later, however, he was transferred and *housed in the comfort of the castle at Abydos*. His followers called the castle Migdal Oz or *the Tower of Strength*. Then Shabbetai began to sign his letters as Jehovah, the God of the Jews—"*I am the Lord your God, Shabbetai Tzevi.*"

Evidently, the world could not piece together the jigsaw to solve the very straightforward puzzle. As we saw in the Gerasene encounter between Jesus Christ and the fierce demoniac living among the tombs, it is never the demoniac that speaks, but the demon or evil spirit that has stolen his body and voice. When Jesus Christ asked his name, the possessed man responded, "My name is Legion; for we are many." *Legion,* therefore, was the collective name by which the evil spirits within the possessed man had identified themselves; it had nothing to do with the actual name of the man himself. There was no doubt that the man, Shabbetai, was a demoniac. Even without being asked, his possessing evil spirit revealed his identity plainly: "*I am Jehovah your God.*"

It was clear that the man, Shabbetai Tzevi, was but another stolen voice and direct epiphany of Jehovah, the name being his personal, pro tem epithet. The signs were so many and so clear:

- Shabbetai Tzevi was widely acclaimed by worldwide Jewry.
- There were public processions in his honor.
- There were visions of him *riding on a lion with the seven-headed dragon in his Jaws*. That was another cryptic way of referring to Jehovah, the *lion of Judah*, as the beastly head of the seven principalities. Revelation 12:3

refers to him as the *"great red dragon, with seven heads ... and seven diadems upon his heads,"* and Revelation 17:13 says, "These are of one mind and give over their power and authority to the beast; [so that] they will make war on [Jesus Christ,] the Lamb."

- There were visions of him seated upon the throne of the world.
- He was housed in the Tower of Strength.
- He was associated with the cryptic year of 1666.
- He officially signed his name as Jehovah—"**I am Jehovah your God, Shabbetai Tzevi.**"

That was the closest Jehovah really came to helping the Jews realize that he, and not Jesus Christ, is their personal messiah.

When in September 1666, Jehovah/Shabbetai was brought before the Sultan in Edirne for his *cryptic trial*, he finally disclosed his current mission. He had actually appeared to lead the Jews and their worldwide religious surrogates into joining forces with Islam, his newest religion of *unconditional surrender*. As a formality, the Sultan gave him the choice between conversion to Islam and death. He chose Islam, and he was immediately released. Thus, Jehovah/Shabbetai practically acted the position of *Apostate Messiah* of the Jews, just to show them the example. He was simply telling the Jews to accept his new religion of Islam or face his wrath.

Of course, he had told them in advance that he would be moving over to a certain "new people." Hence, he appeared to abrogate Judaism officially, while carrying his temporarily disfranchised Jews along. Jehovah's prophecy through Ezra read: "Announce to my new people that I will give them the kingdom of Jerusalem, which I had planned to give to Israel." [2 Esdras 2:10 (GNB)] Evidently, he knew well in advance that the Jews would never readily go along with him on that one. But he made his point clearly as the *Apostate Messiah* of the Jews. Whether the Jews are willing to admit it openly or not, Judaism and Islam are one; Jehovah is god to both. Jehovah asked

Muhammad to say to the Jews (or the People of the Book), "We believe in that which hath been revealed unto us and revealed unto you; our God and your God is one, and unto him [Jehovah] we surrender. [Qur'an 29:46]

Following the Jewish rebellion against Rome that began in AD 66, the Roman forces under Titus Flavius Vespasianus besieged and destroyed the city of Jerusalem in AD 70. He virtually reduced the Jewish Temple of Jerusalem to ashes to pave the way for the "official" transfer of the Temple Mount to Jehovah's "new chosen victims," the Muslims. Accordingly, the Muslim caliph, Umar I, entered Jerusalem in AD 638, and officially claimed the custodianship of the Temple Mount for the Muslims, as prophesied. Muslims call it *al-Haram ash-Sharif*—"The Noble Holy Place." Both Arab and Jewish sources confirm that after the symbolic conquest of Jerusalem by the Muslims, the Jews themselves led the conquerors to the site of the Holy Rock and the Temple yard, and actually helped to clear away the debris.

The *Dome of the Rock* was subsequently built on the Temple Mount between AD 685 and AD 691 by the 10th Muslim caliph Abd al-Malik ibn Marwan, not as a mosque for public worship, but purely as a *mashhad*—a religious monument for pilgrims. It was, most especially, a symbol of the "new" Islamic custodianship over the Temple Mount. Al-Aqsa mosque was later built on the same site during the rule of the Umayyad prince al-Walid 1 (705–715), and that decisively finalized the Islamic takeover of Jehovah's so-called *Noble Holy Place*. There was no doubt, therefore, that the Jewish authorities clearly understood the message that Jehovah/Shabbetai ministered to them.

Let me briefly recall the historic fact that Jehovah had literally made the Jews pay with the blood of their nation for the custodianship of the Temple Mount. In fact, King David purchased the site from the original Jebusite owner, following an ill-fated national census exercise, which Jehovah had personally *incited* David to undertake. According to the scripture, "The anger of Jehovah was kindled against Israel," and he gave David a choice between three national calamities that he had already planned against Israel: "Thus says Jehovah, 'Three things I offer you; chose one of them, that I may do it to you [and your people]. Shall three years of famine come to you in your land? Or will you flee three months before your foes while they pursue you? Or shall there be three days pestilence in your land?'" [2 Sam. 24:12–13] Being a warrior, David chose the third evil, deciding that it was better to "fall into the hand of Jehovah" than to "fall into the hand of another man."

Jehovah made good his decision and sent a pestilence upon Israel from the morning until the appointed time; and seventy thousand Israelite men died, from Dan to Beer-Sheba. Jehovah's evil spirit of destruction stopped short of destroying Jerusalem when "**Jehovah repented of the evil**" and told him, "it is enough, now stay your hand." Then Jehovah ordered David to set up an altar to him on the very spot by the threshing floor of Araunah the Jebusite where the evil spirit of destruction stopped his carnage. David bought the threshing floor and the oxen for fifty shekels of silver, built the altar to Jehovah, and offered burnt offering and peace offerings. It was on the same spot that David's son and successor Solomon built the first Temple to Jehovah, which was completed in 957 BC. It went through a series of destruction and reconstruction, until the second and last Temple begun by Herod the Great in 20 BC and completed forty-six years later.

Thus, the Jews had a natural right of custodianship over the site, which also happened to be the very spot on Mount Moriah where it was believed that Jehovah had directed Abraham to build the altar to sacrifice his son, Isaac.

Another crucial fact, however, is that Jehovah's eternal dwelling place is on the same spot on the Temple Mount. He personally affirmed that to Solomon during the dedication of the first Temple, saying, "I have chosen and consecrated this house [on this spot] that **my name may be there forever**. My eyes and my heart will be there for all times. ... and the name of the city henceforth shall be, Jehovah is there." [2 Chron. 7:16; Ezek. 48:35] Therefore, whether the Temple Mount is under the custodianship of the children of Israel or the children of Ishmael, and whether the Jewish Temple or Muslim Dome and Mosque stand on the spot, the truth always remains that Jehovah dwells there and the Jews know it.

In fact, Christians and Muslims in the European middle ages also believed the Dome of the Rock itself to be the Temple of Solomon—*Templum Domini*. Consequently, the *Western Wall* or the *Wailing Wall*, which was the only remains of the Jewish second Temple, was made part of the walls surrounding the Muslim Dome of the Rock and Al-Aqsa Mosque in AD 691. That necessarily made the Temple Mount the joint religion monument of both the children of Israel and the children of Ishmael; and that reaffirmed the rabbinic belief that the divine presence of Jehovah never departs from the Western Wall after all.

For the change of a "chosen people," Jehovah also needed to promote for himself a new name, *Allah*, and a new religion of unconditional surrender, *Islam*. Jehovah was only spreading out his dragnet to trap more unsuspecting human spirits. Therefore, whether called Jehovah or Allah, the god of Abraham is still the same *"old dragon with seven heads"* and *"the ultimate dragon with the seven-headed dragon in his jaw"* who vowed to dominate the whole world through his Abrahamic game plan. Jehovah had vowed to either rule over the spiritual descendants of Adam, for obvious reasons, or he would haunt and consume them all. "As I live," he vowed, "surely with a mighty hand and outstretched arm and with wrath poured out, **I will be king over you.**" ... "And I will dash them one against another, fathers and sons together, says Jehovah. **I will not pity or spare or have compassion that I should not destroy them**. ... Behold, I will feed this people with wormwood, and give them poisonous water to drink. I will scatter them among the nations whom neither they nor their fathers have known; and I will send the sword after them, until I have consumed them." [Ezek. 20:33; Jer. 13:14; 9:15–16]

Evidently, Jehovah desires what he can never get, and so he kills and destroys. I just wish that the Jews would for once try to see Jehovah for who he really is. He has always been a false messiah to the Jews, right from the very beginning of their ill-fated national history, indirectly avenging on them his humiliating defeat in the hand of their spiritual precursor, Adam. It is very strange that the Jews do not yet see that Jehovah is the only real enemy they have. He betrayed Israel in Canaan, in Egypt, in Babylon, in Germany at the Holocaust, in the whole of Europe, and in the Middle East. He particularly betrayed Israel regarding the so-called "Promised Land" of rest.

Will tiny Israel ever have rest in the *land that devours its inhabitants* and among their permanently hostile Arab neighbors? Jesus Christ, the Prince of Peace gives definite answer to that; not until they say, "Blessed is he who came to them in the name of the Father." [Matt 23:39] Not until the Jews realize that Jehovah, the god of war, has been their archenemy all alone, and then decisively condemn and finally denounce him for good.

Jehovah/Shabbetai had a clear motive; it was to try his luck once more, with his stage-managed conversion to Islam, to obtain unquestioning submission to his will from the spiritual sons of Adam. Unfortunately for him, all but his most ignorant and self-seeking disciples became disillusioned by his apostasy gambit and lost faith in him completely. In a mood of apparent victory, the rabbis tried to erase the memory of Jehovah/Shabbetai from the earth, but little did they realize that they remained his most ardent disciples. They destroyed all the letters, pamphlets, and tracts about him that they could find. But they destroyed nothing whatsoever in themselves about Jehovah, who was their actual nemesis. Hence, the Jews remained his bondmen, and the universal *maya* remained intact.

Nevertheless, many outstanding Rabbis of the eighteenth century knew that Shabbetai had been Jehovah, their "Messiah." The *Donmeh* (apostates) who followed his example clearly understood and declared that Jehovah, the God of Israel, had indeed descended and been made flesh in Shabbetai to show the Jews the practical example of "unconditional surrender" to his will.

To convince people that he was the one making the statements of authority through the man, Shabbetai, Jehovah finally restored the *demoniac* to his wretched nature immediately after completing his intended mission through his body. Immediately Jehovah stepped out of the man, Shabbetai, he automatically became *healed* and resumed his normal life as an ordinary human being. And inspired by Jehovah, the Sultan, renamed him **Mehmed Effendi**, because the name "Shabbetai Tzevi" was in fact, Jehovah's personal epithet, as made clear by his signature—"**I am Jehovah your God, Shabbetai Tzevi.**"

Finally, the placated Sultan appointed the man, Mehmed Effendi, his personal doorkeeper and provided him with generous allowance. Evidently, the man was being rewarded for his troubles and for the temporary rental of his body and voice, although only for a very short while. Not long after, Mehmed Effendi fell out of favor with the Sultan and was banished. He died in exile, apparently a loyal Muslim, on September 17, 1676, in Dulcigno, Albania. The facts speak clearly for themselves. Jehovah's spirit possessed, used, and dumped Mehmed Effendi to the ultimate disadvantage of his real self.

It is very imperative to mention the man, Adolf Hitler, *the Fuhrer* of the German war experiment, on this page. He was probably the most obvious direct epiphany of Jehovah Sabaoth, as the undisputed *man of war* on earth. The Hindu Trimurti recognizes three aspects of the god of the world—the creative, the preservative, and the destructive—and personifies each as Brahma, Vishnu, and Shiva. All three dwell in Jehovah as the undisputed chief god of the world of humankind.

The Jewish Torah clearly portrays Jehovah as creator, preserver, and destroyer of our world. It particularly distinguishes himself as the ultimate *man of war*, meaning he is directly in charge of all war matters among all peoples on the earth. Jehovah's own words speak clearer: "Behold, I have created the smith who blows the fire of coals, and produces a weapon for its purpose. I have also created the ravager to destroy." [Isa. 54:16] He also says in 2 Esdras 6:1–6 (GNB), "I made this decision before I created the world ... Even then, I decided that since I, and I alone, had created the world, I, and I alone, would bring it to an end."

The Greek *Proteus* is another expression of the complex personality of the principal god of the world. It meant that he could turn himself into "a lion, a dragon, a leopard, a bear, a film of water, and a high-branched tree," or into a human being, as situations warrant. This agrees perfectly with the Torah accounts of his personal definitions of himself. Describing what a typical day of Jehovah could look like, the scripture says, "Terror, and the pit, and the snare ... upon you, O inhabitants of the earth! He who flees at the sound of the terror shall fall into the pit; and he who climbs out of the pit shall be caught in the snare." [Isa. 24:17–18] A typical day of Jehovah is "darkness, and not light; as if a man fled from a lion, and a bear met him; or went into the house and leaned with his hand against the wall, and a serpent bit him." [Amos 5:19] In other words, Jehovah could literally turn himself into a lion, a bear, a serpent, terror, pit, or snare just to foment human calamities.

The Qur'an echoes the same facts. When it says, "Allah is All-embracing," for instance, and that "He is able to do all things," it makes it clear that Allah is *good and evil*, and that he can do and undo. Indeed, it says, "No calamity befalleth save by Allah's leave," and "Naught of disaster befalleth in the earth or in yourselves, but it is in a book [well premeditated] before we bring it into being. Lo! That is easy for Allah." [Qur'an 64:11; 57:22]

Jehovah also spoke of himself repeatedly in the Qur'an as "the best of schemers." In that regard, human beings ought not to be surprised to have encountered him not only as the *Apostate Messiah* of the Jews, but also as *Hitler*, the warmonger. He appears equally in other personalities or roles that seem to help him maintain his barbaric hold on ignorant humans vis-à-vis the raging battle for the spiritual liberation of captive human spirits.

Jehovah is a career warmonger; it is not difficult to notice when he takes center stage in war situations doing what he does best. The subject of war and the language of human brutalization have long been the chief pre-occupation of his lawless regime and his personal area of specialty. He personally approves wars and fighting as very good for human beings because it serves his purpose. "Warfare is ordained for you, **though it is hateful unto you**; he declared for Muslims, "but it may happen that ye hate a thing which is good for you ... Fight in the way of Allah against those who fight against you. ... And fight them until persecution is no more, and religion is **all for Allah**. ... For had it not been for Allah's [way of] repelling some men by means of others, cloisters and churches and oratories and mosques, wherein the name of Allah is often mentioned, would assuredly have been pulled down. **Verily Allah helpeth one who helpeth him [to fight his wars]**." [Qur'an 2:216, 190; 8:39; 22:40] That explains why he trains and loves regular soldiers and religious *shahids* who make up his visible fighting forces.

In Hitler, Jehovah made many crucial points, which are not difficult for spiritually alert minds to recognize. Hitler represented both direct and indirect attack on the effects of Christ's "new commandment" of knowledge, love, and human unity, as well as a frantic attempt at beating enlightened humanity back into the primitive era of sheer barbarism.

The ages of the *Renaissance* and especially the *Enlightenment* in the West brought about the rapid spread of the spirit of positive empathy or fellow feeling among peoples of the world, giving rise to social reforms in many countries. A spirit of true humanitarianism had greatly challenged the inhuman maxims of Jehovah, to the point that the great scientists and philosophers of the nineteenth century had declared Jehovah dead, both within and outside human minds. It had been impossible for clear-thinking people to reconcile the so-called goodness and omnipotence of Jehovah with his consistent devilish outlook. The idea of Jehovah as the truly loving Father who sent Jesus Christ to redeem us from spiritual bondage in the world lacked coherence and in time disintegrated. Philosophers and scientists did their best to save it, but failed, as did poets and theologians. Hence, they concluded that the whole world is practically Godless. In fact, they deemed the belief in Jehovah as *God Almighty* to be "not merely unnecessary but positively harmful" to humankind's spiritual wellbeing.

In Hitler, therefore, Jehovah needed not only to resurrect himself in the human consciousness the best way he knew how, but he also needed to permanently destabilize the social atmosphere that gave rise to the comfort of reason among human beings. He needed, more than ever before, to re-impose on enlightened humanity the vile spirit of mutual distrust and aggressive self-defense. He needed to reinvigorate the natural status quo that ordains various forms of caste systems—racial, social, occupational, and so on—that permanently divided and weakened the humans' collective thrust toward the heavenly ideals of Jesus Christ. He knew that the only way he could reassert his personal control over enlightened humanity was by reindoctrinating the peoples in the art of wars and social strife as a way of life. That way, he would force humanity to abandon moves for international peace and human unity for the destructive and diversionary vocation of a universal arms race.

In Hitler, Jehovah merely displayed the prowess of a seasoned slaveholder, which he is. Knowing the psychology of human weaknesses, it was just a question of him applying the *natural* treatment of slaves to bear on the *Enlightenment* generation who desired eternal salvation from, and the ultimate death of the imposter. Sirach 33:24–28 (GNB) reads:

> "A donkey should be given his fodder and his burden, and he should be beaten. A slave should be given his food and his work, and he should be disciplined. If you make your slave work, you can set your mind at ease. **If you don't keep him busy, he will be looking for freedom.** You can use a harness and yoke to tame an

animal, and slave can be tortured in the stocks. Keep him at work [at war], and don't let him be idle; idleness can only teach him how to make trouble. Work [or war] is what he needs. If he won't obey you, put him in chains."

And so, Jehovah simply appeared in Hitler to keep enlightened human beings busy with wars and matters of war to forestall the rising spirit of international unity, brought about by enduring peace and increasing spiritual awareness. Ushered in by World War I or the Great War, Hitler masterfully consolidated supreme political and military powers in Germany in 1933. He organized one of the most complex military bureaucratic regimes ever known in human history, and singlehandedly initiated World War II for its secret purposes.

It must be confessed that Jehovah's outing in Hitler worked magic for the gods. The two Great Wars came and went, and with them the unique social and spiritual evolutionary thrust that was initiated by the great men of the age of the Enlightenment. The golden *Age of Reason*, which seemed to have triumphed over centuries of superstition and religious bigotry, suddenly relapsed into the darkest *age of ignorance* and military zombiism, characterized by meaningless wars, *"fear of wars and rumors of wars."* As it were, the *Age of Reason* died the death meant for Jehovah and his spiritually enslaving ideals.

Eventually, what seemed like a very peaceful world was transformed into a supercharged theatre of all sorts of wars—the Cold War, Star Wars, Holy Wars, Civil Wars, Limited Wars, Trade Wars, and what have you. Suddenly, men of highly unstable mentality, *possessed* by evil spirits of violence and wars, replaced the sound-minded scientists and great thinkers of repute, and had their fingers on the "red buttons" of weapons of mass destruction all over the world, as commanders-in-chief of various belligerent regimes.

In the Soviet Union, communism—which may have started as an honest attempt at founding a new, open, and equitable society, liberated from the oppressive excesses of capitalism where everybody, working as a team mutually catered for everybody's needs—ended up as a worse kind of close circuit bondage on the people. Lenin himself had assigned major importance to the peasantry in formulating his program, maintaining that it would be a serious error for the Russian Revolutionary Workers Movement to neglect the peasants. In fact, he had envisaged a program of *"peace, land, and bread."* Unfortunately, what started as a noble and direct attempt at bettering the existing plutocratic democracy eventually ended up as a deadly secret cult—a worse kind of oligarchy. Armed with a brand-new agenda altogether, Russian Communism literally banished every bit of truth and justice that stood in its way to the Siberian torture camp.

As it were, the whole world united, as one, in the marshal spirit of the German Fuhrer to suffocate the noble spirit of true communism in the Soviet Union forever, the so-called champions of it being the most adamant totalitarians and die-hard capitalists at heart. Soviet Communism became synonymous with falsehood, cold-bloodedness, and torture. In direct opposition to its true meaning, it became an undisguised system of attack on openness and egalitarianism, and hence, was terminally set against Christ's gospel of love, truth, and the higher life.

Soviet Communism failed because it was communism in word and not indeed. Nevertheless, perfect communism is still the godliest system of communal living, based on true love and universal goodwill. Indeed, communism is the official way of life in heaven. If properly understood and implemented on earth, Jesus Christ's "new commandment" of love is guaranteed to lead to perfect communism even here on earth. In fact, Jesus Christ tells us to pray daily for the model life of heaven, as contained in the words of the Lord's Prayer—"Thy kingdom come, thy will be done on earth as it is in heaven." The will of the Father is for human beings to love and live in peace with one another. If perfect love rules the world, there will be absolute peace; then, the kingdom of the Father will literally be here on earth.

Adolf Hitler was born in 1889 at Braunau am Inn, Austria-Hungary. His father, Alois, born in 1837, was illegitimate and for a time bore his mother's name, Schicklgruber. By 1876, thirteen years before Adolf's birth, Alois had established his claim to a new surname, "Hitler," for its hidden purpose. History has it that Adolf was a school dropout and a struggling young artist. In fact, his early years seemed aimless and frustrated both before and after the deaths of his father and mother in 1903 and 1908 respectively, until the Great War ultimately brought him in line with his exact area of interest for his present outing.

In 1913, at the age of twenty-four, he moved to Munich, Germany, but came back to Austria the following year for military examination. Rejected as unsuitable at the military recruitment in Austria in 1914, he returned to Germany, volunteered for the German army during World War I (1914– 1918), and served the whole war. In the war, he proved beyond doubt that he was born to fight. Except when hospitalized, he was continuously in the front line. Although he was wounded in 1916, gassed in 1918, and was still hospitalized when the war ended in 1918, for him, life could mean nothing without the war. For his exceptional bravery in action, he was awarded the iron cross second class in 1914, and the first class in 1918, which was a rare decoration for a corporal.

Germany lost the war, and the country suffered terribly. Many Germans became jobless and poor due to difficulties arising from Germany's failure to pay all that the Allies demanded as post-war reparation. The people wanted someone to lead them back to glory again, and Hitler was positioned to capitalize on the situation to advance his secret, universal militarization agenda.

After the war, he joined the National German Socialists Worker's Party (or Nazi Party) and soon worked his way to a position of absolute political and military authority over Germany. He became the party president with unlimited powers in 1921, at thirty-two. In

1930, he was elected into political office, and three years later, in January 1933, he became Germany's chancellor. He immediately passed laws giving himself total power and soon became a dictator. He controlled Germany's government completely. Thus, he decisively proved that, far from being aimless in life, he was the meticulous architect not only of his own destiny, but also of the fate of humankind.

In 1923, Hitler staged an abortive military coup in support of General Enrich Ludendorf, for which he was sentenced five years, for treason. He served only eight months of it, and *in comfort at the fortress of Landsbery am Lech*. The time in prison merely turned out to be an *official* timeout within which he prepared the first volume of what amounted to his political and military manifesto or *open agenda*. He appropriately named it *Mein Kempf (My Struggle)*—that is, his cryptic struggle against the new religion of reason and universal friendship. Rather than tarnishing his image, the abortive putsch gave Hitler worldwide fame.

The first volume of *Mein Kempf* entitled *Die Abrechnung* (The Settlement of Revenge)—[*The Settlement of Accounts* or *Revenge against the liberal social reformers*], stated his *religious* racist ideology clearly. In it he made the Aryans the *genius race* and the Jews the *parasite* that must be vehemently discriminated against—though, not according to their *original* "Yahwistic" religion, but according to their *spiritual race*; and of course, according to their *new* religion of reason, which directly undermined the natural harmony of the universal order. Accordingly, Nazism became a revolutionary movement in direct opposition to the positive social revolutions of the seventeenth and eighteenth centuries that were geared toward general social changes and the universal improvement of human dignity.

In his *natural* theory of the *Volk*, Hitler made it clear that the *caste system* is the natural law of human relationship on earth, that inequality between races and individuals are a part of an unchangeable worldly order. On the surface, he held the natural unit of humankind to be the *Volk*. Then, he regarded the "Aryan race" as the greatest and the only creative race on earth—the only source of human greatness and progress—while the Jews, whatever their educational and social development may be, were forever fundamentally different from and inimical to Germans. He also stressed that he stood at the apex of the mysterious universal hierarchy, as the supreme *Fuhrer* or "Supreme Leader or Ruler or God" of the Aryan race. As the first or god of the highest of the human races, he expected people to deduce that he was in fact the "God" of all human races. Unfortunately, not many people understood that riddle then, and even now.

Hitler's *principle of the Volk* was a very simple, but cryptic way of introducing himself as the supreme ruler of the present world order. He divided humankind into two symbolic camps: the *builders of the world*, represented as the **Aryans** (Germans), and the *destroyers of the world*, represented as **Jews** (i.e., spiritual descendants of Adam). Putting it differently, the Germans represented the unrepentant sons of perdition who seek eternal continuation of the world order, while the Jews represented the redeemable sons of the heavenly kingdom who seek to overcome the world. He made it clear that the two are permanently at war with each other and would continue to be until the end of time.

The second volume of Jehovah/Hitler's "Book of struggle," entitled *Die National Sozialistische Bewegung* (*The National Socialist Movement*) simply outlined his political, military, and terrorist strategies for achieving his goal of trying to re-colonize enlightened humanity. *Mein Kempf* ultimately became the sacred scripture of Nazism, which was purely a terrorist, totalitarian mass movement, embodying far more extreme ideas and practices than the Italian Fascism. The party's "socialist" rhetoric was merely a rabble-rousing gambit designed solely to attract support from the German working class. Needless to stress that the political atmosphere prevailing in post-war Germany prepared the perfect grounds for Jehovah/Hitler's totalitarian regime.

Nevertheless, while *the struggle* may have seemed, on the surface, to be of a mere political and military expansionist agenda and a racist attack on the Jews, Polish, Slavs, and social misfits within Germany, Jehovah/Hitler's open *religious agenda* was clearly stated. The main goal of Nazism was to undermine the prevailing spirit of reason and human unity. Its express manifesto rejected rationalism, liberalism, democracy, the rule of law, human rights, and all movements of international cooperation and peace. It stressed instead reliance on primitive human instinct, the subordination of the individual to the state, and the necessity of blind and unswerving obedience to *leaders appointed from above*. It also stressed the inequality of men and races and the right of the strong to rule the weak. It sought to advance an ethic of hardness of heart among peoples.

As the symbolic sap or lifeblood of his earthly regime, Jehovah/Hitler stressed that the Aryan race should never be allowed to be *poisoned* by the transforming thoughts of the *spiritual* Jewish race; that allowing that would literally mean the end of the world. He asserted that it was necessary to completely exterminate the Jews, whom he regarded as the distorters of the harmony of the world order, not only for the sake of Germany, but also for the salvation of the entire human race.

However, in order that people may understand that he spoke not about the physical German people, Jehovah/Hitler made clear statements on the eve of the Allied Rhine crossing that implied that even the entire physical German population should be totally sacrificed for the preservation of the endangered world order. He had issued an order to his forces decreeing *"obstruction by self-destruction,"* stressing that "the battle should be conducted without consideration for our own [human] population." Accordingly, he instructed his regional commissioners, "to destroy all industrial plants, all the main electricity works, water works, gas works together with all food and clothing stores" so as "to create a desert in the Allies' path." He argued that "If the war is lost, the German nation will also perish. So, there is no need to consider what the people require for continued existence." [*Britannica.* 1999 Multimedia Edition. CD-ROM]

Evidently, Hitler was not referring to the physical German people as the sap of human race, because even the total annihilation of geographical Germany could never have meant eternal death of the entire Nordic Aryan race in physical terms. Besides, the physical war was eventually lost, but the German nation remained. In spiritual terms, however, the so-called **Aryan** race will not survive the final battle against universal falsehood when ultimate victory of the **Jews** would bring about definite end of Jehovah's world. This calls for deeper thoughts and understanding.

The physical attributes of Hitler, the man of war, perfectly agreed with those of Jehovah, the god of war. History described him as:

- a gifted mass agitator with an actor's ability to be fully absorbed in the role that he created for himself;
- a shrewd and calculated politician who was aware of the weaknesses of his own position, and who perceived more quickly than anyone else how a situation could be best turned to his own advantage (he personally spoke of himself as the *"programmatic thinker and politician become one"*);
- a master propagandist and a false man of peace;
- a betrayer and a cold-blooded murderer who sacrificed most of his closest companions for his own selfish ends;
- a skilled opportunist and friend of the wicked and the ruthless, who regarded the fascist Italy and aggressive Japan as natural allies;
- a diehard sadist who never really had any interest in the personal benefits of his own faithful operatives, beyond using them in any ways that served only his personal interest;

- a despotic tyrant, "*appointed from above*" indeed.

Hitler wielded absolute, *supernatural* powers over his subjects. His words remained law, even to the point that his followers obeyed his dying instruction that they cremate his remains along with that of his mistress, Eva Braun. Furthermore, when Jehovah/Hitler dictated his last personal will, shortly before his inevitable suicide, he exhibited the supernatural authority of a master making authoritative demands on his subjects. It was a unique will indeed.

He willed nothing of material possession to his relatives or to anyone else, but rather *commanded* world rulers to vigorously continue his cryptic *struggle* against the silent Redeemer of true humanity, against the spirit of liberalism in the West, and against the "harmful" religion of reason originating from the spiritual descendants of Adam. His words reveal his personality clearly: "Above all, **I demand of nation's leaders and followers**, scrupulous adherence to the race laws and to ruthless resistance against the world poisoners of all peoples, international Jewry." [*Britannica*. 1999 Multimedia Edition. CD-ROM]

The world had deemed Hitler defeated in World War II, but in view of the hidden motive of "*the struggle,*" he scored resounding victory over true humanity in his mysterious outing as the *man of war*. Literary critics argued that his "Book of Struggle," *Mein Kempf*, was turgid, repetitive, wandering, illogical, filled with grammatical errors, and that it reflected the work of a half-educated man. Yet they also quickly admitted that it was skillfully inciting and appealing to many discontented people in Germany—the ultra-nationalistic, the anti-Semitic, the anti-democratic, the anti-Marxist, and the military. In other words, despite the sub-intellectual standard of the book, it was overwhelmingly received and acted upon by those for whom it was meant. It was published in two volumes in 1925 and 1927, with a condensed edition appearing in 1930. By 1939, it had sold 5,200,000 copies and had been translated into eleven various languages of the world. How about that for a badly written book by a half-educated man?

Following the Japanese surprise attack on Pearl Harbor on December 7, 1941 that precipitated the entry of the United States into World War II, Hitler suddenly declared war on the United States in solidarity with Japan, despite the fact that his pact with Japan was purely defensive. Political commentators judged that he was "misled by an essentially central European view of world politics." They could not perceive that Jehovah/Hitler was perfectly on course with his hidden mission. His overall aim was to start and spread wars over the entire inhabited world, and not necessarily to win them. Jehovah came in Hitler specifically to jam the heads of nations against nations, and the heads of individuals against their fellows. He succeeded immensely in that regard. With the United States effectively drawn into the war, his mission was fully accomplished.

In summary, the power that Hitler wielded was unprecedented, both in its scope and in the technical resources at its command. His originality and distinctiveness lay in his methods, which were shared in whole or in part by millions of people in Germany and elsewhere in the world. By the time he was *defeated* in the *experimental* physical war against enlightened humanity, he had completely broken down the social structure of the world and redirected the nations' focus on wars and war matters. He singlehandedly inaugurated a new era of mutual distrust and hardness of heart with an even greater potential of abuse of power and military destruction. He made no moral or material contribution to humanity; rather, he almost completely put an end to the great Age of Reason.

The greatest significance of Jehovah/Hitler's success with the World Wars would crystallize in the distant future, with the conglomeration of the final wars that would characterize the final days of the present world order. Then, Jehovah will finally assume the center stage in person as the mysterious Antichrist, directing the dooms' day conflagration from his ultimate throne of terror in Jerusalem. According to the scripture, it will be "a day of wrath ... a day of distress and anguish, a day of ruin and devastation, a day of darkness and gloom, a day of clouds and thick darkness." [Zeph. 1:15] It will be "A day of vengeance, a year of recompense for the cause of Zion. ... says Jehovah, whose fire is in Zion and whose furnace is Jerusalem." [Isa. 34:8; 31:9] Sadly for Jehovah, the same inferno that he would trigger in those evil days would equally consume him and his impure dreams forever, while the sons of resurrection will experience the final spiritual exodus.

The entire Hitler saga was, therefore, a mere controlled experimentation in total mass mobilization of human beings for the ultimate "War of Armageddon." As the facts on the ground show, human beings all over the world have already fully imbibed the spirit of social violence, armed struggles, and wars, and are ready for the ultimate showdown. The world itself is already supercharged with deadly weapons of mass destruction. These are direct outcomes of Jehovah/Hitler's cryptic offensive as the mysterious *Fuhrer* of our lost world.

CHAPTER FOURTEEN

WALKING BY THE HOLY SPIRIT

Every profession has its ethics, just as every home has its own traditions. Before someone can become a marine engineer or marine navigator, for instance, he must first undergo a cadetship program designed to teach him how to live and work onboard the ship. What this means is that the cadet in training begins to live as if he were already onboard before he gets there. In the same way, a royal family sends royal instructors to prepare a maiden that is betrothed to the crown prince on the traditions of the kingdom and on how to live there, even while she is still in her father's house. The aim is to ensure that she would blend perfectly into the *meticulous* kingdom lifestyle when she eventually comes into the family.

Walking by the Holy Spirit is the process of learning and living the heavenly lifestyle, even as human beings on earth, through the divine guidance of the heavenly Christ. The way false life is lived here in the imperfect world is not the way true life is lived in the perfect spiritual kingdom of the Father. It is necessary for anyone aspiring to perfect heavenly existence to learn the norm and indeed begin to emulate the life of perfect heavenly beings in preparation for the ultimate homegoing. There is the need for such a person to learn and live with *new* attitudes that bring him closer to his desired heavenly lifestyle. These facts should be obvious to any reader who has come this far.

Jesus Christ says, "You, therefore, must be perfect, as your heavenly Father is perfect." [Matt. 5:48] No one should expect this to be as easy as a turnkey exercise. It would take a human being an entire lifetime of determination and perseverance to learn and master a few of the simplest steps that lead to perfection. In any case, it is altogether impossible without the special assistance of Jesus Christ who is our heavenly Guide. *Walking by the Holy Spirit* is the practical process of actualizing spiritual rebirth for our fallen, dead spirits. This means that true Christ-followers must first try to understand what *perfection* of the Father means, and then endeavor to live lives that correspond to the proximity of that perfection on earth, even as human beings.

The model prayer that Jesus Christ taught his true disciples reads, "Our Father in heaven, may your name be kept holy. May your Kingdom come soon. **May your will be done on earth, as it is in heaven.**" [Matt. 6:9–10 (NLT)] This was not a prayer for their everyday material needs because he had already assured them that the Father knew and would always supply all their needs as necessary—"for your Father knows exactly what you need even before you ask him!" The *daily* prayer was intended as a permanent reminder to them of the need to try to live in the world the way perfect angels of the Father live in the heavenly household. Every day that the disciples repeated the divine reminder, they strengthened their attitude toward upholding the Father's holiness in the world. They looked forward to the coming of the Father's Holy Spirit of truth into as many human spirits as possible, and they resolved to live, and to help more and more people to live the life of love and holiness, *as it is in heaven.*

Let me quickly correct the wrong impression that most religious people have concerning the coming of the kingdom of the Father into the world. "**May your kingdom come**" does not imply in any way the possibility of the Father eventually unifying his perfect spiritual kingdom with the imperfect *kingdoms* of the world of human beings. That is practically impossible. Spiritual salvation means that the fallen, dead human spirits in the world must return to the Father's heavenly kingdom for ultimate resurrection, not that the Father would eventually abandon his perfect abode and descend into the realm of imperfection to dwell among his sinful, lost sons. A good father saves his wayward son who is entangled with hoodlums from the gang's hideout and brings him home; he does not leave his home to join his lost son in his dungeon. It just does not work that way.

The Father who is light, love, and eternal life can never become one with our loveless material realm of darkness and death. The coming of the kingdom of the Father is personal to individuals. Kingdom of the Father comes the very instant the Father's indwelling Holy Spirit of truth contacts and reawakens the penitent spirit of a true disciple of Jesus Christ. This can be likened to an incoming of an unseen inner glow that portrays general spiritual refinement, manifesting in a new lifestyle on the part of the disciple. Jesus Christ refers to such a state of newness of an individual as someone "being in the Father and the Father being in the person." Therefore, a clear difference exists between the kingdom of the Father that comes into human beings and the kingdom of the Father to which fallen, dead human spirits must ultimately return to as sons of the resurrection.

Jesus Christ already explained this point to some confused Jewish religious authorities who asked him to tell them when the kingdom of the Father would come into the world. Jehovah's end-time prophecies of the last days of the world, when he hoped to establish his kingdom in Jerusalem and rule in human form as the sole king over all human beings, had created this unnecessary confusion in the minds of the Jews. They had believed that Jesus Christ was referring to the same Jehovah's end-time prophecies when he talked about the coming of the kingdom of the Father; evidently, because they did not know that the Father of Jesus Christ was entirely different from Jehovah their god. Yet, Jesus Christ told them plainly that "The Kingdom of the Father can't be detected by visible signs. You won't be able to say, 'Here it is!' or 'It's over there!' For the Kingdom of the Father is already among you." [Luke 17:20–21 (NLT)]

In other words, the coming of the kingdom of the Father does not involve alteration of the physical nature of the realm of darkness or the inevitable fate of the human world in any way. Not at all! The coming of the kingdom of the Father into the world is the coming of the silent heavenly Comforter and Counselor that Jesus Christ promised his disciples—"the Holy Spirit, who leads into all truth."

He added, "*The world cannot receive him*, because it isn't looking for him and doesn't recognize him. But you know him because **he lives with you now and later will be in you.**" [John 14:17 (NLT)]

The kingdom of the Father in the world is the presence of the invisible Supreme Powerbase that inwardly links all reawakened spirits to the heavenly network, guides them through the complex, deadly minefields of present world order, and guarantees that they are returned to their proper dwelling place in the heavenly household of the Father.

We also know what the coming of the kingdom of the Father means from the answer that Jesus Christ gave to the Jews who doubted the source of his power. He made it known to them that his physical presence with them indeed meant that the kingdom of the Father had already come into the world. "But if I am casting out demons by the power of the Father," he said to them, "then **the Kingdom of the Father has [already] arrived among you.**" [Luke 11:20 (NLT)] It was in the same vein that he had said to them earlier, "Truly, I say to you, there are some standing here who will not taste death before they see [recognize] that the kingdom of the Father has come with power." [Mark 9:1] It was obvious, therefore, that the coming of the kingdom of the Father that Jesus Christ spoke about was a profoundly unseen phenomenon that was already initiated with his physical presence on earth. And it has been in active mode since two thousand years ago.

Walking by the Holy Spirit entails overall attitudinal reform; and that requires commitment, self-discipline, and consistency. People who truly choose the heavenly way must accept and key into the right frame of mind. They must persevere in living by Christ's new commandment of love for all, even though doing so can be very difficult in our present wicked world. Even friends of the world who choose the broadway of the haughty one of Eden fully transform into his iniquitous standards. They are highly disciplined in their ritualistic commitments to his violent commandments, and they dutifully fight his unjust cause on earth, even with their wealth and their lives.

Scriptural evidence proves that Abram was a very kind, loving man before Jehovah called him to walk in his ways. Jehovah started by isolating Abram from his natural environment and his family heritage in the *Exalted Father*, and that made it easier for him to transform and alter his general attitude to conform to his own vocational lifestyle. By systematically applying his so-called ten-point reconditioning tests, Jehovah successfully turned the simple, peace-loving Abram into a violent warrior, a compulsive liar, and a murderer, which defined the lifestyle he desires for anyone who must be his follower. Subsequently, he also altered his name from Abram (*the Father is exalted*) to Abraham (*father of material pursuits*) to symbolize the total takeover of the man's mental faculties.

The same was the case with Muhammad of Arabia. He, too, was a very humble, loving man who sought the natural religion of love with which he hoped to improve the barbaric lifestyle of his Qurayshi relatives. Jehovah abducted and bullied him into forsaking his *"quiet, honored way of life"* and taking up his *violent, outrageous* ways. Islamic tradition states that the "recognition of the Divine nature of the call he [Muhammad] had received [from Jehovah] *involved a change in his whole mental outlook sufficiently disturbing to a sensitive and honest mind, and also the forsaking of his quiet, honored way of life*." [Pickthall, Marmaduke, trans. *The Meaning of the Glorious Qur'an*]

Indeed, for a whole thirteen years after his call, Muhammad maintained his pacifist outlook in the unfolding events of his ambivalent new life. Several passages of the Qur'an bear witness that Muhammad and many of his early followers really hated the idea of fighting wars, even in self-defense, until Jehovah inured them to it with his highly inciting revelations. Of course, Jehovah knew that Muhammad naturally hated violence and wars, and so in Qur'an 2:216, he openly decreed war for him and his peace-loving followers, saying, "Warfare is ordained for you, *though it is hateful unto you.*"

He subsequently explained to them why he habitually incited wars among people, while assuring them that he greatly rewards people who fight his cause. He made it clear to them that his entire worldly dreams and enterprise would crumble if he stopped relying on violence and divide-and-rule tactics against enlightened humanity. Qur'an 22:40 reads, "For had it not been for Allah's [method of] repelling some men by means of others, cloisters and churches and oratories and mosques, wherein the name of Allah is oft mentioned, would assuredly have been pulled down. **Verily Allah helpeth one who helpeth him**."

In other words, Allah openly confirms that violent people help his cause on earth, while he, in turn, helps them to achieve their various earthly ambitions. That explains why violent, evil people prosper on earth, while good people suffer and are persecuted. Jehovah's so-called help to his emissaries is a kind of trade by barter. It is strictly conditional; they must be sufficiently violent in their thoughts and actions.

Accordingly, he says, "Of the believers are men who are true to that which they covenanted with Allah. Some of them have paid their vow by death (in battles), and some of them still are waiting; and they have not altered in the least; that Allah may reward the true men [of violence] for their truth [faithfulness]. ... Think not of those who are slain in the way of Allah, as dead. Nay, they are living. With their Lord they have provision." [Qur'an 33:23–24; 3:169]

People who choose the heavenly lifestyle can now appreciate why there must be a total attitudinal reform for the true followers of Jesus Christ. Because Jehovah is a liar, a violent man of war, and a murderer, those who choose his ways must conform to his lifestyle. Jesus Christ, on the other hand, is the Prince of Peace; his way is of true love, peace, and total nonviolence. Obviously, there is no room for a merger between the two opposite lifestyles.

Let me reiterate my previous assertion here that Paul was an outstanding apostle of Jehovah. He said of himself, "I worship the God of our fathers, believing everything laid down by the law." [Acts

24:14] Saul was violent, hostile, bad-tempered, dissenting, proud, and arrogant by nature, and by strict training in the way of Jehovah. The scripture repeatedly shows that he continued to be violent, hostile, bad-tempered, dissenting, proud, and arrogant even after his stage-managed conversion from the violent ways of Jehovah to the meek and peaceful way of Jesus Christ. Remarkably, Jehovah had the man, Saul, renamed Paul, just as he renamed Abram. But Paul simply did not experience the special inner glow of love and peace that would have enabled him to display that unique attitudinal transformation, which distinguished true Apostles of Jesus Christ.

Jesus Christ said that his true disciples are the light of the world, and then he added, "Let your light *so shine* before men." The light of a true Christ-follower is his overall attitude. Without that external manifestation of the blessed inner glow, someone is simply not a true Christ-follower. Paul's overall disposition remained militant throughout his lifetime. The history of the Roman Catholic Church of Jehovah that Paul founded is entirely characterized by extremism, cold-bloodedness, violence, dissension, and worldliness. That speaks clearly of his actual inspiration.

I am sure that people who look at the actual qualities of Paul's personal lifestyle from this point of view will discover that he was indeed antichrist in his general outlook. Multitudes of customary Christians worldwide that prefer to quote and emulate Paul rather than Jesus Christ on matters of spiritual directives, are equally antichrists by religious default. They prefer to live by Paul's subtly misleading injunctions than live by the express instructions of Jesus Christ.

One must speak candidly and directly about this for the benefit of genuine seekers of the heavenly way. Jesus Christ is the sole heavenly Guide for the whole of humankind. People should emulate the life of Jesus Christ rather than looking up to Paul whose lifestyle and personal doctrines starkly contradict his perfect heavenly standards. A true Christian should be Christ-like and not Paul-like in his overall thoughts and actions. It was obvious that Paul was not

Christ-like. *Walking by the Holy Spirit* means living by the blameless precepts of Jesus Christ and following his exact footsteps. It means persistently manifesting the spirit of love, peace, and goodwill toward everyone. In fact, *walking by the Holy Spirit* literally means someone letting Jesus Christ think all his thoughts, utter all his words, and perform all his deeds from within him.

Some people argue that most of Jesus Christ's precepts are very difficult to practice on earth, given the precarious nature of the human situation and that is a fact. However, one can accomplish a lot with his divine assistance. Indeed, Jesus Christ already said it clearly that the race for true spiritual salvation is not easy at all. The choice between the *easy* life of the world that leads to eternal self-damnation and the *difficult* life of self-restraint that leads to spiritual resurrection is indeed the most difficult aspect of human existence.

Nevertheless, that choice must be made by every human being on earth. Emulating the selfless life that Jesus Christ lived on earth is not easy at all; neither is the so-called *easy* life of the world easy. The way to every valuable achievement in this life is always difficult anyway. The Messiah says, "You can enter the Father's Kingdom *only* through the narrow gate. The road that leads to destruction is broad, and its gate is wide for the many who choose that way. But the gateway to life is very narrow and the road is difficult, and only a few ever find it." [Matt. 7:13–14 (NLT)]

There are usually dos and don'ts in every vocation and in every facet of human life. The phrase, 'When in Rome, Do as the Romans Do' reminds people of the wisdom in abiding by the dos and don'ts of any place or circumstance in which they find themselves. Likewise, the heavenly way of Jesus Christ has its dos and don'ts.

Seeking to regain true spiritual life for one's fallen, dead spirit is not a vocation for an unserious mind. Such a person must be genuinely determined. Whoever chooses the difficult, *narrow way* to true life eternal, must also choose to abide by the dos and don'ts outlined by Jesus Christ who is the sole heavenly Guide. In this regard, express words of Jesus Christ completely supersede all subtly misleading doctrines that were dictated by men of contrary inspiration and approved by devious religious institutions on earth. For example, Jesus Christ says, "Unless one is born anew, **he cannot see** the kingdom of the Father." That is not the same as, "Unless one is born anew, the Father will torment him in the lake of fire forever," which customary Christian churches preach. Likewise, there is that subtle intent to mislead the uninformed masses where the scripture says, "Repent or you will perish" and the churches preach, "Repent or you will face the wrath of the Father." The Father holds no grudge or wrath against anyone.

There is an irreconcilable difference between the Father who silently beckons on all of us to 'repent and be saved,' and Jehovah who threatens to 'pour out his wrath on all flesh.' Also, there is marked difference between what Jesus Christ says to genuine seekers of spiritual salvation and what Paul and his Church teach their hypnotized followers. In the examples given above, the Church subtly interpolated the true gospel of Jesus Christ with false assertions designed to foster the Jewish tradition of fear of Jehovah in peoples' minds. The danger in that is that people dominated by irrational *fear of God* will find it nearly impossible to know and realign themselves with the Father who is love. For this reason, most customary Christians find it very hard to understand how the Father can rightly be said to be **perfect and loving**. They find it almost impossible to see any difference between the Father, who cannot do anything evil, and Jehovah, who can be good or evil as circumstances dictate.

The scripture says in James 1:13 that **"the Father cannot be tempted with evil,"** meaning that he can never do anything evil. Of course, that is why the Father is called perfect. This should help people to understand that Paul and the Church preach Jehovah who would torment unrepentant spirits in hell fire forever and not the loving Father that Jesus Christ exemplified on earth. "Be born anew or you will not see the kingdom of the Father" and "repent or you will perish" are both saying that it is up to people to choose eternal life or eternal damnation, in which case people who choose eternal damnation would remain *self-tormented* at the last day. People who suggest that the Father will be the one to torment the unrepentant individuals are wrong. It is like saying that the ever-loving father of the proverbial prodigal son would have continued to torment his lost son if he had failed to repent and return home. The young man was self-tormented in the first instance; and he would have continued to be self-tormented if he did not repent and return home. The choice between eternal life and eternal death is in the hand of every individual human being on earth.

Fallen human spirits are presently self-tormented in the world; they will continue to be self-tormented in the outer darkness if they fail to repent and accept the Father's present offer of a *second chance*. The emphasis here is on **self-torment**; the Father does not torment anyone now, and he will not torment anyone at any time in the future. That is the gospel truth. Jesus Christ explains this crucial issue further in John 12:47–48 and 3:19, saying, "If anyone hears my sayings and does not keep them, I do not judge him; for I did not come to judge the world but to save the world. He who rejects me and does not receive my sayings has a judge; the words that I have spoken will be his judge on the last day. ... And **this is the judgment, that the light has come into the world, and men loved darkness rather than light**, because their deeds were evil." The *gospel of fear and wrath of God,* dictated by Paul and preached by customary Christian churches is of contrary inspiration.

What then are the true **dos** and **don'ts** of the heavenly way of Jesus Christ? The heavenly way is a lifestyle, and one cannot possibly itemize all the dos and don'ts in a small write up such as this one. Nevertheless, the dos can be summarized under three broad headings, namely, "You must be born anew," "You must seek the kingdom of the Father first," and "You must be courageous and speak out for the truth without fear." The don'ts, on the other hand, concern what should be our proper attitude toward the Father's holiness, and toward the unique status of Jesus Christ, our heavenly Restore Guide.

To begin with, the heavenly Messiah says:

- **You must be born anew:** "Truly, truly, I say to you, unless one is born anew, **he cannot see** the kingdom of the Father." [John 3:3]

This is the very first requirement for anyone who is genuinely desiring to be a part of the heavenly exodus. Unfortunately, most customary Christians, especially the so-called born-again ones, do not understand what this means at all. This simply means that one must develop a new lifestyle that corresponds to newness of life in knowledge, love, peace, and total non-violence. He must undergo **a total change of attitude** in his thoughts and actions toward the Father, and toward his fellow human beings. Of course, we already know what Jesus Christ means by *"he cannot see the kingdom of the Father."* This means that any person who does not totally *renew* his general attitude will not be pure enough to receive the Father's indwelling Holy Spirit of truth that is already in the world.

As we have seen, there are only two choices. It is either one chooses the way of Jesus Christ, or he remains in the ways of Jehovah, which is the normal way of the world. *"You must be born anew"* simply means that anyone desiring to join the way of Jesus Christ should completely turn away from his old ways, from the ways of Jehovah. John 1:12–13 (NLT) says the same thing in a different way: "But to all who believed him [Jesus Christ] and accepted him, he gave **the right to become** children of the Father. They are reborn—not with a physical birth resulting from human passion or plan, but a birth that comes from the Father [i.e., a divine inner rebirth]."

In plain words, this means that all human beings on earth are children or followers of Jehovah, the devil; only the ones who accept and live by the Messiah's *new* commandment of love are spiritually *born anew*. Only such people are inwardly rekindled and transformed into true sons of the Father.

Jesus Christ further stresses the need for total self-transformation from the ways of Jehovah in another way. He once said to the multitude, sons of the world that followed him, "If any of you wants to be my follower, **you must turn from your selfish ways**, take up your cross, and follow me. If you try to hang on to your [*old*] life, you will lose it. But if you give up your [worldly] life for my sake, you will save it. And what do you benefit if you gain the whole world but lose your own soul? [Or] Is anything worth more than your soul?" [Matt. 16:24–26 (NLT)]

As we have seen, wherever Jesus Christ stressed the need for people to repent and be born anew, he never mentioned or implied in any way that the Father would torment the people who fail to receive his message of eternal life. What he said repeatedly throughout his earthly ministry was that people who refuse to be born anew will not experience the interim glory of the kingdom of the Father within them now; and in the future, will not be counted worthy to attain the ultimate spiritual resurrection.

Jesus Christ did not come into the world to scare anyone of us back into heaven. Rather, he came to tell us the truth plainly, and to help us appreciate the clear difference between the heavenly life of perfection and the life of spiritual bondage to sin and death in the outer darkness, so that people may choose freely between the two. Hence, the way of Jesus Christ is *the way of truth and life*, not *the way of fear and wrath*.

The heavenly Messiah pinpointed the qualities that a truly born-anew person must exhibit in his general outlook in this life. Because those qualities are alien to the sons of the world, he says that any person desiring the ultimate return to the Father of heavenly life must do his best to emulate him and not any other person. He made that explicit in Matthew 23:8–10 (NLT), saying, "Don't let anyone call you 'Rabbi,' **for you have only one teacher**, and all of you are equal as brothers and sisters. And don't address anyone here on earth as 'Father,' for only God in heaven is your spiritual Father. And don't let anyone call you 'Teacher,' **for you have only one teacher, the Messiah."** Accordingly, he says:

- **You must learn from me:** Because "I am the way, the truth, and the life. No one can come to the Father except through me." [John 14:6 (NLT)] "No one truly knows the Son except the Father, and no one truly knows the Father except the Son and those to whom the Son chooses to reveal him." ... So "Come to me [not to any other person—whether god or man], all of you who are weary and carry heavy [worldly] burdens, and I will give you rest. **Take my yoke upon you. Let me teach you, because I am humble and gentle at heart,** and you will find [eternal] rest for your souls." [Matt. 11:27–29 (NLT)]

  Jesus Christ was a very simple person. He was *humble and gentle at heart*; he was loving and compassionate, and he was a servant-leader. In fact, he effectively exemplified the perfect attributes of the Father in the world and proved himself to be the worthy Prince of Peace. He expects his true followers to be exactly like him, and he says that they can succeed in doing so with his special help and guidance. He became a human being so that he would become the perfect model for sons of the world who genuinely desire true spiritual redemption. He assures the world that the kingdom of the Father is for people who are pure at heart, humble, loving, and peaceable, as he is.

- **You must love one another:** "I have loved you even as the Father has loved me. Remain in my love. When you obey my commandments, you remain in my love,

> just as I obey my Father's commandments and remain in his love. ... There is no greater love than to lay down one's life for one's friends. ... So now I am giving you a new commandment: Love each other. Just as I have loved you, you should love each other. **Your love for one another will prove to the world that you are my disciples.**" [John 15:9–10, 13; 13:34–35 (NLT)]

Love is the hub of the true gospel of Jesus Christ. Love is the source of all existence. Without love, there would be no life. Love is goodness; absolute love is perfection, light, and life. People who seek true spiritual life are indeed seeking to return to the realm of perfection where love is everything. Now, the Father is Divine Spirit whose infinite love perfects the heavenly realm. He is the Source or Tree of love, light, life, and perfection himself. All the perfect spirits in existence reflect his divine nature within his perfect heavenly kingdom. True eternal life is only possible within the eternal realm of the Father's positive influence. Beyond the Father's eternal realm of love, light, and life is the eternal realm of darkness and spiritual death. As fallen, dead spirits, we presently dwell in this opposing realm, and that explains why our lives are naturally dominated by selfishness, jealousy, envy, bitterness of heart, hatred, indignation, anger, wrath, enmity, strife, dissension, wars, unhappiness, worries, pains, and the like.

It should be easy for any clear-thinking person to see from the above that any person or institution that preaches the *wrath of God* is not talking about the Father whose love is absolute. Jehovah, the jealous, bungling god of violence and wars is strictly an inhabitant of this realm of eternal conflicts; customary Christian churches that preach his indignation, anger, and wrath on humanity are certainly on his payroll. The Father's love is infinite and unconditional.

No entity or evil being in existence can offend the Father, not even Jehovah, the haughty *Almighty* that we ignorantly dread as the devil in the world. All the fallen, dead spirits in the world are lost sons of the Father; he loves and feels compassion for both the oppressed and the oppressors alike. He sent Jesus Christ to redeem **all** of us from spiritual self-damnation in the outer darkness. "For the Father so loved [his lost sons in] the world that he gave [sent] his only Son, that whoever believes in him should not perish but have [regain] eternal life," says John 3:16.

Love is the central norm of heavenly life, and that is what the fallen, dead spirits in the world violated in the first place. Receiving Jesus Christ or accepting his gospel of the kingdom means that one has willingly accepted to return to the heavenly norm of unconditional love for all. All that Jesus Christ is saying is that true seekers of heavenly life should keenly practice living the heavenly lifestyle here on earth, even as human beings. The main reason he became a human being was to show us how to live the heavenly life of love and peace on earth as human beings. He exemplified the love of the Father for everyone to see, and he enjoined us to emulate him. He is not telling or expecting any of his true disciples to do what he has not done or to live beyond his personal examples.

For very good reasons, Jesus Christ also says to genuine seekers of the heavenly way:

- **"You must love your enemies and sincerely pray for their good:** You have heard the law [of Jehovah] that says, 'Love your neighbor' and hate your enemy. But I say, love your enemies! Pray for those who persecute you! **In that way, you will be acting as true children of your Father in heaven**. For he gives his sunlight to both the evil and the good, and he sends rain on the just and the unjust alike. If you love only those who love you, what reward is there for that? Even corrupt tax collectors do that much. If you are kind only to your friends, how are you different from anyone else? Even pagans do that. But

you are to be perfect, even as your Father in heaven is perfect." [Matt. 5:43–48 (NLT)]

Jesus Christ loved both the people who loved him and the people who saw themselves as his enemies. He prayed for the people who persecuted and crucified him, stating that they did not know what they were doing. Of course, Jehovah and all his apostles of doom who think that violence can liberate them from their present spiritual quandary are utterly deluded. Only true love can liberate from spiritual death. In the meantime, love is also the ultimate therapy for all forms of worldly problems. When love overwhelms our hearts, we are filled with *the fullness of the Father*, and then our lives naturally become stress-free. Even the slightest degree of loveless thought or action becomes a serious breech in that regard.

Jesus Christ tells us to love and pray for the good of our enemies, because it is to our spiritual advantage that we do so. Indeed, it is so difficult in the worldly setting, for human beings to love their *enemies*, but people who really understand the benefit in doing so will at least try to cultivate the positive attitude. When we hate people who hate us, we personally hinder *the fullness of the Father* within our inner beings; but when we love and pray for them, we retain closeness with the Father and help our misguided brothers improve their spiritual state.

Likewise, when we forgive people for hurts they have done to us, we retain closeness with the Father. Here again, the heavenly Messiah openly abrogates another typical injunction of Jehovah, the god of the world, and gives us his *new* heavenly law of endless forgiveness and total non-violence, "You have heard that it was said [by Jehovah, god of the Jews], 'Eye for eye, and tooth for tooth.' But I tell you, **Do not resist an evil person.** If someone strikes you on the right cheek, turn to him the other also. And if someone wants to sue you and take your tunic, let him have your cloak as well. If someone forces you to go one mile, go with him two miles." [Matt. 5:38–41 (NIV)]

"Love your enemies" and *"do not resist evil persons"* are but extensions of the heavenly norm of love. Naturally, the Jews found the teachings of Jesus Christ regarding love of one's enemies entirely heretical. His idea of regarding non-Jews as their neighbors was also very alien to them. One day, an expert in Jewish religious law asked him, "And who is my neighbor?" As far as the Jews were concerned, no other tribe on earth loved and fought for its own better than the Jews did. One thing Jehovah taught them so well was that their neighbors are only fellow Jews. So many verses of the so-called Old Testaments are explicit about this fact. Some of these verses include: "Do not seek revenge or bear a grudge **against a fellow Israelite** but love your neighbor as yourself." [Lev. 19:18 (NLT)] "At the end of every seventh year you must cancel the debts of everyone who owes you money. ... This release from debt, however, **applies only to your fellow Israelites**—not to the foreigners living among you. ... You may charge interest to foreigners, but you may not charge interest to Israelites." [Deut. 15:1, 3; 23:20 (NLT)]

What human beings do not realize is that the Father does not see tribes or nations of people when he looks down on his fallen, lost sons in the nether world. He does not see geographical lines of divide on maps that make nations out of a homogenous family of fallen sons of heaven. The Father's love knows no such bounds. To him, there are no Jews or Gentiles, no Aryans, Poles, or Africans; there are no white, black, brown, or pink spirits. He loves and cares for all equally and offers his second chance to all and sundry. Jesus Christ said it plainly: "All of you are equal as brothers and sisters."

It is important, therefore, that true seekers of the heavenly life should work out how to separate this truth from the false reality that the world order paints before their physical senses. If they do, they will be able to look beyond worldly boundaries, appearances, concepts, and traditions to the actual nature, stance, and desire of the Father for all of us.

No doubt, the worldly concept of love is entirely misleading. Apart from human beings interpreting sheer sensual passion between men and women as love, the religious notion of Jehovah's conditional affection for people who serve his selfish desires as the perfect love that the Father has for us is indeed blasphemous. Luckily, the scripture captures a slight glimpse of what true love entails in its definition of love and heavenly wisdom. It says, "Love is patient and kind; **love is not jealous** or boastful; it is not arrogant or rude. Love does not insist on its own way **[i.e., love is not self-seeking]**; it is not irritable or resentful; **it does not rejoice at wrong but rejoices in the right**. Love bears all things, believes all things, hopes all things, endures all things. **Love never ends**." [1 Cor. 13:4–8] Judging from the above, Jehovah is completely loveless.

The scripture further compares the *wisdom of the world* and the *wisdom from above*, which is also a manifestation of the love of the Father to the heavenly dropouts in the world, and that should help to paint the correct picture of the purity of the Father's love in our minds. It says:

> "But the wisdom from above is first of all pure. It is also peace loving, gentle at all times, and willing to yield to others. It is full of mercy and good deeds. It shows no favoritism and is always sincere. And those who are peacemakers will plant seeds of peace and reap a harvest of righteousness. ... But if you are bitterly jealous and there is selfish ambition in your heart, don't cover up the truth with boasting and lying. For **jealousy and selfishness are not the Father's kind of wisdom.** Such things are earthly, unspiritual, and demonic. For wherever there is jealousy and selfish ambition, there you will find disorder and evil of every kind [as we have in the world]. [James 3:17–18, 14–16 (NLT)]

Jehovah, the one that religious people revere as *God Almighty* in the world, is everything that true love is not, and his wisdom is strictly "*earthly, unspiritual, and demonic.*" Jehovah is a mere self-seeking, anthropomorphic deity that is completely consumed with jealousy, arrogance, bitterness of heart, wrath, jealous rage, and vengeance. He is the direct opposite of what true love and heavenly wisdom stand for. He says to his followers, "I Jehovah your God am a jealous God, visiting the iniquity of the fathers upon the children to the third and the fourth generation of those who hate me." [Exod. 20:5] Clearly, Jehovah is a self-confessed unforgiving deity. Yet his hypnotized religious followers propagate him as 'the Beneficent, the Merciful'; and as loving and ever forgiving.

Helping human beings to understand that Jehovah is not the Father is perhaps the most difficult aspect of the Messiah's gospel of the kingdom. This is because people who look up to him as *God Almighty* are completely blanked out from the actual love of the Father that enlightens human minds. In this regard, *walking by the Holy Spirit* means that one correctly identifies and walks by the divine guidance of **the true Source of love** and heavenly wisdom, and does not yield to sheer religious infatuation. Let me state emphatically here that Jehovah is **the source of all evils** on earth. The more religious-minded people become, the more unbearable the world will be. *"For wherever there is jealousy and selfish ambition, there you will find disorder and evil of every kind,"* says James 3:16(NLT).

Jesus Christ narrowed down his entire mission in the world to love, beginning with his liberating and life-giving encounter with Adam and Eve in Eden to his Good News messages to the whole world as Son of man. Thus, he brought to bear what ought to have been the focal point of human religion if indeed it were a heavenly institution. If indeed customary Christianity were of Jesus Christ, there would not have been any place for the gospel of jealousy, wrath, and vengeance within its doctrines and preachments.

Responding to a question by a Jewish religious lawyer, regarding the most important commandment in the law of Moses, Jesus Christ made it clear that the heavenly norm is only one, and that is love. The numerous ungodly ordinances decreed by Jehovah through Moses were unwarranted accretions upon the simple heavenly norm.

Jesus Christ answered the lawyer, saying, "You shall love the Father your God with all your heart, and with all your soul, and with all your mind. This is the great and first commandment. And a second is like it, You shall love your neighbor as yourself. On these two commandments depend all the law and the prophets." [Matt. 22:37–40] Galatians 5:14 simply says, "For the whole law can be summed up in this one command: '**Love** your neighbor as yourself.'"

Other *Dos* of the heavenly way include:

- **You must be merciful:** "You must be compassionate, just as your Father is compassionate." [Luke 6:36 (NLT)] Then he added, "Now go and learn the meaning of this Scripture: '*I want you to show mercy, not offer sacrifices.*' For I have come to call not those who think they are righteous, but those who know they are sinners." [Matt. 9:13 (NLT)]
- **You must give the gospel freely because you received it freely:** "And preach as you go, saying, 'The kingdom of heaven is at hand.' Heal the sick, raise the dead, cleanse lepers, cast out demons. **You received without paying, give without pay.**" [Matt. 10:7–8]
- **You must always apply the Golden Rule:** "Do to others as you would like them to do to you." [Luke 6:31 (NLT)]
- **You must be a servant-leader:** "The greatest among you must be a servant. But those who exalt themselves will be humbled, and those who humble themselves will be exalted. ... I tell you the truth, unless you turn from your sins and become like little children [before your heavenly Father], you will never get into the Kingdom of Heaven. So, anyone who becomes as humble [and pure at heart] as this little

child is the greatest in the Kingdom of Heaven." [Matt. 23:11–12; 18:3–4 (NLT)]

- **You must persistently strive for perfection:** "You are to be perfect, even as your Father in heaven is perfect. ... [For,] a tree is identified by its fruit. If a tree is good, its fruit will be good. If a tree is bad, its fruit will be bad. ... Yes, just as you can identify a tree by its fruit, so you can identify people by their actions." [Matt. 5:48; 12:33; 7:20 (NLT)] "A good person produces good things from the treasury of a good heart, and an evil person produces evil things from the treasury of an evil heart. What you say flows from what is in your heart." [Luke 6:45 (NLT)]

The Father is the Tree of love, light, and eternal life; anyone who is truly *born anew* has become his fruit. Because the Father is perfect, if his kingdom truly dwells within someone, his utterances and actions will prove that.

Now, when people have fully recognized the overwhelming importance of true love and inwardly realigned themselves to the true Source of it, they become duly equipped for the next big step toward true spiritual salvation. Anyone who has not crossed the necessary threshold of love is still in darkness, and Jesus Christ says that "he who walks in darkness does not know where he goes." [John 12:35]

The next phase of the battle of salvation is fought against distracting worldly gains, such as material riches, prominence, and dominion. The so-called good things of the world are not only worthless, but also detrimental to the spiritual pursuits of people who are truly walking by the Holy Spirit. They are parts of the programmed obstacles invented by the world to hinder the spiritual salvation of captive human spirits. People who chase after these vanities will most definitely lose the crucial battle for true eternal life. It is to this effect that Jesus Christ asks, "For what will it profit a man, if he gains the whole world and forfeits his life." [Matt. 16:26]

People who are truly *born anew* have acquired the fullness of the Father within themselves. Love for the Father, for Jesus Christ their heavenly Guide, and for their fellow human beings has become their second nature. What such people need next is to remain focused by refusing to be swept away by the meaningless allures of worldly treasures. To such people, Jesus Christ says:

- **You must seek the kingdom of the Father first:** "Don't store up treasures here on earth, where moths eat them and rust destroys them, and where thieves break in and steal. Store your treasures in heaven, where moths and rust cannot destroy, and thieves do not break in and steal. **Wherever your treasure is, there the desires of your heart will also be.** … No one can serve two masters. For you will hate one and love the other; you will be devoted to one and despise the other. **You cannot serve both the Father and Money.** … Seek the Kingdom of the Father above all else, and live righteously, and he will give you everything you need. [Matt. 6:19–21, 24, 33 (NLT)]

When we look at what the love of money and the power of money have done and still do in the world today, it becomes much easier to see why our heavenly Guide, Jesus Christ, spoke strongly against the love of money. When we say, "The love of money is the root of all evils," we speak the truth, but average human beings hardly understand what that means in effect. The root of all evils is not the physical money that we spend on goods we purchase for our basic daily needs, but the concept and premeditated intentions of the inventor of money.

When Jesus Christ said, "You cannot serve both the Father and Money," he means that *Money* is a worshiped entity that is directly opposed to the Father in the world. Similarly, when he said, "give to Caesar what belongs to Caesar, and give to the Father what belongs to the Father," it was the same opposing entity, *Money*, that he referred to as *Caesar*, in his capacity as one entitled to collect tax monies from his human subjects. Now, every human being knows that Jehovah is the principal inventor of the present world order, as well as the worldly concept of money. He is the one who *blesses* human beings with an abundance of money, and it is to him that people pay their religious taxes all over the world. In other words, Jehovah is the *Money* or the *Caesar* that is directly opposed to the Father's divine interest in the world.

According to the Qur'an, "**No calamity befalleth [on earth] save by Allah's leave [consent]**," and "Naught of disaster befalleth in the earth or in yourselves but it is in a Book before We [Allah and his partners in evil] bring it into being." It also says, "Allah is Creator of all things, and he is the Guardian over all things," and that "He is the First and the Last, and the Outward and the Inward [here in the world]." [Qur'an 64:11; 57:22; 39:62; 57:3]

All these agree perfectly with information in the Bible. According to the Bible, "all that is in the world ... is not of the Father but is of the world." [1 John 2:16] Jehovah confirms that by saying, "I am the first and I am the last [in the world]; besides me there is no [other] God." He also says of himself, "I form the light and create darkness, **I bring prosperity and create disaster**; I [Jehovah] do all these things," thus confirming that he is indeed **the source of all evils** on earth. [Isa. 44:6; 45:7 (NIV)]

Now, since Jehovah is the source of all evils in the world, it follows that the love of Jehovah is the root of all evils in the human situation. The love of Jehovah turned the peace-loving Abram into a compulsive liar and murderer; it turned him into a lover of worldly treasures. The love of Jehovah made Jephthah murder his only daughter, and it made King David dance naked before his subjects in the streets of Israel. The love of Jehovah made the Jews war against their neighboring nations, and created so much bad blood that today fuels the endless wars and ghastly *intifada* that go on in the Middle East. The love of Jehovah made Jewish religious leaders and their Roman cohorts persecute and murder their sinless Messiah and most of his harmless disciples in cold blood. The love of Jehovah made the Catholic Church of Rome burn at the stake so many innocent translators of the Bible and other advocates of the true gospel of Jesus Christ. The love of Jehovah was also the driving force behind the atrocities of the Roman Catholic Crusaders and the Inquisitions.

The love of Jehovah made Muhammad take to arms, although his inner self hated doing so. Of course, the history of religious *holy wars* proves that there has never been a time in the history of humankind when evil had been so decisively committed against defenseless communities of people except when done on the strength of the aggressors' love for Jehovah, the god of the world.

Usually, people argue that they need a lot of money to be able to worship and do the works of *God*. Indeed, most of us pray for riches, feeling that when we become very rich, we will be able to build mosques or church premises for *God*, and establish foundations for orphans and the destitute people in society. We see, however, that Jesus Christ counts all those things unnecessary for people who seek the Father. The Father does not dwell in concrete structures built by human hands, but in peoples' spirits. There are simple and more sincere ways people can help the less privileged, without resorting to a public display of religious philanthropy.

The truth is, "people who long to be rich fall into temptation and are trapped by many foolish and harmful desires that plunge them into ruin and destruction. For the love of money is the root of all kinds of evil. And some people, craving money, have wandered from the true faith and pierced themselves with many sorrows." [1 Tim 6:9–10]

The Messiah's answer to the very rich man who asked him what he should do to have eternal life still applies to every rich person on earth today. He told him, "Sell all your possessions and give the money to the poor, and you will have treasure in heaven. Then come, follow me." [Luke 18:22] As expected, the rich man became so sad at the thought of giving up all the worldly treasures he had worked so hard to acquire for himself. Then Jesus Christ stated the hard truth concerning riches and how much a hindrance they are to our true spiritual salvation: "How hard it is for the rich to enter the Kingdom of the Father! In fact, **it is easier for a camel to go through the eye of a needle than for a rich person to enter the Kingdom of** the Father!" [Luke 18:24–25 (NLT)] Therefore, he still says to all who desire perfect heavenly life, "Beware! Guard against every kind of greed. [True] Life is not measured by how much you own." [Luke 12:15 (NLT)]

Craving for money and the flashy material treasures of the world has remained one temptation too many for normal human beings to overcome in this life, and it has to do with the basic programming of the human mind. This is the greatest problem confronting customary Christian ministers today, especially the Pentecostalists. For obvious reasons, they seem to find it difficult to agree with Jesus Christ on issues of material *breakthroughs, monetary empowerment,* and *prosperity*. In fact, the Church preaches nothing else but gospel of material possessions in the name of Jehovah.

The Church ministers find their only justification in the misconstrued alibi that Paul provided them. Paul wrote in 2 Cor. 8:9, "For you know the grace of our Lord Jesus Christ, that though he was rich, yet for your sake he became poor, so that by his poverty you might become rich." Clearly, this verse does not suggest in any way that Christians should pursue riches in the name of Jesus Christ, and some of the ministers know that very well. Hence, when they cite the verse during sermons, they simply say, "Jesus Christ became poor so that we might become rich." This modified rendering alters the actual meaning radically, and with that, they feel justified to override the straightforward precepts of Jesus Christ on the matter. They feel that the verse gives official backing to their gospel of money and the good things of life. Nevertheless, to accept or reject the words of Jesus Christ on any issue is really a matter of choice; the Church ministers make theirs and must live with the ultimate consequence. People who listen to them should make their individual choices as well.

Next, Jesus Christ says:

- **You must be courageous and speak out for the truth without fear:** "When you hear of wars and insurrections, don't panic. Yes, these things must take place first, but the end won't follow immediately. ... Nation will go to war against nation, and kingdom against kingdom. There will be great earthquakes, and there will be famines and plagues in many lands, and there will be terrifying things and great miraculous signs from heaven. But before all this occurs, **there will be a time of great persecution**. You will be dragged into synagogues and prisons, and you will stand trial before kings and governors because you are my followers. But this will be your opportunity to tell them about me. So don't worry in advance about how to answer the charges against you, for I will give you the right words and such wisdom that none of your opponents will be able to reply or refute you! Even those closest to you—your parents, brothers, relatives, and friends—will betray you. They will even kill some of you. And everyone will hate you because you are my followers. **But not a hair of your head will perish! By standing firm, you will win your souls.** [Luke 21:9–19 (NLT)]

This is the final requirement for every person who has truly become *born anew*. It is like when the marine engineer cadet has gone to school, practiced his career on cadet ships under the strict supervision of proficient engineers and risen through the ranks to qualify as a professional chief engineer. He would then take up a position of responsibility on board the ship as head of the engine department, applying what he learned and practiced, supervising the less experienced engine room crew under his command. At that point, what he would need is the courage to confront the challenges associated with his profession and the self-confidence to convey his knowledge to others.

A truly born-anew disciple who has learned from Jesus Christ and shunned the distracting allures of the material world around him needs the special *courage of rock*, the like that the Messiah identified in Simon Bar-Jona, to confront both natural impediments and deliberate afflictions occasioned by the world. He needs the confidence that comes from heavenly knowledge or spiritual insight to defend his convictions and to convey the will of the Father to others who are less informed than he is.

When Simon Bar-Jona had learned from Jesus Christ and had received the kingdom of the Father within his spirit, he was able to testify in the street of Israel, without fear of the Jewish religious authorities, that **'Jesus Christ is the Son of the *Living* Father.'** It was a very dangerous thing to do at the time, when the bloodthirsty religious authorities were seriously sniffing around Jesus Christ and his disciples, seeking evidence that he was indeed "preaching in the name of another *God*" so that they would put him to death, as Jehovah had instructed. Simon's testimony was exceptionally significant and authoritative. It did not only disclose the true nature of Jesus Christ, but it especially distinguished the Father of Jesus Christ as *Living* Spirit, making it obvious that Jehovah, god of the Jews, was but a *Dead* god.

Jesus Christ called the special type of courage displayed by Simon in that circumstance, "*Peter*," which meant "*Rock*." Then, he solemnly added, "on this *rock* [or *courage of rock*] I will build my church [i.e., mission in the world], and the powers of death shall not prevail against it." [Matt. 16:18] Jesus Christ was saying that every true disciple of the heavenly way needs the same special *courage of rock* to withstand the severe trials that the world is bound to mete out on him during his transitory life on earth. Putting it in a different way as he foretold the future for his true disciples, he said, "There will be a time of great persecution. ... But not a hair of your head will perish!" and "**By standing firm, you will win your souls.**"

The most important don'ts of the heavenly way concern what should be our proper attitudes toward the Father's Holiness in the world and toward Jesus Christ, as the sole Guardian of the heavenly way. People who truly walk by the Holy Spirit appreciate the absolute nature of the Father's Holiness, and upholding the honor of that Holiness in their thoughts and actions remains very paramount in their minds. Jesus Christ portrays the importance of upholding the Father's Holiness in the world in the very first sentence of the model prayer that he approved for all his true disciples: "*Our Father in heaven, may your name be kept holy.*"

Normally, human nature takes spiritual matters for granted, and human beings do not seem to understand where to draw the line in trying to pursue and entertain themselves with the wry comedies of this life. Every normal person honors and respects his parents; he does not make jest of their integrity. The Father demands and deserves much more than the type of honor we accord our imperfect human parents. The Father is the epitome of Holiness; no one should desecrate or disrespect his name under any circumstance. This is of extreme importance, not only for people who desire spiritual resurrection, but also for all spirits in existence. Disrespecting, or making jest of the Father's Holiness in the world, is the surest way of remaining spiritually dead forever.

Accordingly, Jesus Christ says:

- **Do not blaspheme against the Father's Holiness:** "I tell you the truth, all sin and blasphemy can be forgiven, but anyone who blasphemes the Holy Spirit will never be forgiven. **This is a sin with eternal consequences.**" [Mark 3:28–29 (NLT)]

In trying to appear most powerful and superhuman in the public's eyes, so many so-called men of *God* today go about performing all kinds of magical feats, while claiming that they are working with the power of the Holy Spirit. Some Church ministers make the Holy Spirit seem just like a major actor in the open-air play they are performing. That has eternal repercussions, which they may or may not be aware of.

Some comedians, too, resort to making jokes with the Father's Holy Spirit in their desperate effort to try to elicit laughter from some incurably miserable audience. Comedy may be nothing but comedy to human beings, but every blasphemous joke has its spiritual repercussions. Besides, we are not here in the world for jokes and foolish laughter. If people understand what the battle for spiritual salvation entails, they will shun all forms of induced gaiety and human fantasies.

- **Do not call anyone father or rabbi in the world:** "Don't let anyone call you 'Rabbi,' for you have only one teacher, and **all of you are equal as brothers and sisters**. And don't address anyone here on earth as 'Father,' for only the Father in heaven is your spiritual Father. And don't let anyone call you 'Teacher,' for you have only one teacher, the Messiah." [Matt. 23:8–11 (NLT)]

Part of the process of remaining focused on whatever one is doing is identifying and holding in constant view the targeted goal. The goal of everyone seeking true spiritual salvation is ultimately reunification with Divine Spirit, with the Father who is the Blessed Tree of eternal life, and with the heavenly household of perfect spirits. No other Father or Tree of Life exists. Having correctly identified their target or spiritual goal, people who genuinely seek the ultimate spiritual reunion with the Father should endeavor to remain focused on him. That is why Jesus Christ wants us to avoid being distracted by seemingly harmless worldly idea of referring to or looking up to some dead entities in the world as fathers or teachers, be they biological or of religious faith. In this battle for spiritual reunion with our true heavenly Father, nothing should be taken for granted.

Indeed, it makes no sense for a person traveling to London to call every transit stopover on his itinerary London. In fact, it could cause him fortunes. I once met three young African stowaways in the streets of Buenos Aires, Argentina. They came up to my colleague and me and introduced themselves; then we sat in a snack shop while they narrated their very pathetic story. They said that they had desired so much to go to America and eventually succeeded in hiding in a ship heading directly to New York. Fortunately, and unfortunately for them, they were discovered some days before the vessel's next port of call, which was Buenos Aires. The captain of the ship, being unwilling to take chances with the American Immigration on stowaway problems, promptly handed them over to the Buenos Aires authorities on arrival.

The boys claimed that they were escapees from the war-torn Liberia and were handed over to the Office of the United Nations High Commissioner for Refugees, (UNHCR), who granted them asylum. During the official interrogations, the boys said that they were heading to New York. Then, the UNHCR offered them a choice between remaining in Buenos Aires or being sent to New York, if they still wished to go there. The boys told us that they saw the beautiful high-rise buildings and the serene environments of Buenos Aires and decided among themselves that that was equally 'New York,' and so they chose to stay on. They were then taken to the refugee camp and there their story ended abruptly, like it ended for most other refugees of this world. Finally, they confessed to us that they had since become so dejected that they were indeed seeking to stowaway back to their homes in Africa. They wanted to know if we could help them, but we told them that our ship was not on African route.

Jesus Christ does not want this kind of dilemma for any of his true disciples in the world. Just as there could be no alternative New York for the three young stowaways, there will never be another Father for any fallen, dead spirit in the world. Every so-called father in the world is false, and calling any entity, person, or thing "father" is an unnecessary self-distraction for any person whose target is truly the heavenly Father of all. I encouraged my children to call me *Dad* or *Daddy*, not father, and I called them my sisters or brothers. Sometimes, my second daughter, Ruby, protested that she was my daughter and not my sister, but I was sure that she would eventually understand that that was what we were in reality—"brother and sister," just as Jesus Christ said.

That brings me to the case of people praying through some dead individuals and other imperfect human beings, looking up to them as *saints* and religious *masters*. Jesus Christ is the sole Messiah and link between the Father and all the fallen, dead spirits in the world. Apart from instructing that his true disciples must never call anyone master in the world, he specifically said that they should ask the Father whatever they need directly **in his name**, and not in the name of any other entity, dead or living. The heavenly Christ resumed his rightful place in the Father's kingdom after his earthly mission, and he has linked all his true disciples unto the heavenly grid. And now that the Father's Holy Spirit of truth dwells within all his true disciples on earth, he simply says that they are divinely connected to the Father through him. He had promised them, saying, "In that day you will know that I am in my Father, and you in me, and I in you." [John 14:20]

The promises he made to his true disciples before he departed from the world still apply to all his true disciples today:

> "Soon the world will no longer see me, but you will see me. Since I live, you also will live. When I am raised to life again, you will know that **I am in my Father, and you are in me, and I am in you**. ... At that time you

won't need to ask me for anything. I tell you the truth, **you will ask the Father directly, and he will grant your request because you use my name.** You haven't done this before. **Ask, using my name**, and you will receive, and you will have abundant joy. ... Then you will **ask in my name**. I'm not saying I will ask the Father on your behalf, for the Father himself loves you dearly because you love me and believe that I came from the Father." [John 14:19–20, 23–23, 27 (NLT)]

Jesus Christ did not leave any room here for people who might eventually decide to ask in the name of Mary, his earthly mother, or in the name of *dead* saints, or in the name of avatars or so-called mystical *masters*. Not surprisingly, the same Roman Catholic Church purported by Paul to be in the name of Jesus Christ, does every other thing in the world but what Jesus Christ says and stands for. People who pray through Mary, saints, fathers, and various religious masters of the world pray to Jehovah and not to the Father. True disciples of Jesus Christ pray *directly to the Father in his name*, just as he instructed, and they always receive the inner satisfaction and joy that he promised to all who love him and obey his words.

- **Do not presume to be greater than your master:** "A disciple is not above his teacher, but everyone when he is fully taught will be like his teacher." [Luke 6:40 (NLT)] A friend once told me about a poll that was carried out by an organization in the United States to determine the most influential persons in the life of humanity. In that poll, Paul was ranked third, while Jesus Christ ranked fifth.

Indeed, most customary Christian are followers of Paul and worshippers of Jehovah; only very few are true disciples of Jesus Christ. Paul did not only arrogate to himself the title of the best *apostle* of Jesus Christ, he also called himself *teacher* and first *father* of all customary Christians, not minding that Jesus Christ had personally instructed his true disciples never to call anyone 'father' or 'teacher' in the world. Paul said to his customary Christian followers, who were supposed to be his 'brothers and sisters,' as instructed by Jesus Christ, "For though you have countless guides in Christ, you do not have many fathers. For **I became your father in Christ Jesus through the gospel.**" [1 Cor. 4:15] Paul was a three-fold religious fraudster; he was a *false apostle* of Jesus Christ, which was why he could call himself *father*, as well as *teacher* par excellence of the gospel of Jesus Christ.

Sadly, most churchgoers interpret Paul's deliberate and consistent disregard of explicit instructions and wishes of Jesus Christ as mere coincidences. They even hold that Paul explained the gospel of Jesus Christ in the world better than Jesus Christ himself. That is sheer aberration. For, a room cannot be more spacious than the house in which it is situated.

Well, the reason Jesus Christ made the assertion that *a disciple could never be greater than his master* was to prepare the minds of his true disciples in advance to be able to pinpoint impostors, like Paul, by their fruits. Bearing in mind the unique position of Jesus Christ as the sole Envoy of our heavenly Father in all matters relating to the spiritual salvation of all fallen, dead spirits in the world, we can readily appreciate why none of his disciples can ever be better informed than he is. The scripture describes Jesus Christ as *"the name above all other names ... in heaven and on earth and under the earth,"* meaning he is the ultimate Teacher and Guide of the heavenly way.

It was also in the interest of helping his true disciples to imbibe the spirit of meekness, humbleness, and servant-leadership that Jesus Christ said, "Take my yoke upon you. Let me teach you, because I am humble and gentle at heart, and you will find rest for your souls. ... The greatest among you must be a servant. But those who exalt themselves will be humbled, and those who humble themselves will be exalted." [Matt. 11:29; 23:11–12 (NLT)] Did Paul really learn anything from Jesus Christ? Not at all! Facts abound that Paul never really knew or understood Jesus Christ. He rather learnt a lot from Jehovah whose ulterior interests he subtly served. Paul was undeniably a full-time apostle of Jehovah.

The above *dos* and *don'ts* are merely a few written reminders for beginners in the heavenly way. People who are truly *born anew* already have the kingdom of the Father dwelling within them. They have become one with the Father and with his Son, Jesus Christ, and as such, are inwardly instructed. Such people have acquired functional conscience and common sense, which are all that the heavenly way requires. As the Messiah promised, the indwelling Holy Spirit of truth is continually guiding them into all the truth from within. They are the people who are truly walking by the Holy Spirit.

WALKING BY THE HOLY GHOST

It is very important for me to differentiate between walking by the Holy Spirit of the Father, meant for true disciples of Jesus Christ, and walking by Jehovah's *Ghostly* spirit of violence and delusion that he prophesied and has now *poured out* indiscriminately upon unsuspecting religious extremists all over the world. Walking by the *Holy Ghost* is not the same thing as walking by the Holy Spirit.

People who walk by the so-called *Holy Ghost* are friends of the world; they collectively serve Jehovah's ungodly interests in their various capacities. They endorse and glorify all the human tragedies of the so-called Old Testament that were willfully instigated by Jehovah against defenseless masses; and while threatening people with Jehovah's impending wrath and apocalyptic doomsday, they propagate the fear of him as the beginning of wisdom. At the same time, they equally preach monetary breakthroughs, worldly goods, prosperity, and happiness in the world. In return, Jehovah rewards them with the treasures of the world, wealth, fame, and public acclaim. In other words, people who walk by the *Holy Ghost* love the world, and the world loves them.

The fruit of the so-called *Holy Ghost* can be seen playing out in most Pentecostal churches all over the world today. The site of a hyperactive Church minister shouting his head off, sweating, and jumping up and down in front of emotionally aroused, noisy congregation, paints the perfect picture of a people possessed by Jehovah's end-time *Holy Ghost.*

People who walk by the Holy Spirit of truth, on the other hand, are friends of Jesus Christ whom the Father has separated out of the world. The world hates them, as it hates their friend, Jesus Christ. They preach disentanglement from *monetary breakthroughs, worldly goods, prosperity, and contemporary happiness in the world.* They preach the love of the Father that drives away all fears, while courageously testifying that Jehovah and all the gods of the world are evil. Certainly, they are not at the center stage of things in the world.

I should state categorically however, that there is no such thing as a "holy" ghost! Every ghost is a ghoul or an evil spirit. No matter how anyone chooses to define a "ghost," it is always associated with the dead, a phantom or a false image of reality. *Encarta Dictionary* defines a ghost as "the supposed **spirit of somebody who has died**, believed to appear as a shadowy form or to cause sounds, the movement of objects, or a frightening atmosphere in a place." In other words, ghosts are strictly associated with dead and evil spirits, and with haunted houses, people, and things. *Walking by the Holy Ghost,* therefore, means walking under the hallucinating influence of a certain domineering ghost that falsely calls himself *holy*. In any case, the thoughts, utterances, and actions of people who walk by the so-called *Holy Ghost* always reflect terror, disaster, death, and repulsive things. On the contrary, people who walk by the Holy Spirit of the Father reflect gentleness, love, peace, and holiness.

Anyone who reads the Bible objectively will observe the consistent difference between the will of Jesus Christ and those of Jehovah, concerning the spiritual salvation of captive human spirits.

The fact that Jehovah and Jesus Christ are directly opposed to each other on this matter is very clear. The express mission of Jesus Christ is to liberate, rekindle, and resurrect dead human spirits and give them eternal life, while Jehovah seeks to eternally hold human spirits in captivity in the outer darkness. Jehovah always offers the false version of whatever our heavenly Messiah stands for, and he has always stated his position firmly in both words and actions. Jesus Christ promises eternal life, while Jehovah vows Armageddon and eternal hell fire for our captive spirits.

The Father sent Jesus Christ into the world to accomplish the spiritual salvation of **all** the lost sons of the Father in it; he, therefore, became the **only true Savior** of the whole world. Accordingly, the Bible unambiguously declares, "There is salvation in *no one else*! The Father has given *no other name under heaven* by which we must be saved." … "Therefore, the Father elevated him [Jesus Christ] to the place of highest honor and gave him *the name above all other names*, that at the name of Jesus every knee should bow, *in heaven and on earth and under the earth*, and every tongue confess that Jesus Christ is Lord [of our spiritual salvation], to the glory of the Father." [Acts 4:12; Phil. 2:9–11 (NLT)]

Now, to counter this unequivocal fact about the divine status of Jesus Christ, Jehovah enslaved the lost sons of Abraham for more than four hundred years in Egypt to break them mentally and spiritually. Thereafter, he stage-managed their ill-fated physical rescue amidst unnecessary cataclysms, just to make himself appear as an alternative savior to the heavenly Messiah that the people were expecting. He succeeded with the battered Israelites, positing them as his official witnesses, and his calamitous outburst in Egypt as the practical example of his power to save. He forgot that salvation by the expected Messiah was to be strictly spiritual; his was purely a military liberation of human exiles on earth, which many brutal military generals like himself have replicated both before and after the Jewish Exodus.

As expected, however, Jehovah went ahead to proclaim himself the only God and Savior in existence, claiming legitimacy by referring to the fatal events of the ill-fated Jewish Exodus. He said, "But you are my witnesses, O Israel! ... You are my servant. You have been chosen to know me, believe in me, and understand that I alone am God. There is no other God—**there never has been, and there never will be**. I, yes I, am [Jehovah], and **there is no other Savior**. First I [sold you into slavery,] predicted your rescue, then I saved you and proclaimed it to the world. No foreign god has ever done this. You are witnesses that I am the only God." [Isa. 43:10–12 (NLT)] "I have been [Jehovah] your God ever since I brought you out of Egypt. You must acknowledge no God but me, **for there is no other savior**." [Hosea 13:4 (NLT)]

Then, Jehovah extended his fictitious claim over the entire human race, boasting and swearing that every knee must bow to him on earth as the only God and Savior in existence. "Turn to me and be saved, all the ends of the earth!" he says, "For I am God, and there is no other. **By myself I have sworn**, from my mouth has gone forth in righteousness **a word that shall not return**: To me every knee shall bow, every tongue shall swear." [Isa. 45:22–23]

But Jehovah's boasting and swearing by his name all turned out to be empty words, as the Bible unequivocally declares that Jesus Christ is the true Savior of the world and that all knees should bow to him and not to Jehovah. Thus, Jehovah's word returned to him void. It is very shameful, indeed, that someone who expects people to accept that he is the *Supreme God Almighty* would make sentences he could not substantiate, even when he had sworn by his own divine integrity.

Today, a customary Christian apologia argues, in defense of Jehovah, that he was the God who elevated Jesus Christ to such *absolute place of honor and relevance* as the *only* true Savior of the world. Surely, such an argument is laughable for a *God* who had emphatically stated that "there is no other God—**there never has been, and there never will be**. ... and **there is no other Savior**," and who had affirmed, "I will not give my glory to anyone else." He did not leave himself any such window of opportunity to retract his words when he *swore by his own name* and declared that *his words in the matter were irrevocable*. The truth is that no normal person elevates his own subordinate above himself under any circumstance whatsoever. Jehovah is simply what he has always been in relation to our heavenly Messiah, a powerless underdog. Worldly religion will never be able to invent any sound argument to alter that truth.

Again, where Jesus Christ promises his true disciples outright spiritual resurrection and ultimate return to their proper place in the heavenly kingdom of their Father, Jehovah promises a refurbished earthly situation to his blind followers. His fictitious promise of *New Jerusalem* on earth that would completely pass away on the last day is a sardonic affront on his followers' common sense.

In the end, the resurrected disciples of Jesus Christ will regain their full spiritual personalities as perfect spirits in the perfect spiritual kingdom of their Father. The scripture confirms that "they cannot die anymore; because they are equal to angels and are sons of the Father, being sons of the resurrection." [Luke 20:36] Meanwhile, the scripture speaks plainly about what life would be like in Jehovah's so-called New Jerusalem. Among other things, it says, "No longer will babies die when only a few days old. No longer will adults die before they have lived a full life. No longer will people be considered old at one hundred! **Only the cursed will die that young!** In those days people will live in the houses they build and eat the fruit of their own vineyards." [Isa. 65:20–21 (NLT)] Jehovah's alternative salvation simply amounts to a repeat of the miserable human experiences on earth.

It is not difficult to see that there is no spiritual value in Jehovah's alternative salvation. People who choose Jehovah's so-called New Jerusalem on earth would remain humans; they would still be born as babies, and they would grow old and die. They would still plant vineyards and depend on organic and synthetic foods to stay alive; they would still build and live in ramshackle houses to protect themselves from unsafe natural environments, and they would still live side-by-side with dumb animals.

Jesus Christ promised to send the indwelling Holy Spirit of truth from the Father as Comforter to his true disciples after his departure from the physical stage of the world. And in line with his shameless ploy of contradicting every perfect idea of our heavenly Messiah, Jehovah equally stated that he would pour out his evil spirit of violence and delusion on the entire human race in the later days. Those later days are already here; and while true disciples of Jesus Christ walk by the Holy Spirit of truth from the Father, deluded followers of Jehovah, the god of Israel, walk by his so-called *Holy Ghost*.

The scripture shows vivid differences between the central substance and motive of Christ's promise of the Holy Spirit of truth from the Father to his true disciples in the world, and those of Jehovah's promise of end-time, indiscriminate outpouring of his ghostly spirit of violence and delusion upon all unguarded human spirits on earth. The reader should closely compare the two eternally opposed promises to understand the express motive of each.

CHRIST'S PROMISE OF THE HOLY SPIRIT OF TRUTH

The words of Jesus Christ are explicit in the verses shown below concerning his ultimate motive:

- "If you love me, obey my commandments. And I will ask the Father, and he will give you another Advocate, who will never leave you. He is the Holy Spirit, who **leads into all truth.** *The world cannot receive him* because *it isn't looking for him and doesn't recognize him.* But you know him because **he lives with you now** and **later will be in you.**" [John 14:15–17 (NLT)]
- "No, I will not abandon you as orphans—**I will come to you.** Soon the world will no longer see me,

but you will see me. *Since I live, you also will live.*" [John 14:18–19 (NLT)]

- "I am telling you these things now while I am still with you. But when the Father sends **the Advocate as my representative**—that is, **the Holy Spirit—he will teach you everything and will remind you of everything I have told you.**" [John 14:25–26 (NLT)]
- "But I will send you the Advocate—the Spirit of truth. He will come to you from the Father **and will testify all about me**." [John 15:26 (NLT)]
- "There is so much more I want to tell you, but you can't bear it now. When the Spirit of truth comes, **he will guide you into all truth**." [John 16:12–13 (NLT)]

It is clear from the above that Jesus Christ was telling his past and present disciples about his **third coming** into the world in his Spirit form to continue his ministry, both in them and through them. Of course, he is the sole Redeemer of the world; hence, even when the world no longer sees him in human form, people who know him, know that he is still personally in charge of his mission in the world as the heavenly Christ. Therefore, the coming Holy Spirit of truth will be none other than Jesus Christ in his Spirit form.

When he dwelt among his disciples in human form, he told them that they knew him [i.e., the Holy Spirit of truth], "because he lives with you now." Then he promised them that he would indeed come back to them in the world after dropping his human garb, albeit in a different form. "No, I will not abandon you as orphans—**I will come to you**. Soon the world will no longer see me, **but you will see me**." Jesus Christ was simply describing the necessary physical transition that he must go through to advance to the next spiritual phase of his divine mission. That people of the world *"will no longer see me, but you will see me"* shows clearly that he is still very much around, albeit in a form that only his true disciples can perceive. He assured them that they would still know him when he returned as the Holy Spirit of truth and dwelt within their spirits, as he dwelt in Adam and Eve during his first coming into the world. "And later **he** [i.e., I, Jesus Christ] **will be in you**," he promised them. Therefore, walking by the Holy Spirit of truth literally means walking by the indwelling heavenly Christ in oneself.

During the **first coming** of the heavenly Christ into the world in the Garden of Eden, he appeared in his Spirit form as the *Holy Spirit of Knowledge*. He dwelt within Adam and Eve, liberated them from Jehovah-imposed state of terminal ignorance, and inaugurated the prophecy phase of his heavenly mission through their family lineage. Adam and Eve were his only disciples in the whole world at his first coming. They received his divine mandate to prophesy, to create awareness of his presence in the world and to prepare the mind of ignorant humanity for his **second coming**, which would be in human form. Adam became the first prophet of the heavenly way, and all the true prophets of the coming Messiah were sons of Adam, from Abel to John the Baptist who was the very last.

The **second coming** of the heavenly Christ, as prophesied by the sons of Adam, was in the human form, and the purpose was to enable all human beings to see, touch, and hear his word of love and life directly from his own mouth. But he assured all and sundry that his Spirit was the sole life-giver to the world. "The Spirit alone gives eternal life. Human effort accomplishes nothing. And **the very words I have spoken to you are spirit and life**," he said. [John 6:63 (NLT)]

The scripture further explains why the Father's Holy Spirit of Knowledge and Word of Life in Eden became human and dwelt amongst us who are filthy sinners. It says, "Because the Father's children are human beings [now]—made of flesh and blood—the Son also became flesh and blood. For only as a human being could he die, and only by dying could he break the power of [Jehovah] the devil, who had the power of death. Only in this way could he set free all who have lived their lives as slaves to the fear of dying." [Heb. 2:14–15 (NLT)]

And "So the Word became human and made his home among us. He was full of unfailing love and faithfulness. And we have seen his glory, the glory of the Father's one and only Son [in the world]," says John 1:14 (NLT).

In other words, our heavenly Messiah is the miraculous manifestation of our heavenly Father's Word of Love and Life, meant for all his lost sons in the world. All living beings in the world are animated by lost spirits who are fallen sons of the Father. These include Jehovah who claims to be *God Almighty* on earth, his companions who claim to be archangels, human beings who have been mystically hypnotized into believing that they are nothing but inconsequential breath of Jehovah, and all other lifeforms in the universe.

As we have seen, our heavenly Messiah was the *Holy Spirit of Knowledge* during his first divine manifestation in Eden. In that capacity, he vanquished programmed human ignorance and promised humanity eternal life in the Father. **"You will not die!"** was his solemn promise to humanity then. Jehovah and his religious cronies branded him serpent and archenemy of humankind because his coming meant spiritual redemption for their ignorant human captives.

Jesus Christ, the heavenly Teacher became his divine epithet during his second coming and the human phase of his mission in the world. He became "the true light that enlightened every man," and continued to assure all the people who believed his original promise of life in Eden that they would not die. "*I am the way, the truth, and the life*," he assured, "No one can come to the Father [the Tree of Life] except through me. ... *I am the resurrection and the life.* Anyone who believes in me will live, even after dying." [John 14:6; 11:25 (NLT)]

Jehovah and his religious cronies still branded him a sinner and archenemy of humankind; they persecuted and crucified him, believing that they could stop his divine mission by so doing.

Unfortunately for them, the Father's Word of Life cannot be killed by dead spirits in total darkness. Thus, divine mission of the heavenly Christ has proved to be unstoppable.

Finally, the *Holy Spirit of truth* is the divine epithet of the heavenly Messiah in the present phase of his mission in the world, and his promise of eternal life to people who believe in him remains unchanged. "Because I live," he assures, "you will live also!" [John 14:19] Therefore, the *Holy Spirit of Knowledge* is the same as the *Holy Spirit of truth, our heavenly Teacher,* our heavenly Messiah, and **Jesus Christ of Nazareth**. This perfectly agrees with the scripture, which says, "Jesus Christ is the same yesterday, today, and forever." [Heb. 13:8 (NLT)] Whatever the epithet has been, **Jesus Christ is indeed one with our unchangeable, loving Father.** He once asked his apostles, "Have I been with you all this time, Philip, and yet you still don't know who I am? **Anyone who has seen me has seen the Father!** So why are you asking me to show him to you?" [John 14:9 (NLT)]

Indeed, Jesus Christ has been with us since he first touched down in the Garden of Eden, and he has worked still to overcome Jehovah's oppressive worldly regime to set our fallen spirits free from spiritual bondage in the world of sin. Ever since the Garden of Eden, he has had only one business in the world—to lead all lost sons of heaven who accept the Father's offer of spiritual resurrection back to the heavenly household of perfect spirits, by guiding them in the way of truth and love. As the scripture says, "**he will guide you into all truth.**" It is very sad indeed that customary Christians who say that Jesus Christ is the same yesterday, today, and tomorrow also say that he was the physical manifestation of Jehovah, the unforgiving, barbaric god of the Old Testament who—according to the scripture—does not change.

JEHOVAH'S PROMISED OUTPOURING OF HIS GHOSTLY SPIRIT

The contrary motive of Jehovah's own promise is clear from his own words in the scripture:

- Then, after doing all those things, **I will pour out my Spirit upon all people**. Your sons and daughters will **prophesy**. Your old men will **dream dreams**, and your young men will **see visions**. In those days I will pour out my Spirit even on servants—men and women alike. And I will cause wonders in the heavens and on the earth—blood and fire and columns of smoke. The sun will become dark, and the moon will turn blood red **before that great and terrible day of Jehovah arrives**. [Joel 2:28–31]

Jesus Christ never promised, and he would never be the one to pour out some ghostly spirit of religious confusion on everybody in the world. He specifically said that his Holy Spirit of truth is not for everyone in the world. In fact, he said emphatically that *"The world cannot receive him, because it isn't looking for him and doesn't recognize him."* The world did not recognize the heavenly Christ when he appeared in Eden as the Holy Spirit of Knowledge; it did not receive him when he manifested as Jesus, the heavenly Teacher, and so it would not receive him when he comes as the Holy Spirit of truth. On the contrary, Jehovah's so-called *Holy Ghost* was to be poured out indiscriminately upon all unsuspecting religious and non-religious persons on earth.

The ghostly spirit that Jehovah would indiscriminately pour out on people would be strictly associated with terror, bloodbath, and disaster, which he had planned against helpless humankind. It would be characterized by "blood, fire, columns of smoke, and a certain terrible day of Jehovah's judgment." For Jehovah, it has been one strategy of shadowboxing after another since his utter humiliation in Eden. The outpouring of his ghostly spirit of hallucination and religious hysteria in the later days would come as a widespread spell of ignorance which would herald a certain doomsday when he hopes to eventually come out from his hiding place to fight his cause in person. This would be Jehovah's last-ditch effort at trying to contradict the mission of the Father's Holy Spirit of truth in the world.

Jehovah successfully cast spell of ignorance on Edenic human beings; he lied about the eternal importance of knowledge, and maligned the heavenly Messiah who inspired the people with the fruit of knowledge. Next, he persecuted and murdered Jesus of Nazareth, all in a hopeless bid to try to stop the Father's mission of spiritual rebirth for fallen, dead spirits in the world. Finally, he is hoping to re-blindfold as many people as possible before a certain doomsday when he hopes to come out from his occult burrow to fight his final battles undisguised, as the dreadful Antichrist. He said himself, "I will take vengeance, and I will spare no man." [Isa. 47:2] So, it would be said of Jehovah in those days, "Like a lion he has [finally] left his covert." [Jer. 25:38] But just as he failed in the beginning, he will ultimately fail in the end.

And concerning the prophesied "**great and terrible day of Jehovah**" that would be preceded by "wonders in the heavens and on the earth—blood and fire and columns of smoke" and "the sun becoming dark, and the moon turning blood red," the Scripture does not leave anyone in doubt as to what Jehovah's real intentions are. The prophecies spoke of Armageddon:

- "**Sound the alarm** in Jerusalem!" Jehovah says, "Raise the battle cry on my holy mountain! Let everyone tremble in fear because the day of Jehovah is upon us. It is **a day of darkness and gloom, a day of thick clouds and deep blackness.** Suddenly, like dawn spreading across the mountains, a great and mighty army appears. Nothing like it has been seen before or will ever be seen again." [Joel 2:1–2 (NLT)]

- **"Say to the nations far and wide: 'Get ready for war**! Call out your best warriors. Let all your fighting men advance for the attack. Hammer your plowshares into swords and your pruning hooks into spears. Train even your weaklings to be warriors. Come quickly, all you nations everywhere. Gather together in the valley.' And now, O Jehovah, call out your warriors! 'Let the nations be called to arms. Let them march to the valley of Jehoshaphat. There I, [Jehovah], will sit to pronounce [martial] judgment on them all.'" [Joel 3:9–12 (NLT)]
- "This is what Jehovah of Heaven's Armies says: 'Look! Disaster will fall upon nation after nation! A great whirlwind of fury is rising from the most distant corners of the earth!' **In that day those Jehovah has slaughtered will fill the earth from one end to the other**. No one will mourn for them or gather up their bodies to bury them. They will be scattered on the ground like manure." [Jer. 25:32–33 (NLT)]
- "**But everyone who calls on the name of Jehovah will be saved**, for some on Mount Zion in Jerusalem will escape, just as Jehovah has said. These will be among the survivors whom Jehovah has called." [Joel 2:32 (NLT)]
- "And **[Jehovah] will be king over all the earth**. On that day there will be one Lord—**his name alone will be worshiped**." [Zech. 14:9(NLT)]
- "In the end, the **enemies of Jerusalem** who survive the plague **will go up to Jerusalem each year to worship the King, [Jehovah] of Heaven's**

Armies, and to celebrate the Festival of Shelters." [Zech. 14:16]

- **"All humanity will come to worship me** from week to week and from month to month." [Isa. 66:23]

Jehovah's looming Armageddon would be his final attempt at trying to reassert his position of authority over Jerusalem and to claim supreme kingship over entire human race via military conquest. As everyone can see, it has everything to do with Jehovah's chronic obsession with power and self-praise on earth. Undoubtedly, Jehovah has no business with the spiritual rebirth of his own spirit, or of any other lost spirit in the world. Neither does he care about the perfect spiritual kingdom of the Father that Jesus Christ promises his true disciples.

Therefore, the sole mandate of the people possessed by Jehovah's so-called *Holy Ghost* of dreams, visions, and prophecies is to proclaim the imminent doomsday of his wrath and vengeance at the height of his frustration with his inability to stop the will of the Father in the world. People who walk by Jehovah's *Holy Ghost* are to announce his projected program of evil that will culminate in his days of *great tribulation* on defenseless sons of men; "such as has not been from the beginning of the world until now, and never will be," says Matt 24:21.

The words of the prophecies are plain, and the difference is very clear. People who walk by the *Holy Ghost* preach the fear and wrath of Jehovah, while people who walk by the Holy Spirit of truth preach the special love of the Father that casts out all fears. No honest person on earth can possibly mistake Jehovah's end-time doomsday dance of shame and human destruction for our heavenly Messiah's gift of the life-giving Holy Spirit of truth that is to enlighten the sons of men unto eternal spiritual rebirth.

CONCLUSION

Readers who have come this far would have gained good insight into some complexities of the expanding universe, the human world, and human existence. The universe is a grand Sheol, a howling 'prison of darkness' for dead spirits. It is a malignant tumor that evil spirits who were evicted out of the heavenly realm of perfect spirits erected within the eternal, infinite realm of darkness to serve as an alternative homeland. Organic lifeforms serve as alternative to true life of perfect spirits, but they represent various levels of spiritual death. The world of humans is a prison within the grand Sheol, and human nature is a second degree of spiritual death.

Just like the proverbial prodigal son, all spirits within the universal contraption are *self-afflicted* at various levels of consciousness within their shared netherworlds. They are all in *self-captivity*, especially because the Father's free offer of outright spiritual redemption remains open to all and sundry. Spiritual rebirth, therefore, means liberation from *self-affliction,* resurrection to one's original nature as perfect spirit, and outright return to the realm of perfect spirits.

Again, just like the proverbial prodigal son, it is entirely our prerogative to choose spiritual rebirth or not; to choose whether to return to our truly loving Father and to our heavenly household or not. The Father's free offer of spiritual redemption is unforced; it is entirely volitional. The Father did not send Jesus Christ into the world to scare anyone of us back into heaven.

Rather, Jesus Christ came into the world to reveal forbidden truths about our current situation, to help us understand where we are, why we are suffering and dying in the world, and how we can bring an end to our self-afflictions. He came to help us appreciate the difference between truth and falsehood, light and darkness, heavenly life of perfection and life of spiritual bondage to sin and death in the outer darkness; so that people might choose freely between the two poles of reality. More importantly, Jesus Christ came to help us distinguish between our truly loving heavenly Father and all the dead entities venerated as *Gods Almighty* in our present worlds of darkness.

But choosing spiritual rebirth is not that simple, and readers who have come this far would have understood why it involves serious battles against certain actors and institutions that are terminally opposed to people who truly opt for that. Choosing to return to his loving father was straightforward and easy for the proverbial prodigal son because his slave master was not opposed to his choice and so, did not fight to stop him. While the Father and Jesus Christ work still to help captive human spirits to attain spiritual rebirth and outright exodus from the world, Jehovah, the so-called archangels, worldly religions, underworld institutions, states and non-state actors fight tooth and nail to thwart our chances and perpetuate our captivity and spiritual death.

But the people who choose Jesus Christ and spiritual rebirth should not be deterred by empty threats posed by Jehovah and his vicious worldly institutions; they should be resolute and persevering. The battle may be very hard, but it is winnable. True friends of Jesus Christ are already divinely indemnified. "But not a hair of your head will perish!" he assures them, "**By standing firm, you will win [spiritual rebirth for] your souls**." In fact, Jesus Christ affirms that he had already overcome the world on behalf of all the people who choose and follow his divine guidance. "I have said this to you, that in me you may have peace. In the world you have tribulation; **but be of good cheer, I have overcome the world**." Jesus Christ also reassures all his true followers, saying, "I am the resurrection and the life. **Anyone who believes in me will live, even after dying**. Everyone who lives in me and believes in me will never ever die." [Luke 21:18-19; John 16:33; 11:25-26(NLT)] And finally, he says to them, "Truly, truly, I say to you, he who hears my word and believes him who sent me, **has eternal life; he does not come into judgment, but has passed from death to life.**" [John 5:24]

SELECTED BIBLIOGRAPHY

The Holy Bible:
Revised Standard Version (RSV)
New Revised Standard Version (NRSV)
Good News Bible – With Deuterocanonical Books/Apocrypha (GNB)
New International Version (NIV)
New Life Translation (NLT)
King James Version (KJV)
The Meaning of The Glorious Qur'an, Text and Explanatory Translation by Marmaduke Pickthall, Taj Company Ltd.
John Fowles, "*The Aristos*," Jonathan Cape, London 1965
Karen Armstrong, "*A History of God*," Ballantine Books, New York, 1994
Britannica CD 99 Multimedia Edition
Encarta Premium 2006

www.ingramcontent.com/pod-product-compliance
Lightning Source LLC
LaVergne TN
LVHW042250070526
838201LV00089B/104